Milady's

Hair Removal Techniques

A Comprehensive Manual

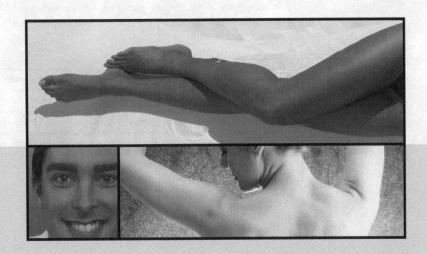

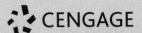

Australia • Brazil • Mexico • Singapore • United Kingdom • United States

**Milady's Hair Removal Techniques:
A Comprehensive Manual**
Helen R. Bickmore

President: Dawn Gerrain

Director of Editorial: Sherry Gomoll

Acquisitions Editor: Stephen G. Smith

Developmental Editor: Judy Aubrey Roberts

Director of Production: Wendy A. Troeger

Production Editor: Eileen M. Clawson

Text Design and Composition: Stratford
Publishing Services

Marketing Specialist: Sandra Bruce

Cover Design: Suzanne Nelson, essence of 7
design

For product information and technology assistance, contact us at
Cengage Customer & Sales Support, 1-800-354-9706
For permission to use material from this text or product,
submit all requests online at **www.cengage.com/permissions**
Further permissions questions can be emailed to
permissionrequest@cengage.com

ISBN-13: 978-1-4018-1555-4

ISBN-10: 1-4018-1555-3

Cengage
20 Channel Center Street
Boston, MA 02210
USA

Cengage is a leading provider of customized learning solutions with office locations around the globe, including Singapore, the United Kingdom, Australia, Mexico, Brazil, and Japan. Locate your local office at **www.cengage.com/global**

To learn more about Cengage platforms and services, register or access your online learning solution, or purchase materials for your course, visit **www.cengage.com**.

Notice to the Reader
Publisher does not warrant or guarantee any of the products described herein or perform any independent analysis in connection with any of the product information contained herein. Publisher does not assume, and expressly disclaims, any obligation to obtain and include information other than that provided to it by the manufacturer. The reader is expressly warned to consider and adopt all safety precautions that might be indicated by the activities described herein and to avoid all potential hazards. By following the instructions contained herein, the reader willingly assumes all risks in connection with such instructions. The publisher makes no representations or warranties of any kind, including but not limited to, the warranties of fitness for particular purpose or merchantability, nor are any such representations implied with respect to the material set forth herein, and the publisher takes no responsibility with respect to such material. The publisher shall not be liable for any special, consequential, or exemplary damages resulting, in whole or part, from the readers' use of, or reliance upon, this material.

Printed at CLDPC, USA, 07-24

Contents

SECTION IV
Introduction to Permanent Hair Removal   151

SECTION V
Laser and Light-Based Epilators   235

Foreword

This book serves as an invaluable tool in offering individuals the opportunity to expand their hair-removal techniques to include other hair-removal services. In addition to offering instruction and basic information on temporary and permanent hair-removal methods, it highlights the important factors to consider when offering treatment to clients. I am a client of the author's, and I enjoy the confidence and convenience of being treated by a professional who is well educated and skilled in temporary and permanent hair-removal techniques. Her individualized approach reflects in her writing, and she tells how to identify any medical condition by seeking medical professionals.

In summary, this book is a very comprehensive and beneficial guide to the causes of hair growth, the histology of skin, and practicing safe and sound methods of sanitation, sterilization, and hygiene. In addition to providing the necessary academic background, this book helps readers identify their levels of understanding and the textbooks and review articles required for further information.

— Shagul Anwar, MD

Preface

When I trained to become a beauty therapist (esthetician) in England 25 years ago, I had the option of adding the skill of electrolysis to my classes. I took that opportunity and found it to be a satisfying and financially rewarding one. I also provide waxing services, and I have found that there is a good marriage between the two.

When clients come in to see me for first-time leg or bikini waxes before vacation, I take the opportunity to introduce those clients to other services and to establish those clients as ongoing and/or long-term ones. When I feel the results would be stunning, and that the service may be something the clients will want to continue, I may offer clients a complimentary eyebrow wax. Those clients may decide to have their eyebrows shaped permanently with electrolysis, or they may have concerns with facial hair that they have been reluctant to talk about. The latter clients I can start on electrolysis programs, liberating them from the cycle of daily tweezing.

Many clients visit the spa for lip and chin waxes. These visits I view as opportunities to educate clients on the benefits of electrolysis. I always refuse to wax the chin and the sides of the face, knowing the problems that doing so can cause further down the road. Many clients are grateful for the personal interest I show in them and their hair-growth issues, not just for the immediate future but long term. I will wax the upper lip, for perhaps the last time, and start electrolysis on the chin or face, moving to the upper lip in the weeks down the road as the early anagen hairs become visible, ensuring a successful treatment.

For clients who seek to wax large body areas and who show an interest in laser hair removal or electrolysis, I analyze the target areas. If I find that the clients are good candidates for laser hair removal, I refer them to a trusted, local dermatology office that does laser hair removal. After two or three laser hair-removal treatments, those clients return to me to permanently eliminate their few remaining hairs with electrolysis. The dermatology office also refers clients to me who are poor candidates for laser hair removal.

Most female clients who receive electrolysis on their faces use other hair-removal methods on other parts of their bodies. For electrologists with open appointments, these clients are opportunities to provide additional, convenient services; increase the client base; and generate revenue.

The purpose of this book is to bring together all hair-removal methods in the hope that those contemplating licensure in one method will see the benefits of becoming knowledgable and licensed in another.

This book is divided into six sections. Section I contains the sciences related to hair growth and removal, whatever the method. Section II explains the hair-removal methods people currently use on their own, as well as the lesser-known methods of threading and sugaring. Section III offers a detailed, instructional guide to all aspects of waxing, to be used with formal classroom training. Section IV contains an introduction to electrolysis, to be used with formal training, additional reading, and the equipment-manufacturers' manuals. Section V contains an introduction to laser hair removal, also to be used with formal classroom training and equipment manufacturers' specific guidelines. Finally, Section VI offers insights into the business side of developing, owning, and operating a business and the importance of licensure and professional ethics.

I hope that a "marriage" can be made between the many aspects of hair removal, and offering every client the most suitable treatments in a convenient and professional setting by becoming a *hair-removal specialist*.

— Helen R. Bickmore

Acknowledgments

First and foremost, I offer my heartfelt gratitude to my husband, Lee, for "picking up the slack" with the home and children and for giving me the support and encouragement I needed to complete this task. I'd also like to thank my three lovely children, Matthew, Kate, and Harry, for their patience and long suffering during those many evenings and weekends I had to lock myself in the study.

I'd like to thank my Acquisitions Editor, Stephen Smith, and Developmental Editor, Judy Aubrey Roberts, for giving me a new challenge to rise to and for their confidence in me, as a first-time author, to be able to complete and deliver this project. In addition, I'd like to thank the Delmar Learning production team, Judy, Courtney Van Auskas, Eileen Clawson, and Wendy Troeger, for their knowledge, experience, and direction and for being such an enjoyable and delightful group of people with whom to work.

Thank you also to Jean Claude and Anne Marie Simille, my employers, for their support, understanding, and patience as I juggled this project with my work in the spa and for offering their spa for photographs. Many thanks to my colleagues, friends, and clients at the Jean Paul Spa for their feedback, encouragement, and willingness to model for photographs. In particular, I'd like to thank esthetician Kathleen Schneider for being the first to read rough drafts of the manuscript in its earliest stages and to give helpful feedback. Thank you, Marisa Clark, Denise Eisley, and Luba Yafayev.

I offer many thanks and much appreciation to the following individuals for independently reviewing portions of the manuscript:

Shagul Anwar, MD
Aaron Arnell, Cosmetology Careers
Deborah Beatty, Columbus Technical
    College
Grace Birch,
    Salt Lake Community College
Dean Charlotte Borste, PhD
Lenore Brooks, Brooks & Butterfield
    Ltd.
Melissa Chapman,
    York County School of Technology

Ari Fisher, PA (laser practitioner)
Puja Gupta (esthetician, threader)
Mayron Heimlich, DC
    (Texas Electrology Supply Company)
Terri Lounsberry (CPA)
Rochelle McCartney
    (esthetician and electrologist)
Darlene McGee, RPh
    (pharmacology)
Elizabeth Myron, Amber Products
Martha Phillips, Ford Beauty Academy

Rose Policastro,
   Capri Institute of Hair Design
Linda Rice, Grace College
   of Cosmetology
Annette Sebuyira (biology instructor)

Robert Shoss, MD
   (dermatology)
Madeline Udod,
   Eastern Suffolk County BOCES

Last, but not least, thank you to two dear friends, Sarah Holle and Carole Valera, for their encouragement and kind, supportive words when I hit a low ebb.

About the Author

Helen Bickmore received her diplomas for Beauty Therapy (esthetics), Body Treatments, Massage, and Electrolysis in 1979 through both the London College of Fashion and the City and Guilds of London Institute (CGLI).

Bickmore is a New York State Licensed Esthetician and Massage Therapist (LMT) and is a Certified Professional Electrologist (CPE) with the American Electrology Association (AEA), as well as a Certified Medical Electrologist (CME) with the Society of Clinical and Medical Hair Removal, Inc. (SCMHR).

Bickmore has taught esthetics at the former Scarborough Technical College, now the North Coast College in Yorkshire, England, and over the years has worked in salons and had her own business in the United Kingdom and United States. Currently, Bickmore is a spa director and continues to serve a large clientele.

In addition, Bickmore has reviewed manuscripts, written articles, appeared on television news programs, given workshops, and served on a number of panels. She resides in Albany, NY, with her husband of 17 years and their three children.

SECTION I

Scientific Considerations

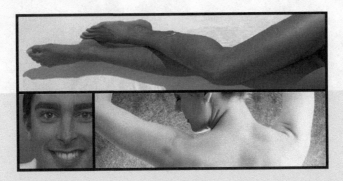

The first section of this book describes all the components that relate to hair growth and the conditions that affect hair growth. This section begins with an in-depth look at the integumentary system, including the structure of the skin and its functions, and continues with the structure of the hair, the hair follicle, and its growth cycle.

Following the anatomy and physiology of the hair and skin, this section delves into some of the major disorders and diseases of the skin that pertain to the hair-removal specialist. Specialists will learn how to recognize these diseases and disorders, how they are caused, how they may be treated, and when to seek professional or medical help.

Of great importance to hair-removal specialists is the study of the endocrine system. This system controls and directs the flow of the hormones that affect hair growth throughout the body. Once specialists understand the endocrine system, they can understand the causes of hirsutism,

hypertrichosis, and other hair-growth conditions. With this knowledge, specialists can advise and treat clients.

Also of great importance to hair-removal specialists is the appropriate use of hygiene, sanitation, and sterilization. To appreciate the importance of these elements is to know and understand pathology and bacteriology.

Putting all this knowledge together, specialists will be sufficiently educated with the background knowledge necessary to continue learning about the various methods of hair removal and their impact on the skin and hair.

CHAPTER 1

Anatomy and Physiology of the Hair and Skin

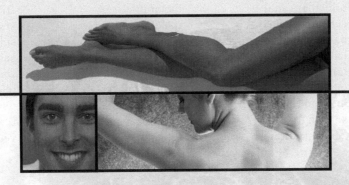

Chapter Outline

Learning Objectives ■ Key Terms ■ Introduction ■ The Structure of the Skin
The Structure of Hair ■ The Stages of Hair Growth ■ The Functions of the Skin
Conclusion ■ Endnotes ■ Discussion and Review Questions ■ Additional Readings

Learning Objectives

By the end of this chapter, you should be able to:

1. Name the layers of the epidermis.
2. Name appendages within the dermis.
3. List the major functions of the skin.
4. Name components of the pilosebaceous unit.
5. Name the three stages of hair growth.

Key Terms

absorption	dermis	keratohyalin granules	sebaceous glands
acid mantle	desquamation	Langerhans' cells	sebum
adipose tissue	dilation	lanugo	secretion
amino acid tyrosine	eccrine	leucocytes	stratified epithelium
anagen	eleidin	lymph	stratum basale
apocrine	epidermis	lymphocytes	stratum corneum
arrector pili	epithelial tissue	malpighian	stratum germinativum
axillae	excretion	medulla	stratum granulosum
basal zone	external root sheath	Meissner's corpuscles	stratum lucidum
catagen	follicular canal	melanin	stratum mucosum
club hair	germinal zone	melanocytes	stratum spinosum
collegenous	hair follicle bulb	mitosis	subcutaneous tissue
connective tissue	hair matrix	Pacinian's corpuscles	subcutis
constriction	horny zone	papillae	sudoriferous glands
cortex	integumentary system	papillary layer	telogen
cosmeceuticals	internal root sheath	pheromones	terminal hair
cuticle	keratin	pilosebaceous unit	tyrosine
dermal papilla	keratinization	reticular layer	vellus

Introduction

This chapter covers the **integumentary system,** which is the structure of the skin and its various layers; the **pilosebaceous** (pye-luh-seh-BAY-shus) **unit,** which is the hair follicle and its appendages; and the responsibility of the skin as the body's largest organ to perform multiple functions. This chapter also describes the structure of hair and its various stages of growth.

The Structure of the Skin

Healthy skin has elasticity and, when pinched or pulled, quickly reverts to its normal shape. It feels cool and soft to the touch and slightly moist. Its color derives from a combination of melanin produced in the **stratum germinativum** (jer-mi-nuh-TIV-um); carotene, a yellowish pigment; and the concentration of blood vessels found in the dermis (Figure 1–1). It is approximately a fifth of an inch thick at its thickest, on the soles of the feet, to a twelfth of an inch at its thinnest, on the eyelids.

The skin is the body's largest organ in surface area covering up to 20 square feet on the average person. It is made of **epithelial** (ep-ih-THEE-lee-ul) **tissue** and **connective tissue** and consists of three main layers:

1. epidermis
2. dermis
3. subcutis or subcutaneous layer

The Epidermis

The **epidermis** (ep-ih-DUR-mus) (Figure 1–2) consists of layers made of **stratified epithelium** (ep-ih-THEE-lee-um). The outer layers are dead and cornified. Skin cells divide in the lowest layer and migrate upward to replace the dead skin cells that have been shed. As the cells move upward, they are filled with a protein substance called **keratin** that helps pro-

integumentary system
the skin and its accessory organs, such as the sebaceous and sweat glands, sensory receptors, hair, and nails

pilosebaceous unit
the entire hair appendage, including the sebaceous gland and the arrector pili muscle

stratum germinativum
the lower level of the epidermis where cell division occurs

epithelial tissue
the tissue that forms a thin protective layer on bodily surfaces

connective tissue
fibrous tissue that binds, protects, cushions, and supports the various parts of the body

epidermis
the thin, outermost layer of the skin

stratified epithelium
layers of tissue that lack blood vessels; acts as a surface barrier

keratin
a protein found in the skin that helps guard against invasion

FIGURE 1–1
The layers of the skin

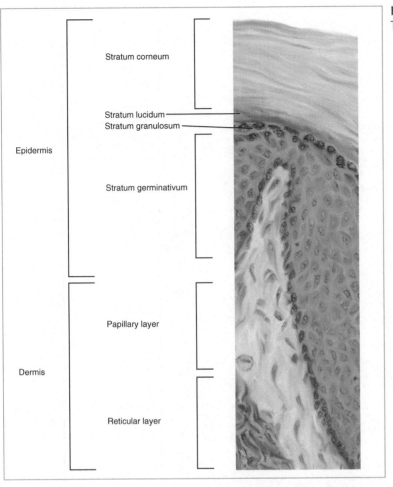

keratinization
the change of living cells to
dead ones

horny zone
the outermost portion of
the epidermis

germinal zone
the layer of skin where cells
divide

stratum corneum
outermost layer of dead skin
cells

sebum
fatty or oily secretion of the
sebaceous gland that lubricates
the hair and skin

stratum lucidum
clear, transparent layer of the epidermis; found under the stratum
corneum

eleidin
clear, lifeless matter deposited in
the form of minute keratohyalin
granules in the protoplasm of
living cells

keratohyalin granules
granules found in living cells that
contribute to the keratin content
of dead, cornified cells

tect the skin against invasion. The process of living cells moving upward and changing to dead cells is known as **keratinization** (kair-uh-tin-yz-AY-shun).

The many epidermal layers are divided into two main zones:

1. **horny zone**
2. **germinal** (JER-muh-nul) **zone**

The Horny Zone

The horny zone, the outer portion of the epidermis, is divided into three layers of differing cells:

1. stratum corneum
2. stratum lucidum
3. stratum granulosum

The outermost layer of the skin is the **stratum corneum** (STRAT-um KOR-nee-um). This outermost layer of dead skin cells is constantly shed, even through the gentle friction of changing clothes. These are flat and without nuclei. These cells are predominantly bound by **sebum**, the skin's natural lubricant. However, this is not enough to prevent the regular shedding of dead skin cells.

The Stratum Lucidum.   Below the stratum corneum lies the **stratum lucidum** (LOO-sih-dum). This layer gets its name from the transparent nature of the cells that contain **eleidin**, a clear substance derived from **keratohyalin** (keh-rih-tuh-HY-a-lun) **granules**, which allow light to pass through them. The cells in this layer also lack nuclei, and they lose their shape. The stratum lucidum is only present in the palms of the hands and the soles of the feet where the epidermis is thickest. It is not found in thin skin.

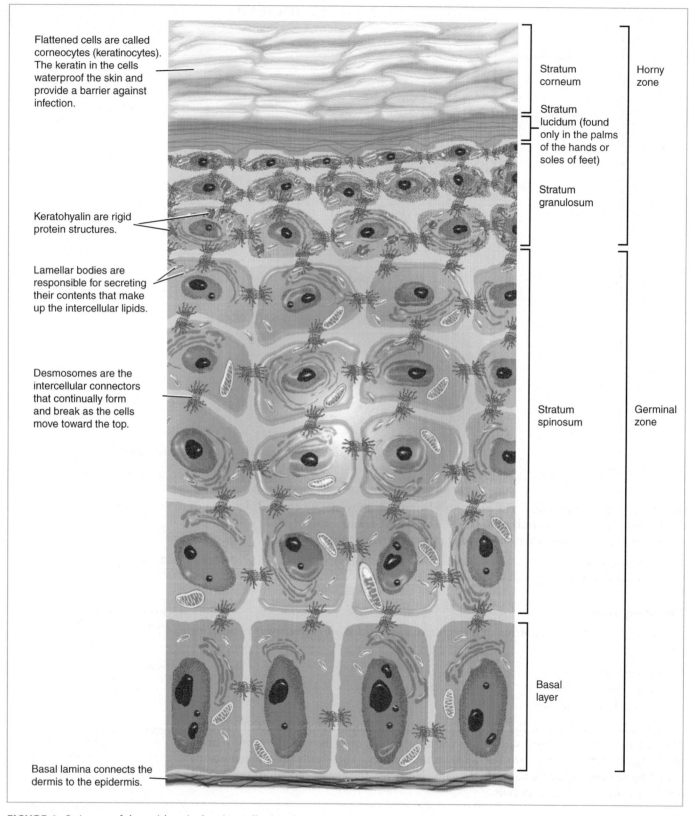

Flattened cells are called corneocytes (keratinocytes). The keratin in the cells waterproof the skin and provide a barrier against infection.

Keratohyalin are rigid protein structures.

Lamellar bodies are responsible for secreting their contents that make up the intercellular lipids.

Desmosomes are the intercellular connectors that continually form and break as the cells move toward the top.

Basal lamina connects the dermis to the epidermis.

Stratum corneum

Stratum lucidum (found only in the palms of the hands or soles of feet)

Stratum granulosum

Stratum spinosum

Basal layer

Horny zone

Germinal zone

FIGURE 1–2 Layers of the epidermis showing cell migration

The Stratum Granulosum.   At the bottom of the horny zone lies the **stratum granulo-sum** (gran-yoo-LOH-sum), also known as the granular layer. Unlike the flatter stratum corneum, the stratum granulosum cells have a distinct shape. The lower cells have nuclei and are still living. As these cells are pushed upward by new cells, they lose their nuclei and die. This layer gives the skin its opaque appearance due to the presence of keratohyalin granules in the cytoplasm. This layer varies in thickness. It is at its thickest on the soles of the feet, followed by the palms of the hand, and it is at its thinnest on the eyelids. Persistent friction and pressure cause areas to thicken for protection and form calluses, as found on the soles of the feet, elbows, and knees.

The Germinal Zone

Two main layers of differing cells make up the germinal or, as it is also known, the living or **basal** (BAY-zul) **zone**:

1. stratum spinosum
2. stratum germinativum

Stratum Spinosum.   The **stratum spinosum** (spee-NOH-sum) is also known as the prickle cell layer because of the cells' prickly shape. They are living cells, each containing a nucleus. Each cell is attached to the cells around it by prickly shaped fibers. Many books refer to the **stratum basale** and the stratum spinosum together as forming the stratum germinativum.

Stratum Germinativum.   The stratum germinativum is the lowest layer of the epidermis and is in contact with the dermis. It is the layer in which cell division called **mitosis** (my-TOH-sis) takes place and where new epidermal tissue is formed and begins migrating to the surface of the skin, replacing the dead skin cells that have been shed. This **desquamation** (des-kwuh-MAY-shun) process takes approximately 28 days—much less in babies and younger children and longer in mature adults, particularly people in their late twenties and older.

In the stratum germinativum are **melanocytes** (muh-LAN-uh-syts). Ultraviolet rays from sunlight react with the **amino acid tyrosine** (TY-ruh-seen) found in the melanocytes and produce **melanin** (MEL-uh-nin), a dark pigment that gives skin its color and protects the dermis from ultraviolet radiation and sun damage. Approximately one in every ten cells in this layer is a melanocyte. The color of the skin depends on the melanin produced. Generally, people of different races have approximately the same number of melanocytes. People with dark skin have melanocytes that are more active and produce more melanin.

Stratum Mucosum.   The **stratum mucosum** (myoo-KOH-sum), combined with the stratum germinativum, is known as the **malpighian** (mal-PIG-ee-un) layer. The stratum mucosum is only a single-cell layer above the stratum germinativum, and there is a difference of opinion as to whether it should be considered a separate layer or part of the stratum germinativum.

The Dermis

The **dermis** (DUR-mis), often called the *living layer* or "true skin," is made of dense connective tissue. It is also divided into layers called the **papillary** (PAP-uh-lair-ee) **layer** and the **reticular** (ruh-TIK-yuh-lur) **layer** (Figure 1–3).

The Papillary Layer

The papillary layer, not to be confused with the **dermal papilla** (DUR-mul puh-PIL-uh) at the base of the hair, lies directly below the epidermis and is made of elastic **collegenous** (kahl-EJ-uh-nus) and reticular fibers that are cone-shaped, finger-like projections called **papillae** (puh-PIL-ee), which protrude upward, into the epidermis, locking the two layers together. Intertwined in this layer are superficial capillaries looped around the papillae. The papillary layer also forms the connective tissue sheath around hair follicles. **Meissner's corpuscles** (MYS-nurz KOR-pus-uls), which are the tactile nerve endings sensitive to touch, are in this layer.

---

stratum granulosum
the granular layer of skin found at the bottom of the horny zone

basal zone
live layer of dividing cells that continuously change and push upward

stratum spinosum
the superior layer of the stratum germinativum; named for its shape and spiny, thorn-like protrusions; also known as the "prickle cell layer"

stratum basale
single cell layer that is the deepest layer of the epidermis

mitosis
the process by which a cell divides into two daughter cells

desquamation
the act of exfoliating dead skin cells

melanocytes
melanin-forming cells

amino acid
units of structure in protein that help break down simple sugars and fats

tyrosine
an amino acid present in melanocytes

melanin
grains of pigment that give hair and skin its color

stratum mucosum
single-cell layer of the epidermis; found above the stratum germinativum

malpighian
a skin layer made of the stratum mucosum and the stratum germinativum

dermis
underlying or inner layer of the skin

papillary layer
the most superficial layer of the dermis

reticular layer
a deep layer of the dermis; composed of dense bundles of collagen fibers; contains vessels, glands, nerve endings, and follicles

dermal papilla
small, cone-shaped indentation at the base of the hair follicle that fits into the hair bulb; also called the hair papilla

collegenous
fiber made of protein that gives the skin its form and strength

papillae
cone-shaped, finger-like projections that protrude into the epidermis

Meissner's corpuscles
nerve endings in the skin that are sensitive to touch

The Reticular Layer

The thickest layer of the skin, making up the greatest portion of it, is the reticular layer. The reticular layer is composed of dense bundles of collagen fibers. These fibers run in parallel layers and are denser closer to the papillary layer; they thin as they incorporate into the fatty **subcutaneous** (sub-kyoo-TAY-nee-us) **tissue**. In the reticular layer are numerous appendages:

> arrector pili muscles
> blood vessels
> fat cells
> hair follicles
> lymph vessels
> nerve endings
> sebaceous glands
> sudoriferous glands

Blood and Lymph Supply. A vascular network of arteries and veins circulate their way into the dermis, where they branch off into smaller capillaries at the hair follicles, the hair papillae, and the skin's various glands.

As the blood supply circulates through the skin via tiny capillaries, it transports the oxygen-rich blood and nutrients essential for growth; reproduction; and tissue repair of the skin, hair, and nails.

Lymph glands produce lymph, which is made of white blood corpuscles and plasma. Vessels carrying the lymph, which contains waste products, salts, and nitrogenous wastes, run parallel to the blood supply and return to the deeper lymph nodes, where the lymphatic fluid is filtered for excretion.

subcutaneous tissue
the fatty layer beneath the dermis that gives the body smoothness and contour; contains fats as an energy source and acts as a protective cushion for the outer skin; also called adipose or subcutis tissue

lymph
colorless, watery fluid that circulates through the lymphatic system; similar in composition to blood plasma

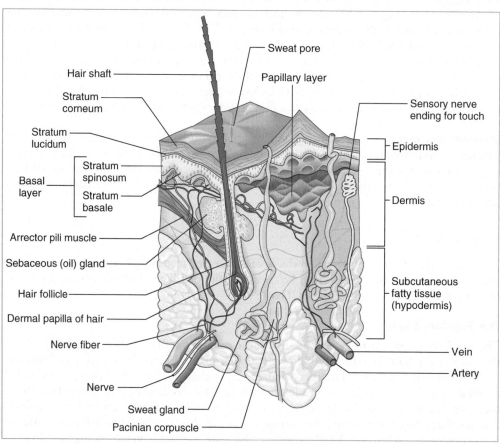

FIGURE 1–3 Structures of the skin

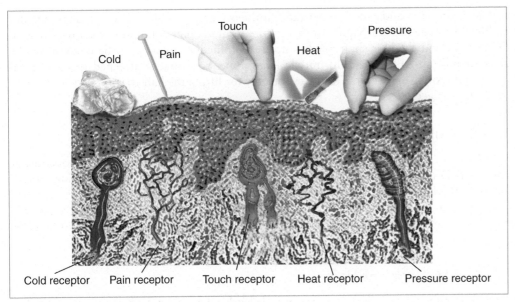

Touch
Pressure
Cold
Pain
Heat

Cold receptor   Pain receptor   Touch receptor   Heat receptor   Pressure receptor

FIGURE 1–4 Sensory nerve endings in the skin

Sudoriferous Glands.   The sudoriferous glands, the sweat glands, are under the control of the sympathetic nervous system. They are found deep in the dermis and have tubular ducts extending all the way up to the pores in the epidermis. There are two kinds of sweat glands: (1) apocrine and (2) eccrine.

The Apocrine Glands.   The **apocrine** (AP-uh-krin) glands, found in the genital area and in the **axillae** (AG-zil-ay), usually open into hair follicles. During perspiration, water, salts, cellular waste, and fatty substances emit from these glands and combine with bacteria at the skin's surface to create body odor. Apocrine glands are also believed to excrete **pheromones**, which are thought to play a role in sexual attraction.

The Eccrine Glands.   The **eccrine** (EK-kreen) glands are found all over the body but in increased numbers on the forehead and the palms of the hands and the soles of the feet. They excrete mainly water with a little salt, urea, and other water-soluble substances.

Sebaceous Glands.   The **sebaceous** (sih-BAY-shus) **glands** are found all over the skin. They are mainly, though not always, appendages to the hair follicles and open into the shafts of hair follicles. These glands are found in greater numbers on the scalp, the T-zone (forehead, nose, and chin), and the cheeks. The sebaceous glands vary in size and shape and in their production of a waxy, oily substance called sebum, which lubricates the skin. The endocrine system influences these glands, which are most active during puberty.

Nerve Endings.   Nerve endings carry impulses to the brain. They are found at various levels of the skin and have different shapes, depending on the jobs they must do (Figure 1–4). As mentioned previously, Meissner's corpuscles are the most superficial and are responsible for touch, as opposed to **Pacinian's** (puh-SIN-ee-unz) **corpuscles**, which are round and lie much deeper in the dermis so that more pressure is required to register sensation. Also closer to the surface is the pain receptor. Below the pain nerve endings are the receptors for heat, which are threadlike, and those for cold, which are round.

Hair

The hair, also called the pilosebaceous unit, is discussed in greater depth later in the chapter. Suffice it to say that the hair and its follicle are major appendages to the structure of the skin (Figure 1–5). Hair is found all over the body, with the exception of the soles of the feet and the palms of the hand. A great deal of hair on the body is invisible to the naked eye. Hair is denser on the head and limbs, and, after puberty, in the groin area and in the

apocrine
glands in the axillae and groin that secrete sweat and substances that produce body odor when contaminated with bacteria

axillae
armpits

pheromones
chemicals produced by humans and other animals that, when secreted, influence other members of the same species

eccrine
glands throughout the skin that excrete mainly water and salt

sebaceous glands
oil glands of the skin connected to hair follicles

Pacinian's corpuscles
nerve endings found deep in the skin that are receptive to pressure

axillae. Hormones and genetic inheritance influence hair growth at different ages in males and females. The root or papilla of the mature **terminal hair** is found in the lower part of the dermis, and the hair shaft reaches up to its follicular opening in the epidermis. The **arrector pili** (ah-REK-tohr-pi-li) muscle is an appendage that is attached to the dermal papilla and to the hair shaft. This is responsible for lifting the hair to trap a layer of air on the skin's surface.

terminal hair
hair found on the scalp, arms, legs, axillae, and pubic area (post-puberty)

arrector pili
an appendage that is attached to the dermal papilla and to the hair shaft

adipose tissue
connective tissue in animal bodies that contains fat

The Subcutaneous Layer

At the base of the dermis is a layer of fatty tissue called the subcutaneous layer, subcutis, or **adipose** (AD-uh-pohs) **tissue**. This layer separates the dermis from the underlying musculature of the body and helps the skin to move over it. This layer also varies in thickness depending on the individual's sex, age, and overall health. Many of the arteries, veins, and lymphatics circulate through this area, as do nerve endings and an abundance of fat cells.

The Structure of Hair

To remove hair successfully, it is important to clearly understand the hair follicle and different stages of hair growth. Healthy hair is continually growing, shedding, and being replaced.

    To understand the physiology of the hair and its follicle, it is best to study it initially as one unit in its active stage. The hair sits in a pocket in the skin. Imagine a finger poking a balloon so the balloon indents (Figure 1–6).[1] The surface area of the balloon depresses around the fingertip and back upward, to the surface. In a similar fashion, parts of the epidermis go down around the base of the hair and back upward, to the surface.

FIGURE 1–5
Cross section of the hair follicle and skin

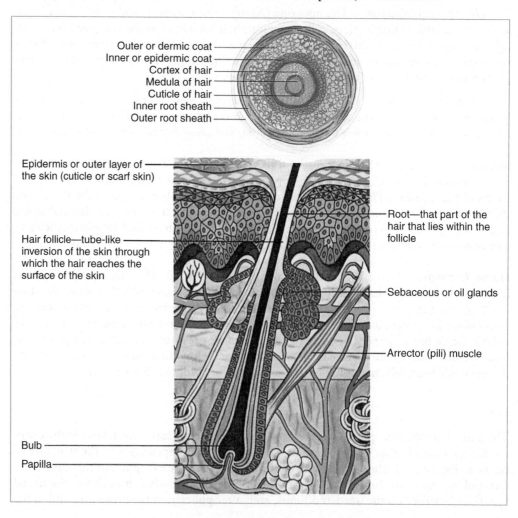

Outer or dermic coat
Inner or epidermic coat
Cortex of hair
Medula of hair
Cuticle of hair
Inner root sheath
Outer root sheath

Epidermis or outer layer of the skin (cuticle or scarf skin)

Hair follicle—tube-like inversion of the skin through which the hair reaches the surface of the skin

Root—that part of the hair that lies within the follicle

Sebaceous or oil glands

Arrector (pili) muscle

Bulb
Papilla

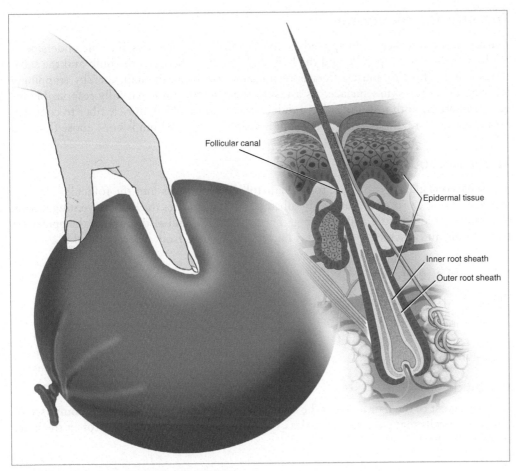

FIGURE 1–6 Balloon diagram of hair follicle

The Follicular Canal and Sheaths

The space the finger occupies in the balloon model, equivalent to the space the hair occupies, is known as the **follicular** (fah-LIK-yuh-lar) **canal**. The outer sheath of the canal is formed from the basal cell layer. The inner side of the follicular canal, which is made of horny epidermal tissue, is called the **external root sheath**.

The Hair Shaft

The hair shaft is lined with epidermal tissue and in full-grown, active-hair stage extends downward, through the dermis to the subcutaneous tissue. The epidermal cells are responsible for producing the hair follicle and the **hair matrix**. The base of the follicular canal widens to something called the **hair follicle bulb**. The bulb, the area where the hair grows, contains the dividing cells of the hair matrix that produce the hair and the protective external and **internal root sheath**. The internal root sheath is sometimes visible on a tweezed hair, looking to the naked eye like a clump of petroleum jelly around the base of the hair. It protects the hair up as far as the sebaceous gland. At that point, it disappears.

The Dermal Papilla and Papillae

The dermal papilla at the base of the hair bulb is an indentation which, as mentioned previously, is the layer of dermal tissue that attaches itself to the epidermis with protrusions called papillae. These papillae contain the blood supply needed for providing nutrients for growth as well as the hormones that stimulate hair growth. This indentation is also called the papilla.

---

follicular canal
the depression in the skin that houses the entire pilosebaceous unit

external root sheath
the inner side of the follicular canal which is made of horny epidermal tissue

hair matrix
the germinating center of the hair follicle where mitotic activity occurs

hair follicle bulb
the bulbous base of the hair follicle that houses the dermal papilla

internal root sheath
the innermost layer of the hair follicle, closest to the hair

The Arrector Pili Muscle

The arrector pili muscle is an appendage to the hair that attaches itself to the underside of the hair at the dermal papilla and the hair shaft, midway between the bulb and the sebaceous gland. This tiny muscle fiber is responsible for lifting the hair, thereby trapping a layer of air on the skin's surface. As a result, the arrector pili is partially responsible for heat regulation. Both fear and cold stimuli cause the arrector pili muscle fiber to contract, lifting the hair straight upward. The result is visible as "goose bumps" or "goose flesh."

The Sebaceous Gland

The sebaceous gland is attached to the hair follicle and opens into the follicular shaft. It secretes sebum, a protective fatty, oily substance that lubricates the hair, preventing it from becoming dry and brittle and breaking. The sebaceous gland also prevents the epidermis from drying and cracking and prevents bacteria and germs from entering the skin.

Layers of the Hair

Three layers compose the hair (Figure 1–7):

1. cuticle
2. cortex
3. medulla

The Cuticle

cuticle
the outermost layer of hair consisting of one overlapping layer of transparent, scale-like cells

The outermost of the hair layers is the **cuticle** (KYOO-tih-kul). The cuticle is composed of transparent cells that overlap like scales. The purpose of the cuticle is to protect the inner layers of the hair.

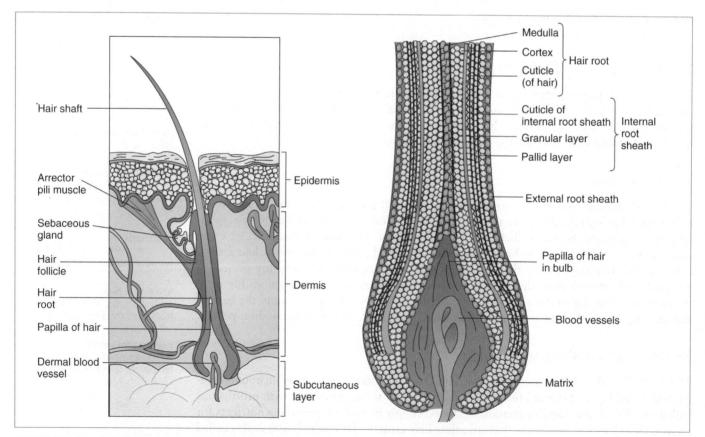

FIGURE 1–7 Hair follicle structure relative to the sebaceous gland

The Cortex

Below the cuticle lies the **cortex** (KOR-teks). This middle layer is made of elongated cells of fibrous tissue and the pigment that gives hair its color. The cortex is also the layer that gives hair its strength and elasticity.

cortex
the middle layer of the hair; a fibrous protein core formed by elongated cells containing melanin

The Medulla

The innermost layer of the hair is the **medulla** (muh-DUL-uh). Made of round cells, the medulla is also called the pith or marrow. Fine hair lacks the medulla, but the medulla can be found in all wavy hair. In general, the curlier the hair, the stronger the medulla.

medulla
the innermost layer of hair; composed of round cells; often absent in fine hair

Types of Hair

There are three main types of hair (Figure 1–8):

1. lanugo
2. vellus
3. terminal

Lanugo

Lanugo, soft, downy hair, is also called fetal hair because it is on fetuses in utero and on infants at birth, covering their bodies and scalps. It may contain pigment and be light or dark. Lanugo often sheds a few weeks after birth. The part of the scalp that rests on the crib mattress often loses lanugo first due to friction. Eventually, the permanent hair begins to grow in.

lanugo
soft, downy hair present on fetuses in utero, and infants at birth

Vellus

This is often confused with lanugo, but **vellus** is present through adulthood. It is fine, short, and often called "peach fuzz." Vellus often has no pigment or medulla. Women are believed to have 55 percent more vellus than men, and it can be found on women's faces where men produce beard and mustache hair at puberty onward.

vellus
fine, short hair with no pigment, found mainly on women's faces; also referred to as "peach fuzz"

Terminal

Terminal hair is the longer, coarser, pigmented hair that covers the scalp and is found on the arms and legs of both males and females. At puberty, it is also found in the groin area and axillae of both males and females, as well as on the face of men and occasionally the chest and back.

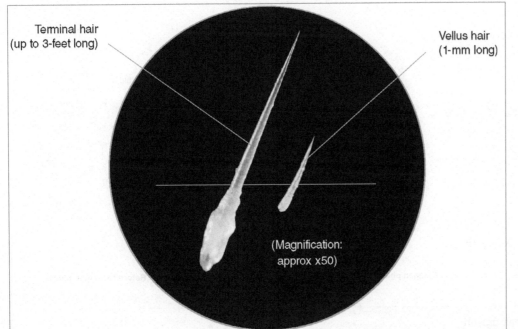

Terminal hair
(up to 3-feet long)

Vellus hair
(1-mm long)

(Magnification: approx x50)

FIGURE 1–8
Terminal hair and vellus

Hair follicles can produce vellus or terminal hair, which can be affected by age; genetics; health; and the hormonal changes of puberty, pregnancy, and menopause.

The Stages of Hair Growth

There are three main stages of hair growth (Figure 1–9):

1. growing
2. transitional
3. resting

anagen
the growth phase in the hair cycle in which a new hair is synthesized

catagen
the transition stage of the hair's growth cycle; the period between the growth and resting phases

telogen
the resting phase of the hair follicle in its growth cycle

The percentage of hair in each stage, and the length of time hair may be in a stage, varies for different parts of the face and body. The three phases, **anagen** (AN-uh-jen), **catagen** (KAT-uh-jen), and **telogen** (TEL-uh-jen), can be easily remembered in their growth sequence by using the acronym ACT.

Anagen: The Growing Phase

Anagen is the hair's active growing phase, when the hair follicle is at its deepest. At this stage, the hair matrix is active, encapsulating the dermal papilla, and the bulb of the hair is visibly darker. Anagen can be affected and altered by the health of the individual, by the use of certain drugs and medications, and by pregnancy. Once a growing anagen hair has reached its full length, it can remain there, depending on location, for varying amounts of time—a few weeks on the fingers to eight years on the scalp.

Catagen: The Transitional Phase

Catagen occurs when the hair follicle separates from the dermal papilla. The follicle shrinks to about a third of its anagen size. A thin cord of epidermal tissue attaching the follicle to the dermal papilla retracts upward, with the dermal papilla. Catagen is the shortest hair-growth phase, lasting for only a few days up to a few weeks. Only a very small percentage of hairs are at this stage at any given time.

It is more difficult to recognize the bulb in catagen, because it is somewhere between the anagen and telogen stages and must be plucked to be observed. What can be observed is that there is a slight reduction in the pigment of the hair, due to a reduction of melanin in the bulb.

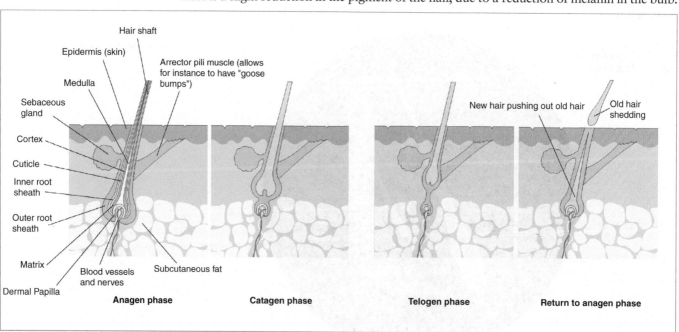

FIGURE 1–9 The three cycles of hair growth

	Percent Telogen	Percent Anagen	Percent Catagen	Percent Uncertain	Duration on Telogen	Duration on Anagen	Number Follicles per sq. cm	Hair Growth Rate	Total Number Follicles in Area	Depth of Terminal Anagen
HEAD										
Scalp	13	85	1–2	1–2	3–4 months	2–6 yrs	350	0.35 mm		3–5 mm
Eyebrows	90	10			3 months	4–8 wks		0.16 mm		2–2.5 mm
Ear	85	10			3 months	4–8 weeks				
Cheeks	30–50	50–70					880	0.32 mm		2–4 mm
Beard-chin	30	70			10 weeks	1 year	500	0.38 mm		2–4 mm
Mustache/upper lip	35	65			6 weeks	16 weeks	500			1–2.5 mm
BODY										
Axillae	70	30			3 months	4 months	65	0.3 mm		3.5–4.5 mm
Trunk	NA	NA					70	0.3 mm	425,000	2–4.5 mm
Pubic area	70	30			3 months	4 months	70			3.5–5 mm
Arms	80	20			18 weeks	13 weeks	80	0.33 mm	220,000	
Legs and thighs	80	20			24 weeks	16 weeks	60	0.21 mm	370,000	2.5–4 mm
Breasts	70	30					65	0.35 mm		3–4.5 mm

TABLE 1–1 Hair growth table[2]

Telogen: The Resting Phase

By the time the catagen hair becomes a telogen hair in its resting phase, the follicle is one-third its original anagen size. The base of the hair looks like a club, from whence it gets the name **club hair**. The bulb is usually white. The now-shrunk dermal papilla is separated from the hair follicle and is only attached by the thin cord of epidermal cells. It will be released by the end of the telogen phase.

club hair
hair that has lost its root structure and that, when shed from the follicle, exhibits a round shape

Hair Growth

Understanding hair growth is still an incomplete science, but there are documented, strong scientific findings that help explain the effects of certain elements on hair growth. Hair grows faster in the summer, for example. Good health improves hair growth. Young people experience more hair growth. In contrast, there is an increase in the number of telogen hairs during illness, after childbirth, and when an individual is experiencing stress. Table 1–1 gives average measurements of the hair in its various stages in various parts of the body. While not absolutely accurate for any particular individual (hair growth is affected by illness, medications, stress, pregnancy, and so on), this table can help explain what is potentially happening in a hair follicle in a particular part of the body any given time. Excess androgens may certainly stimulate terminal hair to regrow faster, meaning a shorter telogen phase.

The Functions of the Skin

As the body's largest sensory organ, the skin has multiple functions, including protection, heat regulation, **excretion**, **secretion**, **absorption**, sensation, and the synthesis of vitamin D. Hair plays an important role in many of these functions. Healthy skin should have hair.

excretion
the act of discharging waste matter from tissues or organs

secretion
the process of producing and discharging substances from glands

absorption
the uptake of one substance into another

Protection

Skin covers the body and protects it against the environment and the invasion of bacteria. Normal skin is usually not sterile and is often covered by legions of bacteria. These bacteria are generally noninvading and nonpathogenic. The skin has a built-in protective aid known as the **acid mantle**, which has the appropriate pH of 5 to 5.6 (7 is neutral). The

acid mantle
the bacteria-killing layer made of sweat and lipids

acid mantle is caused by the combined activity of the sweat and sebaceous glands. Perspiration is acidic. As it lies on the skin's surface, it can act as a bactericide by inhibiting the growth of bacteria. (However, this is not true of areas of higher perspiration, like the axillae and groin area, where the skin is softer and where there is less acidity in excessive perspiration, allowing bacterial growth.)

Reactions, often inflammation, swelling, and welts, occur when an unwanted organism invades the skin. Unwanted organisms are recognized by the **Langerhans' cells** in the epidermis that warn against invading microorganisms. **Leucocytes** are released to engulf and destroy the invading organism. The reaction may seem extreme, but it is the skin's natural way of preventing the spread of infection to the surrounding tissue.

Starting with the outermost layer of the epidermis, the horny layer acts as a barrier against bacterial invasion and water absorption. The skin is waterproof, in part due to the aid of sebum secreted from the sebaceous gland that lubricates and waterproofs the epidermal layers and makes the skin soft and supple. Sebum also prevents drying and cracking and thereby prevents bacteria and germs from entering the skin and, in turn, the body. Adult sebum is also believed to be fungicidal and may play a role in preventing some types of ringworm. When intact, the skin also prevents harmful fluids from entering the body. It not only prevents water from entering the body, it prevents water (trans-epidermal water loss), blood, and lymph from leaving the body.

The germinal layer, particularly the stratum germinativum, contains melanin-producing melanocytes that protect the body from harmful ultraviolet radiation. People with dark skin get better protection from ultraviolet radiation and generally have fewer incidences of skin cancer.

The adipose tissue in the **subcutis** (sub-KYOO-tis) cushions the body from falls, protects against minor trauma, and provides a source of energy.

The lymphatic system acts as a second line of defense against bacterial invasion. Lymphatic fluid and lymphocytes are produced in the lymph nodes. **Lymphocytes** are the only cells in the fluid and are transported through lymph vessels, where they engulf bacteria and are carried to the lymph nodes for filtration and draining of waste products.

Heat Regulation

A healthy body temperature is usually around 98 degrees Fahrenheit (37 degrees Celsius). As changes occur in the environment, the body adjusts with various mechanisms to counteract those changes and to maintain a safe and appropriate temperature. The skin plays a vital role in maintaining the body's temperature and homeostasis. It does so in numerous ways that all work together to help keep the body at a safe and healthy temperature. These ways include evaporation, perspiration, radiation, and insulation.

Evaporation of perspiration on the skin's surface produces cooling, also known as thermoregulation. Radiation from constriction and **dilation** (dy-LAY-shun) of tiny blood vessels, called capillaries, affect body temperature. The dilation or expansion of capillaries causes the surface heat of the body to be reduced through radiation, visible in some skin types as a flushed pink appearance (e.g., in the face). Conversely, the **constriction** or contraction of capillaries slows blood flow, preserving heat and giving the skin a bluish tint. The arrector pili muscle fiber is stimulated by the body when the body feels cold or experiences fear, contracting and lifting the hair, which then traps a layer of insulating air on the skin's surface. Even sebum, which is produced in the sebaceous gland, plays a role in heat regulation, lubricating the hair, keeping it supple, and preventing the hair from becoming brittle and breaking so that the hair will be able to do its job. The adipose tissue of the subcutis also acts as an effective insulator, keeping the body warm.

Secretion and Excretion

The sebaceous glands, as mentioned earlier, secrete sebum, the skin's natural lubricant. During perspiration, salts, urea, and other waste material are excreted through the **sudoriferous** (sood-uh-RIF-uh-rus) **glands** and rise to the surface of the skin.

Langerhans' cells
cells found in the epidermis that warn against the invasion of microorganisms and respond to that invasion

leucocytes
white blood cells or corpuscles

subcutis
a layer of subcutaneous tissue

lymphocytes
cells produced in the lymph nodes, spleen, and thymus gland that produce antibodies capable of attacking infection

dilation
the process of widening or expanding

constriction
the process of narrowing

sudoriferous glands
the skin's sweat glands

Sensation

Through the skin's ability to register sensation the body experiences heat, cold, pain, pressure, and even an annoying itch. Whereas a minor burn can be very painful, a third-degree burn that damages nerves can leave the skin numb, without sensation, once the tissue has healed.

Absorption and Penetration

The skin can absorb oil- and fat-based substances to differing levels, but it cannot absorb water. Pharmaceutical topical creams and lotions, which can effect dramatic changes in the skin, can penetrate the dermis and absorb into the blood supply. For this reason, these creams and lotions require medical guidance and physicians' prescriptions to be obtained and used. **Cosmeceuticals**, which contain no drugs or medications that could cause drug interactions or carry warnings against usage if pregnant or nursing, may have deeper absorption qualities than standard over-the-counter cosmetics. They are believed to be able to effect greater change in the skin than drugstore brands. Cosmeceuticals are obtained from, and require the professional guidance of, a dermatologist, plastic surgeon, or skin-care professional.

cosmeceuticals
products that fall between the categories of pharmaceuticals and cosmetics and that generally have a higher level of absorption than standard cosmetics

 ## Conclusion

Understanding the anatomy and physiology of the skin and hair is fundamental for any hair-removal specialist, regardless of hair-removal method. A good education in the anatomy and physiology of skin and hair is the foundation on which to build all aspects of hair removal.

You should now be able to appreciate the delicate nature of skin; identify the various methods of hair removal; understand how the skin can be easily traumatized; and appreciate the skin's tremendous capacity to heal itself, fight infection, and recover from the many abuses it confronts daily.

 ## Endnotes

1. Described by R.N. Richards, M.D., and G. E. Meharg, R.N., in *Cosmetic Medical Electrolysis and Temporary Hair Removal.* 1997. Toronto, CA: Medric Ltd.

2. From *Cosmetic and Medical Electrolysis and Temporary Hair Removal.*

 ## Discussion and Review Questions

1. What are the three main layers of the skin?
2. Into which two zones is the epidermis divided?
3. Name two layers of the epidermis.
4. In which layer are melanocytes found?
5. What are the two layers of the dermis?
6. What is a sudorific gland?
7. What is a Pacinian's corpuscle?
8. Where is the hair matrix?
9. What are the three stages of hair growth?
10. Name at least five functions of the skin.

 ## Additional Readings

Lees, Mark. 2001. *Skin Care: Beyond the Basics.* Clifton Park, NY: Milady, an imprint of Delmar Learning.

Milady's Standard Comprehensive Training for Estheticians. 2003. Clifton Park, NY: Milady, an imprint of Delmar Learning.

Milady's Standard Cosmetology. 2004. Clifton Park, NY: Milady, an imprint of Delmar Learning.

CHAPTER 2

Skin Disorders and Diseases

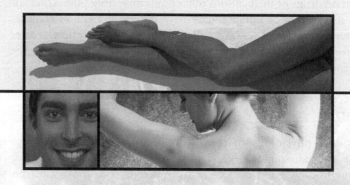

Chapter Outline

Learning Objectives

By the end of this chapter, you should be able to:

1. Understand and identify the most common skin disorders and diseases in the salon or hair-removal clinic.
2. Determine the severity of a condition and whether the condition contraindicates service.
3. Advise a client to seek medical evaluation appropriately.

Key Terms

abscess
acne rosacea
anaphylactic shock
basal cell carcinoma
bulla
crust
dermatologist
dermatology
eczema
epinephrine
erythromycin
excoriation

fissure
herpes simplex
impetigo
keloid
keratosis
lesions
macule
malignant melanoma
milia
mycoses
necrotic
nodule

papule
parasite
pediculosis
pustule
ringworm
scale
seborrhea
septicemia
squamous cell carcinoma
staphylococci
streptococci
systemic

tumor
ulcer
urticaria
vasodilation
verucca plantaris
verucca vulgaris
vesicle
wheal

Introduction

Hair-removal specialists see and touch a lot of skin on various parts of the body. Recognizing **lesions** (LEE-zhunz), skin disorders, and diseases help hair-removal specialists know when it is possible to provide a service, when service is contraindicated, and when to encourage clients to seek medical attention. The purpose of this chapter is to help hair-removal specialists recognize some of the skin disorders and diseases and know when it would be unwise to perform a service or when to refer out for medical attention. It is not designed to educate to the level of treating such disorders or diseases.

lesions
structural changes found in tissue that result from trauma or disease

Skin Diseases and Disorders

The science of diagnosing skin diseases and disorders is called **dermatology**, and the physician who specializes in the treatment of skin diseases is called a **dermatologist**. Hair-removal specialists should recognize common skin disorders and diseases, but some disorders and diseases may not be textbook cases in appearance. When in doubt, hair-removal specialists should always err on the side of caution and leave diagnoses to dermatologists.

dermatology
the branch of medical science that relates to the diagnosis and treatment of skin conditions

dermatologist
a physician whose medical expertise is diagnosing and treating skin conditions

Lesions

A lesion is a structural change in tissue caused by trauma or disease. Lesions can be categorized three ways depending on severity (Figure 2–1):

1. primary
2. secondary
3. tertiary or vascular

Primary Lesions

Primary lesions, the first recognizable signs of skin disease, may range from flat, nonpalpable changes in skin color to elevated, palpable, solid masses. These types of lesions include a:

- **Macule** (MA-kyool), which is a small, discolored spot or patch on the surface of the skin that is neither raised nor sunken (e.g., a freckle)
- **Papule** (PA-pyool), which is a small, elevated pimple in the skin that contains no fluid but that may develop pus
- **Wheal** (WHEEL), which is an itchy, swollen lesion that lasts only a few hours (e.g., a hive or an insect bite)

macule
a spot or discoloration level with the skin; a freckle

papule
a small, elevated pimple in the skin; contains no fluid but may develop pus

wheal
an itchy, swollen lesion caused by a blow, scratch, or pressure

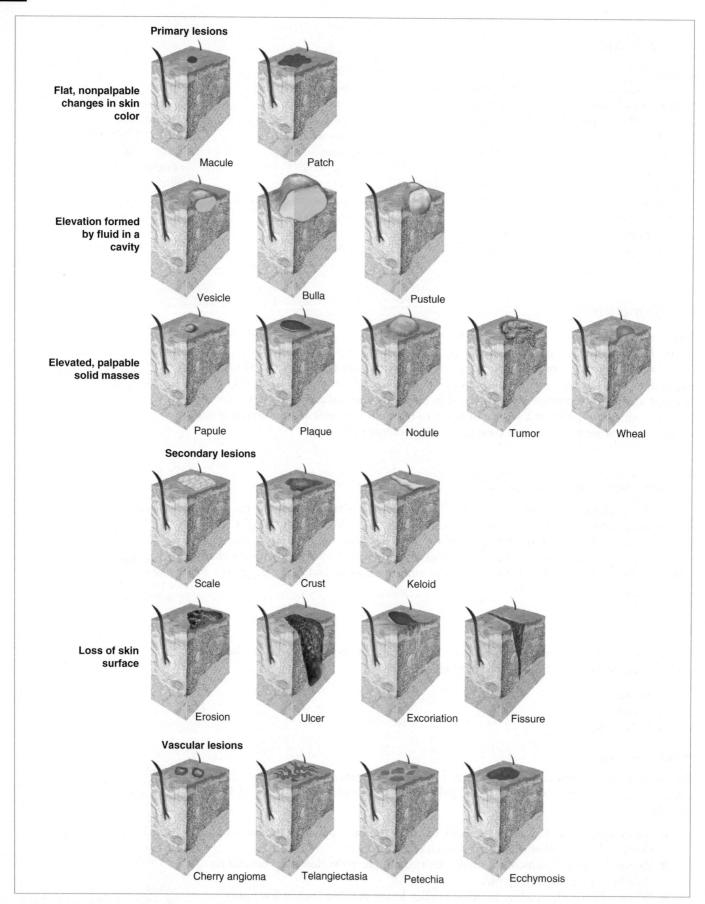

FIGURE 2–1 Three types of skin lesions

- **Nodule** (NAHJ-ool), which is a solid lump larger than a papule (see preceding) that projects above the surface or lies within or under the skin and that varies in size from a pea to a hickory nut
- **Tumor** (TOO-mur), which is an external swelling that varies in size, shape, and color
- **Vesicle** (VES-ih-kuhl), which is a clear-fluid-filled blister within or just beneath the epidermis (e.g., a poison ivy blister)
- **Bulla** (BULL-uh), which is a blister containing watery fluid that is larger than, but similar to, a vesicle (see preceding)
- **Pustule** (PUS-chool), which is a pus-filled skin elevation with an inflamed base

Secondary Lesions

Secondary lesions are primary lesions that have progressed to later disease stages. Secondary lesions are usually characterized by material buildup on the skin and include a(n):

- **Scale**, which is a dry or greasy accumulation of epidermal flakes (e.g., abnormal or excessive dandruff)
- **Crust** (scab), which is an accumulation of serum and pus, mixed perhaps with epidermal material (e.g., a sore scab)
- **Excoriation** (ek-skor-ee-AY-shun), which is a skin sore or abrasion produced by scratching or scraping (e.g., a raw surface due to superficial skin loss after injury)
- **Fissure** (FISH-ur), which is a crack in the skin that penetrates the derma (e.g., chapping on hands or lips)
- **Ulcer** (UL-sur), which is an open lesion on the skin or mucous membrane that is accompanied by pus and loss of skin depth
- **Scar** (**keloid**) (KEE-loyd), which is likely to form when a skin condition that has penetrated the dermal layer has healed

Tertiary Lesions

Tertiary lesions, also called vascular lesions, are tissue changes characterized by tiny blood vessels that have ruptured into the skin. The term *tertiary*, while still used today, is something of a misnomer as vascular lesions can also be primary and secondary lesions. Examples of vascular lesions are telangiectasia (Figure 2–2) and ecchymosis.

Infectious Skin Diseases

There are four categories of infectious skin diseases:

1. bacterial
2. fungal
3. parasitic
4. viral

Bacterial Skin Diseases

A bacterial infection can easily cross contaminate the surrounding area, or affect another individual who is exposed to the microorganisms. In the case of a severe infection, the invading microorganisms may enter the bloodstream causing **septicemia** (sep-tih-SEE-mee-ah). Treatment often requires the use of antibacterial ointments or oral antibiotic medication.

nodule
a solid lump (larger than a papule) that may project above the skin or lie below it

tumor
an abnormal swelling or enlargement that can be malignant or benign

vesicle
a small blister filled with clear fluid

bulla
a large blister containing a watery fluid

pustule
a small, round, raised area of inflamed skin filled with pus

scale
a thin plate of horny epidermis

crust
an accumulation of serum and pus, sometimes mixed with epidermal material

excoriation
abrasion or scratch on the skin

fissure
a cut or crack in the skin

ulcer
an open lesion on the skin or mucous membrane of the body; not caused by a wound

keloid
the skin or film that forms over a wound; contracts to later form a scar

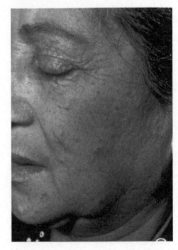

FIGURE 2–2 Telangiectasia

septicemia
occurs when a bacterial infection enters the bloodstream; also known as blood poisoning

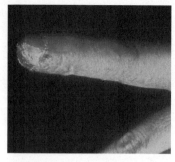

FIGURE 2–3 Impetigo

impetigo
a contagious infection of the skin; visible as brownish scabs mainly around the mouth and nostrils

streptococci
spherical bacteria that causes such diseases as scarlet fever or pneumonia

staphylococci
bacteria typically occurring in clusters; inhabits the skin and mucous membranes

abscess
an enclosed, pus-containing cavity

necrotic
pertaining to dead tissue surrounded by living tissue

mycoses
another name for fungal skin infections

ringworm (tinea corporis)
a parasitic disease and its appendages; presents as circular patches

parasite
an organism that lives and feeds off another organism

pediculosis
louse infestation

Impetigo.   Impetigo (im-puh-TEE-go) (Figure 2–3) is an acute and highly contagious skin infection, found mainly on the faces and hands of children. It is caused by the **streptococci** (strep-toh-KOK-eye) and **staphylococci** (staf-uh-loh-KOK-eye) organisms. With this infection, the area is red and covered with vesicles that ooze and form yellowish crusts.

Abscess.   Also called a boil or a furuncle, an **abscess** (AB-ses) is caused by bacterial organisms like staphylococcus due to a contaminated foreign body, like a splinter. The center of the infection becomes **necrotic** (nuh-KROT-ik), forming pus. The pressure of the well-formed infection makes it very painful to touch. In severe cases, it requires lancing (surgical evacuation) by a physician to release the pus.

Fungal Skin Diseases

Fungal infections are also called **mycoses**. They are generally not as contagious as bacterial infections, unless the immune system is suppressed. Treatment is often slower than bacterial infections (depending on the severity) and requires the use of antifungal prescription medicines.

Ringworm.   Ringworm (tinea corporis) (Figure 2–4) is a highly contagious skin infection that presents with red patches of scaly, blistering skin on hairy aspects of the arms, legs, and scalp. Occasionally, ringworm infections form on nonhairy areas of the skin and can be observed as ring-shaped, red lesions. The fungi feed on dead skin cells and perspiration. This condition causes itchiness and a desire to scratch. Scratching, the leading cause of spreading this disease, also causes soreness to the infected area, possible secondary infection by bacteria, scarring, and permanent hair loss.

Parasitic Skin Diseases

These diseases are infestations of parasites. A **parasite** is an organism that lives on another organism and derives its nourishment to grow and reproduce from that organism.

Pediculosis.   Commonly known as a louse infestation, **pediculosis** (puh-dik-yuh-LOH-sis) is classified into three groups:

1. head lice
2. body lice
3. pubic lice

These infestations feed on human blood. While head lice are not a sign of poor hygiene, body lice generally are. Head lice transfer indirectly from head to head. Pubic lice spread generally by sexual contact. All are treatable with an assortment of shampoos and pre-

FIGURE 2–4
Ringworm
(tinea corporis)

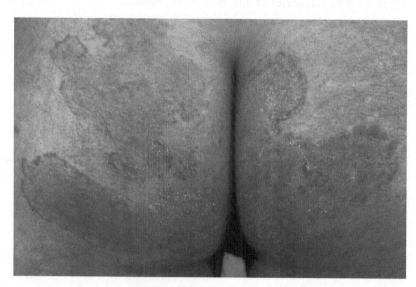

scription lotions and creams. It is important for the hair-removal specialist to appreciate the importance of fresh protective coverings and drapes for each client, as well as things like hair clips and bands to prevent the spread of pediculosis, because it may not be apparent to the technician (or client) that the condition is present.

Viral Skin Diseases

Some viral skin diseases are more bothersome and contagious (herpes simplex) than others (warts), but all viral skin diseases should be avoided and the client referred to a physician for the appropriate treatment.

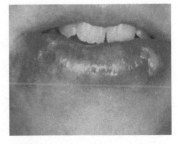

FIGURE 2–5 Herpes simplex

herpes simplex
a virus causing cold sores

Herpes Simplex.   Also called a cold sore, the **herpes simplex** viral lesion (Figure 2–5) forms around the lips. These lesions present as clusters of weeping vesicles that eventually form scabs. The virus can remain dormant in the body for a long time before manifesting. The lesions often flare up at times of stress or illness (e.g., a cold), during menstruation, or after excessive sun exposure. During a flare-up of herpes simplex, the client should not be treated near that area. If the client is prone to cold sores, a prophylactic medication can be taken a few days before receiving a service to prevent an outbreak.

Verucca Vulgaris.   Commonly known as a wart, **verucca vulgaris** (vuh-ROO-kuh vul-GAYR-is) is a virus causing the buildup of keratinized cells into nodules variable in size from a few millimeters to a few centimeters. This condition is most commonly found on the hands, particularly the fingers, and is most prevalent in children. Scratching the warts causes them to spread. While they sometimes disappear spontaneously, they often require over-the-counter medications or treatment from the physician for removal.

verucca vulgaris
a viral infection that causes the buildup of keratinized cells; commonly known as a wart

verucca plantaris
a viral infection found on the soles of the feet; commonly known as a plantar wart

Verucca Plantaris.   Commonly known as plantar warts, **verucca plantaris** (vuh-ROO-kuh plan-TAR-us) is found on the soles of the feet. Unlike the verucca vulgaris, which is raised, the verucca plantaris burrows its way deeper into the skin the longer it is present. These warts can become extremely painful when left untreated. The earlier they are treated, the more superficial they are and the easier they can be treated with over-the-counter medications that break down and slough off the keratinized cells and draw out the warts' cores. When left untreated too long, these warts may need to be excised by a physician or podiatrist.

Allergy-Based Skin Diseases

Allergic or hypersensitive reactions can be caused by multiple factors, including those that are topical, ingested, or inhaled. These factors include chemicals; food and drugs; excessive heat exposure; and plant, animal, and insect exposure. Most allergy-based skin disorders are noncontagious. Poison ivy and poison oak, in contrast, are contagious.

urticaria
the itchy response to an allergen that causes mast cells to release histamine; commonly known as hives

Urticaria

Commonly known as hives, **urticaria** (ur-tuh-KAYR-ee-ah) is the itchy response to an allergen that causes mast cells to release histamine. When this happens, the blood vessels dilate and plasma proteins in the blood and fluids permeate, creating wheals, which are rounded elevations defined by red borders and pale centers. It is this reaction in the tissue that causes extreme itchiness.

eczema
an inflammatory itching disease of the skin

Eczema

Also known as contact dermatitis, **eczema** (EG-zuh-muh) (Figure 2–6) is one of the noncontagious skin conditions. It usually appears with redness (erythema), flakiness, and itching, as well as a combination of papules and vesicles. Eczema's slight redness and flakiness do not prohibit infected areas from being treated, but weeping lesions should be avoided.

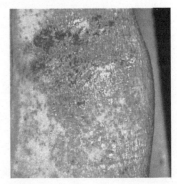

FIGURE 2–6 Eczema

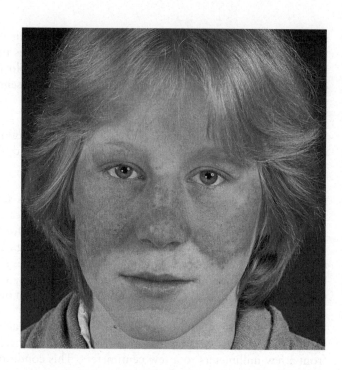

FIGURE 2–7 Lupus butterfly rash

Autoimmune Skin Diseases

Autoimmunity is a condition in which the body's immune system cannot distinguish between foreign antigens and the body's own cells.

Lupus

Lupus gets its name from the Latin term *lupus* (meaning "wolf") due to the red butterfly mark on the face that resembles marks that may appear after a wolf attack (Figure 2–7). Lupus affects women predominately, and its symptoms may include joint pain and swelling and visible blood vessels around the nail cuticles. In serious cases, lupus may affect the nervous system and kidneys. There are two forms of lupus:

1. systemic
2. discoid

Systemic Lupus Erythematosus

systemic
pertaining to or affecting the body as a whole

Systemic lupus erythematosus (SLE) is a serious form of lupus that also affects internal organs. This disease is controlled with steroid therapy.

Discoid Lupus Erythematosus

Discoid lupus erythematosus (DLE), the less serious form of lupus, primarily affects the skin of the face, arms, and back with red patches, folliculitis, lesions that are round and firm. This condition is aggravated by ultraviolet light (UVA and UVB).

Chemical-Causation Disorders

Chemical-causation skin disorders result from dyes, hair colors, synthetic materials, detergents, petroleum by-products, metals in things like costume jewelry, perfumes, and cosmetics.

People who know their allergies and the severity of their allergic reactions, particularly their reactions to certain drugs, should carry documentation. Those who suffer extreme, even life-threatening, reactions should carry **epinephrine** (ep-ih-NEF-run) kits to prevent **anaphylactic** (an-uh-fuh-LAK-tik) **shock** when exposed to triggering allergens.

Food-and-Drug Causation Disorders

The foods most commonly causing allergic reactions, usually through ingestion, are milk, strawberries, peanuts, sesame, and shellfish (iodine). Common allergy causing drugs are **erythromycin** (uh-RITH-roh-MY-sun) and penicillin.

Heat Causation Disorders

While some people who are hypersensitive to the sun's rays develop skin reactions more severe than sunburn, others may develop a rash commonly called "prickly heat." Prickly heat manifests as redness and hundreds of minuscule bumps on the skin, particularly in the folds of the skin.

Plant Causation Disorders

The most common plant causing allergic reactions is perhaps the stinging nettle, which in Latin is *urticara*, the name of the skin disorder (see preceding). Poison ivy and poison oak both fall into this category. Contact with plant resins causes an itchy rash with an abundance of blisters and hives that can develop a few hours to a few days after contact. Cortisone cream is the usual method of treatment.

Hormonal-Induced Skin Disorders

Many people experience skin disorders due to hormonal changes. While these disorders can be aggravated or improved by external influences and topical preparations, the causes of these disorders are systemic, meaning they stem from the body as a whole.

Acne

Acne usually occurs during puberty and continues, when left untreated, through adolescence and into adulthood. Disfiguring scars and skin pitting can result. Adult or mature-onset acne can occur in adulthood, even if acne did not present at puberty.

Acne Terms

Blackheads—Trapped sebum that becomes oxidized keratin on the skin's surface and blackens; also called comedoes

Comedoes—Blackheads (see preceding)

Whiteheads—Accumulations of keratinized cells and sebum enclosed in blind ducts that, when newly established, are hard and white like tiny pearls and that, with time, soften and yellow; also known as **milia** (MIL-ee-ah)

Pimples—Small whiteheads (see preceding) that are slightly red, indicating infection and some pus

Pustules—Whiteheads (see preceding) that are obviously yellowish, red, and swollen, indicating considerable infection and pus

Cystic acne—Inflammations and pockets of pus and fluid that are farther under the skin than pustules (see preceding)

Milia—Whiteheads (see preceding)

epinephrine
a synthetic form of adrenaline that relaxes the airways and constricts blood vessels; used to treat asthma and reduce blood loss

anaphylactic shock
a sudden and potentially fatal allergic reaction in someone sensitive to a particular substance

erythromycin
an antibiotic used to treat a broad range of bacterial infections

milia
a whitehead of keratinized cells and sebum formed in a blind duct of the epidermis

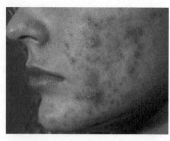

FIGURE 2–8 Acne vulgaris

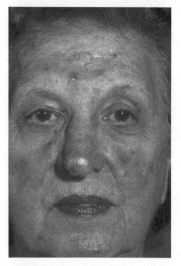

FIGURE 2–9 Rosacea

acne rosacea
a form of acne usually occurring in adults (as opposed to adolescents), visible as ruptured and dilated capillaries usually around the nose and cheeks

vasodilation
the widening of the blood vessels or arteries that increases blood flow

seborrhea
an oily condition caused by overactive sebaceous glands

Acne Vulgaris

Acne vulgaris (Figure 2–8) is a condition that affects adolescents mainly, appearing in puberty. It presents in varying degrees of severity, from a few blackheads and an occasional pustule (acne simplex) to acne vulgaris in which the face and possibly the neck, chest, and back are covered with blackheads (comedoes), whiteheads, pimples, and pustules. The cause is an overproduction of sebum from the sebaceous glands.

Acne Rosacea

Acne rosacea (ro-ZAY-see-uh) (Figure 2–9) is often called adult-onset acne because it rarely occurs in women under age 30. Acne rosacea can be affected by hormone levels, whether through pregnancy, birth-control pills, or menopause. It is noninfectious, generally affecting the nose and cheeks and, in more extreme cases, the chin and forehead. Acne rosacea presents with superficial blood vessels, broken veins, papules, and pustules. It is often associated with seborrhea, although the skin surface can look quite dehydrated.

Flare-ups, causing **vasodilation** (vas-oh-dih-LAY-shun), can result from stress, spicy foods, strong cheese, caffeine, alcohol, and extreme cold and heat.

Seborrheic Dermatitis

Also known as common dandruff, seborrheic dermatitis can be found on the scalp as well as on the face, ears, and even eyebrows. It is caused by **seborrhea** (seb-oh-REE-ah), the oversecretion of sebum from the sebaceous glands in combination with excessive flaky scales. It is noncontagious.

Psoriasis

The cause of psoriasis, a chronic disease, is unknown, but it is believed to be hereditary. Psoriasis is aggravated by stress and the lack of sunlight. It presents with red patches and distinctive borders that are covered with shiny, white scales that are usually found on the elbows and knees, but that can also be found on the scalp, trunk, and limbs.

Skin Cancer

Skin cancer is rising significantly in the United States, faster than any other type of cancer. When caught soon enough, skin cancer is the easiest cancer to treat. No part of the body is immune from skin cancer, but the most common areas have been exposed to the most sun (i.e., the head, neck, face, and hands).

The primary cause of skin cancer is damage from ultraviolet light. Skin cancer grows more prevalent as the ozone layer diminishes, offering less protection.

Skin cancer does not discriminate based on age, sex, or race. Although no one is immune from skin cancer, some people are more at risk than others. Those people can be

---

Genetic Factors of Skin Cancer
- Family history of skin cancer
- Fair skinned, with a tendency to freckle easily
- Light hair, particularly light blonde
- Light eyes (i.e., blue or green or a combination)
- Moles, significant in number, or of an unusual shape, color, or size*

*Most moles are benign skin tumors that occur during the excessive growth of melanocytes, causing the excessive production of melanin. This results in the growth of the mole or nevus. Moles are not present at birth, instead starting development during childhood. While most moles remain benign, some become malignant and therefore should be monitored for changes.

Lifestyle Causes of Skin Cancer

- Frequent blistering sunburns, especially before age 12
- Excessive outdoor exposure where the face and/or body are unprotected
- Geographic location (e.g., high altitudes and locations close to the equator)
- Excessive exposure to radiation from tanning booths or from sun lamps used to treat acne

divided into two groups: (1) those genetically at risk and (2) those whose lifestyles put them at risk. Those at greatest risk, of course, are those who belong to both categories.

Types of Carcinoma

The three types of carcinoma, which vary in severity and cure rate, are:

1. basal cell carcinoma
2. squamous cell carcinoma
3. malignant melanoma

Basal Cell Carcinoma

Basal cell carcinoma (Figure 2–10), the most common type of skin cancer, usually occurs in fair-skinned people who do not tan and have been sunburned. This type of cancer is considered the least dangerous, because it progresses slowly and usually without metastasizing (i.e., spreading from its original site). When left unchecked and untreated, however, basal cell carcinoma can grow deep into the tissue and bone below the skin, causing considerable damage and disfigurement.

basal cell carcinoma
the most common type of skin cancer

Squamous Cell Carcinoma

Squamous (SKWAY-mus) cell carcinoma (Figure 2–11), the second most common cancer, is usually found on the face, particularly on the lips and ears. Squamous cell carcinoma often starts as solar or actinic keratosis (kair-uh-TOH-sis), which is rough, scaly red or brown patches of skin. It is more serious than basal cell carcinoma, because it spreads, including to places like the lymph nodes and internal organs. As a result, it can be life threatening when left untreated. Once it is recognized and diagnosed, however, it is treated fairly easily and successfully.

squamous cell carcinoma
the second common form of skin cancer; usually found on the lips and ears

keratosis
growth of hornlike tissue on the skin

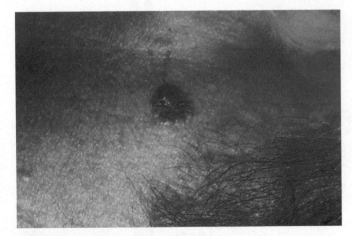

FIGURE 2–10 Basal cell carcinoma

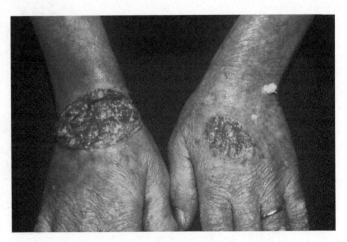

FIGURE 2–11 Squamous cell carcinoma

Malignant Melanoma

Malignant melanoma (Figure 2–12) is a form of skin cancer, and is by far the most dangerous because it is highly malignant and metastasizes early. It forms from the melanocytes in the epidermis. It also may develop from a mole. A change in the size, shape, and color of the growth, and itchiness or soreness in the same area, are causes for concern. Left undetected, malignant melanoma metastasizes quickly and aggressively, spreading to the lymph nodes and other organs. Early detection is crucial for the successful treatment of malignant melanoma. Nothing can replace regular screenings by a dermatologist, but the hair-removal specialist can perform a valuable service for regular clients by knowing the ABCDs of skin-cancer recognition, determining potential problems, and advising clients to seek further medical evaluation when appropriate.

malignant melanoma
the most dangerous form of skin cancer, forms from the melanocytes in the epidermis

FIGURE 2–12 Melanoma

The ABCDs of Cancer

Asymmetry—a growth that, when divided in half, has two mismatched halves

Border irregularity—Ragged or uneven edges that are blurred and poorly defined

Color—Uneven black, brown, and tan coloring; other colors, like red, white, and blue, can also be interspersed in the growth; any change in the color of a preexisting mole or lesion

Diameter—Any growth larger than the top of a pencil eraser, which is approximately 6 millimeters in diameter; any unusual or sudden increase in size should also be checked

---

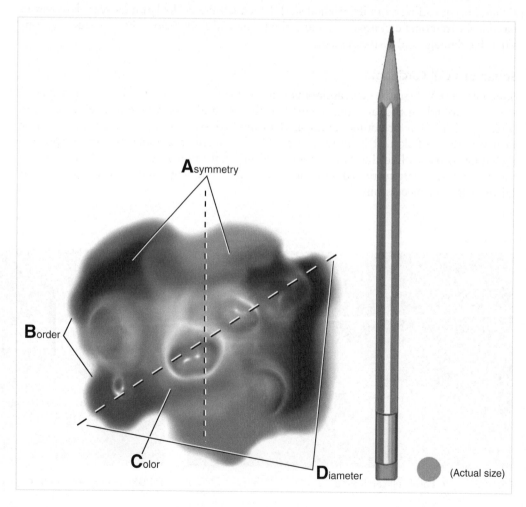

FIGURE 2–13
ABCDs of skin cancer

Conclusion

No matter how skilled a hair-removal technician is, nothing replaces knowledge, especially when it comes to recognizing noninfectious disorders and, more importantly, infectious diseases. While it helps to recognize allergic reactions or noninfectious disorders that may be contraindications, hair-removal specialists must recognize infectious diseases to ensure clients' safety and well-being and to advise clients to seek medical attention when appropriate. Hair-removal specialists should keep books like this one readily available in the hair-removal salon or clinic for reference. Knowing this material is one of the ways in which a hair-removal *technician* or *operator* becomes a hair-removal *specialist*.

 ## Discussion and Review Questions

1. Name one bacterial infection.
2. On what do parasitic infestations feed?
3. What is the common name for herpes simplex?
4. List the ABCDs of skin-cancer recognition.
5. How do a pustule and a blackhead differ?

 ## Additional Readings

Lees, Mark. 2001. *Skin Care: Beyond the Basics.* Clifton Park, NY: Milady, an imprint of Delmar Learning.

Milady's Standard Comprehensive Training for Estheticians. 2003. Clifton Park, NY: Milady, an imprint of Delmar Learning.

CHAPTER 3

The Endocrine System

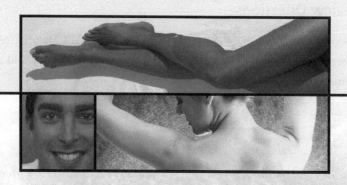

Chapter Outline

Learning Objectives ▪ Key Terms ▪ Introduction
Glands of the Endocrine System ▪ All Components of the Endocrine System
Conclusion ▪ Discussion and Review Questions ▪ Additional Readings

Learning Objectives

By the end of this chapter, you should be able to:

1. Understand the basic functions of the endocrine system, including the endocrine glands and the **hormones** (HOR-mohnz) they stimulate or are stimulated by.
2. Identify the main diseases and disorders caused by any malfunctioning of the endocrine system that relate to the hair-removal specialist.

Key Terms

acromegaly	edema	hypothalamus	parathyroid glands
Addison's disease	endocrine system	hypothyroidism	pineal gland
adenohypophysis	endocrinologist	inhibin	pituitary gland
adrenal cortex	endometrium	interstitial tissue	progesterones
adrenal glands	enzymes	islets of Langerhans	prolactin
adrenal medulla	epinephrine	lactogenic hormone	promine
anabolic steroids	estradiol	Leydig cells	prostaglandins
androgens	estrogens	luteal phase	seminiferous tubules
blastocyst	exocrine	luteinizing hormone	steroids
chorionic	glucagons	melatonin	thymosin
somatomammotropin	glucocorticoids	metabolism	thymus
corpus luteum	glycogen	mineralocorticoids	thyrotropic hormone
corticosteroids	goiter	myxedema	thyroxine
cretinism	gonadotropic	neurohypophysis	vasopressin
Cushing's syndrome	hormones	norepinephrine	
diabetes insipidus	human chorionic	oxytocin	
diabetes mellitus	gonadotropin	parathormone	

hormones
substances produced by the endocrine glands which have a regulatory or stimulatory function (e.g., on metabolism, as chemical messengers)

Introduction

Because hair growth is stimulated by the **endocrine** (EN-duh-krin) **system,** the endocrine system is an important aspect of human anatomy and physiology for the hair-removal specialist to understand. Understanding how this system works helps explain the causes of hair growth, the abnormalities of hair growth, and the appropriate times to refer clients to physicians.

The endocrine system is complicated and can be intimidating to learn. The information in this chapter is not needed for examinations in the field of waxing, but it is required to a lesser degree for electrolysis. The material in this chapter serves as reference for those taking continuing-education courses or reading related articles. This chapter is designed to give a clear outline of the most important components of the endocrine system as those components pertain to the hair-removal specialist. The information in this section is to be used as a tool when advising clients on hair problems. Leave medical diagnoses, prognoses, and treatment prescription to trained medical professionals. When appropriate, however, recommend that clients get some kind of testing from their physicians or an **endocrinologist** (en-duh-krin-AHL-uh-just). An endocrinologist is a physician who specializes in the treatment of endocrine system disorders.

endocrine system
relating to glands that secrete hormones into the lymph or bloodstream

endocrinologist
a physician who studies and treats endocrine disorders

Glands of the Endocrine System

The endocrine system (Figure 3–1) is a system of glands that secrete or excrete chemical substances in the body. These substances affect growth, sexual development, the digestive system, **metabolism** (muh-TAB-uh-liz-um), and overall well-being. They keep the bodily functions in balance and working in harmony. A malfunction in one part of the endocrine system often causes another part to malfunction.

Two types of glands are found in the body:

1. **exocrine** (EK-suh-krin)
2. endocrine

metabolism
ongoing series of chemical interactions taking place in living organisms which provide the energy and nutrients needed to sustain life

exocrine
relating to glands that secrete through a duct to the suface of an organ (e.g., sweat glands or salivary glands)

Exocrine Glands

The exocrine glands are small, tubelike ducts that secrete into cavities and produce mucus or **enzymes** (EN-zymz), as found in the digestive system, or they may secrete nonenzymatic substances, as is the case for the sebaceous glands and the mammary glands. These glands also excrete waste material (e.g., through the sweat glands and the liver).

Endocrine Glands

The endocrine glands are sometimes part of a larger organ and sometimes constitute organs themselves. These glands secrete substances called hormones directly into the bloodstream, stimulating the target organ to further activity or causing the organ to secrete into other parts of the body. The hormones are often called chemical messengers. Hormones may aid in the production of other hormones or be antagonistic and work to stop or slow the production of other hormones.

enzymes
complex proteins produced by living cells that promote specific biochemical reactions by acting as catalysts

FIGURE 3–1
The endocrine system

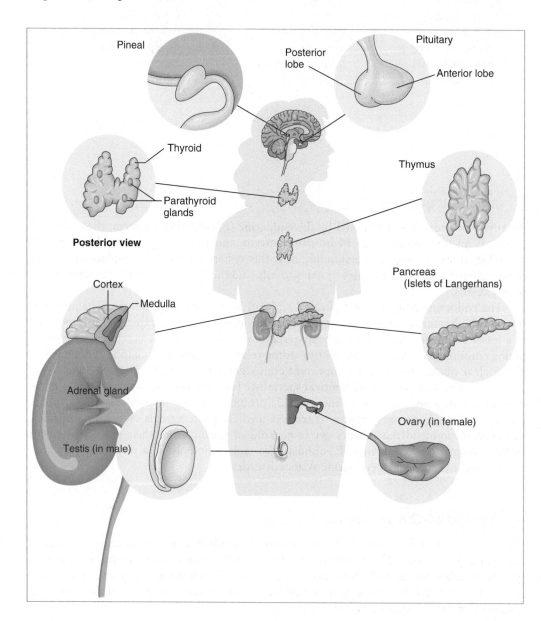

All Components of the Endocrine System

The following describes the endocrine system from head to toe.

The Brain

The following organs are located in the brain and are part of the endocrine system:

- hypothalamus
- pituitary gland
- neurohypophysis
- adenohypophysis
- pineal gland

The Hypothalamus

Although the **hypothalamus** is considered to have ultimate control over a major portion of the endocrine system through the pituitary gland, it is not considered an endocrine organ.

The Pituitary Gland

Divided into two main portions, the **neurohypophysis** and the **adenohypophysis**, the **pituitary gland** is located at the base of the brain. Together these two portions produce more than 15 hormones.

The Neurohypophysis.   The neurohypophysis or pituitary lobe produces two hormones: (1) **oxytocin**, to stimulate the muscles of the uterus to contract during childbirth and to expel milk from the nipples during lactation, and (2) the antidiuretic hormone (ADH) or **vasopressin** (va-SO-pruh-sun), an antidiuretic that causes water to return to the bloodstream, which causes the concentration of urine. A vasopressin deficiency causes **diabetes insipidus** (in-SIP-uh-dus).

The Adenohypophysis.   The adenohypophysis or anterior pituitary lobe is also known as the "master gland" of the endocrine system, although this title is somewhat inaccurate as this gland is in turn controlled by the hormones of the hypothalamus. In fact, although its secretion controls the actions of certain organs, it is in turn affected by the various glands it controls. The adenohypophysis is found in the anterior portion of the pituitary gland and is served by portal veins from the hypothalamus. The adenohypophysis produces at least the seven following hormones.

1. adrenocorticotropic hormone (ACTH), which controls the adrenal cortex and produces **glucocorticoids** and sex hormones
2. **thyrotropic hormone** (TSH), which controls the thyroid gland
3. growth hormone (GH), which affects skeletal development, and which, in excess production in childhood causes gigantism and a dwarfism deficiency, and in adulthood causes **acromegaly** (ak-ro-MEH-juh-lee)
4. melanocyte stimulating hormone (MSH), which stimulates melanocyte production in the germinating layer of the epidermis that causes skin to tan and brown or freckle; its production is inhibited by the hormones of the adrenal cortex
5. follicle stimulating hormone (FSH), which is a **gonadotropic** hormone that affects the ovarian follicles in women and stimulates seminiferous tissue in men
6. **luteinizing hormone** (LH), which like FSH (see preceding) is also a gonadotropic hormone that stimulates ovulation and the interstitial tissue in the male testes where testosterone is produced
7. **lactogenic hormone** (LTH), which stimulates the mammary glands to produce milk; estrogens from the ovaries inhibit LTH production

hypothalamus
area on the underside of the brain which controls involuntary bodily functions, such as body temperature and hormone release

neurohypophysis
the posterior lobe of the pituitary gland which secretes such hormones as vasopressin

adenohypophysis
the anterior portion of the pituitary or master gland, which produces at least seven hormones

pituitary gland
located at the base of the brain, this gland produces hormones that affect all other glandular activity

oxytocin
hormone released by pituitary gland which stimulates contractions of the womb during childbirth and triggers milk secretion during nursing

vasopressin
hormone produced by the pituitary gland which constricts the arteries, raises blood pressure, and reduces the volume of urine excreted by the kidneys

diabetes insipidus
disorder of the pituitary gland caused by a deficiency of vasopressin that causes the body to produce large amounts of urine

glucocorticoids
hormones that control the metabolism of carbohydrates, proteins, and fats

thyrotropic hormone (TSH)
hormone produced by the adenohypophysis which controls activity of the thyroid gland

acromegaly
an adult disease caused by the overproduction of growth hormones, which results in the enlargement of various body parts

gonadotropic
acting on or stimulating the gonads

luteinizing hormone (LH)
hormone produced by the pituitary gland which causes the ovary to produce eggs and secrete progesterone

lactogenic hormone (LTH)
hormone that causes the mammary glands to produce milk

pineal gland
small, cone-shaped organ of the brain that secretes the hormone melatonin

melatonin
hormone secreted by the pineal gland which helps to regulate biorhythms

thyroxine
principal hormone secreted by the thyroid gland which stimulates metabolism

goiter
enlargement of the thyroid gland which appears as swelling in the front of the neck

hypothyroidism
condition resulting from a deficiency in the production of thyroid hormones

cretinism
congenital, abnormal condition marked by physical stunting and mental retardation; caused by severe hypothyroidism

myxedema
disease caused by an underactive or atrophied thyroid gland, which may cause sluggishness or weight gain

parathyroid glands
four small glands that lie in or near the walls of the thyroid gland

parathormone
hormone secreted by the parathyroid

thymus
organ in the base of the neck that is involved in the development of immune-system cells

promine
hormone released by the thymus which affects general growth

thymosin
hormone released from the thymus which influences the development of T cells in the thymus

adrenal glands
glands on top of each kidney that are made of the cortex and medulla

adrenal cortex
one of two main sections of the adrenal glands, which produce hormones called steroids

adrenal medulla
one of two main sections of the adrenal glands, which secrete epinephrine and norepinephrine

The Pineal Gland

The **pineal gland** secretes the hormone **melatonin**, which is inhibited by light and is at its maximum blood concentration at night. Melatonin helps to regulate biorhythms. The pineal gland is thought to play a role in the reproduction and maturation of the gonads.

The Neck

The glands in the neck, the thyroid gland and the parathyroid glands, are also part of the endocrine system.

The Thyroid Gland

The thyroid gland is found on either side of the trachea and larynx. The thyroid produces a group of hormones that contain iodine, the most common of which is **thyroxine**.

Thyroxine controls many metabolic processes, like heart rate, blood pressure, and the basal metabolic rate (BMR). It also affects fertility and mental acuity. A deficiency of iodine and an overactivity of the hormone secretions can cause the glands to swell, which causes a condition known as **goiter** (GOYT-ur). The underactivity or **hypothyroidism** of this gland causes a condition called **cretinism** (KREE-ti-niz-um) in children and **myxedema** (miks-uh-DEE-muh) in adults, as well as a low BMR and weight gain. Hyperthyroidism also produces a condition known as Graves' disease, which causes an increase in the heart and metabolic rate, weight loss, excessive sweating, and the bulging or protruding of the eyeballs from their sockets.

The Parathyroid Glands

There are usually four small, flattened glands. **Parathyroid glands** are found virtually imbedded in the posterior and lateral sides of the thyroid. These glands secrete **parathormone**. Also called parathyroid hormone (PTH), parathormone is responsible for maintaining a constant level of calcium in the blood by acting on the bones, intestines, and kidneys.

The Chest

Located in the chest, the thymus is part of the endocrine system.

The Thymus

The **thymus** lies behind the sternum. It is largest in infancy, growing more slowly than the body and gradually degenerating from puberty onward, replacing its lymphoidal cells with adipose tissue. Its importance lies in early development during infancy and youth, when the body grows rapidly and immunity develops. Before birth, the thymus is the major source of lymphocytes, the precursor cells from which the spleen and lymph nodes form. Two hormones are released from the thymus: (1) promine and (2) thymosin.

Promine affects general growth. **Thymosin** affects the growth of lymphoid tissue producing T cells (thymus-dependent cells). The T cells continue to be stimulated by the hormones of the thymus even after they have left it.

The Abdomen

The hormone producing glands of the abdomen consist of the adrenal glands and the pancreas.

The Adrenal Glands

Adrenal glands sit atop the kidneys like caps, one per kidney. The adrenal glands have two main sections: (1) the **adrenal cortex** and (2) the **adrenal medulla**.

The Adrenal Cortex.   The adrenal cortex produces more than 50 adrenal cortical hormones called **steroids**. Steroids are divided into three groups:

1. **Mineralocorticoids**, which control the mineral and salt content of cellular fluids. Excess mineralocorticoids can lead to the retention of body fluid, called **edema**.
2. Glucocorticoids, which affect the metabolism and the amount of blood glucose. They increase in activity in response to stress. They also depress pituitary secretions of ACTH, TSH, and MSH.
3. Sex steroids, which supplement in weaker degrees the sex hormones secreted by the gonads (i.e., the ovaries and testes).

The Adrenal Medulla.   The adrenal medulla secretes two main substances, **epinephrine** and **norepinephrine**, together more commonly known as adrenalin. Epinephrine is involved in the breakdown of **glycogen** in the liver; norepinephrine causes general vasoconstriction.

Hypersecretion of **corticosteroids** results in **Cushing's** (KUH-sheengz) **syndrome**, often caused by a tumor on the adrenal cortex. The result is muscle weakness, a puffy appearance in the face, obesity, hirsutism, and **diabetes mellitus** (MEL-uh-tus).

Inadequate secretion of glucocorticoids and mineralocorticoids causes **Addison's** (AD-duh-sunz) **disease**, which causes muscle weakness; low blood pressure; anemia; and hyperpigmented areas on the face, neck, and arms.

The Pancreas

The pancreas lies behind the stomach and contains the **islets of Langerhans**, which are endocrine glands that secrete the hormones insulin and **glucagons**. The level of sugar in the blood is lowered by insulin, which causes the body's cells to store it as glycogen. Glucagon raises the level of sugar in the body. Together insulin and glucagons help the body to maintain a balanced level of sugar in the blood. Lack of insulin causes diabetes mellitus.

The Groin Area

The sex organs in the groin area, also known as the gonads (testes and ovaries), secrete sex steroids. In males the sex hormones are known as **androgens**; in females they are known as **estrogen** and **progesterone**. Females also produce androgens in much lesser quantities than males; males likewise produce female hormones in much lesser quantities.

The Female.   The parts of the female reproductive organs that produce hormones are the ovaries, the sacs or ovid organs where the ova or eggs are formed (Figure 3–2). All the eggs a woman will have are in the ovaries before birth and are released one at a time approximately every 28 days between puberty and menopause. The ovaries produce hormones that are responsible for developing the female sexual characteristics (Figure 3–3). The **corpus luteum** also releases hormones. It is the lining of the empty follicle of the ovary that produces yellowish cells that also release the hormones.

Stimulated by the gonadotropin releasing hormone (GnRh), which is secreted by the hypothalamus, the anterior pituitary releases FSH and LH. Due to FSH stimulation, the follicles mature and secrete increasing amounts of **estradiol**. On the thirteenth day of an average cycle, the rise in estradiol stimulates a rise in LH secretion from the anterior pituitary, in what is known as positive feedback. By Day 14, the follicle is ready to ovulate (i.e., to release an egg). Following this, the empty follicle is now affected by the LH, causing the empty follicle to become the corpus luteum, which produces and releases estradiol and progesterone. This aids in the thickening of the tissues lining the wall of the uterus in preparation for the possible implantation of a fertilized egg and in preparing the mammary glands for lactation, recognized in women by fuller and more tender breasts during the latter part of the monthly cycle and during pregnancy. With the secretion of progesterone and estradiol during the formation of the corpus luteum, also known as the **luteal phase**, FSH and LH levels drop in what is known as negative feedback. When LH

steroids
chemical substances produced by the adrenal cortex

mineralocorticoids
hormones secreted by the adrenal cortex which control electrolyte and fluid balance in the body

edema
abnormal buildup of excess interstitial fluid between tissue cells

epinephrine
adrenaline hormone secreted by the adrenal medulla

norepinephrine
hormone secreted by the adrenal medulla which is the principal transmitter of sympathetic nerve endings supplying the major organs of the skin

glycogen
compound stored in the muscles and liver which is easily converted to glucose as a source of energy

corticosteroids
hormones produced by the adrenal glands

Cushing's syndrome
condition caused by excessive production of corticosteroids, resulting in obesity and muscular weakness

diabetes mellitus
disorder caused by inadequate insulin production (Type 1) or a decreased cellular sensitivity to insulin (Type 2)

Addison's disease
a disease caused by the underactivity of the adrenal glands, which causes low blood pressure and weakness

islets of Langerhans
cluster of endocrine cells found in the pancreas which secrete insulin and glucagon

glucagons
hormones produced by the pancreas which raise blood sugar levels by helping to convert glycogen to glucose in the liver

androgens
male sex hormones responsible for developing secondary sexual characteristics

estrogen
steroid hormones produced in the ovaries which stimulate the development of female secondary sexual characteristics

progesterone
sex hormones produced in the ovaries which prepare the womb for the fertilized ovum

corpus luteum
the empty follicle of the ovary

estradiol
estrogenic hormone produced in the ovaries

luteal phase
phase in the menstrual cycle that occurs after the release of an ovum

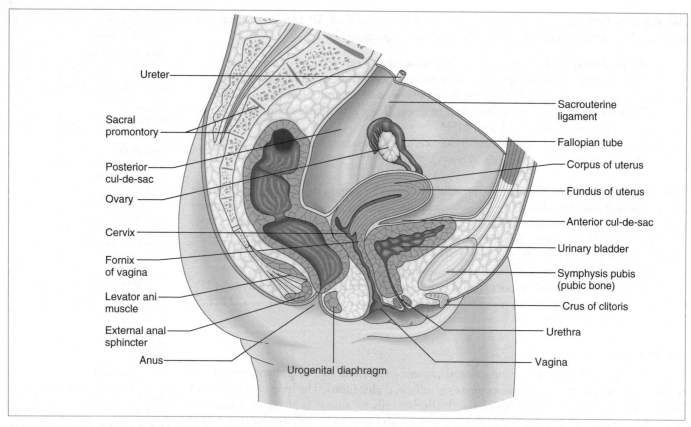

FIGURE 3–2 Structures of the female reproductive system

blastocyst
embryo at the stage where it implants in the wall of the uterus

endometrium
mucous membrane that lines the interior aspect of the uterus; thickens in the latter part of the menstrual cycle

human chorionic gonadotropin
hormone secreted by the blastocyst which stimulates the production of estrogen and progesterone needed in pregnancy

drops, the luteal phase ends, and estradiol and progesterone levels drop. When this happens, menstruation begins, as does a new cycle.

When an egg is fertilized by a male's sperm, it becomes a **blastocyst** and implants in the lining of the uterus, which is called the **endometrium**. The cells of the blastocyst secrete the **human chorionic gonadotropin** (hCG). This is the hormone that is detected in pregnancy tests for a positive reading for pregnancy. The hCG acts like LH.

Hormone	Function
ESTROGEN	1. Affects the development of the fallopian tubes, ovaries, uterus, and the vagina
	2. Produces secondary sex characteristics:
	• broadened pelvis, making the outlet broad and oval to permit childbirth
	• the epiphysis (growth plate) becomes bone and growth ceases
	• softer and smoother skin
	• pubic and axillary hair
	• deposits of fat in the breasts and development of the duct system
	• deposits of fat in the buttocks and thighs
	• sexual desire
	3. Prepares the uterus for the fertilized egg
PROGESTERONE	1. Develops excretory portion of the mammary glands
	2. Thickens the uterine lining so it can receive the developing embryo egg
	3. Decreases uterine contractions during pregnancy

FIGURE 3–3 Functions of estrogen and progesterone

The placenta is formed from tissue from the endometrium. The placenta secretes **chorionic somatomammotropin** (hCS), which acts like **prolactin** and GH and estradiol. The high levels of estrogen that are secreted by the placenta inhibit the action of the milk producing prolactin until after the infant is born.

Labor is stimulated by the secretion of oxytocin from the posterior pituitary and also from the stimulation caused by the release of **prostaglandins** from the uterus. They are believed to affect each other with positive feedback, causing the uterine muscles to contract in a manner necessary for the expulsion and delivery of the infant. When estrogen levels drop after delivery, prolactin stimulates milk production and the baby's sucking reflex on the nipples stimulates oxytocin secretion, causing the "let down" action of the milk into the mammary glands and out through the nipples.

The Male. The male reproductive system (Figure 3–4) is significantly less complicated with regard to the study of hormones, as the hormones serve to produce the sperm to fertilize an egg. In the female, hormonal activity must respond to the possible fertilization, growth, development, and birth of a fetus, followed by lactation to feed and nourish the infant.

The parts of the adult male reproductive system that produce the male hormones called androgens are the testes and the interstitial tissue.

The hypothalamus releases GnRH, which stimulates the anterior pituitary to produce FSH and LH, which stimulate their respective targets in the testes. There are two compartments of the testes: (1) **seminiferous tubules**, where sperm forms, stimulated by FSH, and (2) the **interstitial tissue**, which contains the **Leydig cells**, which secrete testosterone, the major androgen. The secretion of testosterone by the Leydig cells is stimulated by LH. The testosterone then inhibits LH secretion in a negative feedback relationship. The seminiferous tubules produce a hormone called **inhibin**, which is thought to inhibit FSH production, again in a negative feedback relationship.

chorionic somatomammotropin
hormone secreted by the placenta

prolactin
hormone produced by the pituitary gland which stimulates lactation and progesterone secretion

prostaglandins
fatty acids resembling hormones which are released from the uterus

seminiferous tubules
part of the male reproductive system that produces and carries semen

interstitial tissue
tissue lying between parts of an organ or between groups of cells

Leydig cells
cells in the interstitial tissue (see preceding) of the testes which secrete testosterone

inhibin
hormone secreted by the testes and ovary which inhibits the production of FSH in the pituitary

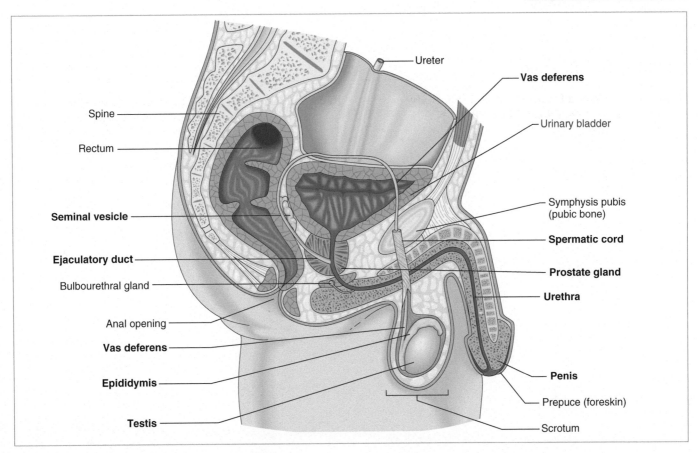

FIGURE 3–4 Structures of the male reproductive system

The development of the male secondary sexual characteristics of facial hair and the "breaking" or deepening of the voice are brought about by the stimulation of androgens at puberty. The effect of androgens on protein synthesis, affecting bone growth and muscle development, leads to the androgens occasionally being called **anabolic steroids**. It is androgens in the blood that search out target receptors in the body. The target area most notable to the hair-removal specialist is the pilosebaceous unit (i.e., the hair follicle).

anabolic steroids
naturally occurring hormones that promote tissue growth

Conclusion

Female hormones fluctuate in their levels at different stages in the woman's life, such as at the onset of puberty, during the menstrual cycle each month, during pregnancy, and during menopause, when estrogen levels rapidly decline. Testosterone levels remain high and stable for the most part from puberty onward and decline very gradually and very slightly in men over 50.

There have been many advances in the field of endocrinology, with many improved and sophisticated readings of hormone levels in the blood, allowing for more accurate diagnosis in diseases that, among other things, cause excessive and unwanted hair growth. A basic understanding of the endocrine system fosters an understanding and recognition of diseases and disorders that cause excessive and unwanted hair. The following chapter addresses those diseases.

Discussion and Review Questions

1. What is the main difference between an exocrine gland and endocrine gland?

2. Which gland is known as the "master gland"?

3. Hypothyroidism causes what condition in adults?

4. Which two main substances does the adrenal medulla secrete?

5. Does FSH cause the hair follicles to produce terminal hair?

Additional Readings

Senisi Scott, Ann, and Elizabeth Fong. 1998. *Body Structures and Functions*. Clifton Park, NY: Delmar Learning.

Redmond, Geoffrey. 1995. *The Good News About Women's Hormones*. New York: Warner Books, Inc.

CHAPTER 4

Hirsutism and Hypertrichosis

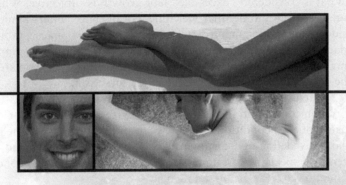

Chapter Outline

Learning Objectives ■ Key Terms ■ Introduction ■ Hypertrichosis
Hirsutism ■ Hair-Growth Diseases, Disorders, and Syndromes
Conclusion ■ Discussion and Review Questions ■ Additional Readings

Learning Objectives

By the end of this chapter, you should be able to:

1. Identify the basic causes of hirsutism.
2. Explain the basic causes of hypertrichosis.
3. Differentiate between the two conditions of hypertrichosis.
4. Recognize when a condition may signal the need for further medical evaluation.

Key Terms

acromegaly
adrenocortical
adrenogenital syndrome

Archard-Thiers syndrome
cortisol
hyperglycemia

polycystic ovarian
    syndrome
Stein-Leventhal syndrome

syndrome
virilism

 ## Introduction

What is considered "excessive" hair growth is subjective. What one person may consider unacceptable another may welcome. For instance, a fair-skinned, blonde woman may consider a few nonpigmented velli along the lip line unacceptable. Another fair-skinned but dark-haired woman might have dark, terminal hair on the upper lip and face in the adult-male, sexual-hair-growth pattern and envy the former woman. The former condition may be considered hypertrichosis, the latter, hirsutism.

Hirsutism and hypertrichosis are often grouped, discussed, and treated as the same problem or condition. However, there are some significant differences in regard to the cause of each condition and how each should be treated. The purpose of this chapter is to carefully define and distinguish between hypertrichosis and hirsutism so that the hair-removal specialist can understand and recognize the two conditions and the right course of action to treat the offending hair.

 ## Hypertrichosis

The word *hypertrichosis* stems from the Greek *hyper,* meaning "over," and *trichosis,* meaning "hair"—an overabundance of hair. Hypertrichosis is therefore excess hair growth on any part of the body that is subjectively abnormal for the age, sex, race, and culture of the individual (Figure 4–1). The type of hair in this condition is usually terminal, does not necessarily grow in the adult-male, sexual-hair-growth patterns, and is not stimulated by male androgens.

Causes of Hypertrichosis

- Genetically inherited and/or particular to race
- Natural life occurrences (e.g., puberty, pregnancy, menopause)
- Reaction to certain medical procedures
- Result of some cancer treatments
- Reaction to certain prescription medications, especially steroids

---

 ## Hirsutism

Hirsutism (Figure 4–2) is the term for terminal hair growth in women that is caused by excessive male androgens in the blood. In this condition, hair does grow in adult-male, sexual-hair-growth pattern.

Causes of Hirsutism

- Stimulation of male androgens at puberty
- Drugs affecting endocrine system, increasing the percentage of male androgens
- Diseases and disorders of the endocrine system

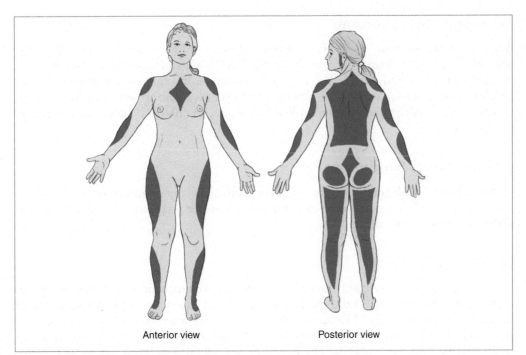

FIGURE 4–1
Body areas prone to hypertrichosis

Anterior view   Posterior view

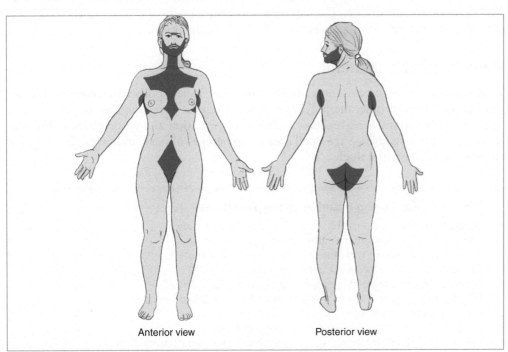

FIGURE 4–2
Body areas prone to hirsutism

Anterior view   Posterior view

Hair-Growth Diseases, Disorders, and Syndromes

A **syndrome** (SIN-drom) is a group of symptoms that, when combined, characterize a disease.

syndrome
a group of signs and symptoms that together characterize a disease or disorder

Acromegaly

Acromegaly is caused by the excessive release of growth hormone (GH) by the anterior pituitary gland, usually due to a tumor. In childhood, acromegaly can cause gigantism. If the body is mature at the onset of the increased hormone production, the result is enlarged hands, feet, and face. Poor vision or blindness may also ensue, and excessive androgen production can cause hirsutism (see preceding).

acromegaly
disease afflicting adults caused by the overproduction of growth hormones; results in the enlargement of the bones of the hands, feet, jaw, nose, and ribs

adrenogenital syndrome
condition caused by the malfunctioning of the adrenal cortex, causing a block in cortisol synthesis and androgen overproduction

virilism
development of male secondary sex characteristics considered unusual in women culturally

cortisol
steroid hormone secreted by the adrenal glands in response to tissue damage; causes inflammation; also called hydrocortisone

Archard-Thiers syndrome
rare syndrome caused by the combination of Cushing's syndrome and adrenogenital syndrome (see preceding); also called the diabetes of bearded women

adrenocortical
androgens produced by the cortex of the adrenal glands

hyperglycemia
abnormally high level of sugar in the blood

Stein-Leventhal syndrome
see polycystic ovary syndrome

polycystic ovary syndrome
disorder affecting women caused by androgen overproduction in the ovaries; presents varied outward signs, including hirsutism and obesity

Adrenogenital Syndrome

Adrenogenital syndrome, also called adrenal **virilism** (VEER-ul-iz-im), results when the adrenal cortex malfunctions and blocks **cortisol** (KOR-tih-sawl) synthesis and causes an overproduction of androgens. The outward symptoms in children are the precocious development of the sex organs, deep voices, and excessive hair growth. In adult women, adrenogenital syndrome causes diminished breast size, an enlarged clitoris, and hirsutism (see preceding).

Archard-Thiers Syndrome

Archard-Thiers syndrome is a rare syndrome caused by the combination of Cushing's syndrome (see following) and adrenogenital syndrome (see preceding). It is also called the diabetes of bearded women.

Cushing's Syndrome

Cushing's syndrome develops from chronic excess of **adrenocortical** androgens or glucocorticoid hormones, which raise the blood sugar level. In excess, these hormones cause **hyperglycemia** (hy-pur-gly-SEE-mee-uh) due to hypersecretion by the adrenal cortex. Outward signs of Cushing's are an enlarged face ("moon face"), neck, and trunk; rounded shoulders, weak abdominals, and hirsutism (see preceding). The limbs remain unaffected. Women cease to menstruate. The skin tends to bruise easily and heal poorly, making it difficult to treat women with this syndrome who have hirsutism.

Stein-Leventhal Syndrome

Stein-Leventhal syndrome is now more commonly called **polycystic ovary syndrome** (PCOS). In this syndrome, the polycystic ovary produces excess androgens. The inward signs of this syndrome are irregular or absent menstruation and cystic ovaries. The outward signs of this syndrome are small breasts, sometimes obesity, and, often, hirsutism of the face, neck, chest, and thighs.

Common Drugs Causing Hirsutism and Hypertrichosis

Anabolic steroids (can cause hirsutism; multiple manufacturers)
Brevicon (causes hirsutism; manufactured by Syntex)
Corticosteroids (creams can cause hirsutism; multiple manufacturers)
Cyclosporin (an immunosuppressant; causes hypertrichosis)
Diazoxide (for treatment of hypoglycemia; causes hypertrichosis)
Dilantin (causes hypertrichosis; manufactured by Parke Davis for seizure control)
Loestrin (causes hirsutism; manufactured by Parke Davis)
Minoxidil (stimulates hair growth; causes hypertrichosis)
Prednisone (causes Cushingoid state; causes hirsutism; manufactured by Roxane)
Premarin (causes hirsutism; manufactured by Wyeth-Ayerst)
Provera (causes hirsutism; manufactured by Upjohn)
Tagamet (causes hirsutism; manufactured by Smith, Kline, and French)
Tamoxifen (for treatment of breast cancer; causes hirsutism; various manufacturers)
Thorazine (used to treat nausea and pediatric psychotic behavior; causes hirsutism; manufactured by Smith Kline Beecham)

Conclusion

A female client may present with a condition of considerable hairiness throughout her body but, given the client's race and culture, it may not be considered either a problem or unattractive, and she may be physically very healthy. This is *hypertrichosis*—hairiness that does not follow the adult sexual hair growth pattern. Another female client may present with a beard, and after questioning it is revealed that she has diabetes. Upon thorough examination, an endocrinologist may discover that the client has a rare disorder called Archard-Thiers syndrome. The woman's beard is hirsute and, with medical treatment and hair removal, the condition can be rectified.

A woman's upper lip hair should not be called a mustache. It is quite simply upper lip hair.

 ## Discussion and Review Questions

1. List three causes of hypertrichosis.
2. Name the two main causes of hirsutism.
3. Name three common syndromes that cause hirsutism.
4. What is the more common name for Stein-Leventhal syndrome?
5. List the three inward and two outward signs of Stein-Leventhal syndrome.

 ## Additional Readings

Edsell, Linda. 1984. *Female Hirsutism: An Enigma*. St. Louis: Pulsar Publishing Co.

Owens, Shelby. 1989. *About That Hair*. Pensacola, FL: author.

Redmond, Geoffrey, 1995. *The Good News About Women's Hormones*. New York: Warner Books, Inc.

CHAPTER 5

Bacteriology, Sanitation, and Sterilization

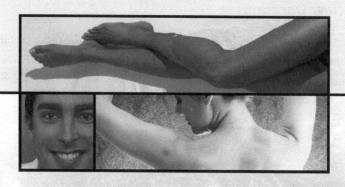

Chapter Outline

Learning Objectives ■ Key Terms ■ Introduction
Pathology and Bacteriology ■ Sanitation and Sterilization ■ Conclusion
Discussion and Review Questions ■ Additional Readings

Learning Objectives

By the end of this chapter, you should be able to:

1. Differentiate between pathogenic and nonpathogenic organisms.
2. Describe the three different types of bacteria and the diseases they cause.
3. Differentiate between bacteria, fungi, and viruses.
4. Describe hepatitis and HIV, how they are spread, and how transmission can be prevented.
5. Understand disease causation and prevention.
6. List the various methods of sterilization and disinfectants as they pertain to the salon/clinic.
7. Apply the principles of hygiene, sanitation, sterilization, and good housekeeping to the salon/clinic.

Key Terms

AIDS	cilia	hypha	psychrophiles
algae	cocci	isolyser	saprophytes
amoeba	coccus	lancets	sepsis
anaphoresis	diplococcus	mesophiles	spirillum
antibiotics	endospore	microbiology	spore
antiseptics	ethylene oxide	microorganisms	staphylococcus
asepsis	extremethermophiles	microbes	streptococcus
autoclave	flagella	motility	syndrome
bacillus	fungi	parasites	thermophiles
bacteria	fungistats	pathogenic	ultrasonic
bacteriostats	glutaraldehyde	personal service worker	virus
biohazardous	hepatitis	(PSW)	
cataphoresis	HIV	protozoa	

Introduction

Learning about microorganisms and understanding their relationship to disease causation, transmission, and prevention are paramount to the hair-removal specialist—for personal health and safety and for the health and safety of clients. A hair-removal specialist is considered a **personal service worker (PSW)**, meaning that the services the specialist provides bring the specialist into close contact with individuals, allowing for the possibility of the transmission and spread of contagious diseases, usually through coughing and sneezing, unclean hands, instruments and work areas, and the sharing of eating and drinking utensils. Electrologists are at further risk through possible contact with blood plasma and other bodily fluids, as are, to a lesser degree, waxing technicians.

The sterilization and sanitation of all instruments and work areas is possibly the most important concern for hair-removal specialists. In this chapter are the important aspects of microbiology and disease causation, as well as the sanitation and sterilization requirements of each aspect of hair removal. Following the guidelines in this book can considerably reduce the risks of disease transmission and cross-contamination.

Pathology and Bacteriology

Why is it important to understand pathology and microbiology? As a PSW, it is important to ask, "What surfaces or equipment do I touch in my treatment area?" and, "What surfaces and tools do my clients come into contact with?" As you look around the treatment area and see the surfaces and hair-removal tools that are in human contact by multiple people during the day, it is also important to envision those surfaces as contaminated with millions of microorganisms and possibly bloodborne pathogens that are invisible to the naked eye. By studying just a few of the more common bacteria and viruses, you will hopefully understand the importance of sanitation and sterilization and have a vision of the enormity of the invisible world of microbiology and its impact on our everyday lives.

Microbiology

Microbiology (my-kroh-by-OL-uh-jee) is the branch of biology that deals with **microorganisms** (my-kroh-OR-gah-niz-ums) and their effects on other living organisms. These microorganisms, or **microbes**, include **bacteria** (bak-TEER-ee-ah), **fungi** (FUN-ji), **viruses** (VY-rus-es), **protozoa** (pro-toh-ZOH-ah), and **algae** (AL-jee). There are two classifications of bacteria: (1) **pathogenic** (path-uh-JEN-ik), which are harmful and disease causing, and (2) nonpathogenic, which are harmless, helpful, and useful.

personal service worker (PSW)
an individual whose work brings the individual into direct contact with other individuals (e.g., health-care professionals and allied-health workers)

microbiology
the scientific study of microscopic organisms and their effects

microorganisms
tiny organisms such as viruses, protozoa, or bacteria that can only be seen under a microscope

microbes
microscopic organisms, especially those that transmit disease

bacteria
single-celled parasitic micro-organisms with no nuclei or organized cell structure responsible for decay, fermentation, and many plant and animal diseases

fungi
organisms that reproduce by spores (see following) and live by absorbing nutrients from organic matter

virus
a minute particle that lives as a parasite in plants, animals, and bacteria; diseases caused by viruses are also called viruses

protozoa
single-celled organisms (e.g., amoeba)

algae
mainly aquatic, plant-like organisms that lack leaves, roots, and stems

pathogenic
causing or able to cause disease

Pathogenic bacteria are in the minority. Most bacteria are nonpathogenic and are found in the air, water, all over our bodies (including in the mouth and in the intestines), and on virtually every surface. Most even benefit us and are found in many foods (especially dairy products), in alcoholic beverages (e.g., yeast), and in medicines (e.g., **antibiotics** [an-tih-by-AHT-iks]). Microbes called **saprophytes** (SAP-ruh-fyts) are essential for decomposing waste and dead matter, feeding on them. Saprophytes are used to create fertilizer. However, if certain other types of unwanted bacteria enter the body, they may cause disease and are then known as pathogens. Pathology is the scientific study of the nature of disease and its causes, processes, development, and consequences.

Bacteria

Bacteriology is the study of bacteria (also called germs), especially in relation to medicine and agriculture. A bacterium is a single bacteria cell visible only through a microscope. It takes approximately 2,000 bacteria cells to cover the head of a pin. Bacteria reproduce and spread rapidly because they can double in number approximately every 20 minutes to an hour, depending on the type of bacterium and its environment. As bacteria reproduce and multiply, they may become a colony. To thrive, bacteria generally require damp, warm, dark places with a food source, although some types can thrive in dry, cool, well-lighted places. Most common bacteria or microbes thrive in temperatures ranging from 26 to 38°C (98.6°F), but some bacteria thrive outside that range.

Bacteria can be categorized into four groups according to the range of temperatures in which they thrive best:

1. **Psychrophiles** (SAY-kro-faylz) require cold temperatures of 0 to 20°C/32 to 69°F and lurk in the dark corners of refrigerators.
2. **Mesophiles** (MES-oh-faylz) grow best between about 25 to 45°C/78 to 112°F.
3. **Thermophiles** (THER-moh-faylz) grow optimally between 50 to 80°C/123 to 178°F.
4. **Extremethermophiles** (eks-treem-uh-THER-moh-faylz), like those in hot springs, grow best between 80 to110°C/178 to 230°F.

Similarly, microbes have different optimal pH requirements (the acid/alkaline mantle). Each bacterium has an optimum range of these conditions within which it grows at a maximum rate. In some cases, this may be a fairly broad range; some bacteria grow maximally over a 5 to 10 degree temperature span. In other cases, the range may be quite narrow; the temperature allowing growth spans only a few degrees. This is important for understanding the potential for bacterial growth in wax.

Bacteria can reproduce every 20 minutes. When conditions are unfavorable for reproduction, a bacterium will form a suit of armor called a **spore** to protect itself until more favorable conditions for reproduction and growth are met. Spores can remain for long periods in an inactive state and still be transmitted to others, thereby finding environments more suitable for growth. Some spores can form a highly protective structure called an **endospore**, though not all bacteria have this ability. Endospores allow bacteria to resist the detrimental effects of certain environmental factors, such as heat, antiseptics, disinfectants, and antibiotics. The ability to kill the endospores along with the other bacteria allows for complete sterilization.

Pathogenic bacteria have three basic shapes (Figure 5–1):

1. **coccus** (KOK-us) (plural **cocci**), or round
2. **bacillus** (bah-SILL-us) (plural bacilli), or rod shaped
3. **spirillum** (plural spirilla), or corkscrew shaped

Coccus.   The coccus bacteria produce pus in those they infect. Common cocci include:

1. **diplococcus** (plural diplococci), which grows in semicircular pairs and causes pneumonia.
2. **staphylococcus** (plural staphylococci), which grows in bunches and is found grouped in small areas, visible as folliculitis, abscesses, boils, or pimples.

---

antibiotics
substances that can kill or inactivate bacteria in the body; derived from microorganisms or synthetics

saprophytes
microbes that obtain food from dead or decaying organic matter

psychrophiles
organisms that grow optimally at lower temperatures, between 0 and 20°C

mesophiles
organisms that grow optimally between 25 and 45°C

thermophiles
organisms that grow optimally between 50 and 80°C

extreme thermophiles
organisms capable of growing at extremely high temperatures (between 80 and 100°C)

spore
a protective structure produced by algae, fungi, and some protozoa

endospore
the inner layer of the wall of a spore

coccus
spherical microorganism, especially bacteria

cocci
plural for coccus, a pathogenic bacteria

bacillus
an aerobic, rod-shaped, spore-producing bacterium

spirillum
spiral-shaped bacterium

diplococcus
a common type of cocci that grows in semicircular pairs

staphylococcus
a bacterium that typically occurs in clusters resembling grapes, normally inhabits the skin and mucous membranes

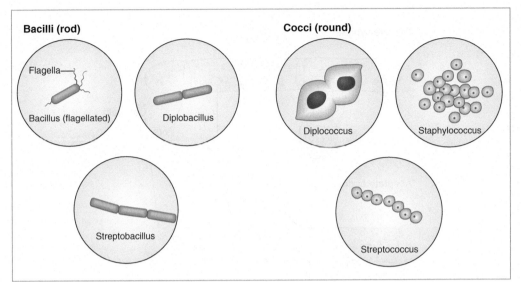

FIGURE 5–1
General forms of bacteria

3. **streptococcus** (plural streptococci), which grows in chains, affecting a large area, and is present in blood poisoning and strep throat. Coccus bacteria are not self-propelling and are instead transmitted through air, in dust, and the substances in which they are found.

Bacillus. Bacilli, the most common pathogenic bacteria, is the most harmful and the most difficult to destroy. Bacilli produce tuberculosis, tetanus, diphtheria, and typhoid fever. Bacilli have **flagella** (fluh-JEL-uh) or **cilia**, which are hairlike projections that propel the bacteria through liquids. This self-propulsion is called **motility**.

Spirillum. The spiral-shaped spirillum can be divided into subgroups that produce such diseases as syphilis and cholera. Treponema pallidum, one such subgroup, is responsible for the sexually transmitted disease (STD) syphilis. Another subgroup is Borrelia burgdorferi, which causes Lyme disease.

Pathogenic bacteria may enter our bodies through the mouth, nose, eyes, and ears as well as through broken skin, causing a bacterial infection. The infection may be localized, in the form of pus made of bacteria, blood cells, decayed tissue, and other waste matter, or it may be carried through the bloodstream causing a general infection to the body.

Fungi

Fungi are plant or vegetable **parasites** (PAR-uh-sayts). They are found in the form of yeasts, molds, and mildews. Like bacteria, many are useful and beneficial. Yeast is used as a raising agent in bread making and for fermenting wines. Molds are introduced into certain cheeses, forming the distinctive blue stripe of blue cheese, and, of course, both mushrooms and penicillin are derived from fungi. Fungi are nature's main decomposers.

A spore, the reproductive part of a fungus, produces a colorless and elongated appendage called a **hypha** (plural hyphae) (Figure 5–2). It is the hypha that invades the body's tissues, like the skin, causing such diseases as athlete's foot or ringworm. Upon being inhaled, it attacks the tissue of the lung, causing chest ailments.

Viruses

Virus (Figures 5–2 and 5–3) is the Latin word for poison. Viruses are subcellular forms of life without nuclei, cytoplasm, or cell membranes. A virus is 50 times smaller than a bacterium. Viruses cannot live or reproduce on their own. They are parasitic and must acquire hosts. Once acquiring living cells as hosts, viruses begin to multiply in vast numbers, causing damage, if not death, to the invaded cells.

Although small, simple, and fragile, viruses can wreak havoc on tissue. A virus consists simply of an outer coat of protein and, on the inside, DNA or RNA. Viruses are

streptococcus
a spherical bacterium, growing in pairs or chains, that often causes disease (e.g., scarlet fever, strep throat, pneumonia)

flagella
hairlike projections found on bacilli that self-propel them through liquids

cilia
tiny, thread-like structures used by bacilli to propel themselves through liquids

motility
movement by independent means

parasites
plants or animals that live on or in other, larger host organisms in ways that harm or do not benefit the host

hypha
the elongated appendage of a fungal spore

FIGURE 5–2
Fungal spores and hyphae

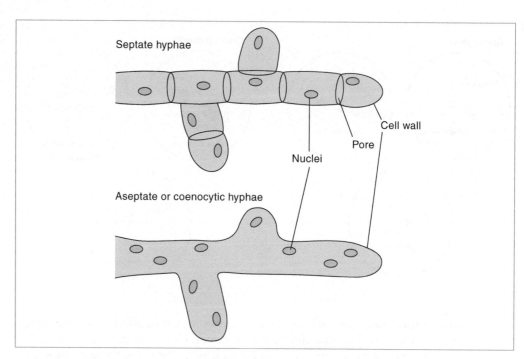

FIGURE 5–3
Highly magnified virus

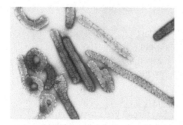

difficult to treat or control, because no known antibiotics destroy them. Usually, the symptoms the virus has caused are treated, not the virus itself, although bacterial infections can develop from a virus that can be treated with antibiotics. The most common virus of greatest concern to the hair-removal specialist is hepatitis. Other viruses include the common cold, influenza, measles, chicken pox, mumps, genital herpes, herpes simplex (cold sores), mononucleosis, and HIV. Respiratory viruses like colds and flu are spread through hand-to-hand contact. Others require the direct contact of blood or body fluids of an infected person to another person. Instruments contaminated with blood or body fluids containing the virus can also infect another unsuspecting individual.

Protozoa

Protozoa are single-cell animal microbes found in water, foods, plants, blood, and body fluids. Some are parasitic, living on the human body. Common human parasites are **amoeba**, causing amoebic dysentery, and mosquitoes, whose bites may cause malaria.

Hepatitis and HIV

The two most important viruses for hair-removal professionals to be aware of are **hepatitis** and **human immunodeficiency virus** (**HIV**), the virus that causes **Acquired Immune Deficiency Syndrome** (**AIDS**). While HIV is not a very resilient virus and generally difficult to transmit, the ramifications from being infected are so serious that it is essential that the virus is addressed and understood. In comparison, the hepatitis virus, although transferred in a similar manner, is more resilient and can also have devastating effects on an individual infected with it.

Hepatitis

Hepatitis is an inflammation of the liver that is caused by alcohol abuse, medications, injury, and certain viruses. There are four main types of infectious hepatitis viruses:

1. hepatitis A virus (HAV)
2. hepatitis B virus (HBV)
3. hepatitis C virus (HCV)
4. delta hepatitis virus (HDV)

HDV is spread only when HBV is present.

amoeba
single-celled organism found in water and in damp soil

hepatitis
inflammation of the liver causing fever, jaundice, abdominal pain, and weakness

HIV
virus that destroys the immune system's helper T cells, the loss of which causes AIDS (see below)

AIDS
Acquired Immune Deficiency Syndrome, a syndrome affecting the body's immune system; caused by HIV

HAV. Formally called infectious hepatitis, HAV is more serious in adults than in children and is easily treatable, often causing no permanent liver damage. Ingesting food or water that has been contaminated with feces containing the virus spreads HAV. This is a typical restaurant/food handling problem in which hands are not washed after using the restroom.

HBV. Formally called serum hepatitis, and more serious than HAV, HBV is transmitted in the same ways as HIV (see following), mainly through contaminated needles, as well as through saliva, semen, and vaginal fluid. This virus is also more resilient than HAV (see preceding).

HCV. Until fairly recently, HCV was known as non-A/non-B hepatitis. Although it is not considered as devastating as HBV, it is as readily transmittable through blood and saliva.
The ways in which hepatitis is spread are:

- Sexual intercourse with an infected person without the use of a condom
- Sharing of needles (commonly occurring among drug users)
- Needle-stick accidents, which occur with health-care workers and electrologists
- Transmission during pregnancy and birth from mother to child
- Blood transfusions (but, due to improved screening, the risk of transmitting hepatitis through blood transfusion is very low in the United States)
- Personal contact with an infected person through nonintact skin contacting the nonintact skin of an infected person and sharing razors or toothbrushes, which transmits the virus in saliva

Because people may carry hepatitis without showing any outwardly visible symptoms, the hair-removal specialist must assume that each client might be infected. The Centers for Disease Control (CDC) has provided guidelines called "Universal Precautions" (see the following section) to be followed under the assumption that people are equal-opportunity carriers of diseases like HIV and HBV. Notable symptoms for hepatitis include a low-grade fever, headache, muscle ache, fatigue, loss of appetite, nausea, vomiting, or diarrhea. Dark urine, pale feces, abdominal pain, and the yellowing of the skin and the whites of the eyes may characterize later stages of hepatitis, along with cirrhosis (scarring) of the liver. HBV is the hepatitis virus of greatest concern to the hair-removal specialist because it is transmitted through blood and the hair-removal specialist will at some point be in close proximity to a client's blood.

HBV Vaccination. To reduce the risk of contracting hepatitis B, electrologists and hair-removal specialists should take vaccines. The HBV vaccine is recommended by both the Immunization Practices Advisory Committee and the Occupational Safety and Health Administration (OSHA). This involves three or four dose vaccinations, depending on the drug company's vaccination type and program. In the three-dose series, there is usually 1 month between the first and second vaccination and 3 months between the second and third vaccination. In the four-dose series, a follow-up vaccination is usually given 12 months later. It is also important to follow the CDC recommendations listed later in this chapter to avoid spreading hepatitis.

HIV

HIV is the virus that causes AIDS. AIDS is a **syndrome**, not a disease. A syndrome is a collection of signs and symptoms that warn of a disease. For example, a sore throat, fever, and aching joints are a collection of symptoms that warn that one may have an influenza virus. AIDS is a collection of symptoms that show that the body cannot protect itself from infection or disease. It should be noted that it is not possible to catch a syndrome; therefore, one cannot catch AIDS. However, one can acquire HIV, the virus leading to AIDS. HIV is very fragile and not easily spread. This virus can be acquired through:

- Sexual intercourse with an infected person without the use of a condom
- Sharing of needles (commonly occurring among drug users)

syndrome
a group of signs and symptoms that together characterize a disease or disorder

- Transmission during pregnancy and childbirth, from mother to infant (the milk of an HIV-infected mother has also been shown to sometimes transmit HIV to uninfected babies)
- Blood transfusions (but, due to improved screening, the risk of transmitting HIV through blood transfusion is very low in the United States)
- Personal contact with an infected person through nonintact skin contacting the nonintact skin of an infected person, where blood literally flows from one person to another

HIV cannot be transmitted through:

- Blood donation*
- Insect bites
- Casual contact (hugging, kissing, sweat, tears, or saliva)
- Airborne means (e.g., sneezing, air conditioners)
- Surfaces (e.g., phones, doorknobs, toilets)
- Food and water

Because the route of hepatitis and HIV transmission is nearly the same, and because HBV presents a higher risk of infection than HIV, the CDC has adopted the HBV model as the "worst-case" scenario in the transmission of infectious diseases that include HIV. Although no cases, to date, have been reported of hepatitis or HIV transmission from electrolysis or other forms of salon hair removal, the potential is there and therefore the guidelines laid out by the CDC should be followed.

Sanitation and Sterilization

Along with the information in this chapter, when considering guidelines for sanitation and sterilization it is important to know the policies, requirements, and guidelines specified by your state, as well as the CDC and OSHA for the different areas of hair removal (e.g., waxing, electrolysis, and laser), for personal protective equipment (e.g., lab coats, gloves, goggles, and drapes), and for the sterilization processing of instruments that may contain bloodborne pathogens.

Sanitation

Most infections can be avoided or controlled by proper public sanitation and good personal hygiene. Sanitization is the significant reduction in the number of pathogens on a surface through cleaning. It is not the total elimination of pathogens. Some pathogens will remain on the surface. Meticulous cleaning is essential before disinfecting or sterilizing to remove any debris.

Hand Washing

The importance of washing hands before and after each client cannot be overly stressed (Figure 5–4). This is the first line of defense in preventing the transmission of bacteria and infections. Correct hand washing removes microorganisms from the skin's surface. Washing hands in front of clients instills confidence in those clients that you follow all necessary guidelines for safe hygiene and sanitation. It is therefore paramount that each treatment room be equipped with its own hand-washing basin, complete with hot and cold running water, soap, paper towels, and a pedal trash bin.

According to CDC Guidelines for Hand Washing and Hospital Environmental Control, plain soap can be used for hand washing in this type of environment, but it should be in a pump bottle, not a bar that can sit in a dish with residual, possibly contaminated, water.

---

*Electrolysis clients who are considering donating blood should, when asked by the Red Cross if they have had electrolysis in the past 6 months, inform the Red Cross that only disposable, single-use needles were used, if that was the case.

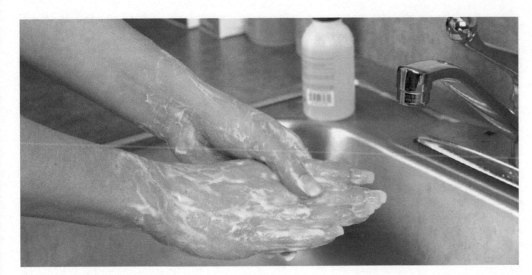

FIGURE 5–4
Proper hand-washing procedure

The following procedure for hand washing is recommended:

1. Remove all jewelry from hands and wrists.
2. Wet hands with tepid water.
3. Apply liquid antibacterial soap and lather for 10 to 15 seconds, approximately the time it takes to sing "Happy Birthday to You." Vigorously rub all the hand's surfaces, paying special attention to fingernails and the area between the fingers.
4. Rinse thoroughly under a continuous stream of running water until all lather is removed.
5. Dry hands thoroughly with clean, disposable paper towels.
6. Use paper towels to turn off faucets.
7. Discard paper towels in a lined foot-pedal bin.

Wash hands:*

- Before and after each client.
- Before and after vinyl or latex gloves are worn.
- If there has been a need to leave the treatment room or to touch a door handle during service.
- Immediately after accidental contact with blood or other bodily fluids.
- After using a tissue to wipe mucus from the eyes, nose, or mouth.
- After using the hands to cover the mouth for a cough or sneeze. A sneeze, when not contained, can travel 12 feet, spreading millions of microorganisms.

Gloves

Gloves are essential to electrologists, but they remain a personal preference for many waxing technicians. Gloves may be required by state boards regulating these services, so check with them and follow their guidelines. Some waxing technicians wear gloves the entire time they are in contact with their clients' skin. Some wear one glove on the hand that comes into contact with the skin when applying pressure to the skin after the wax is removed. Still others choose not to wear gloves.

It is worth noting that blood spots do appear in waxed areas. If there is any chance that the skin on the technician's hand is broken, even in the form of a hangnail, *gloves should be worn*. If you are a waxing technician starting out in this field, wear gloves with every client. Students should get used to wearing gloves with every client. Before long,

---

*When liquid soap pump bottles must be refilled, they should be thoroughly washed so that old soap does not remain for a lengthy period. The pumps, as well as the outsides of the bottles, should also be removed and washed.

Universal Precautions of Glove Use

- A new pair of gloves should be donned with each client.
- Gloves should be discarded when they are torn or punctured. Hands should be rewashed and a new pair of gloves donned.
- Gloves should be powder-free vinyl, because wax can break down and release the protein in latex gloves.
- The client should be questioned for any allergy to latex (see the accompanying section). If the client is aware of such an allergy, it will probably be brought to your attention when you put on gloves.
- Gloves should be worn during the cleaning and handling of forceps and other instruments.
- Gloves should always be worn when handling such chemicals as disinfectants and antiseptics.
- Gloved hands should not be washed. This will cause "wicking," the weakening of vinyl that allows substances to penetrate the microscopic holes that otherwise would not have leaked. When gloves become contaminated during service or treatment, they should be discarded, the hands washed, and new gloves donned.

---

gloves will become second nature and you will feel undressed without them! This standard also lets clients know that you follow Universal Precautions.

Latex Allergy.   Considering the amount of time you will spend wearing gloves, switching to a latex-free environment is a positive move for your health as well as the health of clients who may have a latex allergy. Repeated, long-term exposure to latex can create an allergy that can present, on the less severe end, as a mild rash or dermatitis to a severe allergic reaction that includes the respiratory symptoms of sneezing, runny nose, and itchy

Selection Guide for Gloves Used in Health-Care Settings*

	Barrier Protection	Strength and Durability	Puncture Resistance	Fit and Comfort	Elasticity	Allergenicity
Latex	Long-standing barrier qualities	Strong, natural rubber is durable	Has reseal qualities	Provides comfortable fit	Natural ability due to elastic quality rubber	Contains protein and chemical allergens, low powder is preferred
Neoprene (Chloroprene)	Good but tear resistance is marginal	Strong	Has some puncture-resistant qualities	Provides a good fit, has some elastic ability that enhances fit	Close to latex and allows for flexibility	Contains no latex proteins but has some accelerator chemicals
Nitrile	Resistant to punctures and tears, flexes, and does not develop holes	Strong, has puncture-resistant qualities	Has puncture-resistant qualities	Slightly tighter fit	Less than latex over time tends to shape to wearer's hand	Contains no proteins but contains some accelerator chemicals
Vinyl	Easily breaks during use, baggy	Weak, breaks easily, and punctures	Punctures with sharps	Limited fit, baggy	Dexterity compromised	Contains no proteins but chemical accelerators
Polyurethane	Durable and high puncture resistance	Excellent tear, puncture, and abrasion resistance	Superior to latex for puncture-resistance; mimics nitrile in performance	Good comfort and fit, has latex-like qualities	Elasticity is apparent	Contains no latex proteins and no chemical accelerators
Copolymers (Block Polymers)	Good resistance to tears	Stronger than vinyl, puncture resistance is fair	Easy to puncture	Latex-like fit and comfortable	Elasticity superior to vinyl but below latex	Contains no latex proteins but some chemical accelerators

*By Denise M. Korniewicz, DNSc, RN, FA

watery eyes. Extreme life-threatening allergic reactions do not usually occur at the early stage of latex allergy, but people can develop an extreme latex allergy that can be life threatening. When latex gloves contain powder, the powder absorbs some of the latex proteins, and when the gloves are removed, the powder becomes airborne and is disbursed throughout the room and can also be inhaled.

Antiseptics

Antiseptics are formulated to prevent, retard, or stop bacterial growth. They are not as strong as disinfectants but are safe to use on the skin. An antiseptic sanitizes but does not disinfect. **Bacteriostats** and **fungistats** do not kill germs; they only temporarily inhibit their growth, which will resume once the static properties have worn off.

Disinfection

Disinfection is the term used for the reduction of microorganisms on a surface. However, not all spores will be destroyed, neither will endospores be destroyed. Chemical disinfectants are available in high, intermediate, and low levels of potency and are regulated by the FDA for medical use or the Environmental Protection Agency (EPA) for general environmental surface use. Instructions and guidelines for correct and effective usage can be found on a product's label or insert or on the Material Safety and Data Sheets (MSDSs) (Figure 5–5), which should be available from the manufacturer.

Disinfectants are used for killing bacteria and certain viruses on nonporous surface areas and tools. They are not suitable for use on human tissue. Generally speaking, disinfecting chemicals are too strong for use on the skin. The exception is that a solution of 70% ethyl alcohol or 99% isopropyl alcohol used on the skin will disinfect but not sterilize. Germicidal cleaners can be classified as one-step or two-step cleaners. Most disinfectants we use today are considered one-step germicidal cleaners. They clean, disinfect, and deodorize all at once and are the most convenient to use. Two-step germicidal cleaners require general cleaning before disinfecting, are more corrosive, have a strong odor, and require careful measuring for dilution and use. Chemical disinfectants and germicides do not sterilize an area. Although some of the high-level disinfectants, like **glutaraldehyde** ($C_5H_8O_2$), do an excellent job as germicides, they are not practical as a method for sterilization due to their high levels of toxicity, instability, and the fact that they cannot be biologically monitored. The disinfectant should always be added to the water and not vice versa. In addition, they should be approved by the EPA or the FDA.

Note: All chemicals should be properly labeled and stored in their appropriate containers according to the manufacturers' recommendations for light and temperature. They should be placed on sturdy shelves of the appropriate size and within easy reach to avoid accidental spillage.

Housekeeping

First impressions are important so that clients are confident that they are going to have pleasurable experiences. It is also important that, when clients move into the treatment area, they have safe and sanitary service. A clean, orderly, attractive reception area is an important start, but strict hygiene and sanitation rules should follow in all other parts of the salon, spa, or clinic, with special attention paid to rest rooms and all treatment areas.

Restrooms should be cleaned and disinfected daily and monitored closely throughout the day. They should contain toilet tissue and containers for used sanitary products, have hot and cold running water and liquid soap in a pump bottle, an air drier or paper towels, and a lined pedal bin to house used paper.

Walls, floors, windowsills, and window coverings should all be washed and disinfected regularly. Equipment and work surfaces (carts and cabinets) should be disinfected regularly and between clients.

Regular and routine housekeeping, as well as the proper agents and guidelines, is the only assured way of maintaining a state of **asepsis**, meaning that something is sufficiently clean to prohibit bacterial growth. Failure to follow these guidelines results in possible **sepsis**, which is the presence of pathogenic germs.

antiseptics
agents that prevent or reduce infection by eliminating or reducing the growth of microorganisms

bacteriostats
substances that restrict the growth and activity of bacteria, but do not kill them

fungistats
substances that inhibit the growth of fungi without killing them

glutaraldehyde
an oily, water-soluble liquid used as a disinfectant and biological fixative ($C_5H_8O_2$)

asepsis
condition in which no living disease-causing microorganisms are present

sepsis
the condition or syndrome caused by microorganisms or their toxins in the tissue or bloodstream

Material Safety Data Sheet

May be used to comply with
OSHA's Hazard Communication Standard,
29 CFR 1910.1200. Standard must be
consulted for specific requirements.

U.S. Department of Labor

Occupational Safety and Health Administration
(Non-Mandatory Form)
Form Approved
OMB No. 1218-0072

IDENTITY *(As Used on Label and List)*

Note: Blank spaces are not permitted. If any item is not applicable or no information is available, the space must be marked to indicate that.

Section I

Manufacturer's Name	Emergency Telephone Number
Address *(Number, Street, City, State, and ZIP Code)*	Telephone Number for information
	Date Prepared
	Signature of Preparer *(optional)*

Section II — Hazardous Ingredients/Identity Information

Hazardous Components (Specific Chemical Identity; Common Names(s))	OSHA PEL	ACGIH TLV	Other Limits Recommended	% *(optional)*

Section III — Physical/Chemical Characteristics

Boiling Point	Specific Gravity (H$_2$O - 1)	
Vapor Pressure (mm Hg.)	Melting Point	
Vapor Density (Air - 1))	Evaporation Rate (Butyl Acetate - 1)	
Solubility in Water		
Appearance and Odor		

Section IV — Fire and Explosion Hazard Data

Flash Point (Method Used)	Flammable Limits	LEL	UEL
Extinguishing Media			
Special Fire Fighting Procedures			
Unusual Fire and Explosion Hazards			

(Reproduce locally)

OSHA 174, Sept. 1985

FIGURE 5–5 Sample MSDS product sheet

Sterilization

When learning about sterilization, it is important to understand that a sterile state is a temporary state, one that will be reinvaded by bacteria. Sterilization should be habitual and ongoing.

The goal of sterilization is the complete elimination of all forms of bacteria, especially endospores and viruses. This section, while of importance to the hair-removal specialist in general, is fundamental in the practice of electrolysis.

Sterilization Agents

There are two groups of sterilization agents: (1) physical and (2) chemical.

Physical Agents.   There are four popular physical methods for sterilizing, which use the physical agents of heat, water, and ultraviolet light. The popular physical agents are dry-heat sterilization, steam-heat sterilization, irradiation, and boiling.

Physical agents include:

■ Steam-heat sterilization (moist heat)—The steam-heat method uses an airtight chamber called an **autoclave** (Figure 5–6) to apply steam heat under pressure to instruments. The FDA regulates autoclaves, subjecting implements to the following times and pressures to achieve sterilization:

> **autoclave**
> airtight chamber that sterilizes through the use of steam and high temperature under pressure

■ 15 minutes at 250°F (121°C), 15 psi for unpackaged instruments plus heat-up time
■ 30 minutes at 250°F (121°C), 15 psi for packaged instruments plus heat-up time

■ Dry-heat sterilization (dry heat)—Regulated by the FDA, this forced-air oven is the most popular method in hospitals (Figure 5–7). To sterilize, the implements must be subjected to the following:

■ 340°F (170°C) for 1 hour plus heat-up time
■ 320°F (160°C) for 2 hours plus heat-up time

■ Irradiation (light rays)—Irradiation uses ultraviolet light rays, particularly alpha, beta, and gamma rays, to destroy the microorganisms and spores in an enclosed cabinet. This method is not recommended for sterilizing electrolysis equipment because it is considered ineffective in destroying HBV.

■ Boiling (moist heat)—In boiling, instruments are placed in a vat of boiling water at 212°F for a minimum of 2 minutes.

These methods of sterilization are all designed to kill the spores, endospores, and viruses that antiseptics and disinfectants cannot kill.

FIGURE 5–6 Sample autoclave

FIGURE 5–7 Sterilization lab including a dry-heat sterilizer

Chemical Agents. The two popular chemical methods are soaking in chemical solution, and fumigation, which is the application of gases.

- Liquid—With liquid agents, instruments are submersed in a 2% glutaraldehyde aqueous solution.
- Fumigation—Fumigation uses **ethylene oxide** in a sealed cabinet to sterilize materials that cannot withstand heat or steam.

Glass-Bead Sterilizer—Also known as an endodontic dry-heat sterilizer, the glass-bead sterilizer is no longer approved by the FDA for the sterilization of dental equipment. Once a popular method of sterilization for the electrologist, the CDC now considers this device to be a misnomer, because it does not achieve the necessary level of sterilization. Because some electrologists reuse needles, there is concern that this device will not satisfactorily achieve the necessary results of sterilization for reusable needles.

Sterilization Monitoring and Testing

The CDC, major electrolysis associations (AEA and SCME), and certain states require the monitoring of the sterilization effectiveness of the autoclave or dry-heat sterilizer monthly. This is achieved by purchasing biological testing kits that are placed in the sterilizer for the recommended amount of time and sent in included, preaddressed envelopes to a lab for analysis. If the kit tests positive for microorganisms, you will be notified immediately. Otherwise, written notification is sent acknowledging the effectiveness of the sterilization unit. The written notification should be kept on file for review by inspectors.

- Biological indicators—Regulated by the FDA, biological indicators are commercially formulated devices to test the method of sterilization being monitored to see if conditions were met to achieve sterilization.
- Chemical indicators—Regulated by the FDA, chemical indicators use a color-change process on chemically treated paper strips to indicate if the parameters of heat sterilization have been met. They do not indicate that sterilization has been met.
- Sterilization tape—This tape uses a chemical to indicate that an item has been through a sterilization process, but it cannot indicate if the item is in fact sterilized.
- Spore test—A spore test is used to establish that a sterilizer is functioning correctly (i.e., destroying all microorganisms and spores).

Sterilization of Electrolysis Equipment

Certain instruments used in the practice of electrolysis may become contaminated with blood and body fluids. Therefore, these instruments require sterilization. Because many of the states have different rules and regulations governing the sterilization practices of the electrologist, the guidelines and standards in this section are based on those recommended by the AEA and the Society of Clinical and Medical Hair Removal (SCMHR). Both organizations can be contacted for their recommended safety control standards.

Noncritical, Semicritical, and Critical Items

Items are listed as noncritical, semicritical, and critical depending on their exposure to blood and body fluids. Understanding the three different variables determines what level of sanitation and sterilization is required for an item (Figure 5–8).

- Critical items—Critical (Category I) items come into direct contact with blood and body fluids, including needles and forceps. Therefore, they should be sterilized according to CDC standards.
- Semicritical items—Semicritical (Category II) items may come into contact with nonintact skin and mucous membranes but do penetrate the skin (e.g., electrolysis probe tips, also called caps). These items should be cleaned and processed correctly before and after use on the client.

CLASSIFICATION	STERILIZATION		DISINFECTION	
	Procedure	Time	Procedure	Time
1. Critical Objects (Enters tissue or comes in contact with blood/body fluids) i.e., epilating needles, comedone extractors	A B C* D E*	Manufacturer's Recommendations (MR) MR MR 6 hours 6 hours		
2. Semicritical Objects (Comes in contact with mucous membranes or non-intact skin) i.e., HF/galvanic electrodes, tweezers	A B C* D* E* F* G*	MR MR MR 6 hours 6 hours 30 minutes 20 minutes		
3. Noncritical Objects (Could come in contact with intact skin) i.e., magnifying loop countertops, machine			G* H* I* J* K* L*	10 minutes 10 minutes MR MR MR MR

Modified from Rutolo, Washington, Guidelines for Infection Control Practice, Association for Practitioners in Infection Control, Inc., January 1990.

A   Heat sterilization (steam or dry heat; see manufacturer's recommendations)

B   Ethylene oxide gas (see manufacturer's recommendations)

C   Glutaraldehyde-based formulations (2%), used at full strength, have been shown to sterilize items if they are soaked for about 7 hours.

D   Demand-release chlorine dioxide. Will corrode aluminum, copper, brass, series 400 stainless steel, and chrome with prolonged exposure.

E   Stabilized hydrogen peroxide 6%. Will corrode copper, zinc, and brass.

F   Wet pasteurization (boiling) at 75°C for 30 minutes after detergent cleansing.

G   Sodium hypochlorite (1,000 ppm available chlorine). Will corrode metal instruments.

H   Ethyl or isopropyl alcohol (70 to 90%)

I   Sodium hypochlorite (100 ppm available chlorine)

J   Phenolic germicidal detergent solution (follow manufacturer's recommendations)

K   Iodophor germicidal detergent solution (follow manufacturer's recommendations)

L   Quaternary ammonium germicidal detergent solution (follow manufacturer's recommendations)

FIGURE 5–8 Classification, sterilization, and disinfection

- Noncritical items—Noncritical (Category III) items only come into contact with intact skin (e.g., epilator cords and the indifferent electrode). Routine, regular cleansing and disinfecting of these items are all that is needed to prevent disease transmission.
- Any implements that are used more than once should be sterilized after each client.
- Any item that is dropped on the floor should be considered contaminated and reprocessed in the manner recommended for that item.

Sterilization Protocol

1. The technician should wear gloves when preparing for sterilization and when placing sterilized items in their storage containers.

ultrasonic
sound waves with frequencies above the upper limit of the normal range of human hearing

2. Implements should be thoroughly washed. An **ultrasonic** (ul-tra-SAHN-ik) cleaner effectively removes debris from instruments using sound waves.

3. Implements should be rinsed clean of cleaning solution by being held under lukewarm, running water.

4. After thorough cleaning, instruments are completely dried with disposable paper towels.

5. Instruments should be placed in the selected sterilization unit following the manufacturer's, FDA, or EPA guidelines and using a chemical indicator.

6. After sterilization, all implements should be kept in sterile, closed containers until needed.

7. Unused implements should be resterilized if they have been in contact with a non-sterile surface, after a 24-hour period, or when the container or packaging has been opened.

Needles. Needles are critical items requiring the strictest protocol for sterilization, because they frequently come into contact with blood from the dermis. Most electrologists use single-use, disposable needles.

- Needles should be stored appropriately away from extreme conditions and moisture.
- The expiration date on the package of the prepackaged disposable needles should be noted and observed.
- Needles with an expired date should be disposed of in a sharps container or an **isolyser** needle disposal unit.
- Needles that are in any way damaged should also be disposed of in a sharps container or an isolyser needle disposal unit.
- After use, needles should be disposed in a sharps box or an isolyser needle disposal unit.
- Multiple-use needles should, immediately after use, be submersed in a holding container of enzyme solution and water and covered until the sterilization process.

isolyser
container used for collecting and disposing of needles

Forceps and Tweezers. Electrologists generally use the term *forceps,* which are made of a surgical steel and can withstand the chemicals and intense heat used in sterilization. Cosmetologists often refer to these tools as tweezers. As tweezers used with a waxing service come into contact with skin tissue and, occasionally, spots of blood, they also should be made of a medical-grade surgical steel that can be thoroughly sterilized without damaging the finish, not the kind sold in drugstores to the general public as personal-hygiene items. This text refers to these tools as forceps, indicating the medical-grade quality of the instruments, which allows them to be sterilized successfully. Forceps are critical items and should be handled in a manner similar to needles (see the preceding).

After treatment, forceps should be submersed in a holding container of enzyme solution and water and covered until the sterilization process. Transfer forceps should be cleaned and dried at the beginning or end of each day and before use when one suspects they have come into contact with contaminates.

Tips (Caps) for Epilator Probes. Tips for epilator probes are semicritical items. After each client, the used tip should be placed in the holding container of protein-dissolving enzyme solution, before sterilizing, and before a new, processed tip is placed on the probe. The tip should also be placed in the holding container when it is dropped, mishandled, or comes into contact with contaminates. To process the tips, hold them under warm, running water while still in the holding tray. The tips should then be placed in the ultrasonic cleansing unit following manufacturer's recommendations. Then, they should again be rinsed thoroughly and dried completely with disposable paper towels. If the tips cannot go into an autoclave unit, they can be sterilized using a freshly made solution of 1 tablespoon household bleach to 1 quart of water, or 1 part household bleach to 99 parts water for at least 10 minutes. The tips should again be rinsed thoroughly under running water and dried completely with disposable paper towels. The solution should be discarded immediately after use. The tips should be stored for use in a clean, covered container to prevent them from coming into contact with contaminates before use.

Anaphoresis/Cataphoresis Rollers. Anaphoresis and **cataphoresis** rollers are semicritical items and are cleaned and processed to the same degree as probe tip/caps.

Indifferent Electrodes. Indifferent electrodes are noncritical items and should be cleaned and treated with a low-level disinfectant after each client or in the event of mishandling (e.g., dropping on the floor).

Epilator Chords and Needle Holders. Epilator chords and needle holders are noncritical items and should be cleaned and treated with a low-level disinfectant after each client or in the event of mishandling (e.g., dropping on the floor).

Eye Shields. Eyeshields are noncritical items and should be cleaned with soap and water, rinsed, and dried thoroughly. If there is reason to believe that the client has conjunctivitis, a sty, or another possibly contagious disorder, the eye shields must be sterilized and the strictest care and attention paid to housekeeping and the avoidance of cross-contamination.

Holding Containers. Holding containers should be cleaned at the start or end of each day and any time they come into contact with contaminates.

Biohazard Symbol

The biohazard symbol (Figure 5–9) is recognized internationally to identify biologically hazardous medical waste material, whether it be gauze contaminated with blood or other body fluids, human surgery tissues, cultures of infectious disease, or implements capable of puncturing the skin.

Sharps Container

The sharps container is used to collect sharp medical waste (e.g., needles and **lancets**). For disposal purposes, they are considered **biohazardous** whether or not they were used or contaminated with blood, body fluids, or other disease-causing contaminants. A full sharps box must be collected by licensed biohazard haulers and destroyed in special treatment facilities (Figure 5–10).

anaphoresis
use of a negative pole to force an alkaline product into the skin, toward the positive pole

cataphoresis
the process of using a positive pole to introduce an acidic product into the skin, toward the negative pole

FIGURE 5–9
Biohazard symbol

lancets
sharp tools used for breaking the skin

biohazardous
relating to toxic or infectious agents that may pose a risk to humans or their environments

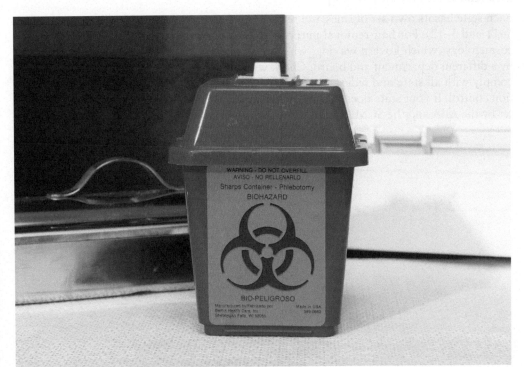

FIGURE 5–10
Sample sharps container

Isolyser Needle Disposal

The **isolyser** method of needle disposal consists of a plastic bottle containing liquid disinfectant. Once filled with needles, a catalyst is added to the isolyser creating a chemical action that causes the liquid to turn to gel. Now a safe solid, the container can be disposed of in the regular garbage.

Universal Precautions

The CDC has published a set of guidelines and controls requiring public service workers to assume *all* human blood and bodily fluids are infectious for bloodborne pathogens, including HIV/HBV, regardless of age, sex, race, and asymptoms meaning without visible symptoms and signs of infection. With this in mind, certain precautions and preventative measures must be taken. These are:

- Hand washing using the guidelines listed previously
- Correct and appropriate use of gloves
- Personal protection equipment (e.g., lab coats, masks, and goggles)
- Correct handling of needles, probes, lancets, and other sharp tools
- Correct disposal of needles, probes, lancets, and anything else contaminated by blood and body fluids

Postexposure Strategies

In the event skin is punctured by a critical item, the following steps should be taken:

1. Politely excuse yourself for a while, without alarming the client.
2. Wash hands thoroughly in continuously running warm water, allowing the puncture wound to bleed out.
3. Apply an antiseptic and a Band-Aid®.
4. Record the client's name, date, and time of the treatment.
5. With skin protected with a Band-Aid® and gloves, resume treatment.
6. Keep an accurate, detailed account of subsequent clients' names.
7. Get tested for HIV/HVB, remembering that Universal Precautions mean that all people are equal-opportunity carriers of these diseases.

Inspections and Sanitation Log

Each state has its own set of rules and regulations for sanitation and sterilization (Figures 5–11 and 5–12). For hair-removal purposes, there are guidelines set up by state boards of cosmetology, which govern waxing, whereas electrology could be licensed and governed by a different department and board. Check with your state licensing board and know and comply with all state and federally mandated laws for sanitation, sterilization, and infection control. If your state does not license the practice of electrology, follow the guidelines set by the AEA and the SCMHR and those described in this book.

Safety and Health Inspection Report

Location: __MCEC__   Inspected by: __DENNIS NELSON__   Date: __12/9/03__

All Salon Areas—Housekeeping and Sanitation

- ☐ OK   Is there evidence the salon has been used for cooking or living quarters?
- ☐ YES   Are all salon areas orderly, dust, insect and rodent-free, clean, sanitary, and well lighted? DISPENSARY—TOO DARK TO READ LABELS IN CABINET ON LEFT SIDE.
- ☐ NO   Are floors swept clean whenever needed and is hair swept up after each client service? Are cotton balls and other materials picked up immediately? CLINIC—HAIR SWEPT BUT NOT PICKED UP.
- ☐ YES   Are floors mopped and carpets vacuumed daily?
- ☐ YES   Are windows, screens and curtains cleaned regularly?
- ☐ NO   Are all waste materials deposited in a metal waste receptacle with a self-closing lid? Are waste receptacles emptied regularly throughout the day? Are hazardous waste containers properly labeled and separated from normal waste as required? LID OPEN—SHAMPOO AREA.
- ☐ YES   Are all sinks and drinking fountains cleaned regularly?
- ☐ YES   Are separate or disposable drinking cups provided for clients and employees?
- ☐ YES   Are hot and cold water faucets clean and leak-free?
- ☐ YES   Are all toilets and washing facilities clean and sanitary? Are toilet tissue, paper towels, and pump-type antiseptic liquid soap provided?
- ☐ YES   Are door handles cleaned regularly?
- ☐ YES   Is food stored separately from salon products? Is there assurance that eating and drinking is done on sanitary surfaces separate from chemical handling or where services are being provided? STUDENTS EATING IN LUNCH ROOM ONLY.
- ☐ YES   Is the work area ventilation appropriate for the services provided and are fans, humidifiers, exhaust and ventilation systems cleaned regularly?
- ☐ YES   Are floors free of water or other substances that could cause a slip, trip, or fall?
- ☐ YES   Are MSDS sheets available for all chemicals used in the salon?
- ☐ YES   Are all chemicals properly stored and all containers labeled? Is the outside of all containers kept clean? MUCH BETTER, UNMARKED WATER BOTTLES IN CLINIC.
- ☐ YES   Is appropriate personal protective equipment (eye protection, gloves, dust and organic vapor masks, etc.) available and used according to manufacturers' directions and salon policy?
- ☐ YES   Does the washing machine provide water temperature of at least 160 degrees Fahrenheit?
- ☐ YES   Is a hospital-grade tuberculocidal disinfecting solution with instructions available for cleaning scissors, combs, brushes, plastic capes, and other materials as required? CURRENTLY USING MARVICIDE.

Emergency Precautions and first Aid

- ☐ YES   Are emergency phone numbers posted where they can be readily found in an emergency?
- ☐ YES   Are fire evacuation procedures posted?
- ☐ YES   Are tornado shelter and fire evacuation locations posted?
- ☐ YES   Are first-aid kits readily accessible with necessary supplies? Is the kit periodically inspected and replenished as needed?
- ☐ NO   Are emergency eye wash bottles provided where chemical handling is done and where chemical services are provided? Is there ready access to a sink with tempered water to completely flush the eyes of hazardous materials? NO EYE WASH BOTTLES IN DISPENSARY.
- ☐ YES   Are exit and warning signs (biohazard, fire door, flammable, or toxic chemicals) posted where appropriate? EXIT SIGNS: 1 IN LAUNDRY, 1 IN LUNCH ROOM (WRONG DOOR), 1 IN CLINIC.

FIGURE 5–11 Professional safety and health inspection report

Salon Self-Inspection Safety and Health Report

Location: _____ Inspected by: _____ Date: _____

All Salon Areas—Housekeeping and Sanitation

☐ Is there evidence the salon has been used for cooking or living quarters?

☐ Are all salon areas orderly, dust, insect and rodent-free, clean, sanitary, and well lighted?

☐ Are floors swept clean whenever needed and is hair swept up after each client service? Are cotton balls and other materials picked up immediately?

☐ Are floors mopped and carpets vacuumed daily?

☐ Are windows, screens and curtains cleaned regularly?

☐ Are all waste materials deposited in a metal waste receptacle with a self-closing lid? Are waste receptacles emptied regularly throughout the day? Are hazardous waste containers properly labeled and separated from normal waste as required?

☐ Are all sinks and drinking fountains cleaned regularly?

☐ Are separate or disposable drinking cups provided for clients and employees?

☐ Are hot and cold water faucets clean and leak-free?

☐ Are all toilets and washing facilities clean and sanitary? Are toilet tissue, paper towels, and pump-type antiseptic liquid soap provided?

☐ Are door handles cleaned regularly?

☐ Is food stored separately from salon products? Is there assurance that eating and drinking is done on sanitary surfaces separate from chemical handling or where services are being provided?

☐ Is the work area ventilation appropriate for the services provided and are fans, humidifiers, exhaust and ventilation systems cleaned regularly?

☐ Are floors free of water or other substances that could cause a slip, trip, or fall?

☐ Are MSDS sheets available for all chemicals used in the salon?

☐ Are all chemicals properly stored and all containers labeled? Is the outside of all containers kept clean?

☐ Is appropriate personal protective equipment (eye protection, gloves, dust and organic vapor masks, etc.) available and used according to manufacturers' directions and salon policy?

☐ Does the washing machine provide water temperature of at least 160 degrees Fahrenheit?

☐ Is a hospital-grade tuberculocidal disinfecting solution with instructions available for cleaning scissors, combs, brushes, plastic capes, and other materials as required?

☐ Are "wet sanitizers" containing disinfecting solution used only for implements to be decontaminated?

Emergency Precautions and first Aid

☐ Are emergency phone numbers posted where they can be readily found in an emergency?

☐ Are fire evacuation procedures posted?

☐ Are tornado shelter and fire evacuation locations posted?

☐ Are first-aid kits readily accessible with necessary supplies? Is the kit periodically inspected and replenished as needed?

☐ Are emergency eye wash bottles provided where chemical handling is done and where chemical services are provided? Is there ready access to a sink with tempered water to completely flush the eyes of hazardous materials?

☐ Are exit and warning signs (biohazard, fire door, flammable, or toxic chemicals) posted where appropriate?

Fire Safety

☐ Are flammable/combustible products and materials (towels, paper, cardboard) stored and handled away from open flame, electrical outlets, and other ignition sources?

☐ Does the salon comply with all local fire codes?

☐ Is the fire alarm system certified as required? Tested at least annually?

☐ Are automatic sprinkler systems (sprinkler heads, water pressure and control valves) free from obstructions and checked periodically?

☐ Are portable fire extinguishers provided in adequate numbers and type?

☐ Are fire extinguishers mounted in readily accessible locations and recharged regularly? Inspection tags marked and current?

FIGURE 5–12 Salon self-inspection report

Walkways, Stairways, and Exits

☐ Are aisles and passageways kept clear?

☐ Are materials and equipment stored such that sharp objects will not interfere with the walkways?

☐ Are standard stair rails or handrails provided for all stairways having four or more risers? Is the handrail capable of withstanding a downward load of 200 pounds?

☐ Are steps provided with a surface that renders them slip resistant? Is the slip resistant material in good condition?

☐ Are all exits kept free of obstructions? Are exits marked with an exit sign and illuminated by a reliable light source?

☐ Are there sufficient exits to permit prompt escape in case of an emergency?

☐ Is the number of exits from each floor of a building and the number of exits from the building itself appropriate for the building occupancy load?

☐ Can exit doors be opened from the direction of exit travel without the use of a key or any special knowledge or effort when the building is occupied?

☐ Are fire doors maintained closed and warnings posted, "Do not block open"?

Ergonomics

☐ Are there heavy objects on the floor or overhead that must be lifted?

☐ Does the working space allow for a full range of work movements?

☐ Is the working point-of-operation at the proper height and adjustable?

☐ Are clippers, scissors, and other tools recommended or provided that maintain a relatively neutral hand and wrist position?

☐ Are armrests and footrests provided where needed?

☐ Where chairs or stools are provided, are they easily adjustable and suited to the task?

☐ Are all written task requirements visible from comfortable positions?

Electrical Safety

☐ Are all electrical tools and implements kept on stands or hangers or otherwise stored properly when not in use?

☐ Are multiple plug adapters prohibited and work stations free from electrical overload (multiple cords plugged into one outlet, or lightweight cords with large appliances with heating elements or motors)? Is the area free from extension cords used as permanent wiring?

☐ Are extension cords limited to one per station, six feet in length, and only in use when providing client services? Are the cords in good condition, not pinched, broken, cracked or covered up?

☐ Are washers, dryers, and other electrical appliances and tools provided with 3-prong plugs or double-insulated?

☐ Are ground fault circuit interrupters (GFCI) provided for areas that are or might become wet?

☐ Are lamps, outlets, extension cords, and other electrical circuitry near flammable chemical handling that could serve as an ignition source?

☐ Are all circuits identified in breaker panel boxes?

☐ Are all unused openings (including conduit knockouts) in electrical enclosures and fittings covered by covers, plugs, or plates?

☐ Are switches, receptacles, etc., provided with tight-fitting covers or plates?

Repairs/corrections must be completed by (date) _____

Report routed to _____ (date) _____

Repairs/corrections have been completed by _____

Signed _____ Date _____

FIGURE 5–12 Continued

Conclusion

Hair-removal specialists must clearly understand the need for proper sterilization and sanitation and can only appreciate its importance by understanding the nature of pathology and disease transmission.

Hair-removal specialists may be in direct contact with dozens of people a week, hundreds of people a month, tens of thousands in a career. For specialists' safety and well-being, they should follow appropriate steps of hygiene and sanitation to the letter. In hair removal, specialists who do not work do not get paid. Staying healthy means no sick days and no loss of earnings.

Clients expect and deserve to be treated in a safe and sanitary environment. They do not expect to be receiving contagions during hair-removal procedures. Not following the mandated guidelines could result in a complaint, which could result in the suspension or loss of a professional license and a lawsuit.

 ## Discussion and Review Questions

1. What is the difference between bacteria and a virus?
2. Name two ways in which HIV can be transmitted and two ways in which it is not.
3. What is the difference between disinfection and sterilization?
4. Name two critical items, two semicritical items, and two noncritical items.
5. Name two FDA/EPA methods of sterilization.
6. Name two acceptable ways of disposing of needles.

 ## Additional Readings

Chesky, Sheldon R., Isabel Cristina, and Richard B. Rosenberg. 1994. *Milady's Playing It Safe.* Clifton Park, NY: Milady, an imprint of Delmar Learning.

Schoon, Douglas D. 1994. *Milady's HIV/AIDS and Hepatitis.* Clifton Park, NY: Milady, an imprint of Delmar Learning.

Milady's Standard Comprehensive Training for Estheticians. 2003. Clifton Park, NY: Milady, an imprint of Delmar Learning.

Nelson, Dennis. 2001. *Safety and Health in the Salon.* Clifton Park, NY: Milady, an imprint of Delmar Learning.

SECTION II

Alternative Methods of Hair Removal

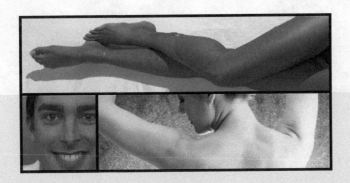

Hair removal has been around for centuries, perhaps, some contend, since the dawn of humankind. Tools once thought to be used for scraping fur from animal skins were discovered to contain human hair and are now believed to have been used as crude razors for shaving the face 20,000 years ago. Threading and sugaring, both ancient methods used in the Middle East, are still used today. Ancient Egyptians waxed hair off with beeswax and sported clean, shaven faces as status symbols. Ancient Sumerians and Romans tweezed eyebrows and facial hair. In the modern United States, people continue to develop and improve hair-removal methods for home use, whether through improved shaving tools, depilatories, or home-waxing products.

This section covers the many home-hair-removal products that are available, how those products work, and those products' effects on the hair and skin. This section also addresses the little-known, alternative methods of hair removal that have been around for centuries in Middle Eastern countries and that are gaining in popularity in Western countries.

By the end of this section, hair-removal specialists should be familiar enough with all these methods and products to be able to answer clients' questions and to offer suggestions.

CHAPTER 6

Home Hair-Removal Methods

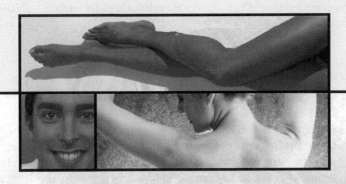

Chapter Outline

Learning Objectives ■ Key Terms ■ Introduction ■ Shaving ■ Tweezing
Chemical Depilatories ■ Bleaching ■ Abrasives ■ Mechanical Epilation
Electronic Tweezing ■ Home Electrolysis Units ■ Hair-Reduction Creams ■ Home Wax Kits
Conclusion ■ Discussion and Review Questions ■ Additional Readings

Learning Objectives

By the end of this chapter, you should be able to:

1. Explain the most popular methods of home hair removal.
2. Differentiate between epilation and depilation.
3. Identify the effects of various hair-removal methods on the skin, hair, and regrowth.
4. Know the pros and cons of each hair-removal method.
5. Advise and educate clients about hair-removal methods.

Key Terms

acute skin disease	eflornithine	keloid scars	radiation
alpha hydroxy acid (AHA)	enzyme	laser	retinoic acid
ammonium bicarbonate	epilation	lidocaine	salicylic acid
androgens	Federal Trade Commission	loofah	scleroderma
benzocaine	(FTC)	lupus	sodium hydroxide
calcium thioglycolate	folliculitis	metabolic activity	sodium thioglycolate
cardiac arrhythmias	Food and Drug	microdermabrasion	stylet
chronic skin disease	Administration (FDA)	ornithine decarboxylase	terminal hair
conductor	hepatitis	oxidize	touchband
depilation	hydrogen peroxide	pseudofolliculitis barbae	tretinoin
depilatory	insulator	(PFB)	vellus

Introduction

Hair removal is a multibillion dollar industry, whether in the form of methods and products used at home or professional services offered in a salon or doctor's office. To be effective in the hair-removal industry, specialists should be well versed in the many home-care methods clients use and those methods' effects on the skin and hair. By understanding these methods and their effects, hair-removal specialists will be able to offer sound advice to clients, explain the problems clients may be having with their home hair-removal methods, and steer clients toward methods better suited to the clients' needs. Home hair-removal methods include shaving, tweezing, depilatory creams, abrasives, bleaching, electronic tweezing, home electrolysis units, hair-reduction creams, and home wax kits.

Shaving

laser
device that uses certain substances to absorb electromagnetic energy and reradiate that energy as a highly focused beam of synchronized, single-wavelength radiation

pseudofolliculitis barbae (PFB)
irritating skin condition of inflamed hair follicles caused by hair removal

folliculitis
inflammation of one or more hair follicles which produces small boils

Shaving is still the most common method of removing unwanted hair, by men and women. However, more and more women are embracing the benefits of professional hair removal and are switching from shaving to waxing, electrolysis, or **laser** hair removal.

Shaving is usually done with a manual or an electric razor on skin that is either wet and lathered or covered with a special foaming product (Figure 6–1). One of the most common problems of shaving is razor burn in the beard area, which can develop into **pseudofolliculitis barbae (PFB)** (SOO-doh-fuh-lik-yoo-LY-tus BAR-bay) (Figure 6–2). This occurs when the shaved-off portion of the hair is sharp. When the hair is also curly, it may turn back into the skin, becoming ingrown and causing an infection. This condition is common in men of African heritage. PFB should not be confused with **folliculitis** (fah-lik-yuh-LY-tis). Unlike PFB, folliculitis can occur with all hair and skin types. It is a condition in which the hair follicles become infected and, often, pus filled due to a bacterial or fungal infection. When chronic, folliculitis can usually be improved by permanently eliminating the hairs from their follicles. To help prevent PFB, it helps to have a less clean shave. Using an electric razor, leave a small amount of hair stubble protruding above the follicle opening. The minor drawback of this method is that the skin feels less smooth, but stubble would soon appear anyway.

Razor induced irritation can also be improved by:

- shaving every other day
- keeping the skin loose (not taut) while shaving
- not shaving over the same area multiple times
- using mild, fragrance-free, antibacterial cleansers
- adding 1 to 2 drops of 100 percent tea tree oil to shaving foam

FIGURE 6–1
Shaving diagram

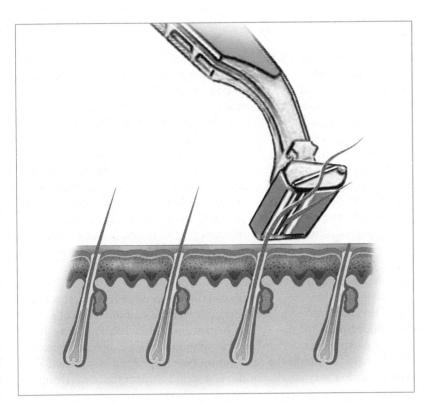

using a fragrance-free aftershave product or a topical solution, such as witch hazel, **alpha hydroxy acid (AHA)** (AL-fah hy-DRAHK-see AS-ud) products, or **salicylic** (sal-uh-SIL-ik) **acid.**

Extreme cases of PFB require treatment with steroids or **retinoic** (RET-in-oh-ik) **acid** (**tretinoin**). Left untreated, unsightly **keloid** (KEE-loyd) **scars** can form on the skin that are far more difficult to improve.

Shaving not only removes unwanted **terminal hair,** it indiscriminately removes finer **vellus** (VEL-us). Shaving stimulates the skin and stimulates hair growth in areas with **androgens** (AN-druh-jenz), like the beard and upper-lip areas. With shaving, even fine vellus with its shallow follicle can develop a deeper follicle and, over time, become terminal hair, thereby aggravating an already undesirable condition.

alpha hydroxy acid (AHA)
acid that occurs from natural products; known for its exfoliating properties on the epidermis (e.g., malic acid from apples, lactic acid from yogurt, glycolic acid from sugarcane)

salicylic acid
acid with antiseptic and anti-inflammatory properties that is extracted from leaves of wintergreen and yarrow and the bark of sweet birch; used to dissolve dead cells on the surface of the skin

retinoic acid
vitamin A derivative that can be added to face creams as a treatment for acne and the visible signs of aging; also called tretinoin

tretinoin
see "retinoic acid"

keloid scars
raised areas of fibrous tissue

terminal hair
hair found on the scalp, arms, legs, axillae, and pubic area (post-puberty)

vellus
fine, generally nonpigmented hair found on the face; often called "peach fuzz"

androgens
male sex hormones responsible for development of secondary sexual characteristics

PROS & CONS

Pros of Shaving

- fast
- inexpensive
- painless
- convenient

Cons of Shaving

- hair grows back coarsely and more stubbly in 1 to 4 days
- when shaving bothersome terminal hair, fine vellus may also be removed, causing a potentially bigger problem
- may cause PFB and ingrown hairs
- may cut the skin, particularly with a dull razor

With shaving, bumps occur as the blunt edges of hair try to push through small follicle openings, where usually fine tips of hair would grow through. Skin rashes may result, often when pieces of a shaved hair fall back into a follicle.

People with diabetes or on blood thinners should not shave, except with electric razors.

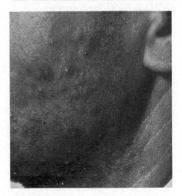

FIGURE 6–2 Folliculitis

Tweezing

Tweezing, usually done with tweezers, is a fast and effective way to remove a small number of hairs (Figure 6–3). The effects of tweezing last longer than the effects of shaving, because the hair is pulled out in its entirety as opposed to simply being cut at the surface of the skin. However, the hair may grow back thicker, more pigmented, and faster the more it is tweezed. Tweezing hair also causes hair follicles to become distorted. These distortions make it difficult for an electrologist to remove hair permanently later.

Tweezing more than a few hairs can be time consuming. When removing undesired hair, it is easy to accidentally remove fine vellus and in so doing stimulate the vellus follicle to create a more obvious, stronger pigmented hair and thereby create a bigger problem.

It is worth noting that the way in which one tweezes a hair affects how the hair may grow back. This is particularly true of eyebrows. When an eyebrow hair is tweezed downward regularly, it begins to grow downward, in the direction in which it was perpetually tweezed. To retrain the growth of eyebrow hair, carefully take the hair in tweezers and gently tweeze the hair in the direction of desired growth. When done regularly, that hair may eventually grow in the desired direction.

Tweezing may be uncomfortable, even painful, usually when done incorrectly. There are many ways in which the discomfort can be reduced. Over-the-counter, topical numbing products containing **lidocaine** (LY-doh-kayn) or **benzocaine** (BEN-zoh-kayn) are effective but must be applied to the area a considerable amount of time before tweezing. Rubbing the area with ice helps to numb the area before tweezing. Another method is to rub the area to be tweezed with a very small amount of lotion to warm the area. Doing so

lidocaine
synthetic local anesthetic drug that may be given by injection or applied to a surface

benzocaine
white, crystalline ester used as a local anesthetic

PROS & CONS

Pros of Tweezing

- minimal cost, after the cost of a good pair of tweezers

Cons of Tweezing

- can be painful
- poor vision may make it difficult to see and clean away unwanted hairs
- eyeglasses for close-up work make it difficult to get to the eyebrows
- can be time consuming in areas of heavy growth
- may cause hair below the skin to break, in turn causing bumps to occur in those follicles as blunt edges try to push their way through small follicles

---

FIGURE 6–3 Tweezing to correct hair growth

opens the follicle and allows the hair to be removed more easily. However, the lotion should be removed from the hair before tweezing because it may cause the forceps to slide up the hair rather than grip it, and this can be painful. The hair should be grasped at the base of the hair where it enters the follicle, rather than at the tip.

Chemical Depilatories

Chemical depilatories come in many different mediums, including creams, lotions, gels, aerosol sprays, and roll-ons. A **depilatory** dissolves the hair just below the skin with the chemicals **calcium thioglycolate** (thy-oh-GLY-kuh-late), **sodium thioglycolate**, and **sodium hydroxide**, agents that have been used for decades in the cattle industry to dissolve the hair on cattle hides.

With chemical depilatories, the keratin in hair is broken down, causing it to weaken and break away (Figure 6–4). The depilatory with the broken hairs forms a jelly-like mass that can be scraped away, or the broken hairs are washed away with the depilatory product. This method washes away more dead skin cells from the surface of the skin than normal washing. New hair, if it was already forming deep in the follicle, may be visible soon after, but if more depilatory product is applied to the area within a month, a skin irritation can

depilatory
substance that removes hair from the body, excluding the hair root

calcium thioglycolate
chemical substance capable of causing the keratin of the hair to degrade

sodium thioglycolate
chemical used to dissolve hair

sodium hydroxide
strong alkaline substance

PROS & CONS

Pros of Depilatories

- relatively inexpensive, though not as cheap as shaving
- can be used in the privacy and comfort of home
- when hair grows back, it is softer than that after shaving

Cons of Depilatories

- results are not as long lasting as waxing
- can have a nasty odor, if not initially, when processing
- can cause skin reactions like contact dermatitis as the skin's natural protective barrier is compromised when the depilatories are washed away
- should not be used on skin that is irritated, broken, or has any signs of pustules or infection

---

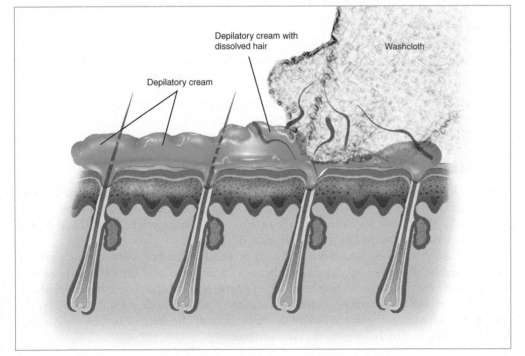

Depilatory cream with dissolved hair

Washcloth

Depilatory cream

FIGURE 6–4
Depilatory cream diagram

occur. This is chemically induced dermatitis. Irritation results because the skin has no chance to replace the normal amount of dead skin cells at its surface, which form skin's protective barrier. This replacement occurs approximately every 28 days.

Chemical depilatories come in differing strengths: a stronger one for the body, arms, underarms, legs, and bikini area and a gentler one for the face. Areas in which dipilatories should be avoided are the eyebrows, nose and ears, skin close to mucous membranes, the vaginal and perineum areas, and any areas in which the skin is broken or irritated. A patch test should be done in an inconspicuous area at least 24 hours before **depilation** to test for an allergic reaction. All the manufacturer's guidelines and instructions should be followed in detail.

depilation
removal of surface hair from the body, excluding the hair root

Bleaching

Although bleaching is not considered a method of hair removal, it is used to reduce the appearance of unwanted hair and therefore merits discussion here. The pigment that gives hair its color is removed by the bleaching agents. **Hydrogen peroxide** (HY-druh-jun puh-RAHK-syd) and the activator **ammonium bicarbonate** (uh-MOH-nee-um by-KAR-buh-nayt) work together as agents to soften, **oxidize** (AHK-sih-dyz), and bleach the hair.

The most popular place for bleaching is the upper lip. Bleaching is also effective on the sides of the face, under the jaw, and on the forearms. It should not be done near the eyes or vaginal area, on cut or irritated skin, or on areas that are sunburned.

If discomfort occurs while the product is still on the area, the product should be removed immediately and the area washed with plenty of cold water. If the bleach gets into the eyes, it should be immediately flushed out with lots of cold water and the assistance of a medical professional should be sought.

Advise clients to do patch tests on small areas (e.g., behind the ear or on an arm at the fold of the elbow) at least 24 hours before using bleach on areas of any significant size. All the manufacturer's guidelines and instructions should be followed in detail.

hydrogen peroxide
unstable liquid compound used especially as an oxidizing and bleaching agent or as an antiseptic

ammonium bicarbonate
white, crystalline solid used in baking powder

oxidize
to react or cause a chemical to react with oxygen

PROS & CONS

Pros of Bleaching

- relatively inexpensive and convenient
- lasts as long as the bleached hair remains in its follicle, which could be up to 16 weeks

Cons of Bleaching

- has a strong, unpleasant odor
- can have a negative effect on the skin, causing irritation, particularly if the product has been left on too long—something people often do for coarse hair
- the pigment of the skin can be altered
- should not be done on skin that is irritated, broken, or has any signs of pustules or infection

---

Abrasives

Abrasives for hair removal come in many different forms but all work in the same fashion. They range from pumice stones and abrasive gloves to small sticks or wands with a sandpaper finish. They work by buffing fine hair from the surface of the skin. They do not remove the hair from below the level of the skin or the root.

The smallest abrasive tool is usually used in small areas. For instance, the abrasive wand is used on the upper lip, while the abrasive mittens are used on the legs. However, these tools are only effective on fine hair, not on coarse hair that has been shaved regularly.

In this method, the skin is held taut with one hand while the other hand glides over the skin in a clockwise and counterclockwise fashion until the hair is buffed away. Care should be taken to stop before the skin is damaged.

PROS & CONS

Pros of Abrasives
- relatively inexpensive
- conveniently used anywhere

Cons of Abrasives
- regrowth is fairly rapid, like shaving
- due to the distortion of the follicle from the varied directions of the abrasive movements, regrowth may be irregular and appear wispy where it once lay flat on the skin
- can be very irritating to the skin
- should not be used by people receiving **microdermabrasion** (my-crow-dur-muh-BRAY-zhun) treatments or who are using Retin A or strong alpha hydroxy acid (AHA) products.
- should not be used on skin with any disorder or disease or on any area with signs of irritation or infection
- should not be used on areas that are sunburned or peeling from the sun

microdermabrasion
dramatic mechanical exfoliation of dead skin cells from the epidermis using tiny crystals

Mechanical Epilation

Mechanical epilation devices use rotating springlike coils to yank hair out (Figure 6–5). **Epilation** (ep-uh-LAY-shun) is like tweezing multiple hairs at once. This device is most commonly used on the legs. It is initially quite painful and may take some time to get used to. Still, clients report that, over time, they get used to the discomfort.

epilation
removal of hair, including the hair root, from the follicle

PROS & CONS

Pros of Mechanical Epilation
- some clients report that their hair regrowth was slower than from shaving and that regrowth was finer and softer
- cost is minimal after the purchase of the device

Cons of Mechanical Epilation
- hair must be at least ¼ inch long
- method is painful and causes unruly hair growth, distorted follicles, and ingrown hairs

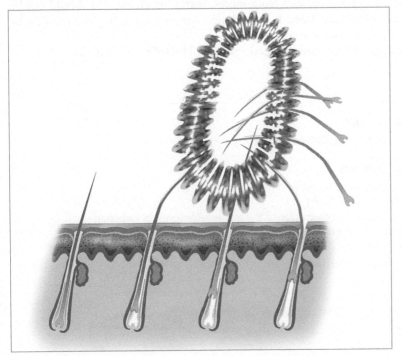

FIGURE 6–5
Electric epilator coils pulling hair

In this method, the rotating coils randomly grip and pull hair out regardless of the hair's direction of growth. This process distorts the hair follicle, causing the hairs to grow back in an unruly fashion. Hairs may also become ingrown.

To use a mechanical epilation device, the hair must be at least ¼ inch long. The skin should be dry, but not so dry that it is flaky. There is less discomfort to the process when the skin is warmed first from a hot bath, which opens the follicles. Using a **loofah** (LOO-fah) in the bath to lift the hairs and exfoliate the skin also helps to achieve better results.

As with any electrical device, the manufacturer's directions and precautions for safety and usage should be followed.

Electronic Tweezing

Electronic tweezers are frequently marketed as a home electrolysis device for the permanent removal of unwanted hair. However, the **Food and Drug Administration (FDA)** does not consider this device a method for permanent hair removal. Manufacturers will often market these devices with "guarantees," but it is important to note that these guarantees are really the warranties—the assurances that the equipment is without defects and will work for a certain period. Such a guarantee has nothing to do with the tool's effectiveness as a device providing permanent hair removal. The FDA and the **Federal Trade Commission (FTC)** have both stated that salons, manufacturers, and distributors may not advertise electronic tweezing as a means of permanent hair removal. Regardless, unscrupulous salons still advertise this method as pain-free electrolysis.

In the electronic-tweezing method, the person grabs the hair to be removed with the electronic tweezers. The electronic tweezers use a high-frequency current that is supposed to radiate for 15 to 30 seconds down the hair shaft, to the dermal papilla, to destroy the hair's root. The problem with this method is that hair is an **insulator**, not a **conductor**. Therefore, the current is easily diverted from its path. Furthermore, the kind of current that would be necessary to destroy the dermal papilla would cause the hair to "singe" and shrivel before getting to the root. In short, this method is basically glorified plucking.

Because electronic tweezers emit measurable levels of **radiation**, they are not recommended for use by women who are pregnant. People who use pacemakers should also not use this device, as it can interfere with the pacemaker, causing **cardiac arrhythmias** (KAHRD-ee-ak uh-RITH-mee-uz). This device should also not be used close to the eyes or to remove ingrown eyelashes, because the levels of radiation can be harmful. This device should also not be used to remove hairs from moles, warts, or areola and should not be employed to remove nasal or ear hairs. It should also not be used in any area with sunburn, an irritation, or a skin disease or disorder.

All manufacturer's guidelines and instructions should be followed in detail.

---

loofah
sponge made from the dried, fibrous interior of an oblong fruit of a tropical gourd; also spelled "loofa" or "lufa"

Food and Drug Administration (FDA)
an agency of the U.S. Department of Health and Human Services which administers federal laws designed to ensure the purity of food, the safety of cosmetics, and the safety and effectiveness of drugs and therapeutic devices

Federal Trade Commission (FTC)
an independent U.S. government agency that works to (1) maintain free and fair competition in the economy and (2) protect consumers from unfair or misleading practices

insulator
material or device that prevents or reduces the passage of heat, electricity, or sound

conductor
substance or medium that allows heat, electricity, or light to pass along or through it

radiation
energy emitted from a source in the form of rays or waves (e.g., heat, light, sound)

cardiac arrhythmias
irregular heartbeats

PROS & CONS

Pros of Electronic Tweezing
- device often carries a 1-year, limited warranty

Cons of Electronic Tweezing
- method is tantamount to tweezing with more costly tweezers
- as does tweezing, distorts follicles
- not advisable for pregnant women due to the measurable levels of radiation
- radiation can adversely affect a person with a pacemaker
- radiation can damage the eyes

Home Electrolysis Units

Home electrolysis devices (Figure 6–6) simply should not be on the market. It takes a considerable degree of skill and experience to know the depth of a hair follicle, the angle at which the hair is growing, and hair's different phases of growth. Even the most skilled electrologists have a hard time working on themselves, because it is difficult to see the angle of the hair without some magnification. It is also difficult to manipulate the hand holding the needle into certain positions on one's own face and body. Failure to achieve an accurate insertion of the needle will not only be ineffective in the destruction of the hair, but could cause significant damage to the skin. Home electrolysis devices should not be used by people with poor vision or unsteady hands, nor should they be used by people who are pregnant or have pacemakers, diabetes, **hepatitis**, blood disorders, **lupus** (LOO-pus), **scleroderma** (sklayr-uh-DUR-muh), or any **chronic skin disease** or **acute skin disease**. Individuals under 18 should not use this device without adult supervision.

In this method, the fingers are moistened with a saline solution (salt and water), which conducts the device's current. The operator then holds a **touchband** and the needle called a **stylet** (STY-let) and inserts the stylet into the hair follicle. The dial on the main device can be adjusted, increasing the strength of current until a tingling sensation is felt. When that sensation is felt, it is presumed that the stylet is at the root of the hair. The position should be held for 15 seconds, at which point root destruction should have taken place. The hair should then "slide" out without resistance using a regular pair of tweezers.

All manufacturers guideline's and instructions should be followed in detail.

hepatitis
inflammation of the liver, causing fever, jaundice, abdominal pain, and weakness

lupus
inflammatory disease affecting connective tissue, joints, and internal organs

scleroderma
disease in which the skin becomes progressively hard and thick

chronic skin disease
illness or condition that lasts over a long period

acute skin disease
disease that is extreme in nature and of short duration

touchband
part of a home-electrolysis device used with a stylet to complete a circuit

stylet
a long, thin, pointed instrument

PROS & CONS

Pros of Home Electrolysis
- device often carries a 1-year, limited warranty

Cons of Home Electrolysis
- it is difficult for a person to achieve an accurate insertion for successful root destruction
- inaccurate application of the current could cause damage, even scarring, of the skin
- many disorders, diseases, and conditions contraindicate this method
- this method is slow and laborious to do on oneself if for more than just a few hairs

---

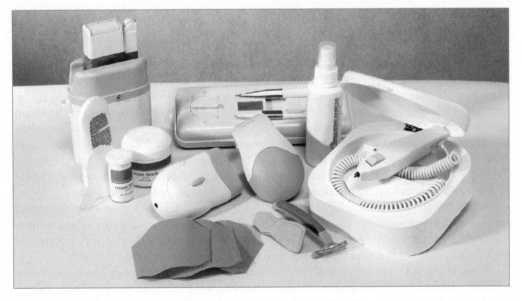

FIGURE 6–6
Home hair-removal supplies

Hair-Reduction Creams

Hair-reduction creams are *not* hair removers. They are designed to extend the time between hair-removal treatments, whether via depilatory creams, waxing, or electrolysis. Most effective hair-reduction creams are available by prescription only. The most common of these is the inhibitor **eflornithine** (ef-LOHR-nuh-theen). This product has been approved by the FDA to slow the rate of hair growth by inhibiting the **enzyme** called **ornithine decarboxylase** (OR-nuh-thyn dee-kar-BOKS-uh-layz), found in human skin. Eflornithine blocks **metabolic activity** in the hair follicle, thereby slowing the hair growth cycle. Eflornithine is applied to the area twice a day. This product should only be used on the face and under the jaw, because these are the areas for which the enzyme was tested and approved. After application, the area should not be washed for at least 4 hours.

It is worth noting that if a person is receiving electrolysis treatments, then the goal is to permanently eliminate unwanted hair, not to drag out the process. To use these creams only delays the permanency of electrolysis. However, if the client cannot get in for follow-up treatments for a number of weeks due to travel, surgery, or whatever reason, this product would be useful. However, the cream must be used for 4 to 8 weeks before results are noticeable. Upon terminating the use of this product, the hair will return to its previous growth cycle in about 8 weeks.

It has not yet been determined if this product is suitable for children or pregnant women.

eflornithine
chemical substance in the commercial cream Vaniqa™; blocks or inhibits hair growth

enzyme
complex protein produced by living cells which promotes a specific biochemical reaction by acting as a catalyst

ornithine decarboxylase
enzyme in human skin that stimulates hair growth

metabolic activity
chemical interactions taking place in living organisms, which provide the energy and nutrients needed to sustain life

---

PROS & CONS

Pros of Hair-Reduction Creams

- easy to use
- effectively extend the duration between visits to the hair-removal specialist, thereby saving money and time
- no other drug interactions have been noted

Cons of Hair-Reduction Creams

- may cause temporary redness, stinging, burning, a rash, or folliculitis
- a prescription is required to obtain these products
- costly without a prescription plan

Home Wax Kits

Never before has there been such a choice of home wax kits available to the consumer. Even professional waxing suppliers are starting to market their wares to the general public. These kits are marketed through infomercials and on the Internet and are popping up on the shelves of every drugstore. These kits range from cold wax to microwaveable wax and stove-top wax. The wax can be applied in different ways—either with a spatula or rolled on directly from the container—and is usually removed from the skin with strips. One would think that these products cut into the business of the hair-removal specialist, but the reality is that the main purpose these kits serve is to illustrate that training and skill are indispensable for a relatively pain-free, problem-free, effective, and long-lasting treatment.

While trained technicians have the skill and speed to safely and accurately apply and remove wax, some areas are just too difficult for technicians to reach, or too uncomfortable for the technicians to wax themselves (e.g., the bikini area). It is also very risky to do one's own eyebrows; hot wax may drop onto the eyelashes or even into the eyes.

Most home wax kits come with instructions, and some of the more costly kits come with informational and educational videos. However, this limited information is no substitute for the hands-on training and experience of a trained professional. By inaccurately applying or removing the wax, the hairs can snap and leave the roots. The broken hair could, in turn, cause folliculitis. There is the potential for individuals to burn or injure themselves, causing bruising, or removing skin with hair if instructions are not followed and the procedure is not administered correctly. Bruising can be around about as long as the area is hair-free. Therefore, the result, for all the trouble, could be no better than shaving.

People who try to wax themselves sometimes end up having to remove the wax in a hot bath or with plenty of lotion, because the anticipation of pain makes it hard to pull the strips off. These people then book appointments at salons to have the jobs finished professionally.

Waxing can be messy in the most ideal professional setting. When done in the home, one must carefully choose the location and take the right precautions at the risk of damaging floors and surfaces. Some hair-removal products are water soluble, which makes cleanup easier, but those that contain resins require stronger solvents to clean from surfaces.

PROS & CONS

Pros of Home Wax Kits

- less expensive than a salon visit
- can be completely private
- can be done when most convenient to the client

Cons of Home Wax Kits

- can be painful
- wax in the wrong direction does not remove hair
- incorrect waxing and removal can break hairs and cause bruising
- wax at the incorrect temperature can cause burning or lift skin or stick to the skin and be difficult to remove
- many areas are difficult to reach
- waxing one's own eyebrows can be dangerous
- can be very messy with a lot of unwelcome cleanup

 ## Conclusion

With the knowledge and understanding of what is available for use in the home to remove unwanted hair, and the effects of those methods on the hair and skin, the hair-removal specialist will be armed with the information to be better able to educate clients and to sell the professional services that best suit individuals.

 ## Discussion and Review Questions

1. What is pseudofolliculitis barbae (PFB)?
2. How do depilatory creams work?
3. Are electronic tweezers effective for permanent hair removal? Why?
4. What is the main active ingredient in hair-reduction creams?
5. List four reasons home waxing kits are not recommended.

 ## Additional Readings

Milady's Standard Comprehensive Training for Estheticians. 2003. Clifton Park, NY: Milady, an imprint of Delmar Learning.

Milady's Standard Cosmetology. 2004. Clifton Park, NY: Milady, an imprint of Delmar Learning.

CHAPTER 7
Threading

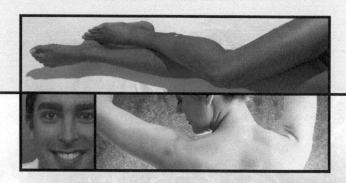

Chapter Outline

Learning Objectives ■ Key Terms ■ Introduction
History and Evolution of Threading ■ Threading Preparation ■ Threading Technique
Conclusion ■ Discussion and Review Questions

Learning Objectives

By the end of this chapter, you should be able to:

1. Recount a brief history of threading.
2. Describe how threading works.
3. Explain the benefits of providing threading as a service.
4. Demonstrate how to prepare the client and administer threading.

Key Terms

Fatlah
Khite
threading

Introduction

Threading, also known as "banding," is a method of hair removal using a looped and twisted cotton thread that is maneuvered by the technician's fingers. The most common area for threading is the face. This is a method, although not common, that is worthy of acknowledgement in this book, because it is a fast, inexpensive method of mass tweezing that does not traumatize the skin. It is a method of hair removal that is worth considering for individuals who have skin-care treatments and products prohibiting waxing. This chapter briefly introduces threading, but this technique is difficult to self-teach and should be learned from an experienced threader.

threading
method of hair removal using strands of thread

History and Evolution of Threading

Threading is a technique of hair removal that has been used for centuries in Middle Eastern countries: Iran, Turkey, India, and Pakistan. In Arabic, threading is known as **Khite** (KYT); in Egyptian, it is called **Fatlah** (FAT-luh). Threading is an inexpensive method of hair removal that has been passed on from mother to daughter over the years. It is a growing practice of hair removal in the United States most commonly found in, but not unique to, predominantly Asian Indian and Arabic neighborhoods. For many, finding an experienced and skilled "threader" is like finding gold.

Khite
Arabic word for threading

Fatlah
Egyptian word for threading

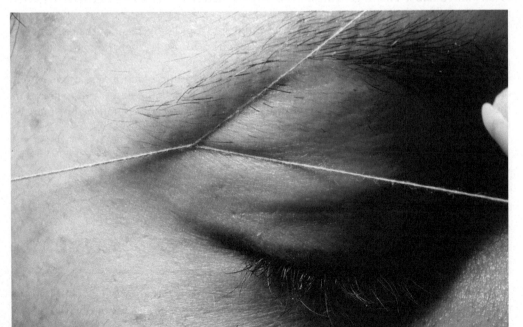

FIGURE 7–1
Example of threading method

Threading Preparation

The practitioner must use a new, clean, and sterile thread for each client. The thread loops can be preformed and sterilized in an ultraviolet sterilizer, then placed in a covered box. The client should be placed in a treatment chair that is lined with a fresh sheet, towel, or paper.

The practitioner should protect the client's hair by wrapping it to avoid snagging any of the hairs on the client's head. The practitioner's hands should then be thoroughly washed.

The area of the client's skin that is to be treated should be cleansed of makeup, wiped with a mild liquid antiseptic, and allowed to dry. Avoid creams that will remain on the hair, because they reduce the effectiveness of the threading.

Threading Technique

The most popular areas for threading are the eyebrows, the area above the eyebrow up to the hairline, the sideburns, the sides of face, the upper lip, the chin, and under the jaw.

The thread should be a strong, cotton, household thread, clean and sterilized. The threads should range in length from 24″ cut to 30″ cut. The shorter threads are easier to control when learning and developing the skill, and they are also better for practitioners with small hands. As the practitioner becomes more skilled, a larger loop of thread is more manageable.

The two ends of the thread are knotted together, forming a loop. The forefingers, middle fingers, and thumbs are placed through each end of the loop in a cat's-cradle fashion. The loop should be twisted at one end multiple times (approximately a dozen times). The twists are then coaxed into the center of the loop, making sure that the knot is at one end, near the fingers, so that it does not interfere with the twisting. Threading is done by placing the upper end of the twist just under the unwanted hairs so that the hairs hang over the twist, then quickly manipulating the twist upward by spreading the lower fingers. This motion entraps or snags the unwanted hair, plucking it out. This motion is followed by quickly spreading the upper fingers, thereby moving the twist toward the lower fingers, dropping some of the plucked hairs. The practitioner then moves quickly to another area of unwanted hairs. The fingers must move rapidly across the area at a rate of one movement approximately every quarter of a second.

As the twist gets congested with hair, it inhibits the rapid movement of the twisting, so a new part of the loop should be twisted or a new thread used. After the service is complete, a soothing lotion may be applied to the skin.

A second, more traditional technique that many threading practitioners use is to put one end of the thread in the mouth, hold the other end in one hand and the looped end in the other hand with the twists still in the middle. The threading is accomplished by maneuvering the head and the looped end of the thread.

Time Allocated for Threading	
Area	**Time in Minutes**
Eyebrows	up to 15
Upper lip	10
Chin	10
Sides of face	20

The cost of thread should be approximately one-third less than waxing. The effect of threading closely resembles the effect of tweezing and, as a result, lasts 2 to 6 weeks.

Threading Indications

■ The most popular areas for threading are the face, including the eyebrows; between the eyebrow and hairline; the upper lip; and the hair along the jaw, under the chin, and on the sides of the face.

Threading Contraindications:

■ broken, irritated skin
■ active eczema and psoriasis
■ active herpes lesion
■ sunburned skin

PROS & CONS

Pros of Threading

■ good alternative for those unable to tolerate waxing on the face due to prescription and other product use (e.g., Retin A, Differin, AHAs) or facial treatments that cause negative reactions when waxed
■ inexpensive, requiring only the use of strong household cotton thread, an antiseptic pretreatment, and soothing after-care
■ minimal product cost service and, when administered by an experienced practitioner, achieved quickly (faster than tweezing) for a high profit
■ discomfort level is usually less than electrolysis and waxing, similar to tweezing, but because it is faster than tweezing, the plucking sensation is more tolerable

Cons of Threading

■ ineffective for large parts of the body
■ can be uncomfortable because the hairs are snagged out of the skin faster than tweezing but more slowly than waxing
■ when not done with care and accuracy, the practitioner may unwittingly remove vellus that was not problematic and in doing so encourage the vellus to grow back irregularly or become terminal hair, thereby aggravating the hair-growth situation
■ because some follicles will become distorted due to the pulling, the regrowth hair may stand in a wispy fashion where it once lay flat on the skin
■ as the hair grows back, folliculitis, pustules, and inflammation that can cause pigmentation problems may increase

 ## Conclusion

When threading is performed by an experienced practitioner, the results are very positive. Threading practitioners who know what they are doing can shape eyebrows beautifully. Threading is a skill that, once learned, takes practice to master but is well worth the effort. Threading is a viable option for clients who cannot tolerate waxing.

 ## Discussion and Review Questions

1. Name two pros of threading.
2. Name two contraindications of threading.
3. Why is threading viable for people who cannot tolerate waxing?

CHAPTER 8

Sugaring

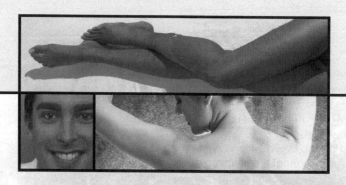

Chapter Outline

Learning Objectives ■ Key Terms ■ Introduction
History and Evolution of Sugaring ■ Sugaring Applications ■ Posttreatment Care
Conclusion ■ Discussion and Review Questions

Learning Objectives

By the end of this chapter, you should be able to:

1. Describe how sugaring is formulated.
2. Explain how sugaring is applied and removed.
3. Understand how sugaring can be effective as a service in the hair-removal industry.
4. Outline how sugaring has evolved to meet U.S. demands for speed, efficiency, and economics.

Key Terms

epilepsy
hemophilia
phlebitis
psoriasis
thrombosis

Introduction

Sugaring is an ancient method of hair removal that has continued to be practiced mainly in the Middle East, North Africa, the Mediterranean region, and Greece. It is fast becoming popular in the United States. Customers like the idea of an ancient, well-used technique and the idea of the sugar paste being 100 percent natural. Sugaring closely resembles waxing in that it grabs multiple hairs and removes them at the bulb. As ancient as the original sugaring method is, it has evolved in the Western world. This chapter addresses the different aspects of sugaring as they have evolved.

History and Evolution of Sugaring

Sugaring is a centuries-old method of hair removal used in the Middle East, North Africa, and the Mediterranean. Sugaring is believed to have been discovered as a form of hair removal in ancient times, possibly by chance, when the sugar paste was formed and used to treat a wound or to dress a burn to help prevent infections from developing and to aid in healing. The removal of the paste would also remove the hair while leaving the skin with very little irritation. Ancient Egyptians believed body hair to be unacceptable and unclean and used various tools, like tweezers and shaving, to remove hair. Sugaring was a faster, less painful, and more effective method that would also have exfoliated the skin, leaving it smoother, more supple, and without stubble. Hair regrowth would have been softer and finer, so it is understandable that sugaring became a lasting and preferred method of hair removal around the region.

While sugaring techniques have remained basically unchanged in many of those regions, when the technique arrived on U.S. soil it started to evolve dramatically. Now there are two very different types of sugaring, just as there is with waxing: (1) the strip-removal method and (2) the nonstrip method. It is important to recognize differences between the two because they have different effects on the skin and hair.

Manufacturers who have jumped on the sugaring bandwagon, due to its low production costs, have begun to distinguish themselves by "improving" the product with additional additives and by promoting the faster method of using strips to remove the sugar paste and wax. The face of sugaring has now changed. What was once a somewhat slow method of sugaring that caused little distortion to the hair follicle by the way it was applied and removed is now applied in the same way as the strip method of waxing, that is, with a spatula then covered with a strip and removed by pulling the strip in the opposite direction of growth. What was once, and still is, marketed as a gentler method of hair removal, causing little irritation to the skin, is now sold in various jars and cans with an array of soothing lotions and gels that are required for after-care. The original method required only a warm, moist cotton or cloth for after-care, but that greatly affects the manufacturer's bottom line. People using Retin A or AHAs may require more soothing agents because those people are more prone to irritation.

The sugaring product is formed by mixing sugar, water, lemon juice, and gum arabic or gum ovaline and heating it until the mixture forms a syrup (Figure 8–1). For sugaring using the hand-application method, the sugar paste mixture should not be too runny. One should

FIGURE 8–1
Key sugaring ingredients

be able to manipulate the mixture into a ball. For sugaring using a spatula and strip, the mixture can be a little thinner, but still not too runny. Most of the sugar paste made and used in the Middle East is 100 percent natural, but companies are now manufacturing what they call "sugaring paste" by adding resins to their products. These products cause confusion, because they are not true sugaring. When 100 percent natural, sugaring is considered hypoallergenic and it is not as irritating to the skin as hot strip wax. Sugar paste is not as hot and does not adhere to the skin like strip wax does. Some sugar paste brands may have gums and resins with fragrances added, which make the paste more irritating to the skin.

It is important to read the product labels and check the ingredients.

> **Simple Recipe for Sugar Paste**
> **Ingredients**
>
> 2 cups sugar
> ¼ cup lemon juice
> ¼ cup of water
>
> All ingredients should be combined and cooked slowly over low heat. The mixture should not be heated above 250°F. A candy thermometer should be used to read the temperature accurately. The mixture should be allowed to cool in a glass jar. It should be used at body temperature when applied by hand or with a spatula.

Sugaring Applications

There are two clearly different sugaring methods: (1) application and removal by hand or nonstrip method and (2) application by spatula and removal by cotton strip.

Application Preparation

Before the treatment begins, the technician should wash hands and apply latex or vinyl gloves. Some technicians doing the nonstrip method apply only one glove to the hand doing the stretching, not to the hand handling the sugar paste, because the gloves make the paste tougher to handle. The gloved hand applies gentle pressure to the skin after each "flick." This may affect the choice of some people to do sugaring as a service.

When hair removal is to take place on the face and the client has not had the service or waxing done in this area before, it is worth doing a patch test first. This tests the client's reaction to the service and whether the client should have the treatment within a day or two of an important engagement. Any reaction, particularly a histamine reaction, will appear almost immediately, and if microorganisms have been introduced to the vulnerable area, pustules may appear up to 48 hours after the treatment. The patch test should be done on the face but in an area less noticeable (e.g., toward the front of the ear).

The sugar paste completely coats the hair shaft and even seeps into the top portion of the hair follicle. It firmly grips the hair from all angles and can be removed quickly in the direction of hair growth, thereby avoiding distortions of the hair follicles and breakage.

Hand Application and Removal

First, the area to be treated should be cleansed with an antibacterial cleanser and freed of dirt, makeup, and lotions in a manner similar to the preparation for waxing.

The skin should feel warm for a more effective and comfortable treatment. If the skin is cool and goose bumps are present, causing the hair to stand upright, this may affect the treatment and cause some hairs to snap and increase discomfort.

Next, the area should be dusted lightly with a gentle powder that is free of chemicals, perfumes, and aluminum that could irritate the skin posttreatment. The powder will absorb any residual moisture, making the treatment more effective.

The sugar paste is then manipulated into a ball. It should be pliable and easy to manage. The paste is pressed and manipulated against the hair growth and back over the top, followed by a quick, flicking motion that is parallel to the skin, pulling the sugar paste off in the direction of hair growth (Figure 8–2). If any hair remains behind, the sugar paste can be reapplied to the area, as it is applied at body temperature.

When that area is cleared, the same ball of sugar can be used to remove hair on the adjacent area, and so on until the service is complete (Figure 8–3). The sugar ball can be used on the same client throughout the service until it becomes so congested with hair that it is rendered ineffective. Then, a new ball of sugar paste should be used. The sugar paste can be used on the face and later the body but not vice versa at the risk of cross-contamination and the potential risk of an outbreak of pustules on the more sensitive skin of the face. For obvious hygiene reasons, the sugar paste should be disposed of after the service and not reused on another client.

Spatula Application and Strip Removal

Application by spatula is done in the same fashion as hot wax: apply in the direction of hair growth, apply the muslin or pellon strip over the top, rub in the direction of growth and quickly pull away against the growth and close to the skin (Figures 8–4 and 8–5). For

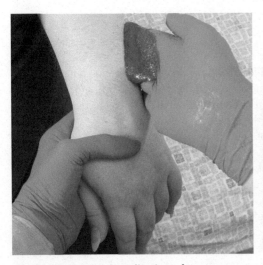

FIGURE 8–2 Hand application of sugar paste

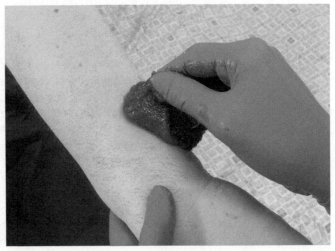

FIGURE 8–3 Manual removal of sugar paste

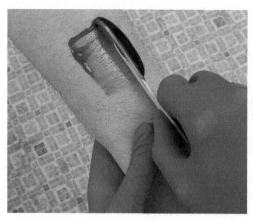

FIGURE 8–4 Spatula application of sugar paste

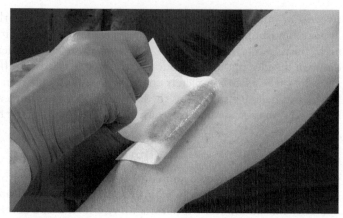

FIGURE 8–5 Removal of sugar paste using a muslin strip

a more detailed description of this technique, see Chapter 11. Some cans of sugaring require the temperature to be hotter than that of the ancient hand-applied method, more like hot wax.

phlebitis
inflammation of the wall of a vein

hemophilia
recessive genetic disorder occurring almost exclusively in males in which the blood clots much more slowly than normal, resulting in extensive bleeding from even minor injuries

thrombosis
formation of presence of one or more blood clots that may partially or completely block an artery or a vein

epilepsy
medical disorder involving episodes of abnormal electrical discharge in the brain; characterized by seizures, convulsions, and loss of consciousness

Indications of Hand-Application Method

- any area may be treated (excluding nostrils, inner ears, genitals, and men's beards) with virgin hair growth of ¹/₁₆ inch
- any area of previously shaved hair or coarser hair of ⅛ inch may be treated

Contraindications of Hand-Application Method

- chapped or broken skin
- sunburned skin; areas should not be sugared until the areas have healed completely
- pimples and pustules
- moles, skin tags, and warts should be avoided
- **phlebitis** (fluh-BYT-us)—physician approval necessary
- diabetes—physician approval necessary
- **hemophilia** (hee-moh-FEE-lee-uh)—physician approval necessary
- herpes, herpes simplex (cold sore)—should not be sugared during an active outbreak
- pregnancy—if the areas requiring sugaring take more than 20 minutes of the client laying flat on the back, the client should wait until after the birth of the baby

Contraindications of Spatula-Applied Method with High Temperature Wax

- sides of face (causing irregular regrowth)
- pimples or pustules
- phlebitis and **thrombosis** (thram-BOH-sis) and any circulatory disorder that is prone to bruising
- **epilepsy** (EP-ih-lep-see)—unless controlled for a long period with medication and depending on the medication, because some epilepsy drugs cause easy bruising; physician's approval must be attained before the sugaring service; the technician should receive a physician's note and have the client sign a release
- diabetes—the client should consult with the physician for the degree of severity and degree of healing
- fractures and sprains—the area should not be sugared until it is completely healed
- hemophilia—clients with this condition should not be sugared in this manner
- herpes, herpes simplex (cold sore)—should not be sugared during an active outbreak; prophylactic medication should be taken before service
- inflamed or irritated skin—should not be treated
- lack of skin sensation—clients should not be sugared this way

- moles, skin tags, and warts—should be avoided
- pregnancy—if the areas requiring sugaring take more than 20 minutes of the client laying flat on the back, the client should wait until after the birth of the baby
- scar tissue, including keloids—should not be sugared in this manner
- sunburn—sunburned areas should not be sugared until the areas have healed completely
- skin disorder (e.g., eczema, seborrhea, and **psoriasis** [suh-RY-uh-sis]) conditions may be treated depending on severity; minimal flakiness of dead skin cells can be sugared, but not if the skin is broken; in mild cases, the skin may benefit from the exfoliating effects of sugaring, but in more advanced stages, broken skin could result, so it is imperative that the technician receives a signed release from the client before the service
- varicose veins—one should not sugar over varicose veins but may treat the surrounding area
- Retin A, Accutane, and Differin—clients using any of these products should not be treated with the higher-temperature sugar paste

psoriasis
skin disease marked by red, scaly patches

PROS & CONS

Pros of Hand-Applied Method

- no risk of burning as it is applied at body temperature
- minimal risk of bruising as it does not adhere to live skin cells and pull at the skin during removal
- due to the application temperature and the fact that it does not adhere to the skin like waxes containing resins, it is considered by manufacturers of sugar paste to be safe to use over areas with varicose veins or spider veins; however, caution, common sense, and good judgment should be used with regard to these conditions
- because the sugar paste does not adhere to live skin cells it will only remove the hair and exfoliate the loose skin cells of the stratum corneum with minimal discomfort and trauma to the skin and can be used safely on dry psoriasis and dry-itch eczema
- because of the temperature and adhesion qualities, the same area can be gone over more than once without the risk of causing irritation and trauma
- because there is no risk of burning or tearing the skin, it is considered safe to use on diabetics; however, a physician's approval should be obtained and a medical release signed
- the hair need only be $1/16$ inch long for removal for virginal (previously untreated) hair
- because the hair is removed in the direction of growth, there is no distorting of the hair follicle or breakage of the hair at the follicle opening
- regrowth hair is lighter, softer, and less dense
- easy cleanup of the equipment, walls, floors, and treatment table, because the paste is water soluble
- easy cleanup for the client
- natural antiseptic properties, inhibiting bacterial growth
- hygienic, because the sugar paste is not reused on other clients
- inexpensive when homemade

Cons of Hand-Applied Method

- slower and more time consuming to perform, especially on large areas
- some minimal discomfort similar, but not as uncomfortable as waxing
- folliculitis and ingrown hairs, although these are considerably less common with this nonstrip method than with both the spatula-applied method and waxing

Pros of Spatula-Applied Method

- no risk of burning, because the paste is applied at a cooler temperature than hot wax
- faster service than the hand-applied method; larger area can be treated at once

continues

- because the sugar paste (if it is resin-free, 100 percent natural) does not adhere to live skin cells, it removes only the hair and exfoliates the loose skin cells of the stratum corneum with minimal discomfort and trauma to the skin and can be used safely on dry psoriasis and dry-itch eczema
- because of the temperature and adhesion qualities, the same area can be gone over more than once without the risk of causing irritation and trauma
- the hair need only be 1/16 inch long for removal for virginal (previously untreated) hair
- regrowth hair is lighter, softer, and less dense
- easy cleanup of the equipment, walls, floors, and treatment table because the sugar is water soluble (when resin-free)
- easy cleanup for the client
- natural antiseptic properties, inhibiting bacterial growth
- hygienic, because the sugar paste is not reused on other clients

Cons of Spatula-Applied Method

- risk of burning if the sugar paste is not tested for appropriate, safe-to-use temperature before application
- some discomfort, similar to waxing
- folliculitis and ingrown hairs
- cleanup may require the use of solvents if resins have been added to the sugar paste

Posttreatment Care

Any remaining sugar paste can be removed from the client's skin with a warm, moist washcloth on large areas or with moist cotton rounds on small areas. The client should not have to leave feeling sticky.

Clients who develop histamine bumps can take an antihistamine if they choose, but they must *not* be supplied by the technician.

Clients should be advised to refrain from using fragrances or deodorants on the treated areas and to avoid the sun or tanning booths for 48 hours after the service.

Clients can usually go 6 to 12 weeks between treatments, although this will vary between individuals and the various parts of the face and body. The more clients are sugared as a method of hair removal, without using any other method in between, the longer those clients will be able to go between services. Sugaring technicians regularly assert that the time between each treatment may increase the more clients use sugaring as their only method of hair removal.

Conclusion

Sugaring is an effective method for hair removal and probably the better choice over hot-strip wax for the face when using the hand-application and removal method, because it does not distort the follicles in this manner. The downside is that this method is much slower than the spatula-application method or waxing, making it more time consuming on large areas and not as cost effective. However, sugaring paste is cheaper to make or purchase and, providing it is 100 percent natural, there is less need for more costly cleaning agents and after-care lotions. Care should be taken to read labels and to choose the most suitable sugaring product.

Discussion and Review Questions

1. What are the three basic ingredients of sugar paste?
2. In which direction is strip sugar paste applied?
3. In which direction is nonstrip sugar paste removed?
4. Name two indications of sugaring.
5. Name two cons of sugaring.

SECTION III

Waxing

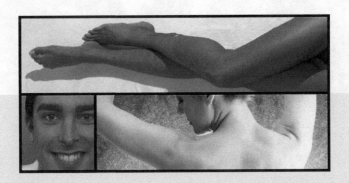

The waxing industry is an ever-growing, ever-evolving, multimillion-dollar industry. Waxing companies continually compete for a piece of the market with new products and new equipment. They promote new techniques, new methods of application, and new trends. Many waxing books and promotional materials adopt a one-product, one-technique approach for all situations and body parts. This book and chapter favor no one method or brand, instead arming the professional waxing technician with the knowledge to make appropriate choices.

The waxing industry is an industry of innovation and controversy: What should and should not be waxed? Is it okay to "double dip"? Therefore, an additional purpose of this section is to address these controversies, thereby enabling technicians to make appropriate choices according to their knowledge and experience and within the confines of their states' licensing regulations.

CHAPTER 9

Introduction to Waxing

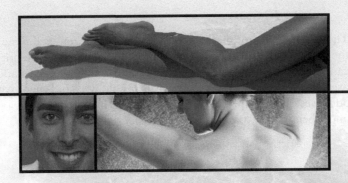

Chapter Outline

Learning Objectives ■ Key Terms ■ Introduction ■ Wax Types ■ The Waxing Consultation
Record Cards and Release Forms ■ Client Expectations ■ Treatment Area Setup
Client Preparation and Treatment ■ Hygiene and Sanitation
■ Conclusion ■ Endnote ■ Discussion and Review Questions ■ Additional Readings

Learning Objectives

By the end of this chapter, you should be able to:

1. List the pros and cons of waxing.
2. List the indications and contraindications of waxing.
3. Offer the most suitable and preferred waxing services to clients.
4. Refer a client to a more appropriate method of hair removal as indicated by the client's profile and hair-growth concern(s).
5. Set up a wax treatment area.
6. Offer appropriate pre- and posttreatment care.

Key Terms

accutane	differin	melting points	sugar wax
amorphous	diopters	muslin strips	synthethic
azuline	ether	pellon strips	tetracycline
benzene	gum rosin	Retin-A	virgin hair
carbon tetrachloride	hard wax	strip method	
crystalline	histamine		

hard wax
depilatory wax used without a strip

strip method
method of hair removal using a strip over the sugar or wax for removal

sugar wax
a hair-removal product that is made primarily of sugar

synthetic
made artificially by a chemical process of synthesis, often to resemble a natural product

benzene
a colorless volatile liquid obtained from petroleum

carbon tetrachloride
an organic solvent

ether
an organic solvent

crystalline
made of or containing crystals or crystal-like structures

amorphous
without a crystalline structure

melting points
temperature at which wax begins to liquefy

gum rosin
a substance produced by distilling resin from living trees; an additive to honey wax

Introduction

There are two major methods of waxing for hair removal. One is **hard wax**, also known as the nonstrip method. The other major wax method is the hot wax or **strip method**. This can include the honey-textured waxes and crème waxes. In addition to those waxes, there are various varieties in between, such as cold wax and **sugar wax**, and many with soothing additives. This chapter covers some of the many types of wax available for hair removal and when those waxes should be considered.

Wax Types

Pure waxes can be grouped according to the element from which they were derived: animal, mineral, vegetable, or **synthetic** (Figure 9–1). All waxes are insoluble in water and soluble in oils and other organic solvents, such as **benzene** (BEN-zeen), **carbon tetrachloride**, and **ether** (EE-thur), but not in alcohol.

The nature of these differing waxes is best defined by referring to their physical properties. Waxes are usually semi**crystalline** or **amorphous** solids that form semiglossy films. They vary in consistency, from fairly soft and malleable to hard and brittle, although when in waxes' molten states are all easily molded. The **melting points** of waxes are generally in the range of 105 to 212°F/40 to 100°C. In the cosmetic, esthetic, and hair-removal industries, waxes are often combined with other ingredients to achieve desired properties (e.g., melting point). Honey wax is the most common wax to which a **gum rosin** is added. This is common with the hot wax/strip method. However, the rosin causes the wax to adhere to the skin (Figure 9–2), causing sensitivity in some clients, particularly to the face and to the more delicate parts of the body, such as the bikini area and underarms. Because

FIGURE 9–1
Samples of hard wax

FIGURE 9–2
Diagram of wax removing hair

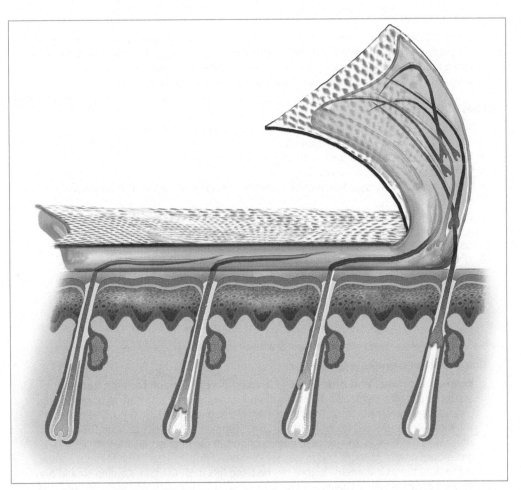

of adverse reactions to the honey wax, particularly in clients using AHAs or prescription skin treatments, wax companies are now manufacturing waxes with **azuline** (AZH-oo-leen), tea tree, and other essential oils to calm the skin and minimize negative reactions. Manufacturers have also reintroduced the hard, nonstrip depilatory waxes that were popular before honey wax, particularly in Europe. Made mainly from beeswax, hard wax became less popular as honey strip wax proved significantly faster, which allowed salons to book more clients and generate better earnings. Hard wax has made something of a comeback, however, because it has proven effective on clients whose specialized skin care could cause problems for strip wax. The unique properties of hard wax have also shown it to be the wax of preference for more delicate parts of the body where the skin may be thin and fragile and the hair coarse, as in the bikini area, or where the hair may grow in multiple directions in the same area, like the underarms.

azuline
a component of the oil extracted from chamomile which has anti-inflammatory properties

PROS & CONS

Pros of Waxing

- Waxing is a relatively fast and efficient way to temporarily remove unwanted hair.
- The technician, with training and practice, can become a "speed waxer," cutting the typical service time in half and increasing profits.
- A shorter waxing time means minimal discomfort to the client.
- Hair regrowth can take 6 to 8 weeks.
- Wax epilates hair, meaning it removes the hair from below the skin, often at the root, without destroying the root. When the hair grows back, it is often softer.
- Many clients experience some reduction in hair growth after multiple wax services. When the hair is removed at the root or papilla, the new papilla must reestablish itself

continues

in the follicle. Not only does this take time, but continual waxing removal may cause the papilla to become weaker, therefore causing extended periods between regrowth and a reduction in hair growth. This is especially apparent in the hair growth on frequently waxed women's legs as those women reach menopause.

Cons of Waxing

- The rosins in wax can adhere to the skin and are the primary cause of irritation.
- The overheating of wax risks irritation.
- When the wax is too cool and goes on too thick, the skin may lift.
- Until skilled with waxing, it can be messy.
- Clients must have a growth length of ½ inch for coarse hair and ¼ inch for rewaxing and fine hair.
- Irregular regrowth can occur after multiple waxing treatments, especially when the hair is removed in the opposite direction. Follicles that grew at a 20-degree angle become distorted by the pulls and start to grow at deeper angles.
- Waxing, when done incorrectly, can cause a 30 percent breakage, and a percentage of those broken hairs will be in the growing (anagen) phase and will be felt within a few days.

Retin-A
a cream containing a Vitamin A derivative and tretinoin; used in the treatment of acne and the reduction of the fine lines associated with aging

accutane
oral medication used for cystic acne

differin
topical cream or gel used to treat acne

tetracycline
a broad-spectrum antibiotic used in acne treatment

Drugs That Contraindicate Waxing

- **Retin-A, accutane, and differin**—Clients using the prescription products **Retin-A**, **accutane** (AK-yoo-tayn), and **differin** will undoubtedly react adversely to facial waxing, because these products cause the skin to become fragile and dehydrated. The reaction will look like a burn and possibly lift the skin. Strip wax should not be used, because it attaches to the skin. Hard wax used with caution can be an effective alternative, depending on the strength and frequency of these products. Hard wax does not adhere to the skin, but as it hardens, it grips the hair and lifts it off the skin. Caution should also be used on areas where clients use any AHA product, particularly glycolic acid, which at 75 percent will scab.
- **Tetracyclin**—Now found in birth-control pills, **tetracycline** (tet-ruh-SY-klyn) can cause an adverse reaction.
- **Blood thinners**—Cumadin and Warfarin, along with drugs to treat epilepsy, cause easy bruising.

The Waxing Consultation

Having a consultation with a first-time client is not only very helpful, it is necessary, especially when waxing the face. When booking new clients, time should be allocated for the consultation. When possible for first-time clients, book 15 minutes for the consultation before booking waxing services of 30 minutes or more. In this way, the specialist can ascertain whether the client has a contraindication, cannot receive the service, or needs a patch test.

The Telephone Consultation

A telephone consultation may be given by the waxing technician or an informed receptionist who books the appointments. During the phone consultation, valuable information can be imparted to the client in preparation for the service. Even if the potential client is receiving dermatological treatments or is using skin preparations that contraindicate the waxing service, it is still often worth bringing the client in for a consultation, because there may be other alternatives. Electrolysis, sugaring, or threading may be options when offered in the salon, or a good professional eyebrow shape with tweezers can be offered.

INDICATIONS & CONTRAINDICATIONS

Contraindications of Waxing

- **Blood and circulatory disorders**—Blood and circulatory disorders, particularly those that cause easy bruising (e.g., thrombosis) are contraindicated.
- **Cancer treatments**—Chemotherapy and radiation may cause increased sensitivity. It would be productive to wait until 6 weeks after the last cancer treatment.
- **Epilepsy**—Epilepsy is contraindicated unless it has been controlled for a long period and with medication that does not cause easy bruising. A physician's approval must be attained before the waxing service. The technician should receive a physician's note and have the client sign a release.
- **Diabetes**—The client with diabetes should consult with the physician for the degree of severity and the degree of healing and sign a release.
- **Fractures and sprains**—The area of fracture or sprain should not be waxed until it is completely healed.
- **Hemophilia**—Clients with hemophilia should not be waxed, because bleeding can occur, especially when removing a high percentage of anagen hairs. The removal of anagen hairs breaks the cycle of blood flow to the dermal papilla and causes bleeding in the follicle.
- **Herpes, herpes simplex (cold sore)**—Clients with herpes should not be waxed during active outbreaks. Prophylactic medication should be taken before waxing.
- **Inflamed or irritated skin**—Inflamed or irritated skin should not be waxed.
- **Lack of skin sensation**—The lack of skin sensation can be due to circulatory problems arising from heart disease, diabetes, or multiple sclerosis. There can be an increased risk of burning, injury, or infection. These clients should not be waxed.
- **Lupus**—Those with mild forms of lupus and not presenting with the rash on the areas to be waxed can be waxed, but it is not advisable. At the very least, these clients should seek referrals from physicians and sign waivers.
- **Moles, skin tags, and warts**—All moles, skin tags, and warts should be avoided. Any mole that looks suspicious; has any of the precancer signs of size, shape, and color; or has hair growing out of it should not be waxed without the permission of a physician. Hair-removal specialists offer a valuable service when they recognize suspicious moles and refer their clients to physicians.
- **Pregnancy**—There is nothing intrinsically wrong with waxing the bikini area or any other area on the pregnant client, but a judgment should be made by both parties jointly and a release form should be signed. If the pregnant client is considered high risk, has high blood pressure or anxiety, it is better to avoid waxing. If the areas to be waxed take more than 20 minutes of the client lying flat on her back, then the client should wait until after the birth of the baby. Prolonged time flat on the back could deplete oxygen to the fetus. Even though there are no recorded cases of infants being harmed because their mothers received wax service, it leaves open the possibility of a lawsuit. The bottom line is to get a physician's permission and have the client sign a release form.
- **Scar tissue**—No scar tissue, including keloids, should be waxed over.
- **Sunburn**—Sunburned areas should not be waxed. Any such area must have healed completely.
- **Skin disorder conditions**—Skin disorder conditions like eczema, seborrhea, and psoriasis may be waxed depending on severity. Minimal flakiness of dead skin cells can be waxed, but not if the skin is broken. Double dipping should be avoided. In mild cases, the skin may benefit from the exfoliating properties of waxing, but in more advanced stages, broken skin could result, so it is imperative that the technician receives a signed release from the client before waxing.
- **Varicose veins**—Technicians must not wax over varicose veins (Figure 9–3) but they may wax surrounding areas.
- **Sensitive areas**—Never wax eyelids, inside the ears or nose, or the areola of the breast.
- **Any uncertain situation.**

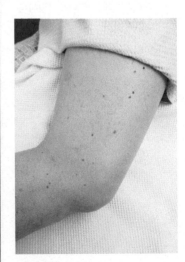

FIGURE 9–3
Do not wax over varicose veins

Other client advice should include:

- The hair to be waxed should be a minimum of ¼ inch long if it is **virgin hair**, meaning that it is previously untreated, or if it is fine regrowth.
- Hair should be ½ inch long if shaven and coarse, which is approximately 10 to 14 days postshaving.
- If possible, the client should lift ingrown hairs 4 days to a week before the service, leaving the hair in the follicle, allowing the follicle to heal and normalize.
- Working the area of the body with a loofah before waxing is recommended, but not on the day of the service, because it is too stimulating.
- Avoid tanning (sun or booths) for 24 hours before and 24 hours after the area has been waxed, or until any redness has completely subsided.

Telephone Consultation tips:
- The hair should be ¼ inch long if virgin, ½ inch long if shaven and coarse, or approximately 10 to 14 days postshaving.
- Release ingrown hairs 4 days before the service.
- Exfoliate the area before but not on the day of service.
- Avoid ultraviolet rays 24 hours before and 24 hours after the service.

The Salon Consultation

The salon waxing consultation is the time for the hair-removal specialist to put forward the most professional image and inspire confidence in the client. This consultation, coupled with a successful service, should gain faithful, regular clients.

To achieve a successful consultation, first impressions are essential and should not be underestimated. The client should be greeted by smiling, helpful, courteous people. When the specialist is booked, the necessary forms can be attached to a clipboard and given to the client while waiting. The specialist should be clean and well groomed and have a friendly, courteous, professional demeanor. The consultation should take place in the waxing area, which should be clean and tidy with no wax dripping down the wax heater and no spatulas in the wax pot.

FIGURE 9–4
A good skin-growth chart should be available for reference during the consultation

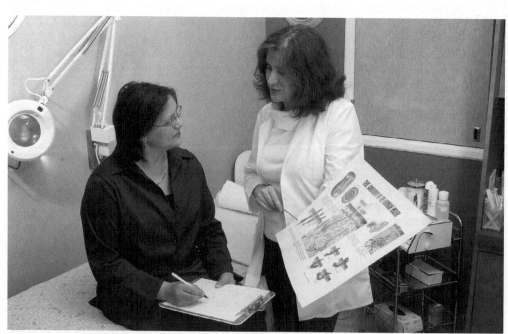

At the start of a salon consultation, it is helpful to have a good skin-care chart that illustrates the different stages of hair growth for reference (Figure 9–4). At this point, the specialist can address the client's completed forms, ascertain in which services the client is interested, and look for any contraindications. If there are no contraindications, it is still important, especially for face waxing, for the client to sign a waxing release form (see following section). By doing this, the client indicates an awareness of the risks that go with waxing and assumes the responsibility of informing the specialist of any changes to the record card.

Next in the consultation, the specialist should inform the client about what the procedure entails and what to expect, as well as give tips for better results. With any face waxing, it is important to ask the new client if the service is for a special occasion. Let the client understand in clear terms that there could be redness and pimples. Then, reiterate, in more depth, the following information imparted during the phone consultation, especially as it relates to hair growth:

- Hair should be a minimum of ¼ inch long if virgin, ½ inch long if shaven and coarse, approximately 10 to 14 days postshaving.
- Release but do not remove ingrown hairs 4 to 5 days before the service, allowing the follicle to heal and normalize.
- Loofah and exfoliate before, but not on the day of, waxing, because it is too stimulating.
- If the skin tends to be dry and scaly, particularly on the legs, lotion can be applied that morning after showering, but not immediately before the service.
- Remind the client to avoid tanning (sun or booths) for 24 hours before and 24 hours after the service, or until any signs of redness have subsided.

Face waxing, which does not include on the eyebrows or upper lip, can create problems for the client. Clients requesting face-waxing services for the first time should be made aware of the pros and cons and possible consequences of face waxing. When clients have not had the chin and sides of the face waxed before, the need for waxing should be determined. Healthy skin is *supposed* to have hair. Vellus is normal and acceptable. Unfortunately, the bright lights and strong magnification of the mirrors in bathrooms create reflections that are often unrealistic, distorted, and illusionary. Have the client look in a regular, handheld mirror an arm's length away and in normal lighting. If the hair is not visible, *it is not a problem.* Any disturbance of that hair could create a bigger problem for the client at some point in the future and cause the client to regret the multiple face waxing services. Discuss other options, like electrolysis, which will eliminate rather than exacerbate the problem.

To close the consultation, always allow time to answer any of the client's questions and to address any concerns. Then, walk the client to the reception area and invite the client to make the appointment.

Record Cards and Release Forms

The client record card (Figure 9–5), when filled out correctly, will contain a wealth of important information, the most crucial being the list of conditions that may contraindicate the service.

Not all clients walking in for quick lip or eyebrow waxes must fill out extensive record cards, especially if they get the service regularly and are just visiting from out of town. However, every client should fill out a simple release form like that in Figure 9–6. It is also important for returning clients to sign release forms each time. Clients continually change their skin-care regimens and could introduce things like glycolic acid or Retin-A, which would cause an extreme reaction to any waxing service. The responsibility cannot be left up to the client to inform the technician of any changes in skin care, therefore, the technician must ask returning clients if there have been any changes and give them the release form to sign.

Client Record Card

Name _____ Date ___/___/___

Address _____

Telephone   Home (___)_____   Work (___)_____   DOB ___/___/___

Do you have a history of the following conditions? Please check those that apply.

☐ Circulatory disorder   ☐ Diabetes   ☐ Epilepsy   ☐ Hemophilia   ☐ Herpes

Skin disorder: ☐ Lupus/DLE   ☐ Eczema   ☐ Seborrhea   ☐ Dermatitis   ☐ Psoriasis

Lack of skin sensation: Location _____ Sunburn: Location _____

Scar tissue: Location _____ Mole(s): Location(s) _____

Fracture(s)/sprain(s): Location(s) _____

Varicose veins: Location _____

Prescription medication(s): _____

Are you pregnant? _____

Face Waxing

Are you currently using any of the following skin-care products?

☐ AHA/Glycolic acid   ☐ Retin-A/Renova   ☐ Accutane   ☐ Differin

Are you currently undergoing any specialized facial/skin treatments?_____
_____

Technician's notes: _____
_____

I understand that it is my sole responsibility to notify the waxing technician of any changes to the above information before any waxing service.

Signed _____ Date_____

Parent or guardian if under 18 years of age _____

Technician's signature_____ Date_____

FIGURE 9–5 The client record card

Client Expectations

Waxing is not without some discomfort, but it is fast and effective. The client's ability to relax will minimize the discomfort.

Erythema

With waxing is the possibility of erythema or redness to the waxed area. If the face is to be waxed, the client should be advised to make the appointment at a convenient time when redness would not be a problem. Clients should not receive facial waxings on the days of important functions. Histamine bumps may occur.

Face Waxing Release Form

Waxing for hair removal, particularly on the face, carries certain risks. These risks may include redness, bruising, and lifting of the skin.

These conditions may be exacerbated by the use of certain pharmaceuticals and cosmeceuticals, particularly those for antiaging and antiacne treatment. Examples of these are retinoids, Retin-A, Renova, accutane, and alpha hydroxy acids (AHAs) like glycolic acid. Face waxing should be avoided when using these products.

Certain prescription medications may aggravate the skin when waxed, particularly those causing photosensitivity (sensitivity to sunlight). Examples of these are many antibiotics, such as tetracyclines, and blood thinners, such as Warfarin, which may cause an individual to bruise easily.

Clients who are receiving esthetic and dermatological peeling treatments may also experience redness and skin lifting from waxing and therefore should avoid waxing while undergoing such treatments.

The use of tanning booths can also contraindicate waxing. Waxing should not be done 24 hours before or after tanning. It should also not be done on an area that still shows an erythema (redness) from tanning.

Because the fields of pharmacology and dermatology are continually changing and expanding, there may be products and drugs that cause negative reactions to waxing that have not been documented.

Client Acknowledgment

- I have read the information on this form and I fully understand the information presented to me.
- I use none of the products known to cause a negative reaction with waxing.
- I am receiving no skin treatments known to cause a negative reaction to waxing.
- I understand that waxing may involve certain minor risks (e.g., redness, sensitive reaction, bruising, and lifting of the skin), and I fully accept all responsibilities associated with these risks.

Client's signature _____ Date_____

Client's printed name _____

Parent or guardian if under 18 years of age _____

Technician's signature_____ Date_____

Technician's printed name _____

FIGURE 9–6 The face waxing release form

Swelling

There may be some swelling after a lip wax. The client should be warned of this and reassured that if it does occur, ice will be provided and the swelling will not last long.

Waxing services can feel more uncomfortable to some clients immediately before and/or after menstruation, so clients can be advised not to book appointments for 3 to 4 days before or after menstruation.

Red Spots

It is important to let clients know that red dots will be visible on waxed areas. These red dots are blood spots. These spots are more pronounced with body waxing than facial waxing. Once the hair has been removed at the root, the base of the hair follicle acquires some blood that would normally feed the hair at the papilla. As there is no longer a hair present, the blood gathers at the base of the follicle. In a few hours, it absorbs back into the dermis. This is a good sign for the client, because it indicates that the hair was "pulled out by the root."

Regrowth

Although waxed hairs usually take from 6 weeks to 3 months to reappear after waxing, depending on the area, it is important to tell clients what to expect with regrowth and when to expect it. Many clients are alarmed after a first waxing experience to see some hairs appear in the week or so following the service. It is worth explaining ahead of time that this will happen and that it is not due to any shortcoming of the waxing service. In fact, these hairs were new anagen hairs lying just below the skin at the time of waxing. As soon as the hair is removed, the hair follicle goes into its resting phase. Therefore, it is wise to ask the first time clients to come back after a few days to a week to remove any hairs that have come through and thereby work to get as many hairs as close to the same cycle as possible.

This will also be true of clients who book their waxing services monthly. Hairs that were waxed away two treatments prior will appear soon after a waxing service. By clarifying this ahead of time with clients, clients will not view this as an excuse for a bad waxing service. Many clients have a hard time keeping a 6-week or 2-month calendar and like to book their waxing services monthly. They should therefore be prepared to experience regrowth from previous services. For clients who are prepared to wait 6 weeks to 2 months between services, it is worth bringing those clients in a week after their first waxing services to wax away new, visible, anagen hairs and to force the hair follicles into close to the same telogen stage as the hairs waxed in the previous week. This will enable clients to experience a greater percentage of hair-free areas over longer periods.

Ingrown Hair Treatment

Good products are now available for the technician to use on and sell to clients to help keep ingrown hairs to a minimum. These products usually contain a high percentage of AHA or salicylic acid. If ingrown hairs do occur, they can be dealt with in a couple of ways.

The first way is for the client to release but not remove as many hairs as possible at least 4 days before the waxing service. The hairs should be released as close to the follicle opening as possible by sterile needle-pointed tweezers and should not be tweezed away but left sticking out of the opening, allowing time for the follicle to heal and normalize around the hair. If the skin is broken and the hair is completely removed, the opening will scab over, a new anagen hair will be trapped under the scab, and it will become ingrown and perpetuate the problem.

Ingrown hairs visible at the start of a waxing service that look like blackheads (Figure 9–7) (this is particularly apparent in the bikini area) usually have follicle openings and can be extracted gently and fairly easily before the service. The technician should wear gloves

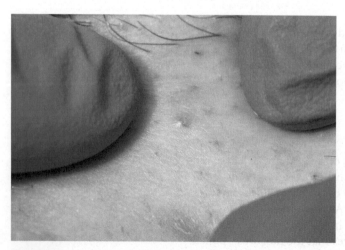

FIGURE 9–7 Sample blackhead type of ingrown hair

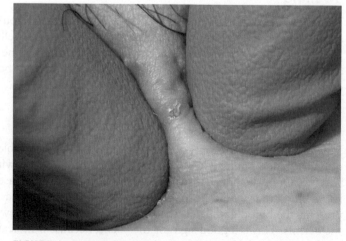

FIGURE 9–8 Extraction of the blackhead type of ingrown hair

FIGURE 9–9 Sample thin line type of ingrown hair

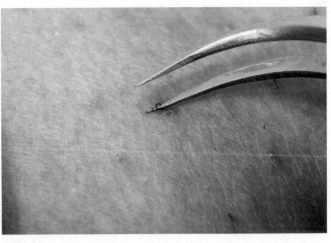

FIGURE 9–10 Extraction of the thin line type of ingrown hair

and wipe the area with alcohol and gently squeeze the blackhead until the hair extracts (Figure 9–8). Once the hair is extracted, it can be wiped away. Because the skin was not broken, the follicle opening was not compromised and does not need time to heal and normalize.

For embedded hair that is visible under the skin as a thin line (Figure 9–9), the technician can release the hair after the waxing service by again wearing gloves, wiping the area with alcohol, and using sterile sharp-pointed tweezers (Figure 9–10). A magnifying lamp can make this procedure much easier. The tweezers should be sharp enough to break the skin as minimally as possible. The hair is released by sliding the tweezers' point underneath it as close to where the follicle should be as possible. The client should be instructed to leave the hair protruding for as long as possible up to 4 days, allowing the follicle to heal and normalize around it. The hair may then be tweezed away days later, when it is healed. Immediately tweezing the hair after breaking the skin causes a scab to form over the opening, and if the hair removed was a telogen hair, there may well be an early anagen hair in the follicle trapped under the forming scab that could become ingrown, perpetuating the problem. The use of needle-pointed tweezers or lancets to break the skin are critical items and may be prohibited by some state licensing boards.

FIGURE 9–11
The waxing treatment room

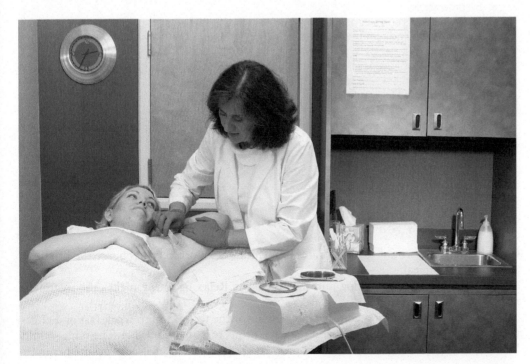

Waxing Materials
- private room that can be locked for clients who must remove clothing or a partitioned area for face waxing
- table at a comfortable working height for the technician
- Stool or step for short clients to get on the table, if necessary
- Paper roll or sheets to cover the table that are changed with every client
- Washbasin, which inspires client confidence when the technician washes hands in front of the client
- Antiseptic cleaner and towels for wiping down counters
- Soap and paper towels
- Disposable vinyl gloves
- Hooks and hangers for clients' clothes
- Washable drapes for the client
- Disposable panties
- Record cards and release forms
- Clipboard and pens
- Diagrams of skin and hair
- Cart, countertop, or cabinet for supplies
- Handheld mirror
- Hair clips
- Lined trash can
- Wax heaters
- Protective collars
- Multiple cans of wax
- Multiple size applicators
- Applicator holder
- Cleansing lotion
- Petroleum jelly
- Pretreatment lotion/witch hazel
- Surgical alcohol
- Antiseptic lotion
- Tea tree oil or other preparatory lotion
- Dusting powder
- **Pellon** (PEL-un) **strips** or **muslin** (MUZ-lun) **strips** in at least two sizes (1" × 3" and 9" × 3")
- Eyebrow brush
- Eyebrow scissors
- Eyebrow pencils and sharpeners
- Electric buzzer, including extra attachments for sterilization
- Tweezers
- Sterilized sharps forceps for removal of ingrown hairs
- Sterilizing unit filled with sterilizing fluid
- Steel dish and lid for sterilized tools
- Tissues
- Cotton in a covered receptacle
- Soothing lotions
- Ice nearby
- Wax cleaner

pellon strips
a soft-woven, paper-like strip used for removing wax from the skin

muslin strips
a thin, plain-weave cotton cloth used for removing wax from the skin

Treatment Area Setup

Good lighting is essential to a waxing treatment area. Fluorescent lights are the brightest and most economical.

Select music that is relaxing and not offensive. Relaxing music makes the treatment more pleasurable.

The table should be at a comfortable height for the technician to work fast and effectively without putting undue stress on the back or posture (Figure 9–11). The table should have a washable, fitted sheet over it for protection. Over the sheet should be a paper liner.

Rolls of paper can be purchased, and most tables have bars in which to attach the paper roll at one end for convenience.

It helps to have a magnifying lamp of at least three **diopters** (DY-op-turz) handy for checking the removal of hard-to-see hairs on the upper lip and brow or for releasing ingrown hairs.

diopters
unit of measurement relating to the power of a lens

The wax heater should be on a paper-lined, rolling cart that can be pulled close to the table to minimize wax spillage.

Client Preparation and Treatment

Wax heaters are usually thermostatically controlled. If they are not, or if there is any doubt, the temperature should be read with a thermometer. Regardless, the wax should always be tested on the technician's skin on the inner forearm before its application on the client. If a piece of muslin is used to remove the test patch on the technician's skin, throw it away. Do not use it on the client.

Positioning

Make sure the table is at a comfortable height for working accurately and efficiently and avoiding fatigue or back discomfort. Check posture. Do not bend over when waxing. Stand close to the area to avoid leaning awkwardly. Make sure there is plenty of space and that the bed is centrally located in the room with easy access from all sides. When the technician is too close to a wall, movement is restricted and the technician cannot follow through with pulls and snaps the hair.

When ready to prepare the client's skin for the service, begin by hand washing in front of the client, drying the hands with a paper towel and using the paper towel to turn off the faucet. Discard the paper towel.

Cleansing

To cleanse and prepare the client's skin, use the waxing manufacturer's prewaxing cleaners. These products are very good for the face as well as the underarm and bikini areas and are usually applied with a piece of cotton. When waxing the face, completely remove makeup from the area to be waxed. This should be done as gently as possible so as not to overstimulate the skin in that area. Makeup can irritate the area being waxed, and oils in makeup prevent the wax from gripping the hair. For larger areas of the body, such as the arms, legs, and back, a spray cleanser is faster and more economical. A spray bottle can contain a waxing manufacturer's product or a general antiseptic product, such as witch hazel. To prepare the limbs, it is faster and more enjoyable for the client when the technician sprays the cleaner on both limbs then wipes in sequence up the limbs with both hands, finishing at the fingers or toes. When preparing the client's legs, the legs should be bent with the knees upward so that the technician can easily reach the underside without inconveniencing the client. Wipe off any excess moisture with two facial tissues, one in each hand.

At this point, a manufacturer's numbing solution or spray may be applied to the area. Take care to completely avoid the eye area with numbing products. The face should never be sprayed with a numbing product. Saturate a cotton square with the numbing spray and gently dab the area of the face with the cotton. The product usually takes 2 to 3 minutes to be effective. Some numbing products have oil carriers, and the oil may prevent the hair from gripping the wax.

Pretreatment

Tea tree oil, which works well as a pretreatment, is an essential oil that evaporates, leaving the skin without a greasy film. It quickly absorbs into the skin, leaving no residue on the hair to inhibit the grip of the wax. Make sure the essential oil is 100 percent tea tree oil.

Many oils on the market may have as little as 5 percent. Tea tree oil has antibacterial as well as soothing and healing properties. The essential oil penetrates to help fight bacteria. It should be applied sparingly to the area, just by sliding a cotton-tip applicator around the lip of the bottle, rather than dipping the cotton tip into the oil, which is wasteful and absorbs more of the essential oil than is necessary.

After cleansing, the area should be lightly dusted with a dusting powder using a piece of cotton. It should be fragrance-free, talc-free, oil-free, and, preferably, corn starch based. The powder serves to absorb any remaining moisture and oil. On larger body areas, if the hair is light and not easily visible, it also helps to mark where waxing has been done and still must be done.

At this point, waxing can begin.

Facial Waxing

Waxing the eyebrows or upper lip can be done during a facial, but it should be done after the cleansing, gentle exfoliation, steaming, and extractions and before the mask. Waxing should not be performed if any aggressive exfoliation has taken place or over an area where extractions were performed. The mask should be soothing. If the indicated mask therapy is not going to be a soothing mask, then a soothing lotion and cool, damp cotton should be applied to the waxed area, avoiding the mask.

Posttreatment

After the hair removal, any residual stickiness should be removed with a soothing wax-removal lotion, which most wax companies manufacture and distribute.

Swelling may result due to the trauma of waxing mainly on the upper lip, more so with strip wax than with hard wax. Swelling can be treated with ice in a bag or cold stones immediately following the service.

histamine
a compound released by the cells of the body's immune system in allergic reactions

Hives can also occur, which is a **histamine** (HISS-tah-meen) reaction. Hives can be avoided the next time if the client takes Benedryl® or some similar product before the service. Many wax companies sell complementing after-care soothing products. Another form of aftertreatment that can be used is salicylic acid, which can sting on initial contact with the skin but then takes away redness in 15 to 20 minutes. For areas that look particularly tender, a cool compress can be made by soaking a clean towel or cotton in a solution made of a tablespoon of baking soda and a pint of water with ice. The compress can be applied to the area for 10 minutes, then removed with any residue. For clients who are prone to breakouts after facial waxing, high-frequency treatments can be applied by a licensed esthetician.

Clients should not take hot baths or use hot tubs the remainder of the day after the service.

Avoid tanning (sun or booths) for at least 24 hours postwaxing or until all erythema has subsided.

Sunless tanning products should not be applied to the skin for 24 hours or until signs of waxing have disappeared.

Clients should not apply perfumed products to the area that was waxed for at least 24 hours.

Hygiene and Sanitation

A clean and sanitary environment is not only important to meeting state requirements, it inspires client confidence. The presentation of the room and technician should reflect a high standard of cleanliness and professionalism.

As the client leaves the room, tools should be washed with a germicidal soap and put in the sterilization unit. Wax spilled on the wax heater should be removed with oil. There are wax-removal products on the market that should not be used on the client and are designed for removing wax from floors and other surfaces. Care should be used with these strong products so as to avoid damaging the finish on the wax heater or removing any lettering and numbering. Throw out any used sticks and strips. Change the paper and/or linen on the table. Change the wax collar and paper under the wax unit if there is wax spilled on them.

Wipe down surfaces and bottles with a disinfectant cleaner. All this can be done in 5 minutes.

As mentioned previously, hands should be washed before and after each client.

Glove Use

The use of gloves still seems a personal preference for many. Some technicians choose to wear gloves the whole time they contact clients' skin. Many still choose not to wear gloves, while others settle for wearing one glove on the hand that contacts the skin when applying pressure to the skin after the wax is removed. It is worth noting that blood spots appear in areas that are waxed. If there is *any* chance that the skin on the hand is broken, even in the form of a hangnail, *gloves should be worn*. Waxing technicians just starting out in the field should wear gloves with every client and get used to wearing gloves with every client. Gloves let clients know that the technician follows Universal Precautions.

A new pair of gloves should be worn with each client. They should be powder-free, vinyl or reduced-protein latex gloves. The client should be questioned for any allergy to latex. Clients who are allergic to latex will probably bring it to the technician's attention when the technician puts on the gloves.

Double Dipping

Double dipping is when the technician takes wax from the pot on a stick, applies it to a client, and returns the stick to the pot for more wax. Many state cosmetology boards do not allow double dipping, although it is practiced commonly in salons across the nation.

As discussed in Chapter 5, to survive and reproduce, bacteria need time and the right conditions: food, moisture, and high temperatures. Other factors affecting bacterial growth and reproduction are pH, oxygen, and light. Most pathogens grow rapidly at temperatures above 40°F/4°C. The ideal temperature for bacterial growth is between 40 and 140°F/4 and 60°C, what Food Safety and Inspection Service (FSIS) calls the "danger zone."

Most disease-causing bacteria are killed at temperatures above 140°F/60°C. The temperature of wax is most effective and comfortable at around 140 to 165°F/60 to 75°C, which means that most disease-causing bacteria are killed in the wax pot. Bacteria are not killed at temperatures below 40°F, but low temperatures slow their growth. Warming a wax pot to between 40°F and 140°F may cause an increase of bacterial growth if bacteria are indeed present in the pot, but as the temperature reaches 140°F, the bacteria start to die.

The fully heated pot is too hot, making it hostile for bacterial growth. Bacteria also need moisture for growth, and there is no moisture in depilatory wax.

Pasteurization, which occurs at 159°F/70°C, renders the Hepatitis B virus inactive, meaning that there is little to no risk of spreading HBV in this manner, nor HIV, which is much less resilient than HBV. The CDC additionally has no record and received no reports of cross-contamination from waxing services. In fact, the CDC does not consider this situation to be enough of a risk to even warrant testing for disease transmission due to waxing services.[1]

After the spatula is coated with wax, it does not contact the skin. Wax glides off the spatula onto the skin as the spatula moves along the skin's surface. The same situation arises during the application of nail polish. The polish alone contacts the nail, and the brush never touches the nail bed, which is why it is acceptable in the beauty industry to not only apply polish from fingernail to fingernail, from toenail to toenail, but from one client to another. It is also acceptable to have nail-polish testers out in the public for randomly testing nail colors. Once an area has been waxed, if hairs remain on the skin, the hairs should be removed only by the wax that is already on the removal strip. The applicator should not contact the newly waxed area and return to the pot.

Tests were carried out using the last ½ inch of three cans of wax with which double dipping was carried out on multiple people, on multiple body parts. The wax was heated to the recommended safe and effective temperature for hair removal. Samples from each can of wax were put into petri dishes to culture for bacterial growth. In addition, a wax sample was taken from a brand-new can of wax and put into its own petri dish to act as a control. The petri dishes were tested after 4 days. No evidence of microorganisms were found under microscopic examination. The test was replicated with the same result. In all eight petri dishes, no microorganisms were found.

Note: Technicians should provide waxing service in the manner laid out by their state licensing boards.

Nondisposable spatulas made of teakwood are becoming increasingly popular, because they can be used repeatedly. Their high-gloss finish prevents the absorption of oils and bacteria. They can be easily cleaned and sterilized, and they do not hold the heat the way metal spatulas can. Teakwood spatulas are available in an assortment of sizes and shapes.

Disposable wood applicators are available in an assortment of sizes for the various waxing services (Figure 9–12). Tongue depressors are commonly used, and while they can be cut to different sizes to reduce the number of sticks used, doing so is not recommended, because doing so can splinter the wood, releasing fine splinters into the wax and risking client injury. The jagged edges of a broken applicator may also scratch the client.

Equipment Maintenance

- Check waxing equipment periodically to ensure the thermostat is working correctly. This can be done using an oven-safe thermometer, which tells if the medium setting is heating the wax to a safe and acceptable temperature.
- Do not clean the wax unit by placing it in water. Unplug it and clean it with recommended solvents.

Safety Precautions

To avoid electrocution:

- As with all electrical salon equipment, keep the wax unit away from water.
- As with any electrical appliance, if it comes into contact with water, unplug it before removing it from the water.

FIGURE 9–12
Different types and sizes of applicators

To reduce the risk of burns, fire, or injury:

- Follow all manufacturer appliance instructions completely.
- Do not use the wax heater if it has a damaged cord or plug, if it is not working properly, or if it has been dropped into water.
- Never leave the wax heater unattended for extended periods while plugged in. Unplug immediately after use.
- Closely supervise the wax unit if it is used near children or invalids.
- Only use the wax heater for its intended purpose of heating wax.

General Equipment Safety

- Do not operate the wax-heating unit if it has a damaged cord or plug, if it has been dropped into water, or if it is functioning improperly.
- Keep the cord away from heated surfaces.
- Do not block the ventilation openings of the wax unit if the unit has them.
- Do not use equipment outdoors or where aerosol sprays are being used.
- Connect the appliance to a properly grounded outlet only.
- Most wax units should have an automatically reset thermal limiter that shuts off the unit. If this malfunctions, it must not be used.
- Do not wrap the cord around the wax unit or bend or twist it.
- Never drop or insert any object into any opening or try to repair it.
- In the event of any malfunction the wax unit should be returned to the manufacturer or taken to the manufacturer's recommended service center for examination and repair.
- Always ground wax heaters. In the event of an electrical short circuit, grounding reduces the risk of electric shock by providing a path of low resistance for the electric current. The plugs on grounded equipment must be plugged into outlets that are properly installed and grounded in compliance with all local codes and ordinances. If there are any doubts or questions regarding the safe grounding of the wax unit, a qualified electrician should be brought in to verify its safety. If the appliance plug does not fit the outlet, the plug should not be modified to fit. Instead, fit a new conforming outlet via a qualified electrician.

Quick Tips

- Exfoliating the skin 48 hours after the service and regularly in the weeks following reduces the chance of ingrown hairs.
- The direction of hair growth may be modified and gradually retrained by waxing the hair in the desired direction.
- Using a spray bottle to spray the cleansing antiseptic on large body areas is a faster method of application. Warn clients to expect the cool mist so they are not startled.

 ## Conclusion

There is nothing more unnerving than causing trauma or injury to a client during a waxing service. It is distressing for the client, who must live with scabbing and/or bruising for a number of days, and if the service was booked before an occasion, it causes further distress and embarrassment at the occasion. The technician can apologize profusely, offer remedies, and not charge for the service. While these are appropriate gestures, they will not undo the damage. These awful incidences can be avoided by following the protocol in this chapter. Certainly, some clients may be unaware of their skin-care product ingredients and are willing to assume the risk; others may fail to accurately report certain factors that may contraindicate the service, but this is out of the technician's control. As long as a full initial consultation has been given to every client, follow-up questions asked at every return visit, and a release signed, the technician is somewhat assured that a correctly applied service will be without adverse effects, other than short-term redness. When protocol and procedures are followed, negative incidences and reactions are considerably reduced and the waxing services will be satisfying.

Endnote

1. Leigh Farrington, MS, CDC Division for HBV.

Discussion and Review Questions

1. What are the two points regarding wax's solubility?
2. What is the general melting point range for waxes?
3. List six contraindications of waxing services.
4. Name a type of drug that contraindicates waxing services.
5. How long should both virgin and previously treated hair be to receive a waxing treatment?
6. What is the most important step to take before touching the client's skin?
7. What are the two benefits of tea tree oil?

Additional Readings

Milady's Standard Comprehensive Training for Estheticians. 2003. Clifton Park, NY: Milady, an imprint of Delmar Learning.

Milady's Standard Cosmetology. 2004. Clifton Park, NY: Milady, an imprint of Delmar Learning.

CHAPTER 10

Hard Depilatory Wax, The Nonstrip Method

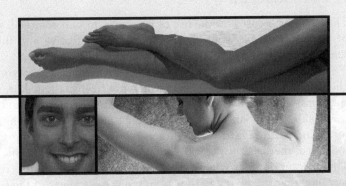

Chapter Outline

Learning Objectives ■ Key Terms ■ Introduction ■ Hard Wax Basics
Hard Wax Application and Techniques for Women
Hard Wax Application and Techniques for Men ■ Conclusion
Discussion and Review Questions

Learning Objectives

By the end of this chapter, you should be able to:

1. List the pros and cons of hard depilatory wax.
2. List the contraindications of hard wax and know when it is the appropriate wax for hair removal.
3. Know the correct method of applying and removing hard wax.
4. Be able to avoid some of the more common mistakes in the use of hard wax.

Key Terms

American bikini wax   carnauba wax   French bikini wax   pubis
Brazilian bikini wax   femoral ridge   glabellar   rosin
candelilla wax

Introduction

This chapter focuses on the use of hard wax in hair removal, including the pros and cons of using hard wax; where hard wax is most effective and the preferred method of hair removal; and when hard wax use is contraindicated.

There has never been a time of more concern to the waxing professional than now, as clients seek advanced skin-care treatments from estheticians, dermatologists, and plastic surgeons, as well as undertake home skin-care regimens that effect more dramatic changes in the skin. Many antiacne and antiaging facial treatments and products create problems for clients with regard to face waxing. Where strip waxing would ordinarily be contraindicated, there are now gentle but effective hard waxes available for use on delicate skin. This chapter outlines when and where hard wax is most effective. It also discusses the correct method of applying hard wax to the various parts of the face and body, as well as tips for a successful service and ways to troubleshoot some of the most common mistakes.

Hard Wax Basics

rosin
a hard, translucent resin derived from the sap, stumps, and other parts of pine trees

candelilla wax
a type of vegetable wax derived from the candelilla plant

carnauba wax
the hardest and most widely used vegetable wax; derived from the leaves of the carnauba palm tree

The melting point of a depilatory wax must be greater than 98°F/37°C but less than 165°F/73.9°C. Because the body temperature is around 98.6°F/38°C, if the melting point were lower, the wax would not solidify. In addition, the wax must be sufficiently firm to grip the hair. A good working temperature for hard wax is between 125°F/51.6°C and 140°F/60°C for application, although it is still all right to use wax up to 165°F/73.9°C considering that the wax cools dramatically, at approximately 7°F/3.9°C per second. As no one wax meets these criteria, depilatory waxes are based on a resin called **rosin** (ROZ-un), often combined with beeswax, **candelilla** (kan-duh-LIL-ah) **wax**, and **carnauba** (kar-NOO-buh) **wax**, to modify their melting points and increase strength (Figure 10–1).

Until the arrival of soft liquid strip wax, hard wax was the most common salon method of hair removal. When strip wax arrived on the market, hard depilatory wax was virtually replaced by it because of strip wax's speed and efficiency. Because time is of the essence to the technician, soft wax with the strip is more practical for large body areas. However, strip wax came onto the market before AHAs, Retin-A, and products and treatments now commonly used for antiaging. Depilatory hard wax is making a strong comeback for use on delicate and fragile skin due to these problems and to hard wax's ability to lift off the skin as it hardens, leaving the skin intact while still gripping the hair.

Strip wax is much hotter and has more of a liquid consistency on application. As it is applied to the skin, it more readily runs to the base of the hair shaft. Because the application temperature of hard wax is somewhat lower and therefore thicker, when it is applied to the skin, it sets faster. Applying wax initially in the opposite direction of hair growth gives the wax the chance to get to the base of the hair first while the wax is still warm. The wax then starts to shrink as it cools. Gliding the wax back over the top of the hair, like frosting a cake, allows for thorough coverage of the hair shaft. Thorough coverage around the hair shaft means a good, tight grip to even the coarsest hairs. Although the wax is usually removed against the hair growth, hard wax can also be removed in the direction of hair growth, especially when it is used with vellus, without distorting the hair follicles.

FIGURE 10–1
Hard wax supplies

There is currently an increase in the demand for the **Brazilian bikini wax**, in which all the hair in the pubic area is removed. The rules of applying and removing strip wax cannot be applied to the labia, but hard wax, with its ability to tightly grip hair without adhering to delicate skin and to remove hair in the direction of growth, makes a Brazilian bikini wax possible.

When first learning to wax with hard wax, it is much easier to start with small sections, even on large body areas. The sections or strips should be no more than 2 inches wide by 4 inches long. With experience and competency, the technician can gradually increase the length of the area to 12 inches for large body areas. A strip should not extend beyond 12 inches long, and the width should remain at 2 inches. The application should always be about ⅛ inch thick on the face to ¼ inch thick on larger body areas, or between three to five coatings of wax. The strip of wax should have a clean, even edge all the way around for a clean removal and be somewhat thicker at the edge, where it will be lifted during removal. Failure to have a clean edge means that little pieces of wax will be left behind, and their removal can annoy the client. Wax will appear shiny and wet and will feel sticky when first applied. When the shine diminishes and the wax looks opaque and maintains a fingerprint, it is ready to lift off. Allowing wax to set for too long causes the wax to become brittle. Such wax breaks and becomes difficult to remove, and it also breaks the hair.

Hard wax should not be overheated. Instead, keep it on a thermostatically controlled timer. It should also not be heated continually for 24 hours. Overheating the pot causes the wax to lose its epilation properties. The wax hardens and becomes brittle too quickly.

Brazilian bikini wax
a bikini wax in which all hair is removed in the pubic region, including hair on the labia and hair between the buttocks

---

PROS & CONS

Pros of Nonstrip Hard Wax

- Hard wax does not distort the hair follicle, because it is removed in the direction of hair growth, not against it, like strip wax.
- Hard wax does not adhere to the skin and therefore causes less irritation than strip wax.
- Hard wax is effective in areas in which the hair grows in multiple directions, like the underarms.
- Hard wax is the most effective wax for using around the labia during the Brazilian bikini wax.
- As with strip wax, regrowth with hard wax is softer and lacks stubble.
- Regrowth generally takes 6 to 12 weeks after hard waxing, depending on the area.
- If hair is left behind after removal, it can be waxed a second time with the hard wax, providing there is no visible irritation.
- Hard wax can be used with caution on clients who use glycolic acid or other AHA skin-care treatments.
- Eyebrows may be waxed with hard wax if Retin-A or other prescription topical and antiacne medicines like Accutane and Differin are being used but have not been applied directly to the eye area and only if a patch test has been performed and the client has signed a release and is aware of the increased risk of a negative reaction. Prescription lotions and creams still migrate somewhat to the eye, causing changes in the integrity of that skin.

Cons of Nonstrip Hard Wax

- The process of waxing with hard wax is slow and laborious and takes considerably longer than strip wax, so it is not preferred for large body areas like the legs and back.
- If hard wax is left to age in heat and new wax is not added periodically, the old wax becomes brittle and loses its removal properties. The wax becomes visibly darker.
- Hard wax is more difficult from which to get good results when a client is menstruating and retains excessive fluids, because the swelling tightens the skin, which in turn causes the hair to shrink into the skin, making it tough to remove.
- With hard wax, the hair cannot be "blended" in the way it can with wax on a strip. This may be a significant enough reason to use the strip wax on areas like the sides of the face or the throat.

If the wax darkens, it has been overheated. To maintain the epilation properties of the wax, add new wax to the pot daily. The wax pot should be kept full and not allowed to get low, because the wax will overheat and burn. The wax should also be stirred regularly to ensure that the older and newer waxes are well blended.

INDICATIONS & CONTRAINDICATIONS

Hard Wax Contraindications

- Inflamed or irritated skin should not be waxed.
- The extensive use of Retin-A and other prescription topical antiacne medicines like Accutane and Differin or glycolic acid or other strong exfoliating treatments contraindicate facial waxing.
- Circulatory disorders that cause easy bruising (e.g., phlebitis and thrombosis) contraindicate hard wax.
- Epilepsy prevents hard waxing, if the medication causes easy bruising.
- Depending on degree of severity and the degree of healing, diabetes contraindicates hard wax.
- Fractures and sprains should not be waxed until completely healed.
- Hemophiliacs should not be waxed.
- Herpes or herpes simplex areas (cold sores) should not be waxed while active. Prophylactic medication should be taken before waxing.
- Lack of skin sensation contraindicates waxing services.
- Moles, skin tags, and warts should not be waxed.
- If the areas needing to be waxed take more than 20 minutes of the pregnant client lying flat on her back, waxing should wait until after the birth of the baby.
- Scar tissue, including keloids, should be avoided.
- Sunburned areas should not be waxed until completely healed.
- Skin disorders (e.g., eczema, seborrhea, and psoriasis) should not be waxed when the skin is broken.
- Varicose veins should be avoided during waxing, although surrounding areas may be waxed.
- The drugs that contraindicate waxing include tetracycline, now found in birth-control pills, because it can cause an adverse reaction with hot wax; blood thinners like Cumadin and Warfarin; and drugs to treat epilepsy, because they cause easy bruising.

Hard Wax Application and Techniques for Women

The Eyebrows

During an eyebrow wax, the client should be lying flat or semireclined. Remove the client's makeup, and clean the area to be waxed with a mild antiseptic cleanser. Apply a very small amount of tea tree oil to the area and allow it to absorb into the skin for a minute. While waiting for the tea tree oil to absorb, test the temperature of the wax on the inside of the wrist. Follow by dusting the area lightly with powder. Analyze the eyebrow using the guidelines in Chapter 11, and decide which shape to create and which hair to remove. With a small spatula, apply the wax to the entire area under the brow, first against the direction of hair growth, then back over the same area in the direction of growth, rather like frosting a cake. A few applications are necessary so that neither hair nor skin is visible through the wax. The strip of wax should have a clean, even edge all the way around for clean removal and be somewhat thicker at the edge, where it will be lifted for the removal. The wax will appear shiny and wet, and it will feel sticky. When the shine diminishes and the wax looks opaque and maintains a fingerprint, it is ready to lift off. Flick up the grasping edge of the wax on the outer edge of the eyebrow and, with a thumb, hold the skin taut. Grasp the wax, and pull quickly against the direction of growth as close to the skin as possible. Immediately apply pressure to the area. Once technicians are proficient in the use of hard wax, they can apply wax to the second eyebrow while waiting for the wax on the first eyebrow to set. When applying wax to the **glabellar** (GLAH-buh-lahr) area between the eyebrows, the same rule applies: Apply the wax first against the growth, then back on top in the direction of growth, and remove against the growth. After the wax has been removed, apply a soothing antiseptic lotion to the area and massage both eyebrows simultaneously finishing with gentle pressure at the temple. A detailed description of how to shape the eyebrows can be found in Chapter 11.

This service should be performed in approximately 20 minutes using hard wax, 30 minutes for complete reshaping.

Avoid waxing the eyebrows if there are signs of irritation or infection, like conjunctivitis.

glabellar
the area above the nose, between the eyebrows

The Upper Lip

The skin of the upper lip is more delicate and sensitive to waxing than is the eyebrow. Hard wax is the preferred choice of wax for this area, although strip waxes designed for the face and sensitive skin also work well. Hard wax is gentle yet effective because it surrounds the individual hairs, gripping them tightly as it sets and lifts off the skin. Another advantage to hard wax is that it can be removed in the direction of hair growth, thereby avoiding the possibility of distorting hair follicles, which happens when removing wax against hair growth.

To remove hair from the upper lip, first cleanse the area to remove any dirt, makeup, and oil. Next, apply a thin coating of tea tree oil to the entire upper lip area with a cotton-tip applicator (Figure 10–2). Allow a moment for the oil to absorb. While waiting for the oil to absorb, test the temperature of the wax by applying a small amount to the inside of the wrist. Dust the area lightly with powder. Stand behind the client at the top of the client's head. Using a small applicator, apply the wax, starting at the outer corner of the upper lip, up against the growth of the hair, to the center and back down to the outer corner, in the direction of hair growth. Avoid getting wax on the lip or in the nostrils. Apply a second coating over the top until it is approximately ⅛ inch thick. Make sure that the area under the nostril is covered and that no hairs are missed on the edge of the lip line. Make sure all edges are even and that the wax is a little thicker at the edge where it will be grasped for removal.

When the hair is fine, it can be removed in the direction of hair growth by pulling downward, from the center (Figure 10–3). However, stronger, more resistant hairs are more successfully epilated by pulling upward, against the hair growth. Apply immediate pressure with the index finger to reduce the smarting sensation. Finish with an application of a soothing antiseptic lotion. This service should be performed in 15 minutes with hard wax.

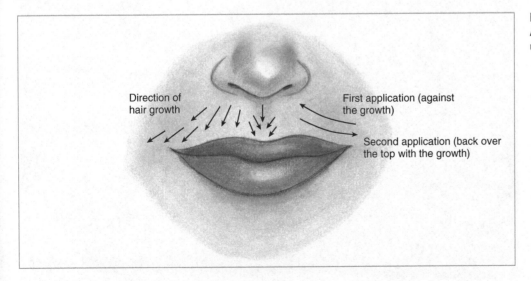

Direction of hair growth

First application (against the growth)

Second application (back over the top with the growth)

FIGURE 10–2
Applying hard wax to the upper lip

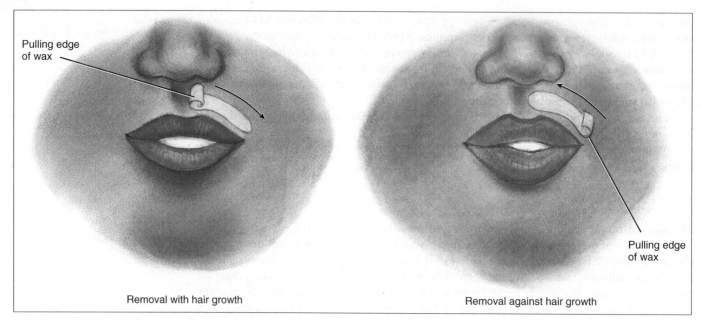

Pulling edge of wax

Pulling edge of wax

Removal with hair growth

Removal against hair growth

FIGURE 10–3 Two different techniques for removing hard wax from the lip

The Chin

Hard wax is an effective method of removing hair from the chin (Figure 10–4) and under the jaw, because it does a good job of gripping the stronger hairs that appear in this area while causing minimal irritation to the skin. Hard wax also removes vellus in the direction of growth without distorting follicles.

Begin the service by cleansing the area and removing any makeup. Dust the area lightly with powder. Ask the client to tilt the head back as far as possible. Decide how many sections of wax must be applied to remove the wax under the jaw and down the throat based on sections of approximately 2 inches by 3 inches, and divide the area accordingly. Stand behind the client, at the top of the head, and apply the wax with a large spatula to the first 2-inch-by-3-inch section, initially against the direction of hair growth, and then back over in the direction of hair growth. Make sure the edges are clean and that the end that will be grasped for removal is thicker. If the hair is vellus that has not been

FIGURE 10–4
Removing hair from the chin

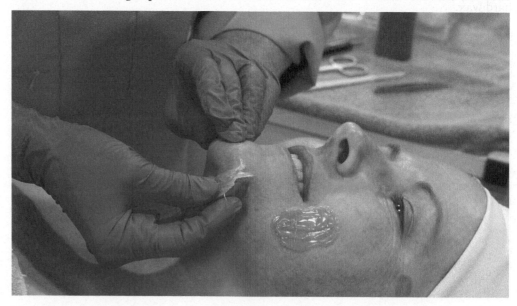

waxed before, it should be removed in the direction of hair growth. If the hair is terminal or has been waxed numerous times in the past against the hair growth so that it stands in a visibly unruly fashion, then the wax can be removed against the hair growth. The skin should always be held taut at the end of the strip where the pull will start and pressure applied immediately after. On completing the underside of the jaw, the chin hair can be removed. Due to the contours of the chin, this area should be waxed in small sections. If there is hair along the jawbone, it can be removed in a sideways fashion, similar to a lip wax. If the hair is fine, the wax can be removed from the center outward, almost in the direction of growth to prevent follicle distortion. This service should be performed in 15 minutes with hard wax.

The Sides of the Face

Waxing the sides of the face, especially against hair growth, can create problems for the client. Educate clients who have not had the sides of the face waxed before and inform them about the consequences. If the hair is strong, the wax should be removed against hair growth. If it is fine, it can be removed with hair growth. If there is visible vellus covering the rest of the face, clearing the area on the sides of the face can leave patchy bald spots that makes the vellus appear more obvious and the face strange.

When waxing the sides of the face, it is worth asking new clients if the waxing is for a special occasion. Let the clients understand in clear terms that they could experience redness and pimples.

Make sure the client's hair is well pinned back. Isolate and determine exactly how much hair is going to be removed from the face. If the sideburns must be shortened, begin by selecting hair equally on both sides of the face to be removed, pinning back the remaining hair. A good rule of thumb is to use the middle knob of cartilage on the inside edge of the ear called the *tragi*. Any hair that is more than ½ inch long should be buzzed or trimmed with scissors to ½ inch. The area should be thoroughly cleansed and free of makeup. Apply a dusting of powder. Turn the client's head to one side, exposing the side that will be waxed first. The technician should stand behind the client at the top of the client's head. Next, apply the wax with a medium-sized spatula, first in the opposite direction of hair growth, then immediately over the top in the direction of hair growth. Apply a second coating until it is approximately ⅛ inch thick. Allow the wax to set, losing its wet appearance. If the hair is strong and terminal, the wax should be pulled off against the direction of hair growth. If the hair is vellus, it can be removed with the hair growth. The skin should be held taut at the base of the pull. Rotate the head to complete the hair removal on the opposite side of the face. Soothe the waxed area with a mild antiseptic lotion. This service should be performed in 15 minutes with hard wax.

The Underarms

To prepare and position the client for underarm waxing, have the client remove the clothing and provide an appropriate drape for a sense of modesty. The client should lie down flat on the table on the back. Always wear gloves, because blood spots form in this area after the hair has been removed. Cleanse the underarms to remove all traces of perspiration and deodorant. If the hair is long so that it curls over, buzz it or trim it to ½ inch long. This will also make it easier to evaluate the different directions of hair growth. Apply a liberal coating of powder. This area should be completely dry for an effective wax removal. Stand behind the client at the top of the client's head. Have the client raise the first arm above the shoulder, placing the palm of the hand under the head. The other hand should reach across the body, and move the breast tissue down and away from the underarm.

Clearly ascertain the directions of hair growth, and identify which section is going to be waxed first. The initial section should be toward the outside edge. If there is a chance of hitting the client in the face, have the client turn the face away. The application of hard wax in this area should be done in small sections of approximately 1 inch by 2 inches.

Apply the wax initially against hair growth, and back over the top with hair growth. A few hairs may grow in different directions in the same cluster. This is an advantage of hard wax. When applied correctly against and then with hair growth, hard wax can cover the entire hair shaft, including hairs growing in different directions. As the wax sets, it shrinks and grips the individual hairs tightly. The wax should be removed against the hair growth in this area. Flick up the edge of the wax where the pull will begin, and hold the skin as taut as possible. Pull the wax away as fast as possible, as close to the skin as possible. Apply immediate pressure. Continue removing the hair in this manner, working from the outside inward. After all the hair has been removed, apply a soothing antiseptic lotion and continue with the other underarm. If the underarm is particularly tender, a cool cotton compress of cold water and baking soda can be applied to the area while the other side is being waxed.

To continue on the other side, have the client switch arms, again placing the hand behind the head and using the free hand to pull the breast tissue down and away from the area. Wax the second underarm, being careful to observe the hair-growth direction, because the directions could differ in the second underarm. Complete the waxing service and soothe the area. Reassure the client that any blood spots are because the hair was removed at the papilla, which is a sign of successful epilation. Let the client know that the blood spots will soon reabsorb into the skin. An application of salicylic acid can be applied with cotton. This helps to remove any redness and bumps and reduces the risk of ingrown hairs.

This service should take between 20 and 30 minutes with hard wax.

Do not wax the underarms if the client has had a mastectomy or suffers mastitis.

The Forearms

Strip wax is the fastest, most effective way to remove hair on the arms. However, because of the pulling direction against the growth of the hair, the hair may start to grow back in an unruly fashion, sticking up. Hard wax or sugaring will prevent unruly regrowth, but both methods are much slower. If the hair growth is strong or already unruly, then strip wax is the better choice. If the hair is fine and virginal, meaning it has not been removed before, it may be worth taking the time to remove the hair with hard wax, pulling it off in the direction of growth.

For hair removal of the forearm, give the client a gown or an apron to protect the clothing. The client should be sitting and the technician standing in front of the client. The forearm should be sprayed or wiped with an antiseptic solution, then dusted with powder. The client should hold the arm outstretched with the palm facing upward. Begin by waxing any unsightly hair on the inside. The hair grows downward, toward the wrist, so the wax should be applied upward first, then downward, following hair growth, removing the hair on that side in one strip. The strip should be 2 inches by at least 4 inches. With experience, the technician can extend this section to 2 inches by up to 8 inches. Begin in the lower half of the inside arm, toward the wrist, where there is less hair. When the wax is set but before it gets hard and brittle, lift the wax at the end farthest from the wrist. With a good grasp, pull off the wax as close to the skin as possible. Apply quick pressure.

The next section to wax should be just above the previous section. After completing the inner arm, the client should turn the still-outstretched arm so the palm faces downward. Holding the arm firmly in place and starting down at the wrist, apply the wax in a strip 2 inches wide and approximately 3 to 4 inches long, depending on the broadness of the arm, across the top of the arm from the outside (little finger side) to the inside (thumb side) and back over the top in the direction of growth, going outside. Once set, flick up the wax on the inside end (thumb side) and quickly pull the wax away, toward the outside as close to the skin as possible. Continue with similarly sized sections all the way up the forearm to the elbow. As the arms broaden, the length of the strip can elongate. Once the technique of waxing with hard wax has been mastered, a 2-inch strip can be left in between, and a second strip of wax can be applied while waiting for the first one to set. The left strip can be waxed after the areas on either side of it. Next, have the client hold the arm straight upward, bent at the elbow, and apply the wax to the side that follows down from the little finger. This can be done in one or two sections. The hair grows downward, toward the elbow. Apply the wax starting near the elbow, working downward, toward the wrist and the back over the top toward the elbow. Remove the wax by pulling from the wrist end upward, toward the elbow. Apply a soothing lotion and continue with the other arm.

The Hands

After completing the arm, proceed to wax the knuckles and hands, if necessary. To wax the hand, take the hand and apply the wax first against hair growth, then with hair growth, which is usually downward, toward the fingers, and angling out, toward the little finger. The entire top of the hand, not including the fingers, can be done at one time. Have the client form a fist by tucking the fingers under, as this tightens the skin. As the client's hand is "floating" without solid support, it is important to have a good grip of the hand when pulling quickly with hair growth. Pressure cannot be applied after the pull, because both hands are occupied. On the fingers, the hair grows toward the middle knuckle, so take one finger at a time, starting at the thumb, and work toward the little finger. Apply the wax to the hair against and then in the direction of hair growth. Once the wax is applied to all fingers, it should have set enough to start removing, beginning again at the thumb and quickly pulling off with hair growth. After removing all the hair, take the hand in a handshake grasp and apply a soothing lotion along the topside, toward the elbow (and shoulder, if upper arm was waxed) and down the underside to the hand. If the hand was waxed, finish by massaging the lotion into the hand and fingers. Proceed to the second arm.

Hair on the lower arm and hand should take approximately 30 minutes to remove.

The Bikini Area and Abdomen

Once more, the technician's standard of professional conduct is most important with the bikini-area and abdomen waxing service, perhaps above all others, due to the issues of modesty and feelings of vulnerability. Confidence and professionalism are paramount. A cheerful and confident professional manner will help put clients at ease. Less anxiety means less discomfort. If unknown at the time of booking, clarify the kind of bikini wax the client would like on entering the wax room. Do not discuss it in the reception area.

The bikini wax comes in three categories:

1. **American bikini wax,** which is the removal of hair exposed at the top of the thighs and just under the navel when wearing a regular bikini bottom
2. **French bikini wax,** which is the removal of even more hair than the American version, including the hair of the anus and labia, leaving only a strip of hair in the front
3. **Brazilian bikini wax,** which removes everything, front to back

A salon can choose its own names for these different bikini waxes, but it is most important that the client and technician both clearly understand what is to be removed and what should be left. Have the drape and a pair of disposable underpants on the table. Inform the client that you will step outside the room for a minute, at which time the client should remove all clothing from the waist down, leaving the underpants if it is for a regular bikini wax or changing into the disposable pair. Reenter the room by knocking first.

Analyze the area, skin, and hair, and ascertain if the client must help with stretching the skin. Always wear gloves for this service.

American Bikini Wax

When doing a regular American bikini wax, strip wax is preferred. Hard wax can be used for a regular bikini wax, but the best combination is strip wax for everything up to but not including the labia. If hard wax is to be used for the complete bikini wax, the following steps should be taken. If the client is wearing her swimsuit or her own briefs, they should

American bikini wax
a standard bikini wax in which hair is removed from either side of the panty line at the top of the thigh

French bikini wax
a bikini wax in which all the hair is removed from the pubic region except for a stripe of hair on the pubis

be protected with a paper towel, with one corner placed down the crotch area, so that two corners can be folded into the sides and the remaining corner tucked over the top. The technician's touch should always be firm and confident.

Using a small applicator, pull out from under the panty line any hair that must be removed. Leave the remainder tucked in behind the panty and give a clean, even line to both sides of the bikini area. If the hair is so long that it curls, trim it to ½ inch. This can be done quickly with scissors for a small amount of hair. If there is a considerable amount, an electric buzzer will be faster. Next thoroughly cleanse the area with an antiseptic cleaner and pat it dry. Then dust the area with powder. Have the client leave one leg straight, and bring the sole of the other foot to the level of the knee. If working first on the right side of the client's bikini area, have the client place her left hand firmly on the paper, fingers straight downward. Ask the client to keep her hands on the paper at all times to avoid getting wax on them and to avoid moving and distorting the line between the hair and paper. The free hand should be placed on the outer edge of the thigh to help pull the skin taut.

Working on the bent leg, apply the wax with the edge of a large spatula in the opposite direction of the hair growth initially, then pass back over in the direction of growth, which is downward, following the panty line. The first application of wax should be to the section farthest away and only up to the **femoral** (FEE-mohr-al) **ridge** in a strip 2 inches wide and 4 to 5 inches long. After mastering the use of hard wax, the technician can leave a 2-inch wide space and apply another strip of wax while waiting for the first application to set. The denser hair on the skin around the **pubis** (PYOO-bus) grows more horizontally and inward, toward the center. In the bikini area where the hair is terminal and strong, the pull of the wax should always be against hair growth. Lift the edge of the strip of wax nearest to the inner thigh. Place the hand firmly on that same end to hold the skin especially taut in this area, and quickly pull the strip of wax back, as close to the skin as possible, in a swift, continuous manner. Do not cut the movement short. Instead, make sure to follow through with the movement, even slightly beyond the placement of wax. Lifting too soon will cause discomfort to the client and could cause a bruise and break the wax. Apply immediate, firm pressure to alleviate the discomfort.

Once all the sections leading up to the panty line have been removed of hair, the hair that grows down from the femoral ridge can be removed. The client should bring the sole of her foot a little higher, to just above the knee. Apply the wax just two-thirds of the way down, first in an upward manner, then in the downward direction of hair growth. Leave enough space at the bottom to place the hand to hold the skin taut. Once the wax is set but still pliable, lift the edge to grasp. Holding the skin as taut as possible, quickly pull the strip straight upward, as close to the skin as possible, and follow by quickly placing the hand firmly on the area for relief. Finally, to finish that side, have the client lift her leg to the chest and grasp it behind the knee. This should expose the last remaining third of the hair that was too near the table to apply wax. This position also ensures that the skin is nice and taut. The wax is applied as before, against hair growth, then downward, with the pull back upward.

The regular/American bikini area with hard wax should take 20 to 30 minutes.

French Bikini Wax

The French style bikini wax is the removal of all hair, front to back, leaving a small stripe, sometimes called a "racing stripe." Follow all the directions for a regular/American bikini wax (see preceding), paying special attention to the cleaning and powdering of the areas to be waxed. Gloves are mandatory for this service.

To remove the hair between the buttocks, there are two positions. Technicians and clients develop their own preferences. In the first position, the client lies flat on the back and raises the knees to the chest and turns the soles of the feet in together. The client can grasp the feet between the legs with one hand, leaving the other hand free to move the panties aside. Hard wax is the preferred wax in this area, although strip wax can be used successfully. The wax is applied upward, against hair growth, then downward, over the top to a small section on the lowest part inside the buttock. Placing one hand at the bottom, pull the strip of wax quickly upward, as close to the skin as possible. Then apply the wax in the same manner to the next section above and so on until the area on that side of

femoral ridge
the ridge at the top of the inner thigh where the pectineus muscle attaches to the pubis forming a visible ridge on the inner thigh

pubis
the joined pair of bones composing the lower front of the hipbone

the inside buttock is cleared of hair. The client should then switch hands, moving the panties to the opposite side and grasping the feet with the other hand. Remove the hair in the same manner as the previous side.

In the second position, the client turns over and kneels. With one forearm resting on the table in front of her, the client has a free hand to move the panties to one side and to help separate the buttocks. The area is then waxed in the same manner as the previous position, except the wax is applied first in a downward direction, then back over the top in an upward direction, and the pull is downward. The client must switch hands when the technician is ready to switch to the other side of the inside of the buttocks.

The final part of the French bikini wax is the removal of the hair around the labia. Only depilatory hard wax should be used in this area. The direction of hair growth on the labia is inward; therefore, the pull in this direction cannot be outward, against the growth. With hard wax, the application can be applied from all directions, allowing for complete coverage to the hair shafts of all hairs. As the wax sets and shrinks, it grips each hair tightly, lifting away from the delicate skin of the labia. The pull of the wax can be made inward or upward, depending on the most obvious pattern of growth. Always remember to apply pressure immediately after each epilating pull. The French bikini area should take about 45 minutes. (See Chapter 11 for illustrations and photos of waxing procedures.)

Brazilian Bikini Wax

For the Brazilian bikini wax, the hair is removed as described for the French bikini wax (see preceding), including the area between the buttocks and the labia. In addition, the hair on the pubis is removed. Because of the direction of hair growth, the coarseness of the hair, and the delicate skin, hard wax should be used for this area. The wax is again applied first against hair growth, then with hair growth. The pull is made against the growth until close to the labia, where the direction of the pull should be straight upward.

Explain to the client that blood spots may appear and are to be expected. This is due to the fact that a rich, healthy blood supply was feeding the hair at the root. Because the hair was removed at the papilla, the blood gathers in the follicle until it realizes that there is no longer a hair there to "feed," at which time it reabsorbs back into the dermis. Blood spots are always *good* signs. With any first-time bikini wax, advise the client to return within 2 weeks for a follow-up wax. After that, the client should have the waxing service every 4 to 6 weeks. A Brazilian bikini wax should take approximately 30 to 45 minutes.

Clean, thick edges are important in this area to prevent annoying little pieces of wax from remaining in the hair. If bits of wax are left behind, gentle oil can be applied to help lift them off. All traces of wax should be removed at the end of the service. Then apply plenty of soothing antiseptic lotion. Salicylic acid can be applied with cotton. This helps to remove any redness and bumps and reduces the risk of ingrown hairs.

The Abdomen

To remove the hair on the abdomen, the client should lie flat on the back, and the top edge of the panties should be protected with a paper towel. Clean and dust the area with powder. If the client's skin is especially loose, in particular after pregnancy and childbirth, the client can help to pull the skin taut, reducing the level of discomfort. Abdominal hair grows inward from both sides, meeting at the center, where it then starts to grow downward. Above and around the navel the hair grows inward, toward the navel. The hair should be removed starting from the area around the navel. Apply the wax to the area, no more than an inch at a time, first against hair growth then following over the top in the direction of hair growth. Lift the edge toward the center, and, holding the skin taut with the free hand, pull the strip against the growth, as close to the skin as possible. Apply immediate pressure after each pull. Work continuously downward until close to the top of the panty line. Have the client hold the paper-lined panty top where removal should end. If the hair is fine, the option of removing the wax with the growth is available to help prevent unnecessary, irregular regrowth. After the hair is removed, remove any trace of wax and soothe the area with lotion. If the client has a pierced navel, to prevent tearing the area around the navel should not be waxed until it has healed to the point at which the ring or bar can be replaced, about 2 months after the piercing.

Allow 15 minutes to wax the abdomen.

The Feet and Toes

Sometimes clients just choose to get their toes waxed without a leg wax. This service can often be included at the time of a pedicure for an additional charge. Make sure the area to be waxed is warm. If the feet are cold, the wax will cool too quickly and become brittle and break without a successful epilation. Apply the wax to the top of the nearest foot, applying it upward in the direction of the leg, then downward, toward the toes. As soon as the wax sets, but before it cools, pull it quickly off, as close to the skin as possible against the growth, which is toward the leg. Apply immediate pressure to the area.

The direction of hair growth on the toes is usually visible. It grows slightly outward on the outer edge and downward, toward the nail in the middle of the toe. Like on the fingers, the wax can be applied to clean, powdered toes one toe at a time, starting with the little toe and working toward the big toe. Once all the wax has been applied, the toes should be ready for hair removal, again starting with the little toe and working toward the big toe. The hair is usually strong, so the pull should be against hair growth. Massage antiseptic lotion into the area to finish.

The Legs

Hard wax is not practical for leg waxing, because it is slower and more laborious than hot strip wax. See Chapter 11 for hair removal from the legs.

 Hard Wax Application and Techniques for Men

The Eyebrows

The glabellar area, often called the "unibrow," can be waxed with hard wax, as can the area under the brow. The client should be reclined or semireclined.

DO'S & DON'TS

Do's of the Hard Wax Nonstrip Method

- Always wash hands before and after touching a client.
- Always apply hard wax first *against* hair growth, then immediately follow over the top *with* hair growth, like frosting a cake or spreading peanut butter.
- Make sure to apply wax a little beyond the area of superfluous hair.
- Use powder to lift hairs and enable wax to get under the hair shaft.
- Always test the temperature of the wax on the inside of the wrist.
- Make sure the wax application is of a manageable size.
- Always hold the skin taut at the end where the pull will start.
- Make sure the strip of wax has a clean, even edge and is thicker at the end where it will be grasped for removal.
- Always discard used wax.
- Frequently stir the hard wax in the pot.

Don'ts of the Hard Wax Nonstrip Method

- Do not allow the wax to overheat and darken and lose its pliancy and removal properties.
- Do not reapply hard wax to an area more than twice in one visit.

Long and unruly brows can first be trimmed with scissors to prevent them from getting in the wax. Avoid overwaxing male eyebrows and giving them a feminine look. To wax and groom a man's eyebrows, first cleanse and dust the area with powder in the usual manner. Apply the wax first against hair growth, then immediately back over in the direction of hair growth. Once the wax is set, quickly pull away against the growth. After completing both sides, move to the center. For men, the eyebrow should always start just to the inside of the corner of the eye; everything else in the glabellar area can be waxed away. This procedure should take approximately 5 minutes.

The Ears

Only the hair on the outer rim and lobes of the ear can be waxed. Never attempt to wax hair inside the ears. Men often trim earlobe hair with scissors, leaving it bristly. Waxing the hair will result in much softer regrowth.

To wax the earlobes and rim, the client can either lie down flat or semirecline. Cleanse and dry the area. Apply the wax to the lobe in an upward then downward direction with a narrow stick. Allow the wax to set. Hold the earlobe taut with the free hand, and pull quickly upward. Proceed to the adjacent area above until all hair has been removed. After completing the second ear, soothe the area with lotion, massaging both earlobes simultaneously for a more pleasurable end to the service.

This service should take 20 minutes to complete with hard wax.

Note: Once the technician masters the technique of waxing with hard wax, a second and third area can be applied with wax while waiting for the first application to set.

WHAT DID I DO WRONG?

Q. *I have a hard time handling hard wax. It always seems to break when I remove it. What am I doing wrong?*

A. The breakage is a result of the wax being allowed to get too cold and hard or applied too thinly. Make sure the wax is at the right temperature when used, not lower than 125°F or 51.6°C. Remember, wax cools at approximately 7°F or 3.9°C per second. Get the application on as quickly as possible so that the underlying layers do not become cold and brittle before the top layer of wax is applied. As soon the wax starts to look opaque, loses its wet-looking shine, and is no longer sticky yet holds a fingerprint, it is time to remove it.

A second reason may be that the wax has been overheated and has either been allowed to remain at a high temperature for too long or has been allowed to get too low in the pot. This is evident if the wax loses its pale color and darkens.

Third, wax loses its removal properties when it gets old. New pieces of wax should be continuously applied to the older wax to restore it.

Q. *I always leave behind bits of wax on the skin and take as long or longer than the hair removal to pick them off.*

A. This happens because you are not producing an even edge when applying the wax. The edge that will be lifted and grasped for the pull should be a little thicker. Make sure your edges are clean and even. To remove any left-behind bits, do not pick away at them, because it is uncomfortable and annoying for the client. Instead, use a light, nonperfumed oil like grapeseed oil and massage the area gently to loosen and remove the bits.

Q. *My walk-in client had a number of breakouts on the upper lip that I waxed within days of receiving the service.*

A. In all probability, the area was not cleansed thoroughly enough. If traces of dirt and makeup remain on the skin, when the soothing lotion is massaged in at the end, it transports microorganisms to the vulnerable follicles and bacterial eruptions can occur. Even if the client is a walk-in, and you are accommodating her in your busy schedule, *all* steps for waxing should be followed, including the pre- and postparts of the service.

Conclusion

Being skilled in the use of hard depilatory wax sets technicians apart as "master waxers," instead of those who are limited to the use of strip wax. The qualities of hard wax make it possible for hair removal in situations that might otherwise contraindicate waxing. Being proficient in the use of different types of wax for hair removal enables technicians to expand their services to clients who may otherwise have to be turned away. The wax industry has now come full circle in its appreciation of the many positive benefits of hard wax and its reintroduction as a waxing service.

 Discussion and Review Questions

1. What is the proper melting point range of hard wax?
2. List three contraindications of hard wax removal.
3. In what direction of hair growth should hard wax be applied?
4. Name two indications that hard wax is the preferred choice for hair removal.
5. Name three reasons hard wax would *not* be the preferred choice of wax.

CHAPTER 11

Hot Wax Strip Method

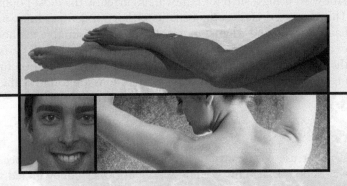

Chapter Outline

Learning Objectives ■ Key Terms ■ Introduction ■ Hot Strip Wax Basics
Hot Wax Application and Techniques ■ Conclusion ■ Discussion and Review Questions

Learning Objectives

By the end of this chapter, you should be able to:

1. List the pros and cons of strip waxing.
2. List the contraindications of strip waxing and explain when it would be indicated as the preferred choice of wax for hair removal.
3. Apply the wax in the correct manner and direction on all parts of the body.
4. Know the most common mistakes in the use of strip wax and how to avoid making those mistakes.

Key Terms

azulene	effleurage	hood	shinbone
blending	glycerol ester	septum	speed waxing
chamomile			

Introduction

Hot wax, using a strip for removal, is currently the most popular method of hair removal. This chapter describes the benefits of hot wax, when hot wax is the preferred choice of hair removal, and when it may not be the most suitable method. It also covers the method of application of hot wax with techniques and tips for all parts of the face and body. Near the end of the chapter is a "What Did I Do Wrong?" section for troubleshooting any waxing mishaps. Review and discussion questions are found at the end of the chapter.

Hot Strip Wax Basics

Wax for use with a strip is a hot wax typically made of beeswax and rosins. Some hot waxes do not actually contain wax, but rather honey mixed with **glycerol ester** of rosin. This kind of wax is fast and effective, and, when used correctly, causes limited discomfort. It is the most suitable method for hair removal on large areas of the body, such as the legs and back. The wax has a liquid-honey consistency, making it fast and easy to apply.

Manufacturers are now producing many other types of hot wax for the more sensitive skin that sports the stubbly coarse hair that still requires the hot wax strip method (Figure 11–1). These new waxes have a more opaque, creamier texture and can achieve a thin, liquid consistency at a lower temperature. They may also contain **azulene, chamomile,** or tea tree oil for their soothing and calming properties.

Hot wax is most commonly applied with a wooden spatula (Figure 11–2). However, on the market now are new methods of application, believed to be cleaner and more

glycerol ester
a refined rosin product that can be mixed with honey to produce a wax-like substance

azulene
an oil that is part of the chamomile essential oil, produced specifically by distillation

chamomile
a composite herb with strong-scented foliage and flower heads that contain a bitter, medicinal substance

FIGURE 11–1
Different hot waxes and wax heaters

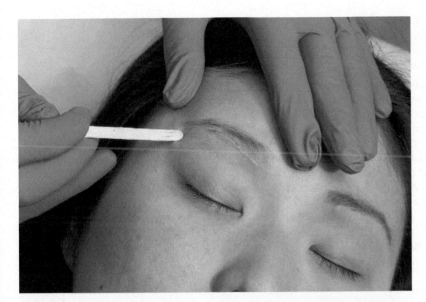

FIGURE 11–2
Applying wax
with a spatula

FIGURE 11–3
Applicator heads

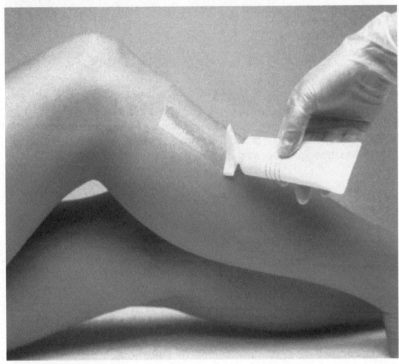

hygienic. These systems use disposable applicator heads or rollers that can be sanitized (Figure 11–3). They also come with prepackaged bottles or tubes of wax.

The disposable applicator used by the PhD system incorporates a back-flow valve, which prevents any back flow of wax into the tube. Because the wax is heated in prepackaged tubes with the applicator head attached to the tube, the technician can work quickly without having to keep returning to the wax pot. However, these applicators do not work for the small areas of the face (e.g., the eyebrows), where the use of a spatula is still the preferred method.

The roller method is portable and convenient, because it eliminates the need for the technician to keep returning to the pot. However, the roller in itself is no different than the spatula as far as hygiene is concerned. The only hygienic difference would be if the client used all the wax in the bottle exclusively. A spatula is still needed for small facial areas. The self-contained application methods can certainly improve the speed of the service, cutting time and increasing profits.

PROS & CONS

Pros of Hot Wax

- Hot wax is quick and easy to use.
- The technician, with training and practice, can become a speed waxer, cutting the typical service time in half and increasing profits.
- A shorter waxing time means minimal discomfort to the client.
- The warmth of the wax opens the pores, making the hair slide out more easily.
- Hot wax epilates hair, meaning it removes the hair from below the skin, often at the root, without destroying the root. When the hair grows back, it is often softer.
- Many clients experience some reduction in hair growth after multiple wax services. When the hair is removed at the root or papilla, the new papilla must reestablish itself in the follicle. Not only does this take time, with continual waxing removal it may cause the papilla to weaken and cause extended periods between regrowth, as well as a reduction in hair growth. This is especially apparent in the hair growth on frequently waxed women's legs as those women reach menopause.

Cons of Hot Wax

- The rosins in hot wax can adhere to the skin and are therefore the primary cause of irritation.
- Until a technician is skilled with the use of hot wax it can be messy, leaving thread-like, sticky trails to be cleaned up.
- An area cannot be rewaxed immediately.
- Hair must be ¼ inch long before rewaxing.
- Strip wax is not the best choice to use on areas with multiple hair directions (e.g., the underarms, where following the directional rules is difficult). Hard wax works better.
- Strip wax is not the best choice of wax when doing a Brazilian bikini wax, because it is impossible to apply the wax in the hair-growth direction and pull away effectively against the growth due to the vaginal opening. Hard wax is the preferred method in this area.
- Regrowth after strip waxing is often irregular. Where the hair, albeit unsightly, once lay uniformly in a certain direction and close to the skin, after removal with the strip it tends to grow back irregularly, standing more upright, in the way it would if one had goose bumps. This is because the hair is removed against its natural growth direction and the follicles that grew at a 20-degree angle become distorted by the pull and start to grow at a deeper angle.

Hot Wax Application and Techniques

The wax should be heated according to manufacturer's specifications, which are usually found on the can of wax or in a brochure accompanying the wax heater. All literature accompanying the equipment should be kept and made available for new employees. If possible, use the wax that goes with the wax heater. If the technician chooses to try a different brand of wax, then a thermometer should be used to test the temperature of the wax and make sure that the wax is at the recommended level. A notation should be made on the pot's dial indicating that level.

Hot wax should be thin enough to run off the spatula easily; its edge should glide along the client's skin, leaving a thin film on the skin.

Even though the wax heater may be thermostatically controlled, it is wise to always test the wax first, on the inside of the lower arm where the skin is more sensitive and where there is no hair. If the wax is the right consistency and at a comfortable temperature, it is safe to use. If the wax is too cool and thick, it will not glide easily onto the skin, and it will pull and possibly lift the skin. It will also be tougher to remove.

Once the applicator has been dipped into the wax, its underside should be scraped on the edge of the wax pot to prevent unnecessary dripping and lack of wax control. Many pots come with scraping bars to allow excess wax to be returned to the pots and not

INDICATIONS & CONTRAINDICATIONS

Contraindications of Hot Wax

- Inflamed or irritated skin should not be waxed.
- Hot wax cannot be used on people who use any glycolic or other AHA skin-care treatments, Retin-A, topical antiacne medicines such as Accutane and Differin or who are receiving glycolic or other strong exfoliating treatments.
- Circulatory disorders that cause easy bruising (e.g., phlebitis and thrombosis).
- Epilepsy is contraindicated, if medication causes easy bruising.
- Diabetes is contraindicated, depending on degree of severity and degree of healing.
- Fractures and sprains should not be waxed until completely healed.
- Hemophiliacs should not be waxed.
- Herpes and herpes simplex (cold sore) areas should not be waxed while active. Prophylactic medication should be taken before waxing.
- Clients with a lack of skin sensation should not be waxed.
- Moles, skin tags, and warts should not be waxed.
- If the areas needing to be waxed take more than 20 minutes of the pregnant client lying flat on her back, waxing should wait until after the birth of the baby.
- Scar tissue, including keloids, should be avoided.
- Sunburned areas should not be waxed until completely healed.
- Skin disorders (e.g., eczema, seborrhea, and psoriasis) should not be waxed when the skin is broken.
- Varicose veins should be avoided, although surrounding areas may be waxed.
- The drugs that contraindicate waxing include tetracycline, now found in birth-control pills, because it can cause an adverse reaction with hot wax; blood thinners like Cumadin and Warfarin; and drugs that treat epilepsy, because they cause easy bruising.

dripped across the treatment area. The applicator should be held at a 45-degree angle to the skin, allowing the wax to glide off it. The applicator should never be placed flat on the skin.

Hot wax is always applied in the direction of hair growth and removed against hair growth. For ease and the client's comfort, the waxing should start where there is no hair at the end of the first epilating pull. It is always better to work from lesser hair growth to denser hair growth. The wax should not be applied to a greater area than is going to be immediately removed. Even with **speed waxing**, the strip should not end where there is still wax (Figure 11–4).

The strip should be placed over the wax, always allowing a sufficient free edge to grasp easily (Figure 11–5). Once the strip is placed over the wax, it only needs to be smoothed or rubbed once or twice to adhere to the wax and be effective. Excess rubbing is only time consuming and annoying to the client, who is braced and ready for that swift pull. Do not prolong the anticipated moment of discomfort by excess rubbing. The rubbing should always be done in the direction of the hair growth. The hand that is not doing the pulling should always be positioned at the free edge end of the strip to hold the skin taut during the pull (Figure 11–6).

The pull of the strip should always be against the hair growth (Figure 11–7). It should be quick and decisive and as close to the skin as possible for minimal discomfort to the client and maximal effectiveness in hair removal. Immediately after the pull, the free hand that was holding the skin taut should be placed quickly on the area that was just worked. On large body areas, this can be done with an almost slapping technique, but not too hard. On a small area, like the face, the hand, or a finger or two should be immediately placed on the area, applying gentle pressure.

Following that, new wax is applied to the next adjacent area, and so on until the job is completed. Placing the used strip over the sticky areas, giving it a quick rub, and lifting it off can remove residual wax from the skin. The same technique can also be used to go back and remove any stray hairs that got left behind. Locate the hair, place the strip over it, and, with a finger, apply some pressure and quickly lift off. Hot wax should never be applied to an area that was just waxed. Along with the hair, a layer of dead skin cells will have also been

speed waxing
technique in which wax is applied to an entire area and removed rapidly with the same strip or a small number of strips

FIGURE 11–4
Muslin placement showing
free edge

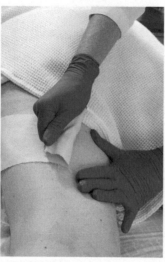

FIGURE 11–5
The free hand should always be
at the end of the free edge to
hold the skin taut

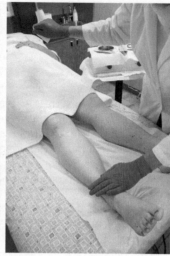

FIGURE 11–6
Proper follow-through
pulling strip

FIGURE 11–7
Incorrect application

removed, compromising the skin and making it fragile and vulnerable. Further waxing may cause significant discomfort, irritation, and redness. Some of the hairs can be tweezed, but if there are too many to tweeze, point out to the client that some new, shorter anagen hairs were not quite long enough, and invite the client to return within a week to clean those areas.

After the removal, the area should be soothed with the appropriate antiseptic lotion.

Hot Wax Strips

Two popular types of strips can be used with hot wax: (1) muslin and (2) pellon (Figure 11–8). The choice is an individual one and can be based on what the technician was trained with or is used to, or on cost effectiveness. The cheapest way of buying strips is to buy the rolls of muslin in bulk and cut the strips. However, time is money, and this may not be cost-effective if it takes time away from clients. When purchasing muslin in bulk, avoid purchasing muslin that has not been treated with a fabric protector or softener, because the wax does not adhere to chemically treated muslin. Pellon strips are preferable

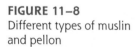

FIGURE 11–8
Different types of muslin
and pellon

for speed waxing as opposed to muslin, because the latter has a tendency to bleed through as the wax builds, making the hands sticky. There are advantages to building the wax on the strip. It is still effective at removing any missed hairs without adding more hot wax to the skin. If the wax starts to bleed through, a little dusting powder can be sprinkled onto the muslin strip to prevent the hands from getting sticky.

The downside to pellon is that, when it is used on an area that is cold, such as the tops of the feet, a thin layer of the pellon can be left behind with the wax. Rubbing the cold area first and warming it can avoid this problem. Both kinds of strips can be used repeatedly during the service and are more effective as there is some wax buildup. The two most effective sizes of strips are 9 inches × 3 inches for the large areas of the torso and 3 inches × 1 inch for the small areas of the face.

Hot Wax Application and Techniques for Women

The Forehead

Many women have asymmetrical hairlines or widow's peaks. They reluctantly wear bangs or style their hair to disguise these irregularities. Waxing is a fast and simple solution to even the hairline. The hair at the hairline that is terminal but soft can be waxed, but as the skin in that area may be delicate, a cream wax or even a hard wax may be more suitable. If the hair is of the same strength as the hair covering the rest of the scalp, and with a deep follicle, then it should not be waxed but eliminated with electrolysis. Following is the procedure:

1. Have the client hold a mirror and together define the desired hairline.
2. With a comb or wooden applicator, isolate the hair that must be removed, and clip back the remaining hair.
3. Trim the hair to be removed to ¼ inch, either with scissors or a hair trimmer.
4. Cleanse, prepare, and powder the area.
5. Ascertain the direction of hair growth.
6. Apply the wax in a small section of approximately 1 inch × 1½ inches, following the direction of growth to a point where it ends in a hair-free zone.
7. Apply the strip, making sure there is enough of the strip at the end that is free of wax so it will be easy to lift and pull. Muslin works better than pellon on small areas that have stronger hair.
8. Quickly rub over the strip, also in the direction of hair growth. Rubbing twice suffices.
9. With one hand, hold the skin taut at the end point, grab the free end, and quickly pull back the strip, following as closely to the skin as possible.
10. Quickly take the hand that was holding the skin taut and apply gentle pressure to the area just waxed.
11. Move to the next adjacent area and so on until the job is complete.
12. Apply a soothing aftercare lotion.

The Eyebrows

For eyebrow service, the client should be semireclined and handed a mirror for viewing the desired shape and any irregularities.

The waxing of every other part of the face and body is purely about hair removal, but the waxing of the eyebrows is also about understanding shape, balance, and the ability to create an illusion. Waxing the eyebrows to remove hair is just one part of the entire picture, because creating the perfect shape for a client takes skill, knowledge, and a good eye.

There are multiple factors to consider when defining the shape of an eyebrow, the first being the age of the client. The sophisticated, thin eyebrow of a woman in her forties may not suit a teenage girl. A more mature woman may benefit from a more obvious arch, especially if her eyes are starting to **hood**, because it gives the illusion of more lift and opens the eyes more. Thinner eyebrows generally suit women with very short hairstyles.

hood
the sagging of skin from under the eyebrow onto the eyelid

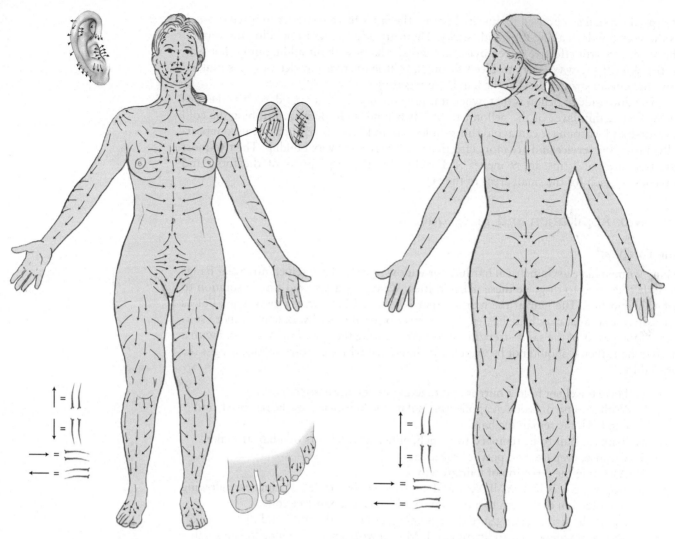

FIGURE 11–9 Hair growth directions, anterior

FIGURE 11–10 Hair growth directions, posterior

FIGURE 11–11
On a round face,
the eyebrow arch should be
defined on the inside of
the pupil

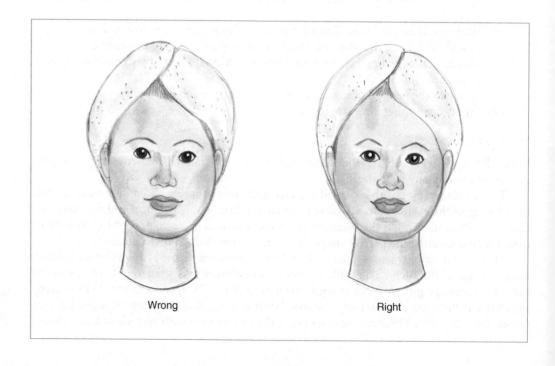

Wrong

Right

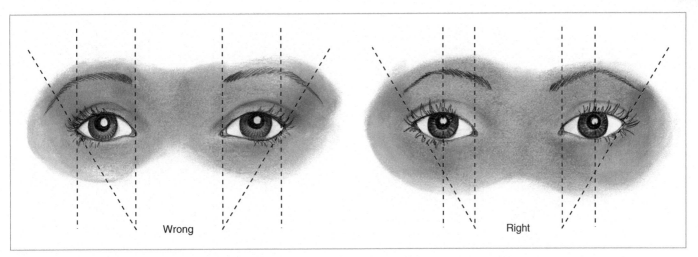

FIGURE 11–12 Diagram showing arch position for wide-set eyes

Also look at what the client is wearing. If the client has full makeup, she probably appreciates a more groomed, sophisticated eyebrow. If there is no makeup, and she typically does not wear makeup, be more conservative with the initial shape, keeping it natural and not too thin. If it is the client's first eyebrow wax, clear communication is important. If it is the client's day off, she may be "dressed down," whereas ordinarily she would sport business attire and a full face of makeup.

Other considerations include the shape of the face and the placement of the eyes. If the client has a round or broad face (Figure 11–11), or if the eyes are set wide apart (Figure 11–12), it helps to bring the point of the arch to the inside of the pupil as the client looks straight ahead. This creates the illusion that the face is narrower or that the eyes are closer together. If her face is narrow (Figure 11–13) or the eyes are close set (Figure 11–14), by placing the point of the arch to the outside of the pupil as the client looks straight ahead the technician can create the illusion that the face is wider or the eyes are more in balance with the face.

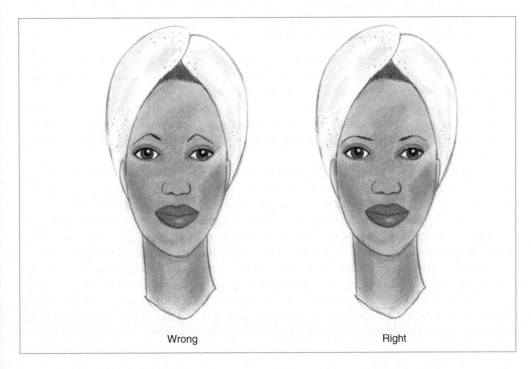

Wrong   Right

FIGURE 11–13
On a narrow face, the eyebrow arch should be on the outside of the pupil

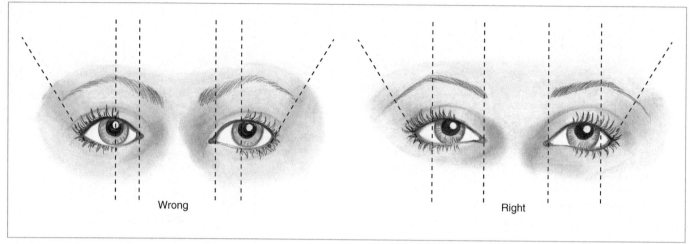

FIGURE 11–14 Diagram showing arch position for close-set eyes

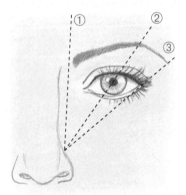

FIGURE 11–15
Use these guidelines when defining the eyebrow shape:
1. Start;
2. Point of arch;
3. End point of eyebrow

When defining the eyebrow shape, the following guidelines should be used (Figure 11–15):

1. **Start**—With the client looking straight ahead, rest a thin, wooden applicator orangewood stick or pencil along the side of the nose, just above the nostril and straight up to the inner corner of the eye. This will determine where the eyebrow should start. Any hair to the outside of the stick should be removed, and any space on the inside should be filled with an eyebrow pencil. Some clients have wider nostrils than others, which could affect the start line. Placing the stick just above the nostril gives a more accurate start point.

2. **Point of arch**—To find the correct point of the arch, for a normal face shape and eye placement, place the stick at the base of the nose and ask the client to look straight ahead. Slide the stick across so that the stick crosses in front of the pupil. The point at which the stick touches the eyebrow is where the point of the arch should be.

3. **End**—To find the correct ending of the brow, the technician should slide the stick, still at the base of the nose, farther around so that it crosses over the outer corner of the eye. The point at which the stick meets the brow is where the brow should end. Any hair that goes beyond the stick should be removed, and any space on the inside of the stick should be penciled in.

There should be a clear ascent from the start to the point of arch and a clear descent from the point of arch to the end. The line should be gradual and tapered. Avoid going from too thick on the ascent to too thin on the descent.

When shaping between the brows, there are also a few factors to consider. A common mistake for brow hair that grows straight up is to simply wax it away, causing the brow line to start farther in than it should when the hairs would be better trimmed around and the corner taken off.

Another point to remember is that hair grows upward between the brows but downward at the top of the nose. Furthermore, when hairs grow inward, they can be removed by tweezing in the direction of the desired new growth rather than being waxed away. This is accomplished by grasping the hair as close to the follicle opening as possible, turning the hair with the tweezers to the new desired direction of growth, then plucking them out. Over time with this repeated method, the hair can be retrained to grow in the desired direction.

Once the desired shape of the eyebrow has been ascertained, the area can be prepared for waxing, first by cleansing the area and removing any makeup from both eyes and from the glabellar, which is the area in between. After this, a little tea tree oil can be applied to all areas with a cotton-tip applicator, to help prevent redness and to provide antibacterial properties. Follow with a little dusting of powder. To wax the brow, use a tiny amount of wax on a thin applicator and separate and pull down, away from the brow line, any hair that must be removed. This can be done with the technician facing the client. The actual waxing is better done standing behind the client. Move the thin applicator with a small amount of wax on it along the underside of the brow, from the start point, following the direction of growth to the end point. Then place the 1 inch × 3 inch strip over the wax, leaving a free edge at the end point to grasp. After two quick strokes, also in the direction of hair growth, the forefinger and middle finger are placed at the end point holding the skin taut, and the strip is pulled quickly backward, against the hair growth and as close to the skin as possible. Gentle pressure is then quickly applied with the fingers that held the skin taut.

This process is then repeated on the other eyebrow. When the second eye is completed, the area between the brows can be waxed, first by applying the wax between the brows in an upward direction, rubbing on the strip twice and pulling down, then removing any hairs at the top of the nose growing downward.

If any wax falls onto the client's lashes, request that the client keep the eyes gently closed. Slide some damp cotton under the client's lashes, then, using a cotton-tip applicator and petroleum jelly, stroke down the lashes until the wax slides off.

After the waxing is complete, tweeze any stray hairs that were not removed or any stubs that were too short to grip the wax. This should be done before any soothing lotion is applied, because the lotion causes the tweezers to slide up the slick hair and not tweeze easily, causing additional discomfort to the client. A soothing lotion can then be gently massaged over the waxed area. When doing this, both hands should massage the lotion into the area simultaneously, finishing with gentle pressure on the client's temples, before lifting. This ensures a pleasant finish to the service.

Allow 15 minutes for a regular eyebrow wax and 30 minutes for an eyebrow shape.

Avoid waxing the eyebrows if there are signs of irritation or infection, like conjunctivitis.

The Upper Lip

With any face waxing, it is important to ask new clients if the service is for a special occasion and to let the clients understand in clear terms that there could be redness and pimples. A cream wax designed for sensitive skin is the wax of choice for this area, because it reduces redness.

The upper lip can be divided into two equal sections for hair removal, divided under the nose. The hair grows downward and outward at a slight angle, following the lip line. Under the nose, however, it grows straight downward. As it is impossible, due to the position of the nose and the mouth, to pull the hair against its growth to remove those hairs, the hair, which is usually fine, is easily removed when pulling across the lip line against the growth with the rest of the hair on that half of the upper lip.

To begin, cleanse the area, apply tea tree oil, then dust the area with powder. Using a medium-sized applicator, apply a thin layer of wax, starting under the **septum** (SEP-tum) of the nose, in a downward, outward direction. It is important to make sure that the area under the nostril is covered and that no hairs are missed on the edge of the nostril. This is an area that should not be immediately rewaxed. Make sure the wax goes as close to the lip line as possible without getting wax on the lips or in the nostrils. There are often nuisance hairs along the immediate lip line and the outside corner of the lip line that stand up and bother clients, especially in rearview or magnifying mirrors. The tissue of the lips is fragile and can be easily lifted. If any wax gets onto the lips, do not remove it with a strip but with either petroleum jelly or a wax-removing lotion for the skin.

Immediately after the wax is applied, place the 1 inch × 3 inch strip over it, leaving enough of a free edge on the outside to grasp. With fingers holding that same outer edge of the lip taut and stable, grasp the strip and pull it quickly across the lip in the opposite direction of hair growth, as close to the skin as possible. Follow through with a quick, sweeping movement, beyond the waxed area.

Quickly apply pressure to the area with the hand that held the skin taut to ease the smarting sensation.

septum
the part of the nose that divides the two nostrils

Proceed to the other side of the lip, and finish by gently massaging both sides of the lip area simultaneously with the hands. Finish by lifting at the corners of the mouth. Offer the client some ice in a baggie if the area remains sensitive or feels puffy.

This service should be performed in 10 minutes.

The Chin

When a client requests a chin wax, it is often considered being not only the chin, but the small area just under the jaw.

Waxing should not be considered the primary choice of hair removal for the chin if the client has never removed the hair with wax before. Waxing, especially with hot wax against hair growth, causes hair on the chin to grow back irregularly, standing, looking wispy. Along with removing the hair that is unwanted, some fine, nonbothersome vellus is also removed, leading to more irregular regrowth. This problem can continue to grow and be aggravated with every waxing service.

The upper lip has two natural boundaries: (1) the lip itself and (2) the nasal fold that runs from the nose and mouth. The eyes also have two natural boundaries: (1) the eye itself and (2) the eyebrow. These boundaries prevent the spreading of regrowth and the need to wax it away. The chin has no such boundaries. The more it is waxed, the more it will need to be waxed, spreading the problem along the jaw and up the sides of the face. As the facial hair is stripped away in one area, the hair adjacent to it appears more obvious and apparent. After multiple wax treatments, a proverbial can of worms opens, and before long the client must deal with things like excessive irregular hair growth that must grow in before it can be waxed again, ingrown hairs, folliculitis, and the risk of injury to the skin as it matures, becomes fragile, and develops liver spots. The client will be unable to use many antiacne or antiaging treatments. Finally, the client will be held hostage to a lifetime of scheduling wax treatments, and the cost it entails. The hair-removal professional will offer a much more worthwhile service by recommending other forms of hair removal, such as electrolysis as a first choice. If the client does not consider that an option, then hard wax or sugaring should be considered, because both techniques remove the hair in the direction in which it grows without distorting the follicle and its regrowth.

If it is ultimately decided that the chin and under the jaw are *both* going to be waxed, the entire area should be cleansed and dusted with powder. Under the jaw should be dealt with first. Ask the client to tilt back the head, then apply the wax to the underside from the jawbone down the throat in the direction of hair growth, which is usually straight downward. Farther down the neck, the hair starts to slightly change direction, growing away from the center of the neck. If there is a considerable span of growth, the area can be divided into two strips in the center. If three strips are warranted, the first strip will be in the center; the second and third will be on either side. After the wax is applied, place the strip over the wax, rub twice in the direction of hair growth, place a hand at the bottom of the throat to ensure that the skin is taut, and quickly pull the strip upward, against the growth. Apply immediate pressure afterward.

Waxing the top of the chin is usually done in two or three sections, depending on the amount of hair growth. Do not cross from one surface or plane to another, which means do not take the wax downward, across the jaw bone, but instead address one surface area at a time. Failing to do this and trying to wax across a plane ignoring the contours of the face makes achieving a successful, clean pull, close to the skin, impossible. Different plains should be dealt with separately. When pulling the strip backward, remember to hold the skin especially tight at the jawbone and to apply direct pressure right after. End the service with a mild antiseptic soothing lotion.

If there are just a few fine but pigmented hairs on the chin between nonbothersome vellus, rather than applying wax to the whole area and stripping the chin of all hair in the path of the wax, dot those hairs individually with wax, leaving as much of the vellus intact as possible. Another technique is to use the wax on the strip left over from the client's lip wax, and, with a finger, press on each hair and quickly pull away, limiting the amount of vellus from being disturbed.

This service should be performed in 10 minutes.

The Sides of the Face

As with the chin, waxing the sides of the face can create problems for the client. If the client has not had the sides of the face waxed before, educate and inform the client of the consequences. As the body's largest organ, healthy skin is supposed to have hair. Vellus is normal and acceptable. Unfortunately, the bright lights and strong magnification of mirrors in bathrooms create often unrealistic, distorted, and illusionary reflections. Have the client look in a regular, handheld mirror an arm's length away and in normal lighting. If the hair is not visible, *it is not a problem*. Any disturbance of that hair could create a bigger problem for the client in the future, and cause the client to regret ever having this service.

The client should understand that, with multiple wax treatments with strip wax, the hair follicles become distorted, causing the hair to grow back irregularly. The vellus that had shallow follicles closer to the epidermis may gradually grow deeper into the dermis and closer to a richer blood supply. As the female client enters menopause and the balance of hormones changes, reducing estrogen and increasing male androgens, these hormones feed the hairs, causing them to become terminal in their growth pattern. In time, the hairs on the chin, with multiple wax treatments, may not be removed with wax, leaving the technician or the client to remove them with tweezers. The extensive regrowth can be unsightly, and ingrown hairs and folliculitis could result. As the client's skin matures, it becomes more fragile, and wax treatments could cause an adverse reaction. The client is then left in a quandary, and the only solution to which is electrolysis, which should have been recommended years earlier when the hair growth was only slight.

If the hair is visible in the preceding situation, and requires removal, electrolysis should be the first choice. If that is not an option, then hard wax is more desirable than strip wax to avoid distorting the follicles and also because the hard wax better grips the stronger hairs of the sideburn but without irritating the skin as much. Sugaring is an option too, if the hair is not too strong.

After learning all the pros and cons, if the client still chooses to proceed with the service, it should be done as follows. Make sure the client's hair is well pinned back. Hand the client a mirror and ascertain exactly what hair is to be removed. If the sideburns must be shortened, begin by selecting the hair equally on both sides of the face that should be removed, pinning back the remaining hair well. A good rule of thumb is to use the middle knob of cartilage on the inside edge of the ear called the tragi. After isolating the hair to be removed (Figure 11–16), any hair that is more than ½ inch long should be buzzed or trimmed with scissors to ½ inch. The area should then be cleansed and dusted with powder.

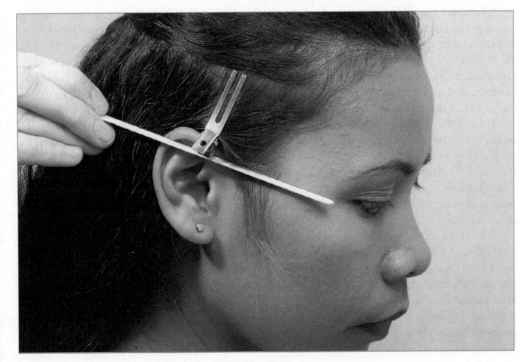

FIGURE 11–16
Isolating the hair for removal

Have the client turn the head to one side. Apply the wax in the direction of growth. If the area to be waxed cannot be done in one pull, begin on the inside edge (toward the nose) first, followed by the area closer to the ear.

Place the wax strip over the area, again leaving enough of a free edge to grasp. Hold the skin taut just below the grasping point and quickly pull back against the hair growth, as close to the skin as possible.

Proceed with the second side in a like manner. Calm the area with a soothing antiseptic lotion.

This service should take between 10 and 20 minutes, depending on whether the hair must be trimmed. More time would be needed if it is the client's first face wax and other suggestions are going to be offered.

The Chest Area

Although the areola should not be waxed, hairs surrounding the areola can be waxed away. They grow in a circular direction, surrounding the areola, but not in any one direction. The different directions of growth should be determined and each hair waxed individually, if necessary. The area should be cleansed and dried. Individually coat each hair with a thin layer of wax in the direction of growth and, using the same size strip that would be used for an eyebrow or a lip wax, gently rub over each hair, also in the direction of growth. Quickly whip back against the growth, holding the skin taut with a couple of fingers at the start of the pull.

Hair can also grow in the chest area upward in the décolleté and downward and inward over the breast and into the cleavage.

The Underarms

There is often asymmetry to the hair growth of the underarms. One side may have two different directions of growth while the other side may have three directions. While strip wax works well on this hair, it must be applied following the different sections of hair growth. If there are different directions in the same cluster, there could be breakage and some hairs left behind. Because the same area cannot be waxed a second time during that service, the remaining hair must be tweezed. Hard wax is very effective in this area, because it goes on against the hair growth, coating the hair in all directions. As the wax hardens, it grips the hair and lifts it away from the delicate skin of the underarms. A more thorough removal is achieved.

Whatever the choice of wax, the preparation of the client is the same. To prepare and position the client for this service, have the client first remove the clothing, and provide an appropriate drape for modesty. The client should lie down flat on the table (Figure 11–17). Wear gloves, because this is an area in which blood spots form after the hair has been removed. If strip wax is going to be used, the area should be cleaned with a mild antiseptic cleanser, and all traces of antiperspirant or deodorant removed. If the hair is long so that it curls over, it should be buzzed or trimmed to ½ inch in length. This will also make it easier to evaluate the different directions of hair growth. Make sure both underarms are dry. To be sure that they are dry, dust them both with powder. Select which underarm is going to be waxed first, and have the client raise that arm above the shoulder, placing the hand behind the head. The other hand should then reach across the body and move the breast tissue down and away from the underarm. Clearly ascertain the directions of growth and which section is going to be waxed first. The initial section should be toward the outside edge. If there is a chance of hitting the client in the face, have the client turn the face away.

The technician should stand behind the head of the client. The wax should be thinly applied with the edge of the spatula at a 45-degree angle in the direction of growth (Figure 11–18). Firmly press the strip over the wax and rub in the direction of growth, allowing enough free edge to grasp at the end. Place the free hand firmly at that same end, holding the skin taut, and quickly pull against the hair growth and as close to the skin as possible. Follow the movement through, close to the skin. Starting to pull upward too soon will bruise the client and/or cause extreme redness. After removal, quickly apply

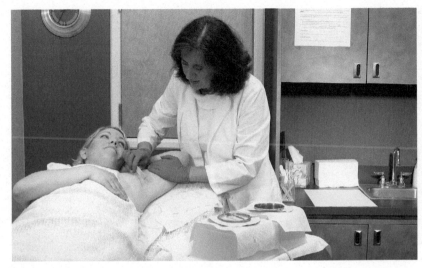

FIGURE 11–17 Proper position of client for underarm wax

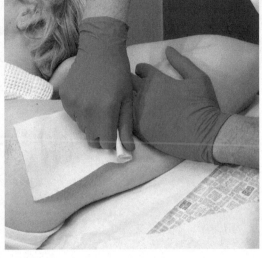

FIGURE 11–18 Wax application to underarm

pressure to the area. Proceed to the next section, repeating in the same manner until the hair has been removed. Apply a soothing lotion to the area. If the underarm is particularly tender, a cool cotton compress of cold water and baking soda can be applied to the area while the other side is being waxed.

To continue on the other side, have the client switch arms, placing the hand behind the head and using the free hand to pull the breast tissue down and away from the area. Wax the second armpit, being careful to observe the hair growth direction, as it could well differ. Complete the waxing service and soothe the area. Reassure the client that any blood spots are due to the fact that the hair was removed at the papilla and that they are a sign of successful epilation. Let the client know that the blood spots will soon reabsorb into the skin. Make sure the client has no residual stickiness in the armpits, because this can make the area feel tender if the skin sticks together. It is also annoying to find clusters of clothing fibers stuck to the area.

This service should take approximately 15 minutes.

Do not wax the underarms if the client has had a mastectomy or suffers mastitis.

The Arms

Strip wax is the fastest, most effective way to remove hair from the arms. However, because of the pulling direction against the growth of the hair, the hair may start to grow back in an unruly fashion, sticking up. Hard wax or sugaring will prevent unruly regrowth, but both methods are much slower.

The Forearms.   For hair removal of the forearm, the client should be given a gown or apron to protect the clothing. The client should be sitting and the technician standing in front of the client (Figure 11–19). The forearm should be sprayed or wiped with an antiseptic solution, then dusted with powder. The client should hold the arm outstretched with the palm facing up. Begin by waxing any unsightly hair on the inside. The hair grows downward toward the wrist, so the wax should be applied thinly and downward, following the growth. Begin in the lower half of the inside arm, toward the wrist, where there is less hair. Apply the strip over the wax, leaving enough of a free edge to grab. Rub just a couple of times, also in a downward motion, then pull the strip away quickly against the growth, but as close to the skin as possible. Apply quick pressure. The next section to wax should be just above the previous section. After completing the inner arm, the client should turn the still-outstretched arm so the palm faces downward. Holding the arm firmly in place and starting down at the wrist, apply the wax across the top of the arm from the inside (thumb side) to the outside (little finger side), the width of the strip. Place

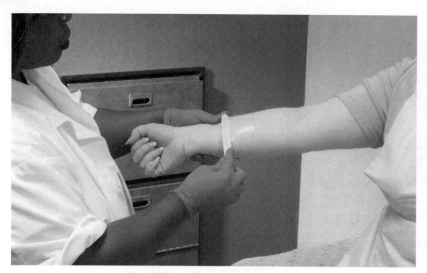

FIGURE 11-19 Proper position of client and technician for forearm wax

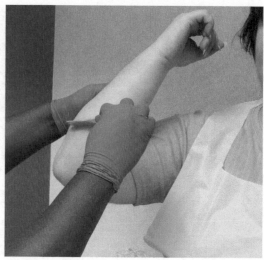

FIGURE 11-20
Bend the arm to remove hair on back of forearm

the strip over the wax, rub twice in the direction of growth, and pull quickly back against the growth. Continue in strip size sections all the way up the forearm to the elbow. Next, have the client hold the arm straight upward, bent at the elbow, and apply the wax to the side that follows down from the little finger (Figure 11-20). This can be done in two sections. The hair grows downward, toward the elbow. Apply the wax to the first section, starting near the wrist, working up, toward the elbow. Proceed in the usual manner.

The Upper Arms.   Most often, the upper arm has just a few hairs right above the elbow. These can often be removed with the wax that is already on the strip. The strip will remove the more obvious hairs, leaving some shorter hairs behind. This technique is known as **blending**, because it produces a gradual link between completely hairless and some hair. If the hair of the upper arm is more obvious and requires complete removal, then the client should relax the arm, allowing the forearm to rest on the lap. The wax should be applied in the direction of growth, which is downward, toward the elbow. The technician should remove the hair in sections starting toward the elbow and working upward toward the shoulder, "blending" if necessary at the top.

The Hands

After completing the lower and upper arm, the technician should proceed to wax the knuckles and hands, if necessary. To wax the hand, take the hand and apply the wax with the growth, which is usually downward, toward the fingers, and angling outward, toward the little finger. The entire top of the hand can be done at once, not including the fingers. Have the client form a fist by tucking the fingers under, because this tightens the skin. Apply the strip over the entire area, and rub in the direction of growth. As the client's hand is "floating" without solid support, it is important to have a good grip of the hand when pulling back quickly against the growth. Pressure cannot be applied after the pull, because both hands are occupied. If the fingers have hair that needs removing and it is only slight, it can often be removed with the wax that is already on the strip. The hair grows toward the middle knuckle, so by taking one finger at a time, pressing the wax onto the hair, rubbing in the direction of growth, and quickly pulling off against the growth the hair can be removed. If it cannot, complete the process by applying the wax. After removing all the hair, take the hand in a handshake grasp and apply a soothing lotion along the topside, toward the elbow (and shoulder, if the upper arm was waxed) and down the underside to the hand. If the hand was waxed, finish by massaging the lotion into the hand and fingers. Proceed to the second arm.

The lower arm should take approximately 15 minutes, the upper and lower, 30 minutes.

blending
using waxed strips (on which wax is present) to remove more developed, longer hairs while leaving some of the shorter hairs

The Bikini Area and Abdomen

The term "bikini wax" refers to the removal of unwanted hair at the top of the leg, below the navel, and in the bikini area. The service was offered for clients in preparation for vacations and swimsuit wear, but now it is a desired service for maintenance year round. Regrowth is often softer, lighter, and less dense when the area is waxed exclusively and regularly. Changes in lingerie styles and the popularity of these styles have also encouraged clients to switch to year-round waxing of the bikini area. Standard, professional conduct is extremely important in this waxing service, perhaps above all others. This is a time when most clients, especially first-time clients, feel the most vulnerable. A cheerful and confident professional manner helps to put clients at ease. Less anxiety means less discomfort. Get comfortable with the idea of bikini waxing so you can make clients feel comfortable with the service. Ask on the phone or in a consultation if clients shave or trim. If not, be prepared to do it.

Show the client into the wax room and clarify what type of bikini wax is desired. There should be a drape and a pair of disposable underpants on the table. Then, inform the client that you will step outside the room for a minute, at which time the client should remove all clothing from the waist down. She may leave on her underpants, if it is for a regular bikini wax, or change into the disposable pair. The client may also keep socks on. Tell the client to get onto the table and to cover herself with the drape. It is, of course, unprofessional to stand and watch the client undress. Give a light tap on the door, and open it slowly, making sure the client is all set before entering. Be professional at all times, avoiding tasteless jokes. After all, when we go to our OB/GYN we do not expect him or her to make tasteless jokes. Never show any kind of shock or amazement on observing the exposed client. Simply make a professional analysis of how you are going to go about the treatment. Analyze the area, skin, and hair and ascertain if you will need the client's help in stretching the skin.

Put on gloves for this service.

The waxing of the bikini area can be classified in three ways:

1. American bikini wax, which is the removal of hair exposed at the top of the thighs and just under the navel when wearing a regular bikini bottom
2. French bikini wax, which is the removal of everything, including the hair of the anus and labia, leaving only a strip of hair in the front
3. Brazilian bikini wax, which removes absolutely everything, front to back

A salon can choose its own names for these different bikini waxes, but it is most important that the client and technician both clearly understand what is to be removed and what should be left.

American Bikini Wax.   When doing a regular American bikini wax, strip wax is preferred. The standard honey style wax works well, but, providing the hair is not too coarse or too short and stubbly, the cream wax also works well. If the client is wearing her swimsuit or her own briefs, they should be protected with a paper towel, with one corner placed down the crotch area, so that two corners can be folded into the sides and the remaining corner tucked over the top (Figure 11–21). Your touch should always be firm and confident.

Using a small applicator, pull out from under the panty line any hair that must be removed, leaving the remainder tucked in behind the panty and giving a clean, even line to both sides of the bikini area. If the hair is so long that it curls, it should be trimmed to ½ inch. This can be done quickly with scissors for a small amount. If there is a considerable amount, then an electric buzzer will be faster. Next, thoroughly cleanse the area with an antiseptic cleaner and pat it dry. The area should then be dusted with powder. Have the client leave one leg straight and bring the sole of the other foot to the level of the knee. If working first on the right side of the client's bikini area, have the client place the *left* hand firmly on the paper, fingers straight downward (Figure 11–22). Ask the client to keep her hands on the paper at all times, to avoid getting wax on them. The free hand should be placed on the outer edge of the thigh to help pull the skin taut. (For incorrect hand placement, see Figure 11–23).

FIGURE 11–21
Proper placement of paper towel in bikini area

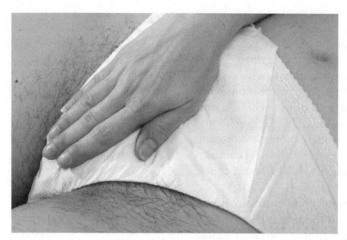

FIGURE 11–22 Correct hand placement for bikini wax

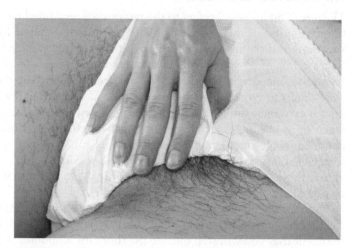

FIGURE 11–23 Incorrect hand placement for bikini wax

Working on the bent leg, apply the wax with the edge of a large spatula in the direction of hair growth. The first application should be to the section farthest away and only up to the femoral ridge (Figure 11–24). The direction of hair growth is usually downward, following the panty line. However, toward the denser hair on the pubis bone, the hair grows more horizontally and inward, toward the center. Place the strip over the wax, leaving space to grab the free edge (Figure 11–25). Rub twice in the direction of growth, then place that same hand firmly at the end of the strip with the free edge. The skin should be held especially taut in this area. Grab the strip and pull backward in a swift, continuous manner, as close to the skin as possible. Do not cut the movement short; make sure to follow through with the movement, even slightly beyond the placement of wax. Lifting too soon will make the client uncomfortable and could cause a bruise. Apply immediate, firm pressure to alleviate the discomfort.

Once all sections leading up to the panty line have been removed of hair, the hair that grows down from the femoral ridge can be removed. The client should bring the sole of the foot a little higher to just above the knee. Apply the wax just two-thirds of the way down in the downward direction of hair growth, leaving enough space at the bottom to place the hand to hold the skin taut. Place the wax strip over the area, again leaving

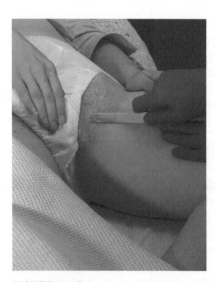

FIGURE 11–24
Bent leg position to remove hair around the femoral ridge

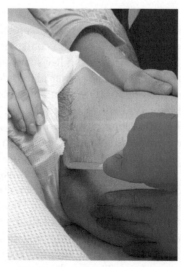

FIGURE 11–25
Applying wax to underside of bikini area

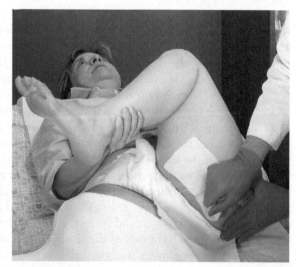

FIGURE 11–26
Leg grasp position for removal of hair in bikini area

enough of a free edge to grasp. Holding the skin as taut as possible, quickly pull the strip straight upward, as close to the skin as possible, and follow by quickly placing the hand firmly on the area for relief. Finally, to finish that side, have the client lift the leg to the chest, grasping at the ankle (Figure 11–26). This should expose the last remaining third of the hair that was too near the table to apply the wax. This position also ensures that the skin is nice and taut. The wax is applied as before, downward, with the pull upward.

If the client is going to have a full leg wax or an upper leg wax and she can maintain this grasp for a little longer, it is an excellent position from which to remove the hairs from the top/back of the thigh, while the skin is tight. Halfway down the back of the thigh, the hair changes direction and grows across from the outside in and should not be removed in this position. One side of the bikini area should always be completed before going to the other side.

The regular/American bikini area should take 15 minutes to wax.

French Bikini Wax.   The French style bikini wax is the removal of all hair, front to back, leaving a small stripe of hair over the pubis sometimes called a "racing stripe." Follow all directions for a regular/American bikini wax (see preceding), paying special attention to the cleaning and powdering of the areas to be waxed. The technician must wear gloves for this service. To remove the hair between the buttocks, there are two positions. Technicians and clients develop their own preferences.

The first position is to have the client lie flat on the back and raise the knees to the chest and turn the soles of the feet in together (Figure 11–27). The client can grasp the feet between the legs with one hand, leaving the other hand free to move the panties aside. Although hard wax may be preferred in this area, strip wax can be used successfully. The wax is applied downward to a small section on the lowest, inside part of the buttock. The strip is placed over the wax and given two firm rubs. Then, placing one hand at the bottom, the strip is pulled quickly upward, as close to the skin as possible. The wax is then applied in the same manner to the next section above and so on until the area on that side of the inside buttock is cleared of hair. The client should then switch hands, moving the panties to the opposite side, and grasp the feet with the other hand. Remove the hair in the same manner as on the previous side.

The second position for French bikini waxing is to have the client turn over and kneel (Figure 11–28). With one forearm resting on the table in front of her, the client has a free hand to move the panties to one side and to help separate the buttocks. The area is then waxed in the same manner as the previous position (see preceding), except that the wax is applied in an upward direction and the pull is downward. The client must switch hands when the technician is ready to switch to the other side of the inside of the buttocks.

The final part of the French bikini wax is the removal of the hair around the labia (see Chapter 10). This area should only be waxed with hard wax, because the direction of hair

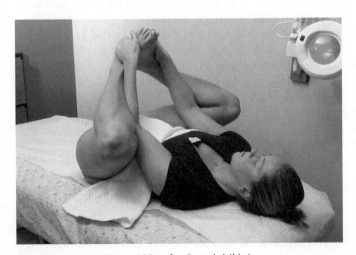

FIGURE 11–27 First position for French bikini wax

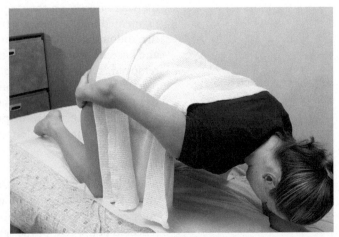

FIGURE 11–28 Second position for French bikini wax

growth on the labia is inward. Therefore, the pull in this direction cannot be outward, against the growth.

The French bikini area should take 30 minutes to wax.

Brazilian Bikini Wax.   For the Brazilian bikini wax, the hair is removed as described for the French bikini wax (see preceding), including the area between the buttocks and the labia. In addition, the hair on the pubis is removed. Because of the direction of hair growth, the coarseness of the hair, and the delicate skin, hard wax should be used for this area. The directions for removal are found in Chapter 10.

Explain to the client that blood spots may appear and are to be expected. This is due to the fact that a rich, healthy blood supply was feeding the hair at the root. Because the hair was removed at the papilla, the blood gathers in the follicle until it realizes that there is no longer a hair there to "feed," at which time it reabsorbs into the dermis. Blood spots are always good signs. With any first-time bikini wax, advise the client to return within 3 weeks for a follow-up wax. After that the client should space waxing service every 4 to 6 weeks.

All traces of wax should be removed at the end of the service using a strip and then plenty of soothing antiseptic lotion. Salicylic acid can be applied with cotton. This helps remove any redness and bumps and reduces the risk of ingrown hairs.

The Brazilian bikini wax should take between 30 and 45 minutes.

The Abdomen.   To remove the hair on the abdomen, the client should lie flat on the back with the top edge of the panties protected with a paper towel. The area should be clean and dusted with powder. If the client's skin is especially loose, in particular after pregnancy and childbirth, the client can help to pull the skin taut, reducing the level of discomfort. The hair in this area grows inward from both sides, meeting at the center where it then starts to grow downward. Above and around the navel it grows inward toward the navel. The hair should be removed starting from the area around the navel. Apply the wax to the area, no more than an inch at a time, following the direction of hair growth. Apply the strip and, holding the skin taut with the free hand, pull the strip against the growth, as close to the skin as possible, applying immediate pressure after each pull. Work continuously downward until close to the top of the panty line. Have the client hold the paper-lined panty top where hair removal should end.

Some clients have a few strong, dark hairs in the center and finer, pigmented hair covering the rest of the abdomen. It is the strong, dark hair in the center clients usually want removed. Unfortunately, waxing the center leaves a bald spot, causing the finer, pigmented hair to be more apparent. The client has a few options. The first and most costly is to remove the hair of the abdomen entirely with laser. The second option is to remove the few strong and bothersome hairs with electrolysis, leaving the remaining finer hair intact. Another option is to dab individual dark hairs with wax and remove them individually, if there are few and doing so not too time consuming. Another option is to apply the wax entirely to the area where the stronger hair is most apparent and remove it all, then with the wax already on the strip, "blend" outward by laying the strip over some of the finer pigmented hairs, leaving a few behind and less of a contrast. The last option is to wax all the abdominal hair, but with the understanding that the hair may grow back irregularly and become more apparent than it was before, requiring constant waxing. After the hair is removed, remove any trace of wax and soothe the area with lotion. If the client has a pierced navel, the area around it should not be waxed until it has healed to the point where the ring or bar can be replaced, usually about 2 months after the piercing. If the area is pulled abruptly, the piercing could tear.

The abdomen should take about 5 minutes.

The Legs

A half-leg wax can vary considerably between an upper leg and a lower leg. The hair of the upper leg may be less dense when compared to the lower leg, but a larger surface area still must be covered, taking more time and using more wax than the lower leg. This should be reflected in the cost of the service and the time allowed for the hair removal. An upper-leg wax or a whole-leg wax does not include the bikini area. That is usually an additional service requiring additional preparation and additional cost, so make sure the client understands that. If the whole leg is going to be waxed, the legs should be prepared by having the client lie flat on the back with the legs flat on the table (Figure 11–29). Mist or spritz the top area with an antiseptic lotion, then dust the entire area with powder. Have the client bend the knees and place the soles of the feet on the table, then apply the lotion and powder as far underneath as possible. To prepare the limbs, it is faster and more enjoyable for the client if the technician works simultaneously by spraying the cleaner on both limbs, then wiping in sequence up the limbs with both hands, finishing at the fingers or toes. Wipe any excess moisture off with two tissues, one in each hand.

The client may now straighten the leg. If the feet and toes are to be waxed with the leg wax, this is a good time to wax them. Make sure the area to be waxed is warm. If the feet are cold the wax will remain behind and not lift off with the strip. Apply the wax to the top of the nearest foot, applying it downward, toward the toes (Figure 11–30). Quickly apply the strip, before the wax cools, and pull it quickly off, as close to the skin as possible. Apply immediate pressure to the area. If there is very little hair in the toes, the wax on the strip may be sufficient to remove those hairs simply by pressing the wax onto the hair and quickly pulling away, making sure that the pressure is in the direction of growth and the pull is in the opposite direction. If there is considerable growth, the growth is usually visible, growing slightly on the outer edge and down toward the nail in the middle of the toe.

Once the foot has been cleared of the hair, start on the inside lower leg at the bottom, by the ankle. Dip the spatula well into the wax so that approximately 3 inches of the spatula are coated in wax. Scrape excess wax off the underside of the spatula, then holding it at a 45-degree angle, and start at approximately 7 inches up from the ankle. Glide the spatula downward with the hair growth for the same 7 inches using the edge of the spatula, allowing a thin layer of wax to slide off it and onto the leg. Apply the strip, leaving enough of a free edge to grab and rub twice in the direction of growth. Place the free hand on the skin by the free edge of the strip, then grab the strip and quickly pull away, against the hair growth and close to the skin. Apply immediate and firm pressure. The next application should be directly above the previous one, proceeding in the same manner until the knee is reached. Return to the bottom of the leg and begin the process again, this time applying the first strip of wax to the area just to the inside of the **shinbone**. Continue removing the hair in the usual manner, in sections moving up the leg again stopping at the knee. Rotate the foot back to the center. Proceed again from the bottom, working in the same-size strips, on the front of the leg, up the shinbone to the knee. Rotate the foot slightly inward. Starting again at the bottom, clear the hair in the same-size strips to the outer side of the lower leg, again working up to the knee.

shinbone
the flat surface of the bone immediately under the skin on the front of the lower leg

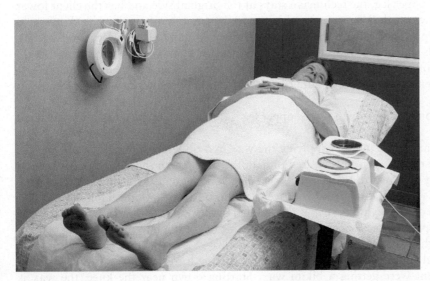

FIGURE 11–29
Preparing the client for leg wax

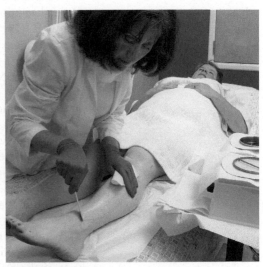

FIGURE 11–30
Application of wax to the lower leg

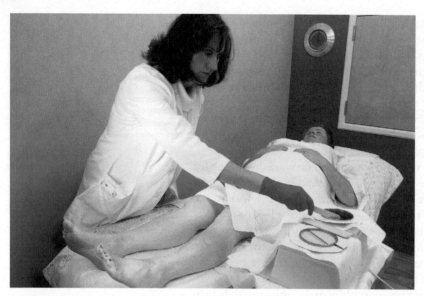

FIGURE 11–31
Wax cart may be moved if reaching across the client is uncomfortable

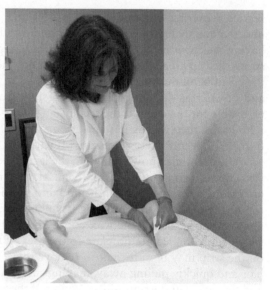

FIGURE 11–32
Technician has less control at the foot of the table

To wax the knees, have the client bend the leg, putting the foot flat on the table. This area has coarse patches of dry, dead skin cells as well as folds of skin on some clients. This position ensures that the skin is tight. Apply the wax in downward, outward sections, from the middle of the knee to the lower half. Apply the strip, rub downward, and remove quickly upward, working around the knee. Next, apply the wax to the top part of the knee in a downward direction to the middle. Apply the strip, rub, and remove it against the growth.

After the knee is completed, move to the upper leg. If the upper leg is not going to be waxed, move to the other side. It helps to move the wax around to the opposite side on a cart if unable to reach over (Figure 11–31). Another option is to stand at the foot of the table, but in this position the technician will be pulling the strip in a direction away from the technician's body and will not have as much control or be able to follow the movement through as easily (Figure 11–32). It is also only a suitable position for the lower leg. There are waxing tables available in which a middle portion at one end drops away, allowing the technician to step in farther. One must be very slender to slip into this middle opening, however.

To wax the upper leg, the technician stays at the original side and has the client lower the leg back downward. When waxing this area, it is very important that the skin is held taut with every pull. The skin on the thigh is often looser than the lower leg, and there are often more folds of skin around the knee, behind the knee, and on the back of the thigh. Where the roll-on applicator may work well on the lower leg, it can be more uncomfortable on the upper leg, because it can drag on the skin and not roll with fluidity if it starts to cool.

The direction of hair growth on the upper leg is downward in the middle and outward on either side.

Begin by waxing the middle, applying the wax in a downward direction, toward the knee. When the middle section is cleared of hair, the outer thigh should then be waxed in sections starting downward, toward the knee. The wax is applied starting at the middle, going outward. Apply the strip and rub over it in an outward motion. Holding the skin very taut on the outer thigh, the strip is then pulled in the opposite direction, back toward the center. This procedure is continued up the outside of the thigh to the point where there is no hair growth at the top.

At this point, ask the client to bend the leg, bringing it to the same position it would be in if the client were getting a bikini wax. Starting down near the knee, the wax is applied from the middle outward. Be careful not to go too far down toward the table, because enough room must be left to hold the skin taut for the pull back upward. Another reason is that the hair at the back of the thigh changes direction, growing up, toward the buttocks, and the flesh from the back of the thigh may be pushed forward when the client is lying on the back. Before pulling the strip upward, make doubly sure that the skin is held as taut as possible. This is an area that can bruise easily if the pull is not swift and clean. Complete the sections of the inner thigh up to the bikini, but not the bikini area, unless that is part of this service.

At this time, ask the client to bring the knee to the chest, if able, grabbing the leg behind the knee. This tightens the skin on the back of the thigh, allowing the removal of the hair back there with less discomfort. This works well for clients who may be overweight or have loose skin. Only the hair growing straight toward the buttocks should be removed in this manner. Any hair growing across the back of the thigh should be removed with the client lying face downward. After completing the inner thigh, move to the opposite side and continue removing the hair in the same manner as the first side. When the hair removal of the front and sides of both legs is completed, lotion should be applied to the waxed areas removing any remaining wax, so that the client does not stick to the paper when turning over.

The client may now turn over for the remaining hair removal on the back of the legs. Have the client hang the feet off the end of the table. More powder should be applied at this time, especially if the client has been perspiring. For the calf, the hair generally grows across the calf from the outside inward. The growth pattern changes behind the knee. Start the first section with the wax following the direction of growth, at the bottom of the lower leg. Apply the wax, from the outside inward. Rub in the same direction. Then, holding the skin taut, pull backward, against the growth. Immediately apply pressure. Continue up the calf in the same manner to the back of the knee. The hair growth pattern can vary at the back of the knee and should be determined at the time of waxing. The same is true for the back of the thigh. Generally, the hair also crosses from the outside of the thigh growing toward the inner thigh for the first half to two-thirds of the thigh. At the top, it often changes direction, growing straight upward, toward the buttocks. Some clients may have a spiraling hair growth pattern on the back of the thigh. Clearly evaluate the hair growth directions and wax following the standard rule for strip wax of applying it in the direction of growth, rubbing on top of the strip in the direction of growth, and removing the strip against the growth. When all hair has been removed from both legs, pamper the client by applying plenty of lotion and using gentle **effleurage** movements. Massage and soothe the legs using upward movements up the middle and a little lighter stroking down the outside.

If the client has poor mobility in the hips and cannot turn the legs inward or outward very easily while lying on the back, it may be easier to first position the client lying face downward, with the feet off the end of the table. This position supports the hip and offers a better range of motion to the client.

The half-leg treatment should take approximately 30 minutes. The whole-leg treatment should take approximately 45 minutes.

effleurage
a rhythmic, gentle stroking of the skin, often just using the fingertips, which does not attempt to move the muscle underneath

Treatment Areas for Men

The areas male clients most commonly choose to have waxed are the back, the shoulders, between the eyebrows, and the outer ear. Some, especially swimmers or body builders, have the chest and legs waxed, too. Occasionally, male clients enter the salon dressed as women and request more extensive waxing. Men requesting sex-change operations are often required to go through psychiatric testing and are asked, before succumbing to major surgery, to live and dress as women for a period. Eventually, these clients may opt for hormone therapy, laser treatments, and/or electrolysis. Until then, however, they may choose to have much of the torso hair waxed away, along with the arm and leg hair. These situations may be awkward for the waxing professional, but they are also awkward for those requesting the services. Confidence, compassion, and professionalism from the technician are paramount. Clearly ascertain from clients which hair they would like to have removed and clearly explain back to the clients what can and cannot be done and what the clients can expect.

FIGURE 11–33 Before eyebrow waxing

FIGURE 11–34 After eyebrow waxing

The Eyebrows

Most of the time, the glabellar area, often called the "unibrow," needs waxing (Figure 11–33).

Occasionally, a little cleaning under the brow is warranted. Often, the brow hairs are long and unruly, and trimming them with scissors can make a big difference in their appearance. Men's eyebrows should not be waxed in the same way women's eyebrows are waxed. Men often do not want a sophisticated look but a more natural look that is simply well groomed. Men do not expect high arches.

To wax and groom men's eyebrows, cleanse and powder the client's eyebrows in the usual manner. Hand the client a handheld mirror and discuss the shape, what should be removed, and what should stay. Using a small amount of wax on the end of a thin, wooden applicator, isolate the hairs under the brow that should be waxed off. Apply the wax in the direction of growth. Apply the strip, also rubbing in the direction of growth, and quickly pull away, against the growth. After completing both eyebrows, move to the center. For men, the eyebrow should always start just to the inside of the corner of the eye; everything else in the glabellar area can be waxed away (Figure 11–34).

This treatment should take approximately 15 minutes.

The Ears

Only the hair on the outer rim and lobes of the ear can be waxed. Never attempt to wax hair inside the ears. Men often trim ear-lobe hair with scissors, leaving it bristly. Waxing the hair will result in much softer regrowth.

To wax the earlobes and ear rim, have the client lie flat or assume a semireclined position. Cleanse and dry the area. Apply the wax to the lobe in a downward direction with a narrow stick. Apply a small strip over the area. Hold the earlobe taut with the free hand, and pull quickly upward. Proceed to the area above. Apply the wax in a downward motion along the rim. Apply the strip, again rubbing downward. Holding the top portion of the lobe taut, pull quickly upward, against the growth. After completing the second ear, soothe the area with lotion, massaging both earlobes simultaneously for a more pleasurable end to the service.

When mastered, 10 minutes should be more than enough time for this service.

The Chest

Before waxing a man's chest, have the client sit on the side of the table and discuss which areas the client would like cleared of hair. Some men book this service wanting abdominal hair or hair in front of the shoulders removed right up to the chest area but leaving the hair on the chest (i.e., above and between the breasts), intact. Make sure the task is clearly understood. Gloves should be worn for this service, because blood spotting is likely.

For this service, the client should be lying flat on the back. Stand at the side of the table for the side that is being worked on, changing sides after that half is completed. When waxing a man's chest, the hair must be approximately ½ inch long. If it is longer than that and curly, it should be trimmed to ½ inch long. When trimming the hair with an electric trimmer, trim it well away from the wax, because the hair will "fly" into the wax pot. Alternatively, make sure the wax pot is covered. After trimming the hair, warn the client that he will feel a cold spray. Spritz or wipe the entire area with an antiseptic liquid like witch hazel. Wipe away any excess with a paper towel, and dust the area with powder. The first application of wax should begin on an outer edge, working upward and inward, toward a denser area. The wax should always be applied in the direction of hair growth, rubbed in the direction of the hair growth, and removed against hair growth. A large strip should be used. As the area becomes dense, the wax applications should be in smaller strips. Remember to apply immediate pressure after each pull. On completion, soothe the entire area with the after-care lotion.

Approximately 30 to 45 minutes is needed for this service, depending on the amount of hair to be removed.

The Back

When men book back waxes, they generally want all the hair removed from just below the waistband upward. If the client is wearing a business suit and will be returning to work, suggest that he remove his pants and upper clothing. Provide a hanger on which to hang the clothes and a towel or drape to place around the waist. Leave the room while the client readies. If the client does not need to remove his pants, have him at least remove the belt from his pants for comfort, then have him lie on the table face downward. His arms should be upward, with the elbows sticking outward. The client should rest the side of the face on the tops of the hands. Place two paper towels along the top edge of the client's pants. If the hair is longer than ½ inch, it should be trimmed. If using an electric trimmer, cover the wax pot or trim the hair well away from the wax. Stand on the same side on which the wax is going to be applied, changing sides after that half is completed. Gloves should be worn for this service, because blood spots are inevitable (Figure 11–35). Warn the client that he will feel a cold spray, then spray the area with an antiseptic. Wipe off any excess moisture with a paper towel, and dust with powder.

Begin the hair removal at the area just above the waistband of the pants. The first application of wax should begin from the outside edge of the torso where the hair growth starts (Figure 11–36). Using a large spatula, dip into a full pot of wax until one-half to two-thirds of the spatula is covered. Remove the spatula, scraping the underside of the spatula on the side of the pot or on the scraping rim that is provided. Using the edge of the spatula, glide inward, following the direction of hair growth toward the base of the spine, allowing a thin layer of wax to cover the area. Apply the strip, leaving 1 inch free edge at the farthest end. Rub the strip twice in the direction of growth, then, with the free hand placed over the base of the spine, and holding the skin taut, quickly pull backward and downward against the growth and as close to the skin as possible. It is important to follow the movement through in a downward motion to where the hair growth started. Quickly apply firm pressure with the free hand. The next application should be right next to the preceding one. If the length of the strip will be too long to do in one try, remove the strip on the outside first. The second strip should be toward the middle, the third strip to the side of the first, and the fourth strip above the third, going to the middle. Continue on in this manner until reaching the top. At the top, the hair starts to grow downward in the center, along the spine. Complete the removal on that side by following the waxing rules and directional changes. Also include at this time, if it is requested, the back of the shoulder. When that side is complete, move to the other side of the table and repeat the process.

With the gloves still on, apply plenty of soothing antiseptic lotion to the area that was waxed. Be careful not to extend beyond that, because there may be a few more strips to do

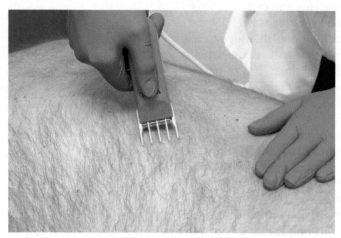

FIGURE 11–35
Position, placement, and preparation of client for back waxing

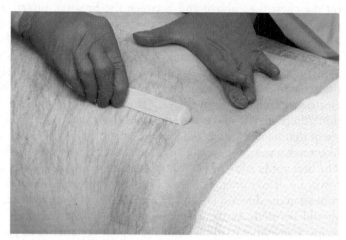

FIGURE 11–36
Initial wax application to back

with the client sitting up. A cool compress soaked in a baking-powder solution can also be applied for a few minutes. It is not unusual for hives to develop in this area. They will subside in an hour or so. Applying a salicylic acid product to the area will help reduce redness and bumps. Because the client cannot see the back, the technician must let the client know when the blood spots have diminished and when it is safe to get dressed. Do not let the client risk getting blood spots all over his clothing. The client should now sit, facing the technician. At this time, with the arms at his side, the rest of the shoulder area can be waxed and any blending toward the front can be done, making sure both sides are balanced and even. The shoulders are waxed in a similar manner to the knees, one surface area or plane at a time and not attempting to round a curve with the strip. The hair on the shoulder usually grows inward to the center of the shoulder from the back and inward toward the center from the front. Waxing the front is considered a separate service (part of the chest wax), but blending a little with wax already on the strip is acceptable.

DO'S & DON'TS

Do's of the Hot Strip Method

- Always wash hands before and after touching a client.
- Use a full pot for large surface areas so that a larger surface area of spatula is covered when dipped into the wax.
- Use the edge of the spatula.
- To clean the spatula, wipe it between two epilating strips.
- Always hold the skin taut at the free edge end of the strip before pulling.
- To ease the client's discomfort, have the client take a deep breath while rubbing over the strip and blow out during the pull.
- Always apply pressure quickly after each pull—gentle pressure for the face and firm pressure for the torso and limbs.
- Tell the client to use no makeup or perfume, and to avoid tanning and hot tubs for at least 24 hours after the service or until any signs of trauma and irritation have been completely eliminated

Don'ts of the Hot Strip Method

- Do not apply wax to an area longer than is going to be immediately removed.
- Do not apply wax to an area that has just been waxed.
- Do not overlap with hot wax.
- Do not wax the areola of the nipple.
- Do not wax inside the ear or nose.

This service should take between 30 and 45 minutes. If the price is listed as "starting from . . . ," it is for two reasons: (1) the task, that is, how much hair there is and how involved the service is going to be, and (2) the speed of the technician. The more experienced and faster the technician, the more the salon should charge.

WHAT DID I DO WRONG?

Q. *When I waxed my client's eyebrows, I lifted off skin when I pulled the strip away, and it later scabbed. What did I do wrong?*

A. The client was probably using a skin-altering product like Retin-A. Assure the client that this was not a burn (unless multiple clients were injured from the same pot). If the skin is fragile and the wax is too cool, it can lift the skin off. A soothing healing product like aloe vera gel can be applied to lifted skin. A topical antibiotic ointment can also be used. Instruct the client that it is important to avoid picking at the scab, because doing so could leave a scar. Neither should the client expose the area to sun until completely healed, because doing so could cause hyperpigmentation. To avoid this, discuss skin-care product usage during the consultation. Find out exactly what the client has been using and always have all clients read and sign releases like the one in Chapter 9.

If the client was not using a product designed to thin the skin, there may be a problem with the waxing technique. The wax should only be applied to the area on the brow bone, not in the socket where the skin is looser. The skin should be lifted and held taut over the brow bone. The wax should be applied thinly. The skin should continue to be held taut for the removal with the pull made low and parallel to the skin. Follow through with the movement, and do not bring upward too soon.

Q. *The wax stayed on the client's skin and did not come off with the strip. What happened?*

A. There are a few reasons wax does not lift off with the strip and stays behind on the skin. The first is that the client's skin may be damp, either from the cleansing/pretreatment product or from perspiration. Before applying the wax, make sure the skin is dry. For a small area, lay a tissue over it to test for moisture. Dust the area with powder.

The second most common reason is that the skin may have been too cool from poor circulation or cold weather. Make sure the area is warm before applying the wax. If not, give the area multiple rubs to warm the area.

Third, wax may have been left behind because the skin was not held taut. This happens in areas where there may be loose skin or folds of skin, like on the back of the thigh and, often, in the bikini area.

Finally, the reason might have been a poor-quality muslin strip or one that had been treated with chemicals like fabric protectors or fabric softeners.

To remove the wax, add no more wax unless either attempts have been tried and failed. Place the strip over the wax at a sideways angle, rub over the strip, and, holding the skin especially taut, pull quickly backward. Applying more wax often increases the problem and should be a last resort. If more wax is applied, it must be applied and removed as quickly as possible while still warm.

Q. *When I waxed my client's bikini area, it bruised in the crease at the top of the leg.*

A. Bruising most commonly happens when the skin is either not held taut enough or the technician pauses during the pull of the strip. Make sure to follow all the way through with the pull, keeping the hand close to the contour of the face or body. Do not lift up and away too soon.

In this instance, bruising occurred because the wax was applied across a plane, that is over two different surfaces at once. The area at the top of the leg to where the underpant line ends should be dealt with in one application, and the area beneath where the underpant lies and where there is more dense pubic hair, separately. Trying to do both planes at the same time, crossing the crease, can result in a bruise.

Q. *When waxing a client's eyebrows, I removed too much hair, leaving a gap in the brow line.*

A. There are three common causes of removing too much hair. The first is that too much wax was applied to the area and, when pressure was applied over the strip, the wax "bled" into an area that it should not have. Wax application should be thin. The second common mistake is that at the point of the arch there are sometimes hairs that grow downward that have roots in the main brow line. If wax inadvertently gets onto the tips of these hairs, these hairs will also come out with the pull, leaving unwelcome "holes." This can often happen with Asian eyebrows. To avoid this, first, using a small stick with just a small amount of stickiness, isolate and pull down the undesired hair, and brush back and away the hair to remain. Petroleum jelly can be applied to the hair that should remain. Third, do not reuse a strip on the eyebrow area, and do not use the test strip used on the inside of the wrist to test the temperature.

Conclusion

Strip waxing has been a popular and effective method of hair removal for three decades, with no signs of letting up. Manufacturers continue to try to improve the wax by making it gentler to use on more delicate areas in response to the needs and wants of clients who use skin care that compromises the delicate epidermal tissue. While strides have been made in this regard, and strip waxes are promoted as kinder and safer for the most delicate skin, proto-col should continue to be followed to avoid unnecessary trauma. With continued practice and mastery in the use of strip wax, the hair-removal specialist can become a speed waxer, someone who offers a great temporary hair-removal service in a short time and with little discomfort to the client. Speed waxers quickly earn the loyalty and continued patronage of clients who appreciate skill and speed.

 Discussion and Review Questions

1. What are the two main components of hot strip wax?

2. Is it acceptable to "double dip"?

3. What are two benefits of applying hot strip wax with an applicator tip or roller?

4. List five contraindications of hot strip waxing.

5. In which hair-growth direction is hot strip wax applied?

6. Describe two situations in which common problems occur in hot strip wax treatments and explain how to avoid those problems.

SECTION IV

Introduction to Permanent Hair Removal

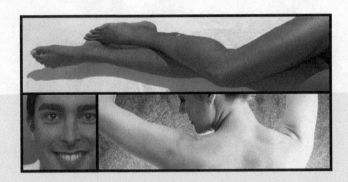

Welcome to the world of permanent hair removal, more commonly called electrolysis. Electrolysis is the only proven method of permanent hair removal recognized by the FDA and AMA. This section addresses all the basic areas pertaining to electrolysis as a method of hair removal, how it is used, indications and contra-indications, and pre- and posttreatment. This section is an introduction to electrolysis and should not be the only tool in learning and developing the skill of electrolysis. Rather, it should be used with formal classroom training.

Three main modalities fall under the "electrolysis" classification:

1. thermolysis
2. galvanic electrolysis
3. the "blend"

Each has a chapter. Electrolysis is the generic term for all three modalities of permanent hair removal, although "true" electrolysis is the galvanic modality. Electrolysist and electrologist are used synonymously to mean someone skilled in using electricity to remove moles, warts, telangiectasia, or hair roots. The terms electrology and electrolysis, however, are *not* synonymous. Electrology is the general study of electricity and its properties, while electrolysis generally has two meanings. First, it means the use of electricity to cause the chemical decomposition of some substance. Second, and more specifically, it means the use of an electric current to remove moles, warts, telangiectasia, or hair roots. Finally, electrolysis can also be

continued

thought of as a specialized case of histolysis, which is defined as the breakdown and disintegration of body tissue.

The first chapter in this section gives an overview of the history and evolution of electrolysis and the different modalities that fall under this umbrella. It also covers electricity as it pertains to electrolysis and focuses on setting up the treatment area and equipment and supplies.

The following chapter addresses all commonalities the three methods share, including the client consultation, contra-indications, positioning, and electrolysis techniques, including the insertion and pre- and posttreatment care.

CHAPTER 12

The History and Evolution of Electrolysis

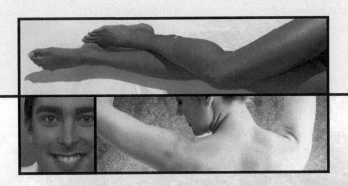

Chapter Outline

Learning Objectives ■ Key Terms ■ Introduction ■ The History of Electrolysis
Electricity and Electrolysis ■ Types of Permanent Hair Removal ■ Equipment and Supplies
Conclusion ■ Discussion and Review Questions ■ Additional Readings

Learning Objectives

By the end of this chapter, you should be able to:

1. Understand the evolution of electrolysis.
2. Name the three modalities of electrolysis and explain how they work to effectively destroy the hair follicle.
3. Describe how to set up a treatment area with the necessary equipment.
4. List the basic differences of various needles.
5. Know how to troubleshoot the most common problems.

Key Terms

alternating current	circuit breaker	electroplated	Ohm's law
ampere	conductor	fuse	phoresis
anaphoresis	converter	galvanic electrolysis	point effect
anions	critical item	histolysis	rectifier
anode pole	diathermy	hydraulic stool	rheostat
Arkansas stone	direct current	insulator	shank
autoclave	electrologist	ionization	thermolysis
blend	electrology	iontophoresis	transformer
cataphoresis	electrolysis	milliamperes	volt
cathode pole	electrolysist	milliamperemeter	watt
cations	electrons	ohm	
circuit			

Introduction

This chapter covers the history and development of electrolysis and how it has evolved over the years into a widely used and accepted method of hair removal.

This chapter also deals with electricity as it pertains to electrolysis and the three modalities of thermolysis, galvanic electrolysis, and the blend and how those modalities work.

Finally, it covers the most practical and effective way to set up a treatment area and discusses the equipment and supplies needed to perform electrolysis services (Figure 12–1).

The History of Electrolysis

electrolysis
the use of an electric current to remove moles, warts, or hair roots

galvanic electrolysis
a modality of electrolysis using direct current (see preceding) with positive and negative poles that causes the production of caustic lye in the hair follicle, which in turn causes the hair's destruction

thermolysis
the breakdown of a substance by heat; as it pertains to electrolysis, used synonymously with diathermy (see following)

In 1869, ophthalmologist Dr. Charles E. Michel began to research a method of safely and permanently removing ingrown eyelashes from his patients' eyelids. Michel devised a method of inserting a surgical needle into the hair follicle that was connected to a dry cell battery by a conducting wire. After applying a measured amount of direct current, he observed that the hair did not regrow. In 1875, he documented and published his findings, and **electrolysis** (ee-lek-TRAHL-ih-sis) was born as a method of permanent hair removal. It was then quickly adopted as a method of treating not only ingrown eyelashes but unwanted facial hair. The process, while effective for one ingrown eyelash, for facial hair it was slow and laborious. By 1916, Professor Paul Kree, in recognizing this inefficiency, developed a more efficient method by using multiple needles at once. **Galvanic** (gal-VAN-ik) **electrolysis**, which uses multiple needles, became the most popular method for decades following and was a major catalyst in the development of electrolysis as a profession for hair removal. A number of years later, in 1923, an article about the use of high-frequency current for hair removal was published by Dr. Bordier, a Frenchman. This application of high-frequency current became known as **thermolysis** (thur-MAHL-uh-sis) due to the heat produced to destroy cells. High-frequency thermolysis was introduced as a much faster method of treating unwanted hair. However, with this method there seemed to be a higher percentage of regrowth, and its effectiveness greatly depended on straight, undistorted hair follicles and an accurate probe and insertion depth to ensure the destruction of the dermal papilla.

By 1938, Henri St. Pierre and Arthur Hinkle introduced a methodology combining the best of galvanic and thermolysis modalities, which they called the "blend" technique. Both galvanic and high-frequency electrolysis could be combined alternately or simultaneously. The resulting technique was faster than the galvanic modality, not quite as fast as thermolysis, but more effectively destroyed the dermal papilla, especially on distorted

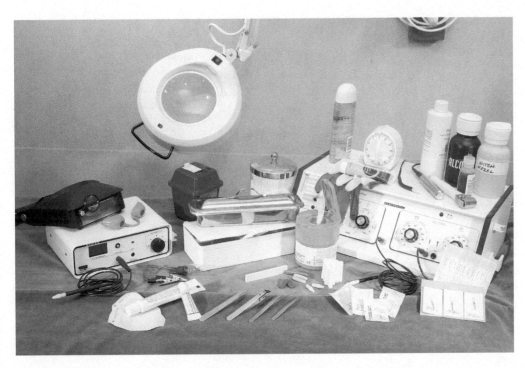

FIGURE 12–1
Electrolysis machines
and supplies

follicles. While thermolysis or **diathermy** (DY-uh-thur-mee) is still the most popular modality used in other parts of the world, the blend method has become the most accepted and popular method in the United States.

Electricity and Electrolysis

To understand electrolysis one must first understand the basics of electricity, or **electrology** (ee-lek-TRAHL-uh-jee) (Figure 12–2), as it is this electrical energy, whether it be direct current (DC) used for galvanic electrolysis or alternating current (AC) used for thermolysis (Figure 12–3) that destroys the dermal papilla in the hair follicle, resulting in permanent hair removal. A clear understanding of electricity ensures a better understanding of electrolysis equipment.

Electric energy can be produced through five main sources:

1. friction
2. magnetism
3. heat
4. chemical reaction
5. atomic reaction

The result of these five sources is the flowing of negatively charged particles called **electrons** (ee-LEK-trahnz) along a pathway called a **circuit** (SUR-kit), by means of a **conductor** (kahn-DUK-tur). A conductor is a substance that allows the free, easy, unrestricted flow of electrons. Examples of good conductors are most metals, especially copper; steel electrolysis probes; saline (water and salt mixture); and the human body. An **insulator** (IN-suh-layt-ur) inhibits or causes resistance to the flow of electrons. Examples of insulators are rubber, plastic, wood (dry), and glass. Hair is also a very poor conductor of electricity and does not withstand heat well, which is why electric tweezers are completely ineffectual as a method of permanent hair removal. The flow rate of electrons can be measured by a unit called an **ampere** (AM-peer). In electrolysis, flow is measured in **milliamperes** (mil-ee-AM-peerz). A milliampere is 1/1000 of an ampere. The **milliamperemeter** (mil-ee-AM-peer-mee-tur) measures current in 1/1000s of an ampere. The quantity of current flowing through a circuit is controlled by a **rheostat** (REE-oh-stat), which is the intensity control dial on the epilator unit.

diathermy
a treatment accomplished by passing high-frequency electric currents to generate heat; as it pertains to electrolysis, used synonymously with thermolysis (see preceding)

electrology
the general study of electricity and its properties

electrons
stable, negatively charged elementary particles that orbit the nucleus of an atom

circuit
route around which an electrical current can flow, beginning and ending at the same point

conductor
a substance that allows electricity to pass through it

insulator
a material or device that prevents or reduces the passage of electricity

ampere
basic unit of electric current that measures the current's force

milliamperes
units of electric current, one of which equals 1/1000 of an ampere (see preceding)

milliamperemeter
a device that measures electric current in units of 1/1000 of an ampere (see preceding)

rheostat
a resistor designed to allow variation in resistance without breaking the electrical circuit

FIGURE 12–2
Diagram of watt including volt, ampere, and ohm

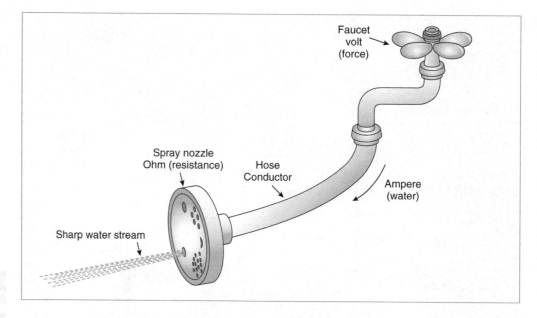

ohm
a unit of electrical resistance

volt
force that is needed to send 1 ampere (see preceding) of electric current through 1 ohm (see preceding) of resistance

Ohm's law
the law of physics that states that electric current is directly proportional to the voltage applied to a conductor (see preceding) and inversely proportional to that conductor's resistance

watt
the unit of power produced by a current of 1 ampere (see preceding) acting across a potential difference of 1 volt (see preceding)

rectifier
an electronic device that converts alternating current (see preceding) to direct current (see preceding)

converter
a device used to change alternating current (see following) to direct current (see following)

transformer
a device that transfers electrical energy from one alternating circuit to another with a change in voltage, current, phase, or impedance

fuse
an electrical safety device that contains a piece of metal that will melt if the current running through it exceeds a certain level

circuit breaker
a device that can automatically stop the flow of electricity in a circuit if there is too much current to operate safely

Other common electrical terms worth understanding when using electrical equipment are:

ohm (OHM)—a unit that measures the amount of resistance, indicating whether a higher voltage is required to push a current through a conductor

volt—the force needed to send 1 ampere of electric current through 1 ohm of resistance

Ohm's law—the requirement of 1 volt to push the current of 1 ampere through the resistance of 1 ohm; voltage = current × resistance

watt—the unit measure of electrical power involving the flow of current along a conductor and the voltage; 1 kilowatt = 1,000 watts

A **rectifier** (REK-tih-fy-ur) converts DC to AC, while a **converter** (kun-VUR-tur) changes AC to DC. A **transformer** (tranz-FOR-mer) increases or decreases the voltage of AC.

Certain safety features prevent electrical damage or injury. The first is a **fuse**. A fuse is a thin wire designed to hold a specific amount of electricity. If more than the desired amount of electricity flows through the fuse, which happens when too many appliances are plugged into the same outlet, the fuse wire overheats and breaks, discontinuing the flow of electricity along the circuit. When the fuse breaks, it must be replaced. Care should always be taken to make sure the correctly sized fuse is used and that the corresponding outlets are not overloaded with appliances generating more electricity than the outlet should handle.

The second safety device is the **circuit breaker,** which is used instead of a fuse. The circuit breaker works by throwing a switch when there is an overload of electricity, thereby discontinuing the flow of current. To restore the flow of current, one simply needs to flick the switch back on. However, one must first make sure that the elements that caused the circuit breaker to throw the switch are eliminated or sufficiently reduced.

Electrolysis equipment should always be plugged into its own socket with a grounded, three-pronged plug. It should never be "stacked" into an adaptor with other electrical appliances, especially large appliances like refrigerators or air conditioners, or even microwave ovens. To do so could affect the even flow of current. If another appliance requires a surge of current, the result could be a reduction of electricity to the electrolysis equipment, requiring the operator to boost the current flow. As the surge ends, excessive current from the electrolysis machine could significantly damage the skin. The analogy is to being in the shower and having another water source (e.g., another shower, dishwasher, or washing machine) using hot water. The person in the shower turns up the hot water.

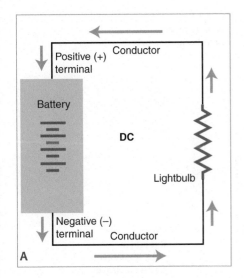

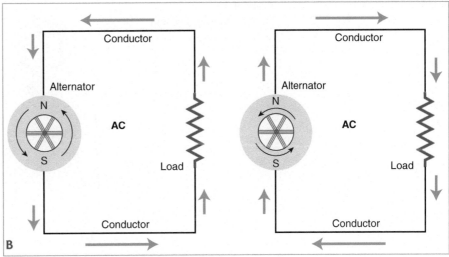

FIGURES 12–3A and B Diagrams illustrating direct current (DC) and alternating current (AC)

When the other source cuts its hot water, there is a sudden burst of hotter water back in the shower, which can be startling and extremely uncomfortable.

There are two types of electricity, based on electron flow:

1. **direct current** (DC), which is the flow of electrons in one direction, even and constant
2. **alternating current** (AC), which is the rapid flow of electrons, first in one direction, then in the opposite direction

An oscillating current is similar to AC except that oscillation has a higher frequency.

direct current
electric current that flows constantly in one direction

alternating current
electric current that regularly reverses direction

Types of Permanent Hair Removal

There are three modalities of permanent hair removal based on the type(s) of electric current that they use.

1. thermolysis, which uses alternating current
2. galvanic, which uses direct current
3. the blend method, which combines alternating and direct currents simultaneously or sequentially

Electricity and Thermolysis

Thermolysis, also called diathermy, shortwave, and radiowave (the same waves in microwave ovens), is a method that uses AC to produce oscillating radio high-frequency waves (Figure 12–4). The high-frequency current oscillates in a range of 3 to 30 megahertz, or 3,000,000 to 30,000,000 cycles per second. The Federal Communications Commission (FCC) has assigned three frequencies for use:

1. 13.56 megahertz
2. 27.12 megahertz
3. 40.68 megahertz

The 13.56 megahertz frequency is used most commonly in electrolysis today. Equipment using an alternative frequency is subject to federal prosecution.

The high-frequency waves travel down the probe and, when the probe is placed in the follicle and surrounded by the moisture of the soft tissue cells, the water molecules of the soft tissue start to vibrate, producing heat. This heat causes tissue damage and can destroy the dermal papilla. The probe itself does not become hot, but the high-frequency

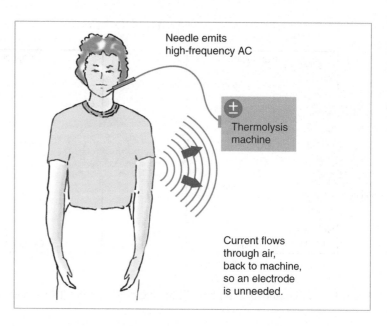

FIGURE 12–4
High frequency on client

Needle emits
high-frequency AC

Thermolysis
machine

Current flows
through air,
back to machine,
so an electrode
is unneeded.

electromagnetic field generates heat through vibration in the water molecules. The moister the tissue, the more heat that can be generated. As there is generally more moisture at the base of the hair follicle, more heat is often generated there. The heat is even more directly targeted to the dermal papilla at the base of the hair follicle if an insulated probe is used, because heat is first produced at the tip, known as the **point effect**. It then rises in a droplet shape toward the upper portion of the hair follicle.

Electricity and Galvanic Electrolysis

To understand galvanic current with regard to electrolysis (Figure 12–5) one must first understand the science of **ionization** (eye-ahn-ih-ZAY-shun) and the use of positive (+) and negative (–) poles to separate substances into ions. An ion is an atom or a group of atoms carrying an electric charge. When negatively charged using the **cathode** (KATH-ohd) pole, the ions are called **anions** (AN-eye-unz), and the process is called **anaphoresis** (an-uh-for-EES-us). When positively charged using the **anode** (AN-ohd) pole, the ions are called **cations** (KAT-eye-unz) and the process is called **cataphoresis** (KAT-uh-fuh-REE-sus). The anode chord for an electrolysis machine is usually red, and the cathode chord is usually black.

This galvanic modality uses DC, which flows in one direction, from the negative pole to the positive pole. The galvanic modality is a product of electrochemistry using electrical energy to bring about a chemical change. This happens when an electrode (e.g., a hand-held metal rod) carrying a positive charge of electricity is conducted by the metals (electrolytes) in the body and the negatively charged electrode (e.g., the probe) is inserted into the follicle. The result is that the current flows from negative to positive and, as the negatively charged probe lies in the follicle surrounded by soft tissue, an electrolytic chemical action, called ionization, occurs in which ions, released from atoms in the tissue, rearrange themselves, forming new substances. Two molecules of salt (NaCl) and two molecules of water (H_2O) in the tissue cells separate and regroup to form one molecule of hydrogen gas, one molecule of chlorine gas, and two molecules of sodium hydroxide (NaOH), also known as lye. Lye formation interests the electrologist, because it is the lye that effectively decomposes the soft tissue.

Electricity and the Blend Method

The **blend** uses the slower but effective method of galvanic (DC) electrolysis with the fast-acting benefits of thermolysis (AC). These two modalities can be applied simultaneously or sequentially, leading with either method. The AC and DC pass down the same needle. The DC cause the production of sodium hydroxide (lye) at the base of the follicle, and the AC action heats up the lye bringing about a faster and more effective destruction of the

---

point effect
the concentration of high frequency current at the tip of the probe

ionization
a process in which an atom or a molecule loses or gains electrons, acquiring an electrical charge

cathode pole
pole used to negatively charge ions

anions
negatively charged ions

anaphoresis
process whereby ions are negatively charged

anode pole
pole used to positively charge ions

cations
positively charged ions

cataphoresis
the process whereby ions are positively charged

blend
method of electrolysis that combines thermolysis (see following) and galvanic electrolysis (see preceding)

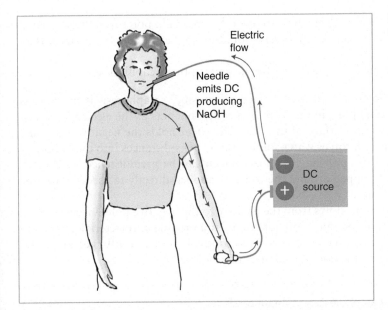

FIGURE 12–5
Galvanic current on client

dermal papilla and tissue of the hair follicle. Conversely, the AC generates heat in the follicle causing increased permeability of the lye produced by the DC. The blend method reduces the treatment time to one-quarter of that of conventional galvanic current alone. Although it is still not equal to thermolysis in terms of time, the "bleeding" effect of the lye in the follicle and the destruction it causes to not only the dermal papilla but to other follicular tissue, with less occurrence of regrowth, makes it most effective.

The thermolysis modality is the easiest to learn but requires greater skill to master, because it requires an accurate probe for successful destruction of the dermal papilla. The galvanic method is the next easiest to learn and understand; the blend technique is considered the most difficult to learn and apply, but it is well worth the effort for its superior results when applied successfully.

The Kobayashi-Yamada Method

Developed in Japan, the Kobayashi-Yamada technique is a method rather than a modality, first recognized generally in 1985 when its results were published in the *Journal of Dermatologic Surgery and Oncology*. Although it is not a method that is well known in the United States at this time, its successful results have caught the attention of electrologists and it is being discussed and debated as viable. This method uses the IME HR-5000 "spark gap" device with an operating frequency of 1 megahertz and 10 to 15 watts (compared to a thermolysis machine of approximately 7 watts), putting the output at two times that of a typical thermolysis machine. It also uses insulated needles and a pole plate that must be in contact with the client's skin. It causes trauma to the skin and can cause scarring unless the technician is extensively trained. For this reason, ice packs and some local anesthesia are recommended during treatment.

Phoresis

Phoresis (fuh-REE-sis) is the scientific term for the process in which chemical solutions can be forced into the unbroken skin using the galvanic current. In electrology and esthetics, phoresis is used in two main forms that are called **iontophoresis** (eye-ahn-toh-foh-REE-sus): (1) anaphoresis and (2) cataphoresis.

Iontophoresis.   Iontophoresis is the esthetic term used for ionization. It is the use of galvanic current to introduce water-soluble products into the skin using the anode (+ pole) and cathode (– pole) with DC.

Anaphoresis.   Anaphoresis is the process of using the negative (cathode) pole to force substances into unbroken skin. The current flows from the negative to the positive pole.

phoresis
process in which chemical solutions can be forced into unbroken skin using galvanic current

iontophoresis
the movement of ions through biological material under the influence of an electric current

Anaphoresis can be used before electrolysis to open the fine, tight pores usually associated with dry skin, to aid in insertion. Anaphoresis should be applied at a lower intensity than cataphoresis.

Anaphoresis should *not* be applied over fragile and ruptured capillaries.

Cataphoresis. Also known as "positive surface galvanism," cataphoresis is the process of using the positive (anode) pole, in the form of a roller that acts as the electrode, to distribute galvanic current to the surface of the skin. The client holds the negative (cathode) pole in the hands. The current forces water-soluble acidic pH substances into the unbroken skin. There are two ways of applying the gauze, which can be premoistened with witch hazel. The gauze can be wrapped around the roller or applied directly to the skin and the roller moved across the gauze.

In this method, the current flows from the positive to the negative pole. In electrolysis, it is used to stop the galvanic action, soothe the skin, and provide antibacterial protection after treatment. It can also be used after waxing to soothe irritated or inflamed areas and as a treatment with a facial. It is not applied after thermolysis.

Differences between Cataphoresis and Anaphoresis

Cataphoresis (Anode)	Anaphoresis (Cathode)
Produces acidic reactions	Produces alkaline reactions
Closes the pores	Opens the pores
Soothes nerves	Stimulates and irritates nerves
Decreases the blood supply	Increases the blood supply
Constricts blood vessels	Dilates blood vessels
Hardens and firms tissue	Softens tissue
Has antibacterial qualities	

Setting Up the Treatment Area

- The treatment room (Figure 12–6) should be large enough for all equipment and still allow room for easy maneuverability around the treatment couch.
- The room should have a good source of natural or artificial light.
- The walls and floors should be washable and easy to sanitize.
- The room should be able to maintain a comfortable temperature control of 72°F.
- The room should contain a washbasin with hot and cold running water, liquid soap, paper towels for drying hands, and a pedal bin for waste.
- The room should have adequate storage in the form of an easy-to-reach cabinet for drapes and supplies.
- The equipment should rest on a sturdy, mobile cart that is easy to clean and sanitize.

FIGURE 12–6
The electrolysis treatment room

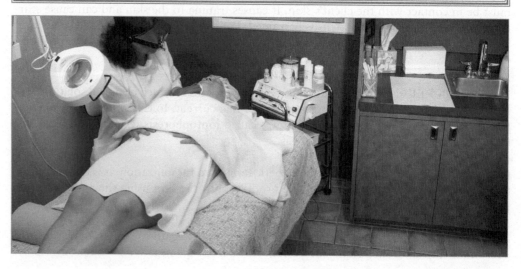

Dual-Roller Iontophoresis.   Iontophoresis uses two ionto rollers for the ionization treatment. One roller is attached to the negative (cathode) pole, the other to the positive (anode) pole. The client need not hold an electrode. Lotions or a gauze soaked in a solution are applied to the skin, and the rollers are passed over the skin, causing ionization.

Equipment and Supplies

The large purchases for an electrolysis treatment room are the electrolysis machine, sterilization unit, treatment couch, operator stool, and magnification lamp. Attending trade shows, conferences, and conventions is a good way of selecting the right equipment for the size of the business and budget. Smaller items like the additional sterilization equipment, probes, and forceps are also available at trade shows and conventions, but can also be purchased from electrolysis supply companies using their catalogues or web sites.

The Epilation Unit

When selecting an epilation unit for purchase, there are a number of considerations:

- First, have a clear idea of how to develop the electrolysis business. Is it just going to be a small, part-time business out of the home or a growing entity with 5 or more full days of treating clients?
- Will the machine be used by one individual or by multiple operators?
- What are the required manufacturing standards for electrolysis machines for where the technician lives, and does the equipment meet those standards? Electrolysis equipment is regulated in the United States by the FDA.
- What is the cost of the equipment? Financing offered by the manufacturer or supply company may mean technicians can purchase the machine they feel most suits their needs.
- Consider the ergonomic design of the machine. Is it clearly labeled and easy to understand? Will it clean easily without wiping crucial numbers and markings off the dials?
- Does the manufacturer offer additional complementary training with the equipment, ensuring that the operator understands all variables of the equipment and is comfortable with those variables?
- Customer service is an important consideration. Does the equipment manufacturer have a toll-free hotline for answering questions and troubleshooting problems? Hotlines help solve problems and avoid having to ship the equipment for repair.
- In the event of a real technical or mechanical problem, know what the warranty covers, including parts and labor.

The Treatment Couch

Treatment beds are now available for every budget, from the basic no-frills model for a startup practice on a limited budget, which costs several hundred dollars, to a state-of-the-art **hydraulic stool**, or a remote-controlled swivel chair for the higher end budget, costing thousands of dollars. A bed is one of the four most important purchases for the treatment room; the others are the epilation unit, the sterilizing unit, and the magnifying lamp. Consider how long clients will sit or lie on the treatment couch and how often. Can the couch facilitate longer sessions? Recognize the positioning features of many beds and how positions affect the technician's ability to perform treatments successfully, efficiently, and without straining, leaning awkwardly, or having to keep moving the bed and disrupting the service. Bad posture not only affects the standard of treatment, it could cause chronic back problems and operator fatigue.

hydraulic stool
a type of stool in which little force is needed to effect a large range of mechanical adjustments

When shopping for a bed, attend conferences, equipment trade shows, and fairs in the industry and test the furniture by sitting in the various working positions and, if necessary, using a second person to help demonstrate access to parts of the face and the ease of transferring down the body to the lower extremities. Test for softness and client comfort. Many salon-supply companies often offer discounted show prices, making such trips worthwhile.

Like the couch, the stool can vary from a basic swivel to a state-of-the-art, hydraulic-performance model. It is worth paying for sturdiness and metal attachments and casters, because plastic pieces tend to weaken and break with use. Other "musts" for the stool are the ability to roll with ease and to adjust height easily.

Magnification Tools

Magnification can come in the form of magnifying lamps or optical aids like headband goggles, loupes, or clip-on specs. Most electrologists use the circular magnifying lamp with the circular fluorescent lightbulb.

Magnifying lamps have many benefits. As well as the obvious magnification, they can provide continuous bright light. They also provide an effective shield when working on a client's face. They can be attached to a wall, to an equipment cart, to an esthetic facial unit, or on a free-standing post for more mobility. The magnifying lamp attached to the wall is restrictive, often requiring the client to reposition and the technician to move the treatment chair to accommodate the lamp. Sometimes, glare from overhead fluorescent lighting can affect the clear view through the lens, in which case the overhead fluorescent light can be switched off using the magnifying lamp to provide the sufficient lighting. There is less of a tendency to develop eye strain or to get headaches from a magnifying lamp, because the eyes are better able to change their degree of focus, which is more difficult with the loupe and other eyewear. Most lamps use 3, 4, 5, or 8 dioptic lenses for magnification. Some specialized models come with additional lenses for even greater magnification.

Eyewear is a little more complicated and requires a period of adjustment. Technicians claim that, after an initial period of adjustment in which they experienced headaches, they got used to the eyewear. Eyewear is available as a loupe that has one lens for each eye and a comfortable headband to keep it securely in place or as a slip-on for regular wear. The technician may flip the lens upward to communicate with the client or to view at distances (e.g., to look at a wall clock or a component on the epilating machine). Also available are the binocular loupes that have two lenses for each eye and therefore greater magnification, approximately three times greater at a distance of 14 inches.

General Magnification Guidelines		
Diopter	Power	Working Distance (Inches)
2	$1^1/_2\times$	20
3	$1^3/_4\times$	14
4	$2\times$	10
5	$2^1/_4\times$	8
7	$2^3/_4\times$	6
10	$3^1/_2\times$	4

At the end of a session, when removing the eyewear, and during the session, if the lenses can be lifted easily off the eyes, it is important to focus on something at a distance to exercise the eye muscles that have been focused on a narrow, limited level.

Sterilization Equipment

For the components of purchasing sterilization equipment, see Chapter 5.

Gloves

Many of the general guidelines for glove usage can be found in Chapter 5, but there are some additional points worth noting with regard to electrolysis:

- Question clients for allergies to latex. When clients do have allergies, they are usually aware of it and will mention them when they see the technician donning gloves. Nonlatex vinyl gloves should be available for clients allergic to latex.
- Gloves should be powder-free.
- Gloves often run big, so technicians with small hands should try extra-small gloves first. For medium hands, try small size, for large hands, try medium, and so on. The gloves should fit snugly to ensure that there is sensitivity at the fingertips, which enables the electrologist to feel any nonpigmented coarse hairs that may not be easily visible. Gloves that are too big and buckled and wrinkled generally afford less sensitivity.
- Purple gloves are effective at helping to see nonpigmented hairs. They make good backdrops for otherwise hard-to-see hairs, as opposed to natural gloves, which are too close in color to light-colored hair.

Probes/Needles

In this book, *probe* means *needle*. This is a purely personal choice, but over the years, the term *probe* has been less nerve wracking to new electrolysis clients. The term *needle* in medical and allied-health services refers to an instrument that injects into tissue (e.g., an immunization shot) or draws out blood and other body fluids. The connotation is one of trauma, leaving some people squeamish. The probe should not puncture the skin at the surface, but instead should slide down an existing opening (e.g., the follicle), where it acts as an electrode. The terms technicians choose are personal preferences.

As the correct pristine, sharp knife for a task is important to a master chef, so should the right probe be to the electrologist. Just as a chef would not try to slice and dice a tomato with a dirty, dull-edged, and damaged knife, neither should an electrologist settle for a contaminated, dull, bent, or weakened probe. The primary consideration must always be that the probe is sterile, whether it is a newly opened, disposable sterile probe or a probe that has gone through complete sterilization. The preferred choice for electrologists today is to use the former: a brand-new, presterilized, prepackaged probe with each client for each visit. The technician should open probes in front of clients, giving the clients peace of mind and confidence in the technician as a professional. Most clients would willingly pay $1 more per treatment for new, disposable probes. Many packages have visible marks of sterilization and expiration dates. If packaging is damaged in any way, or if the date on the package has expired, discard the probes in the sharps box or by another appropriate method as described in Chapter 5. The significance of sterilization and the harmful contaminates and diseases that can be found on used probes are addressed more fully in Chapter 5.

Sterilization aside, the needle (of correct diameter size) should be able to enter and slide down the follicle and, with all other variables in place, apply the necessary amount of current to destroy the dermal papilla and/or the sebaceous gland, a process called **histolysis** (his-TAHL-uh-sis). Many electrologists feel a need to change probes for fresh ones during extended treatments of 30 to 45 minutes or longer, because the probes bend and weaken with use and tissue debris may adhere to the probes' sides, particularly for noninsulated probes, if too much treatment energy is used, rendering them less effective.

While probe length, diameter, tip, and blades can vary, there are only two main types of probes: (1) the one-piece probe and (2) the two-piece probe (Figure 12–7). Both offer variations of length, diameter, tip, and blade.

histolysis
the breakdown and disintegration of bodily tissue

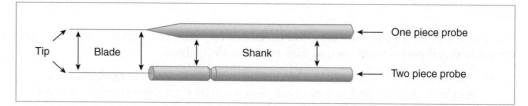

FIGURE 12–7 One-piece and two-piece electrolysis probes with parts labeled

One-Piece Probes

One-piece probes are fashioned from single, solid pieces of steel. They can have tapers that blend gradually into the blade or tapers that cut more abruptly into the blade. The one-piece probe is generally more rigid and less flexible than the two-piece version (see following), but it still has enough flexibility to cover most electrolysis tasks. The one-piece model bends more gently and gradually and is great for coarse hair with deep, straight follicles.

Two-Piece Probes

With the two-piece probe, the blade is attached to the shank by a divot cut out most of the way around the shank, called a crimp. This probe is also called a straight or cylindrical probe. The two-piece probe is generally a little flimsier than the one-piece probe when all other variables (e.g., length and diameter) are equal. The two-piece model bends and "gives" more easily, making it a favorite for experienced electrologists who feel that the thinner-diameter probes contour with the follicle as they slide down. These electrologists claim to "feel" the follicle walls through the probe.

One-piece and two-piece probes alike have several distinct components:

- **shank,** which is what is inserted into the probe holder
- **blade,** which is the gold or steel portion of the probe that is inserted into the hair follicle; it comes in various lengths, diameters, and shapes and is insulated or noninsulated
- **tip,** which is the portion in insulated probes where the current is produced in the hair follicle
- **taper,** which is the graduated link between the shank and the blade, not present on all probes

Insulated Probes

Insulated probes are covered two-thirds of the way down with an insulated plastic coating. They are most effective when using thermolysis modality, because they produce the current and therefore the heat down at the tip of the probe (Figure 12–8). As a result, they apply heat only to the base of the follicle, where it is most desired to destroy the dermal papilla. The sebaceous gland remains unaffected. According to James E. Schuster, MD, because the intensity of heat is three to four times greater at the tip of an insulated probe than on a noninsulated probe, the epilator should be adjusted to reduce the treatment energy when using insulated probes. While there is no electrical reason insulated probes cannot be used with galvanic current, the lye pattern differs with insulated probes. There is one school of thought that, for effective and permanent hair removal, the sebaceous gland should also be destroyed. For this reason, insulated probes are not preferred for the galvanic modality or the blend method. When using an insulated probe of the same diameter as a noninsulated probe and applying the same milliampere, there will be equal strength but greater density of electrons at the tip of the insulated probe, whereas the energy or heat pattern will be disbursed less densely over the length of the noninsulated probes. There may also be some question as to the durability of the insulation on the probe and whether the lye produced by the galvanic current would break it down. Consult with the probe manufacturer to determine if the insulation on the probes could withstand the effects of the lye.

shank
part of the probe that is inserted into the probe holder

Insulated probes come in varied lengths and diameters as well as three shapes: (1) tapered, (2) cylindrical, and (3) bulbous.

Tapered Insulated Probes.   Tapered should be the first choice when using thermolysis, because it produces the best point effect. Considered sturdier than the two-piece cylindrical, the tapered insulated probe is more suitable for long sessions.

Cylindrical Insulated Probes.   The popular standard, two-piece, cylindrical probe, like the tapered probe, works well with thermolysis. If the insulation can hold up to the lye produced by the galvanic current, the cylindrical probe is suitable for the blend technique.

Bulbous Insulated Probes.   Insulated bulbous probes, which create the greatest amount of lye at their tips, are effective with galvanic current. For those who believe that permanent destruction of the hair follicle must include destruction of the sebaceous gland, bulbous probes are not the probes of choice. For those who feel that only the destruction of the dermal papilla is necessary, these probes are a good choice.

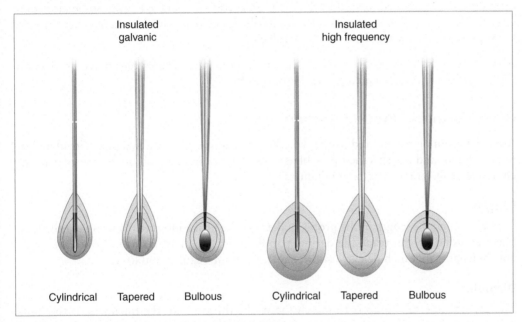

FIGURE 12–8   Heat and lye pattern on insulated probes

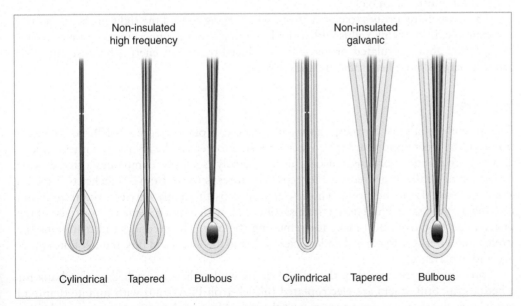

FIGURE 12–9   Heat and lye pattern on non insulated probes

Noninsulated Probes

Like cylindrical probes, noninsulated probes come in varied lengths, diameters, and the three following shapes:

1. tapered
2. cylindrical
3. bulbous

Tapered Noninsulated Probes. Tapered probes are not suitable for galvanic current because they are wider at the top and therefore generate a stronger lye gradient closer to the surface of the skin at the opening of the hair follicle, where it is least desirable and least effective.

Cylindrical Noninsulated Probes. Cylindrical probes are preferred for use with galvanic current, because they evenly distribute lye throughout the hair shaft.

Bulbous Noninsulated Probes. The noninsulated probes with the bulbous tips offer little difference when compared to the cylindrical probes using galvanic. Some electrologists feel the tip makes insertions into small follicles difficult, while others believe the tip helps prevent perforating the base of the follicle.

All three noninsulated probes can be used with thermolysis. The pattern of lye production differs with each noninsulated probe (Figure 12–9).

Other Factors in Probe Selection

After determining the desired probe, whether it be a one piece or two piece, insulated or noninsulated, and the specific tip or blade, the other remaining factors to consider in the choice of probe are its length and diameter.

Length

When selecting the length of the probe, make sure the probe inserts fully into the follicle so that the probe tip can reach the dermal papilla in its late-anagen stage. Probes are available in lengths that include extra short, short, medium, regular, and long.

Diameter

The general rule of thumb is to match the probe thickness to the thickness of the hairs being epilated. Probe sizes come in 0.002, 0.003, 0.004, 0.005, 0.006, and 0.007, which is 2 to 7 thousandths of an inch.

There are many probes to choose from when trying to find the right probe for a task. For example, if removing vellus with a shallow follicle on the upper lip using thermolysis, use a 0.002 short, insulated probe with a reduced-treatment energy, because the finer probe generates more heat than the thicker probe.

Forceps

Forceps come in almost as many shapes and sizes as probes (Figure 12–10). For the electrologist, the most important factor when choosing forceps is the ability to withstand sterilization frequently. For this reason, most electrolysis-supply companies offer a wide variety of medically approved steel forceps. The forceps range from 2¾ inches to 5 inches long; most are 4¼ inches long. The 2¾-inch forceps fit snugly between the thumb and forefinger of the same hand doing the insertion and, with a quick maneuver or twist of the fingers, can be moved into place for removing the hair. The second hand maintains the stretch and offers greater speed and efficiency. Using the forceps in this manner takes practice and experience.

electroplated
an object coated with some substance by electrical means

Some forceps are smooth at the tip and shank while others are etched on the shank for a better grip. Still others are **electroplated** (uh-lek-troh-PLAY-tud) with minute diamond particles at the tip for a more sure grip of the hair. Most of the forceps recommended for

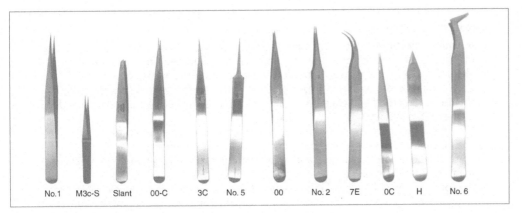

FIGURE 12–10
Different types of forceps, or tweezers

electrologists have very, very sharp tips to grip the finest hair as close to the follicle opening as possible, without snagging or tweezing adjacent hairs. Despite this, some electrologists still prefer the slanted tip, which is suitable in areas where hair growth is not dense. Some forceps curve or bend at the top and are excellent for releasing long, imbedded, ingrown hairs.

Forceps Maintenance and Repair

To maintain the forceps' sharp points and effective gripping action, store them with their protective guards on. The guards, however, withstand only **autoclave** (AW-toh-klayv) and chemical sterilization. When the tips become damaged, usually from dropping, they can be repaired using a natural stone, like **Arkansas stone**, available from electrolysis supply companies, or a simple piece of fine sandpaper.

autoclave
a strong, steel container used for steam sterilization

Arkansas stone
type of stone used to smooth or sharpen another object

Inward Bend.   If forceps are bent inward (Figure 12–11), they can be repaired by sandwiching sandpaper between the two tips with the bent portion of the tip resting on the gritty side of the paper, squeezing the two tips together as hard as possible, and dragging the tips across the paper. If both tips are bent inward, simply fold the sandpaper so that both tips can drag across the paper.

Outward Bend.   If forceps are bent outward (Figure 12–12), they can be repaired by placing the bent tip directly on sandpaper, placing the paper on a hard surface, and dragging the tip across the paper. Repeat until under a magnifier the problem is corrected.

Electrolysis forceps are classified as a **critical item**, because they come into contact with blood and body fluids. As a result, they must be cleaned and sterilized as discussed in Chapter 5.

critical item
an instrument that comes into contact with blood or other bodily fluids

FIGURE 12–11 Repairing inward bend of forceps

FIGURE 12–12 Repairing outward bend of forceps

Care of the Equipment

- As with all electrical equipment, the electrolysis unit should be properly grounded and in an outlet designated for its use only and with no adjustments made to the plug.
- The unit should be kept away from direct heat (e.g., sun or heaters).
- Units should be kept well away from water. If a unit comes into contact with water, it should be turned off and checked for damage by a licensed electrician recommended by the unit manufacturer.
- The unit should never be opened by an untrained or unlicensed electrician.
- The unit should be kept free of dust and have adequate ventilation.
- Cords should be kept untangled and away from items and edges that might weaken them or cause them to fray.
- Do not clean the unit with volatile chemical substances or water. Chemical substances can remove important markings, and water can enter the unit, damaging it internally.

Troubleshooting Problems with Electrolysis Equipment

No current is being produced at the probe.
- Is the machine plugged in and turned on?
- Is the machine receiving power from the outlet? If not, check the outlet with another appliance.
- Does a fuse need replacing, or has a switch flipped at the circuit breaker?

The power indicator light is on, but no current is producing at the tip.
- Are all dials (rheostat) where they should be?
- Is the footswitch connected properly to the machine?
- Is the needle holder cord properly connected to the machine?

There is still no current.
- Does the indicator light come on when depressing the footswitch? If the light fails to come on, the problem is with the footswitch or the footswitch cord or adaptor that plugs into the epilator. If the light does come on, the footswitch is working and the problem lies elsewhere, possibly in the needle holder or the handheld electrode or their respective cords and adaptors. Further isolate the problem by eliminating the handheld electrode, unplugging it, and switching it to thermolysis mode.
- Does the probe produce current in thermolysis mode? If yes, the problem was with the handheld electrode and most probably the cord, which should be replaced. If no current is produced at the probe in thermolysis mode, then there is a very good chance that the problem lies with the needle holder and/or the cord. The needle holder and cord should be replaced and retested. It is always worth having spare cords to prevent having to cancel clients, which inconveniences those clients and sacrifices revenue. If there is still no current at the probe in thermolysis mode, then an additional test can be done with a small lightbulb.

Other Supplies

The following supplies should be available in the treatment room or easily accessible. Additional housekeeping/cleaning supplies should be kept separately.

- chart of skin and hair
- license, diplomas, professional affiliation certificates, if not displayed in the reception area
- client health/treatment record form
- additional literature (e.g., before and after-care instructions)
- spare cords and electrodes for galvanic machine
- sterile container with lid for storing sterile tools
- container for contaminated tools
- sharps container or isolyser
- spare needle-holder cords
- 12 assorted needle-holder caps
- ultrasonic unit with protein-dissolving enzyme detergent
- scissors
- laundry hamper

- paper drapes or towels
- bolster or pillow
- clock
- timer
- mirror
- two covered jars containing lip rolls, cotton rounds, and cotton squares
- Menda™ or another bottle dispenser for alcohol and other antiseptic
- eye shields
- Arkansas stone and fine sandpaper
- gentle cleanser and makeup remover
- antiseptic lotion
- anesthetic cream or lotion
- ice and ice bags
- after-care lotions
- after-care camouflage product
- cleaning/disinfecting supplies for use between clients

Bulb Test

A test bulb (Figure 12–13) can be purchased from any electrolysis-supply company. It works by clipping one clip to any metal portion of the electrolysis unit and the second clip to the metal portion at the end of the probe (with the plastid cap removed). The current is applied by depressing the footswitch. If the lightbulb lights, the needle cord is working well. If the bulb does not light up, there could be a rupture in the needle cord that is preventing the current from flowing freely to the tip of the needle. The needle cord needs replacing.

A busy electrolysis business with a supply of replacement cords and even a small piece of backup equipment benefits should a significant problem with the main epilator require shipping it across country for repairs.

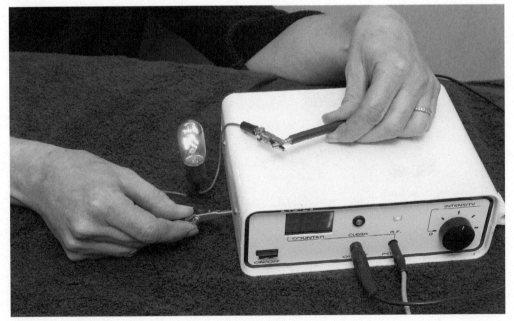

FIGURE 12–13
Testing the equipment using the test bulb

electrologist
someone skilled in the use of electricity to remove moles, warts, or hair roots; synonymous with electrolysist (see following)

electrolysist
someone skilled in the use of electricity to remove moles, warts, or hair roots: synonymous with electrologist (see preceding)

Conclusion

You may have already decided to become an **electrologist** (ee-lek-TRAHL-uh-just), or **electrolysist** (eh-lek-TRAHL-ih-sist), or you may be working in another hair-removal field and are considering the benefit of adding electrolysis to your skill as a hair-removal specialist. Electrolysis is a valued service that can only complement and enhance other hair-removal services. This chapter and those that follow should, when paired with formal classroom training, provide an opportunity to establish a lucrative and rewarding career as an electrologist *and* a hair-removal specialist.

Discussion and Review Questions

1. Name three of the five sources that can produce electric energy.
2. What is Ohm's law?
3. Name a good conductor and a poor conductor.
4. What is a milliampere?
5. What is the difference between AC and DC?

6. What is cataphoresis?
7. What is the difference between insulated and noninsulated probes?
8. In the United States, who regulates electrolysis equipment?

Additional Readings

Bono, Michael. 1994. *The Blend Method*. Santa Barbara, CA: Tortoise Press.

Gallant, Ann. *Principles and Techniques for the Electrologist*. Cheltenham, U.K.: Stanley Thornes (Publishers) Ltd.

Glor, Fino. 1987. *Modern Electrology*. Great Neck, N.Y.: Hair Publishing, Inc.

Hinkle, Arthur Ralph, and Lind, Richard W. 1968. *Electrolysis, Thermolysis, and the Blend*. Los Angeles, CA: Arroway.

Meharg, G. E., R.N., and Richards, R. N., M.D. 1997. *Cosmetic and Medical Electrolysis and Temporary Hair Removal*, 2e., Toronto, Ont: Medric Ltd.

CHAPTER 13

Selecting the Right Modality and Treatment Application

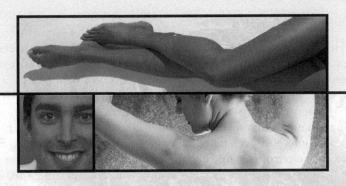

Chapter Outline

Learning Objectives ■ Key Terms ■ Introduction
■ The Client Consultation ■ Selecting the Right Modality
The Treatment ■ Posttreatment ■ Treatment Techniques ■ Carpal Tunnel Syndrome
Conclusion ■ Discussion and Review Questions ■ Additional Readings

Learning Objectives

By the end of this chapter, you should be able to:

1. Conduct a client consultation.
2. Select the best modality for a client's treatment.
3. Know theoretically how to deliver electrolysis to all areas of the face and body.
4. Understand, theoretically, basic electrolysis techniques.
5. Know how to provide appropriate pretreatment and after-care, including advising clients on home care.

Key Terms

acne vulgaris	divot	hirsute	prilocaine
arnica montana	EMLA	hyperpigment	steroid dependent
auditory meatus	erythema	isopropyl alcohol	dermatoses
auricle	eschar	Novocain™	tragus
carpal tunnel syndrome	ethyl alcohol	occlusive dressing	vasoconstriction
cortisone	grand mal	petit mal	working point

Introduction

This chapter builds on all the physical sciences covered in previous chapters, concentrating on the client. This chapter focuses on electrolysis as a hair-removal service, from background theory to the more practical selection of modality and client preparation. This chapter also addresses after-care and home-care recommendations.

Important considerations in permanent hair removal are pros and cons. When selecting the most suitable modality of electrolysis, it is paramount to be aware of and discuss indications and, even more important, contraindications and how they affect the decisions of both electrologist and client. This chapter delves into those areas and helps the electrologist guide the client through a successful consultation and, eventually, a treatment program both parties are happy with.

When assessing a client for electrolysis, have a current, accurate, and complete health history. If the client lists medications, clearly record those medications. Do not assume

---

PROS & CONS

Pros of Electrolysis

- Electrolysis is currently the only proven method of permanent hair removal recognized by the FDA.
- Electrolysis can be performed successfully on all types of hair: blonde, dark, gray, straight, curly, vellus, or terminal.
- Electrolysis can be used effectively on all skin types and with all races: dry, oily, or mature.
- Electrolysis can be performed on all parts of the face and body, except for the inside of the nose or the inside of the ear.
- Electrolysis can remove hairs with great precision, one at a time, making it a great choice for shaping eyebrows.

Cons of Electrolysis

- Electrolysis requires the client to stop other forms of hair removal on the areas to be treated other than trimming or shaving. It is difficult for some people to allow hair to grow in before treatment.
- Electrolysis is seen as costly to some who consider tweezing free and who do not appreciate the negative, long-term impact of tweezing.
- Electrolysis can cause discomfort.
- Regularly scheduled appointments can be difficult for busy people. To succeed, electrolysis requires a commitment to the program of treatments and a temporary reorganization of time and priorities.
- Electrolysis treatments can cause redness (erythema), bumps, and swelling.
- Makeup should not be worn for 24 hours after the treatment, which may be difficult for some women.
- Extensive electrolysis work may take months, even years, to complete.

INDICATIONS & CONTRAINDICATIONS

An indication is a sign or symptom that something exists or is true. With electrolysis it is the sign that there is a condition of superfluous hair that is treatable. A contraindication is a condition, disease, or medication that precludes the client from temporarily or permanently receiving electrolysis.

Indications for Electrolysis

Indications for electrolysis would be unwanted hair, regardless of texture or pigment, on any part of the face and body except the inside of the nose and the inside of the ear.

Contraindications for Electrolysis

Besides the conditions, diseases or medications that may temporarily or permanently preclude a client from receiving electrolysis, some situations may allow the electrologist to proceed with caution, with the approval of or under the direction of the client's physician. A contraindication may be temporary, like a sunburn, long lasting, an example being pregnancy, in which the service can be given postpartum, or a permanent contraindication like diabetes mellitus which is a chronic disorder.

---

medications treat only obvious and well-known conditions. For example, Minoxodil is a vasodilator used to treat hypertension, but it has now become more recognized for restoring hair growth.

Acne Vulgaris

Individuals with **acne vulgaris** (ACK-nee vul-GAR-is) should receive no electrolysis in the vicinity of the affected area due to the high presence of bacteria and the possibility of cross-contamination. In addition, acne vulgaris is a painful condition, and electrolysis only adds discomfort to the already traumatized area. Certainly, electrolysis helps control acne outbreaks by eliminating hairs that get trapped in the infected follicles and by providing galvanic current, which destroys sebaceous glands in the hair follicles. However, treatments should be held off until the active outbreak has passed and there is little sign of infection. The client should be referred to a dermatologist and receive a course of facials to control the condition as soon as possible.

> **acne vulgaris**
> the "common acne" characterized by blackheads and pimples; found most commonly in teenagers and young adults

Asthma

While asthma does not preclude electrolysis, caution should be exercised. This illness is nervous in origin, and those with it may be prone to attacks when feeling anxious about the procedure. The frequency and severity of attacks should be documented and may help determine if electrolysis can be given. Every step should be made to relieve any apprehension and anxiety the client may experience. Treatments should start at a low current level and progress cautiously.

Blood Pressure

Clients with blood-pressure problems may be treated with electrolysis, but caution should be used when treating those with high blood pressure problems, particularly when those clients show anxiety.

Deep Brain Stimulator (DBS)

In December 2002, the FDA put out a warning to all medical workers to be on the alert for patients with deep brain stimulator (DBS) implants and to avoid treating those patients with diathermy. The risk of exposing a patient to a diathermy treatment, who has this implant, is serious injury and possibly death. The DBS acts like a regulator for the brain, to stabilize the tremors associated with diseases like Parkinson's. Patients are asked to avoid shortwave diathermy treatments, which may cause the metal implants and associated leads to heat. The FDA has listed certain equipment it considers a threat, and diathermy epilation units are not listed. However, as studies in this area are still inconclusive, it is prudent to treat no individuals with these implants until research is complete and there is conclusive evidence that it is safe to treat these individuals.

Diabetes

Considerable care should be taken in treating a client with diabetes, also known as diabetes mellitus. The severity of this illness, including the kind of treatment the client receives for it, should be well documented. Include whether the disease is controlled by diet and exercise, with an insulin pump, or regular insulin injections. The lower extremities should never be treated with electrolysis, because the loss of some sensation to the skin makes it difficult to judge appropriate levels of intensity. Also, the skin has diminished ability to heal. While these problems are more severe in the lower extremities, they also affect other parts of the body, including the face. The need for meticulous hygiene, sanitation, and sterilization cannot be overemphasized. The client should be advised of the importance of following home-care procedures to promote faster healing in a condition that otherwise heals poorly. Guidance or a referral from the client's physician is necessary.

Epilepsy

grand mal
a serious form of epilepsy in which there is loss of consciousness and severe convulsions

petit mal
a form of epilepsy marked by episodes of brief loss of consciousness without convulsions or falling

Both **grand mal** (GRAHND MAL) and **petit mal** (puh-TEET MAHL) attacks can be triggered by electrolysis current. If the seizures are infrequent and controlled by medication, it is possible to perform electrolysis on these clients, particularly if the unwanted hair is emotionally stressful for the client and there is a real need for the service. However, clients with epilepsy *must* be evaluated by their physicians before receiving electrolysis treatment. The physicians will determine if the treatments would be safe. Receive the physicians' approvals in writing.

Heart Conditions

People with heart conditions can receive electrolysis, but they should do so with the knowledge of, and supervision of, their physician. Physician approvals must be in writing. Clients wearing pacemakers should not receive the galvanic or blend method unless the positive electrode is placed so the flow of current does not pass through or near the pacemaker. See Chapter 15 for further details on safe placement. If the client is to receive thermolysis, the technician should be sure that the high frequency of the epilator will not interfere with the pacemaker, which can happen if the pacemaker is "synchronous," that is, it stimulates the heart on demand, as opposed to asynchronous, which delivers a constant rate of electrical stimuli to the heart. Never treat a cardiac patient without the full and written consent of their cardiologist. The treatments should be short. People with heart conditions often present with poor circulation and bruise more easily. Medications for the condition may affect blood clotting.

Metal Implants

Metal implants may include pacemakers, pins, rods, plates, and intrauterine devices (IUDs). When using galvanic current, the client may feel discomfort, so the pathway for the hand-held electrode should be positioned such that the current does not pass near any metal implants. Thermolysis may be a better choice of modality.

Skin Disorders

Most skin disorders like sunburn or acne are temporary in nature and only the area affected need be avoided. Other skin disorders, like herpes, may be contagious and the client should not be treated even in areas where the skin is not affected. Other skin disorders may be indicative of a serious chronic disease like lupus, that contraindicates electrolysis.

- **Acne**—Skin with the occasional acne pimple can be treated with electrolysis, as long as the affected area is avoided. Acne vulgaris, as mentioned previously, should be completely avoided.
- **Cold sores**—People with active outbreaks of herpes and presenting with cold sores should not be treated with electrolysis. A prophylactic medication can be taken before an appointment.
- **Eczema**—The area of eczema outbreak should not be treated with electrolysis, but other areas of the face and body not so affected can be treated.
- **Inflammation**—Any areas of inflamed skin (**erythema** [er-uh-THEE-muh]) should not be treated with electrolysis until the skin has healed.
- **Moles**—There is no documentation that treating a mole with electrolysis causes problems, but because there is always the chance that the mole could be cancerous, clients should have their moles checked first and receive the consent of their physicians to have the moles treated.
- **Sunburn**—Sunburned areas should not be treated with electrolysis until the sunburn has subsided and the skin has returned to normal.

erythema
redness of the skin as a result of the widening of small blood vessels near the skin's surface

Doctors' Consent

Any time there is a condition that may be contraindicated or questionable for treatment, clients must always receive consent in writing from the clients' physicians. There could be serious legal ramifications were something to happen, even if it was not triggered or affected by the electrolysis. Always follow protocol to avoid a damaging lawsuit. If there is any question of a client's well-being, do not provide the service. Advise the client of other options.

Exercise vigilance with clients' health and well-being. Do not try and make a diagnosis beyond your expertise. Instead, know when to refer to physician for further evaluation.

The Client Consultation

The client consultation is the first opportunity the electrologist gets to demonstrate professionalism to the client. It is a time to acquire important information from the client, before organizing a treatment plan, as well as to explain the process of electrolysis to the potential client and answer any questions the client may have. No new client should be treated without a consultation first, even if the client has had electrolysis in the past. Clients' medical histories change.

Usually, the first point of contact between the potential client and the electrolysis clinic is by telephone. If the electrologist does not answer those calls personally, instead leaving that task to a receptionist or another employee, that individual should be trained and informed well enough to answer basic questions (e.g., qualifications and professional associations of the electrologist, different modalities, the use of disposable needles). However, responding individuals should make no promises or suggestions of how long it will take to rid the potential client of unwanted hair that has not yet been seen by the electrologist. In a polite and friendly manner, the potential client should be invited to make an appointment for a consultation, which will be an opportunity to view the facility and have questions answered in more detail.

For efficiency, have the potential client arrive 5 to 10 minutes early to fill out paperwork. This allows the electrologist to use the consultation time to examine the client's skin and the hair-growth area to be treated, to discuss the recommended course of action, and to answer questions. Even though this is a consultation and not a treatment, it is important that, once in the treatment room, all aspects of sanitation and hygiene apply. There should be fresh linen or paper on the treatment couch, and the electrologist should wash the hands, especially if the client's skin is going to be touched. Next, the electrologist should go over the consultation form step by step (Figures 13–1 and 13–2), making sure everything is clear and accurate. Finally, the electrologist should have the client sign and date the form in the electrologist's presence.

After a brief review of the consultation form, the electrologist should turn the focus to all aspects pertinent to the treatment, posttreatment and home care, checking the "Instructions" section on completion. These aspects follow briefly and in more detail later in the chapter:

■ Address any contraindications that may be apparent, and discuss the client's medical history and prescription medications.
■ Once satisfied that the medical history is in order and clearly understood and that electrolysis is indicated as the best solution for permanently removing the

Electrical Epilation Consultation/Record Form

Name _____ Date _____

Address _____

Telephone   Home (___)_____ Work (___)_____ DOB ___/___/___

Referred by _____ Attending physician _____

Medical History: Allergies (especially latex) _____

Infectious diseases _____ Nervous disorders _____

H/L blood pressure _____ Heart disease/pacemaker _____

Hormone therapy _____ Thyroid condition _____

Epilepsy _____ Asthma _____

Diabetes _____ Pregnant _____

Hepatitis A, B, or C _____ Metal implants (piercing) _____

Deep brain stimulator (DBS) _____ Other _____

OB/GYN History _____

Medications _____

Area(s) to be treated _____

_____

Skin type _____ Hair pelosity _____

Previous Hair Removal

Temporary means of hair removal _____ Frequency _____

Permanent means of hair removal _____

Date began _____ Last treatment _____ Approximate number of treatments _____

Instructions   Before treatment _____ After treatment _____

Topical anesthetic _____

I, the undersigned, do hereby certify that the answers to the above questions are correct to the best of my knowledge.

Signature _____ Date _____

Signature of parent/guardian if under 18 years of age _____

FIGURE 13–1 Consultation and Client Record Form – front view

unwanted hair, explain the proposed treatment and what to expect. Have a chart illustrating the cross section of the skin with the pilosebaceous unit and the three different stages of hair growth.

- Discuss the recommended modality, how often the client should come in for treatments at the start, and how long each treatment session should be for optimal results.
- Discuss regrowth, as well as what the client is permitted and not permitted to do (e.g., no tweezing the area, only trimming or shaving). Although shaving is an acceptable temporary method, it is not recommended on women's faces if there are nonpigmented vellus mixed with unwanted terminal hairs. The vellus may become pigmented and stronger. Trimming terminal hairs with scissors is better.

Date	Treatment Time	Modality	Current Intensity	Current Duration	Needle Size(s)	Area(s) Treated	Additional Comments

FIGURE 13–2 Consultation and Client Record Form – back view

■ Advise the client of the things that will help make the treatment more comfortable, like avoiding caffeine in the hours preceding the treatment and allowing plenty of time to get to the appointment so there is no stress or anxiety. Advice may include using a topical anesthetic to help dull the sensation of the current, particularly on the upper lip.

■ Next, explain the potential skin reactions of the session, and allow the client to schedule appointments accordingly (e.g., not immediately before an important board meeting if the upper lip is going to be red and puffy and no makeup can be applied). When discussing the most suitable appointment time, point out that makeup is not recommended for 24 hours after the treatment.

■ Explain the importance of a strict home-care routine that will aid in the healing process and prevent unwanted skin reactions.

■ Finally, make sure the client understands the fee for the service and explain the option of purchasing a package of services at a discount, if this is something that the facility offers.

At the end of the consultation, assure the client that electrolysis is a process that works and that, although it may take some time, it is worth the commitment. It can eliminate unwanted hair growth once and for all!

COMMONLY ASKED QUESTIONS

Q. *What is electrolysis?*

A. Electrolysis is the permanent removal of unwanted hair by sliding a tiny probe, the approximate thickness of a hair, down the hair shaft to the root of the hair where a quick pulse of current is applied, resulting in the coagulation of the blood supply to the hair and the destruction of the root.

Q. *Is electrolysis permanent?*

A. Yes. The FDA and AMA recognize electrolysis as the only proven method of permanent hair removal. Once the blood supply to the hair has been destroyed at the root, hair will no longer grow from that hair follicle.

Q. *Where on the body can electrolysis be done?*

A. Electrolysis can be done on any part of the face and body where there is unwanted hair, except the inside of the nose and the inside of the ear.

Q. *Does electrolysis hurt?*

A. Generally, electrolysis does not hurt, but certain parts of the body are more sensitive to the current than others—for instance, the upper lip. For more sensitive areas, or for people with lower discomfort thresholds, there are various topical anesthetic creams that can be used to numb the area(s) to be treated.

Q. *Will I be red after the treatment?*

A. There may be some redness in the area. In the case of the upper lip, particularly if extensive work has been done, some people may experience mild puffiness for a short while. Usually, any reaction is gone in an hour or two.

Q. *How long do the treatments usually take?*

A. Treatments usually range from 15 minutes to an hour, depending on the amount of hair that must be removed and the person's tolerance for a longer session.

Q. *Will there be any permanent marks on the treated area?*

A. No. In the hands of a well-trained and skilled electrologist, whose instructions for after-care are followed, there should be no lasting marks or scars.

Q. *Will there be regrowth?*

A. Some regrowth is possible, particularly with (telogen) hairs that were not in the best stage for permanent removal (the best stage is the growing or anagen stage). Shaving or trimming the area 2 days before ensures that the electrologist can observe and remove only hairs in the growing stage. Occasionally, a hair root may receive sufficient treatment energy to release the hair and damage the root but not completely destroy it. A finer hair may regrow.

After-Care/Home Care

Meticulous after-care is essential to speeding the healing process and to avoid pimples. Clients' hands should be washed thoroughly and clean before touching the treated area. Explain to clients that the current, when applied to the follicle, destroys bacteria in the follicle. Antiseptics applied before and after the treatment temporarily remove bacteria from the skin's surface. If little pustules become apparent in the days after the treatment, microorganisms may have been introduced in the day or two after the treatment, when the skin was still vulnerable and healing. These microorganisms may have been introduced through:

- touching the skin with unclean hands, which is easy to do if it was a habit to feel for the hairs (e.g., while driving)
- saturating the skin with water, thereby transporting microorganisms down into the follicle
- using face creams that have been contaminated by dipping fingers directly into the pot rather than using a spatula
- makeup that has been contaminated by touching fingers to the lip of the bottle or using dirty sponges
- hair, particularly if it contains some product that goes onto the pillow, which then contacts the face and transports microorganisms to the vulnerable areas of the face and neck

Skin Cleansing

Cleansers should be fragrance-free and designed for sensitive skin. Masks and rich creams should be avoided for 48 hours.

Avoid saturating the face with water for 24 hours after the electrolysis session. Body areas can generally be washed after 12 to 18 hours. Water too readily transports microorganisms down into an already vulnerable area. The face can be cleansed with appropriate lotions and removed with damp cotton or tissues. For the body, a perfume-free body wash or a gentle germicidal soap like Safeguard™ can be used. If the client has been in the habit of sticking fingers into the jar of face cream, recommend a fresh face cream and spatula, especially for the few days following the treatment when the skin is most vulnerable to infection.

Medicated Creams

Mild first-aid or antibiotic creams, such as Neosporin™ or Bacitracin™, can be applied, but not steroid creams like **cortisone** (KOR-tih-sohn). Cortisone creams should not be used or recommended for after-care for any client requiring their use for 2 weeks or more. Long-term use of cortisone creams could cause the skin to develop **steroid dependent dermatoses**, meaning that the irritation could return, necessitating further use of the cream. It is lengthy and bothersome to "wean" the skin of cortisone dependence.

Makeup Removal

Avoid makeup for at least a day. Instruct the client to apply clean and sterile makeup. If the makeup may have been compromised with fingers or a well-used sponge, it may be worth purchasing new, "clean" makeup for the duration of the treatment. Avoid putting fingers to the bottle opening and contaminating the whole bottle. Also, avoid makeup sponges unless they are washed thoroughly after each use or disposed of and replaced regularly. These are good hygiene habits to develop regardless of the reason. Cake makeup that uses sponges is generally more clogging and tougher to clean, so avoid it, if possible. Makeup removal should be gentle and done with products that are perfume-free and designed for sensitive skin.

cortisone
a hormone secreted by the adrenal gland used to treat rheumatoid arthritis and allergies

steroid dependent dermatoses
a condition in which the long-term overuse of topical steroid creams causes the skin to require continued usage to keep the offending condition away

Hair

If the client is prone to breakouts on the face or neck after electrolysis, and all previous steps are being used to prevent the breakouts, another consideration may be the hair. If the client wears product in the hair, the product will pick up dirt and pollutants from the environment. The dirt and grime often get transferred to the client's pillowcase and in turn to the client's skin. Because it is not recommended to saturate the face after the treatment, the client should not shower and wash the hair. Instead, the client can put a sleeping cap over the hair and use a clean, fresh pillowcase for the 2 or 3 nights following the treatment, until the skin has healed.

Ultraviolet Exposure

hyperpigment
producing too much pigment; causes brown spots on the skin

Tanning in a tanning booth or natural sunlight should be avoided while undergoing regular electrolysis treatments, meaning treatments once every 2 weeks. If there is any erythema to the skin, tanning may cause the skin to **hyperpigment** (hy-pur-PIG-ment), and produce brown spots. Advise clients to protect their skin from any ultraviolet rays with a sunscreen of at least SPF 15. SPF 30 can be used on the body, but it is generally too clogging for the face. Using an SPF 15 and reapplying it after a few hours is as effective as the SPF 30, but less clogging.

Bleaching Creams

Hair can be bleached, carefully following manufacturer's instructions, but not for at least 48 hours after the treatment or if the area is still showing signs of irritation.

Postelectrolysis Regrowth

There are two main types of regrowth: (1) apparent and (2) actual.

Apparent Regrowth

Apparent regrowth is not true regrowth. It is simply hair that is now noticeable but was not noticeable before (e.g., a follicle in the telogen phase with no observable hair may suddenly produce a new anagen hair). This often is the case with new clients who had previously waxed or tweezed the hairs, sending the follicles into a telogen stage where it could be weeks, even months, before the follicle shows a new anagen hair. As a result, as clients cease all other methods of hair removal, they should be warned that it will appear that they are producing more hair as those resting follicles slowly produce anagen hairs. Another consideration is that after the more noticeable coarse hair has been removed, clients begin to notice the finer, previously less noticeable hair.

Actual Regrowth

Actual regrowth occurs in a hair follicle that has been unsuccessfully treated with electrolysis. The cause of this is an inaccurate insertion in which the dermal papilla is missed, a distorted follicle that was ineffectively treated with thermolysis, or an inadequate treatment energy, either from insufficient current intensity or insufficient duration. Tell the client that, for the destruction of as many hair roots as possible, resulting in minimal hair regrowth, the current must be at a certain level, which may involve minimal discomfort.

There should be no more depilatories or waxing to the area being treated, and *no more tweezing*. Tell the client that to continue to tweeze any hair extends the time it will take to complete the process, because tweezing forces hairs into a resting stage and depending on the area, may take up to 3 months before the follicle produces a new hair that can be treated, prolonging the electrolysis. Let the client know what the tweezing costs per session, and they will soon break the habit. Tell clients that they may trim the hair close to the skin. Recommend baby nail scissors with blunt tips. Reiterate the importance of trimming or shaving a couple of days before the treatment session.

Pain and Discomfort

Pain perception and pain thresholds differ considerably from individual to individual, as does the type of pain. A woman can give birth to baby after baby after baby without as much as an aspirin but require a topical anesthetic for electrolysis on the upper lip. Pain thresholds and perceptions are as unique, individual, and varied as hair-growth patterns. It is therefore crucial not to presume that clients can tolerate certain levels of discomfort. Do not dismiss the clients' reference to discomfort or they will not remain your clients for long. It is also important to be honest about potential discomfort and to suggest help for alleviating discomfort. Questioning clients about pain during the consultation prepares the client and allows the technician to make suggestions. Generally speaking, older women have higher pain thresholds, but this may change if a woman has high anxiety or other nervous disorders. Young women often have slightly lower thresholds that are exacerbated if they are "high strung." Men at the outset often portray "bravado" and the ability to tolerate any kind of discomfort, but do not be fooled. Men are often the first to give up on programs of treatments if their comfort levels are not established.

"Peaches!"

A client entered the salon ready for a treatment, with preapplied topical anesthetic, anticipating pain, making faces and saying, "I know it's going to hurt like the dickens. I just got my period!"

With the current intensity barely high enough to desiccate the dermal papilla, this client vocalized her discomfort with, "Oh! Ouch! Yikes! Oooh! That hurts!" and waved her hands around. I asked her to think of something comforting at the moment. She suggested "peaches—fuzzy, juicy, delicious peaches" I asked her to say "peaches" every time she felt the current, in place of the anguished words of pain. At first she'd say, "Ouch! Peaches!" I then suggested she say "peaches" with me as I applied the current. After a few minutes, the client completely relaxed and not only ceased the rhetoric of pain but stopped saying "peaches," too. This client now realizes that her *perception* of pain is a big part of the problem in experiencing discomfort, so it is now much easier to change that perception by starting the treatment session vocalizing "peaches" and eliminating the pain rhetoric. Try to encourage clients to avoid using words that are associated with pain. Ask clients to state a number from 1 to 10 to indicate their comfort levels, 10 being the worst pain, 1 being no pain.

Certain areas are generally more sensitive to stimulation and therefore more uncomfortable. These areas are often around body orifices (e.g., the groin, eyes, ears, nose, and mouth). The increased sensitivity offers warning and therefore hopefully protection. Under the nose and around the mouth, the sensitivity facilitates the pleasure of kissing; if you are a Maori from New Zealand or an Eskimo, rubbing noses is a similar sign of affection. The flip side is the increased sensitivity experienced from the application of the current or a jab from an incorrect probe. Therefore, it is not unusual for an anesthetic to be prescribed for these areas.

Anesthesia

At this time, electrologists have no authority to inject an anesthetic like **Novocain**™ (NOH-vuh-kayn) to block pain, but there are some effective topical numbing products that are available with or without prescription. In the United States, the most popular prescription-required topical anesthetic used by electrology clients today is eutectic mixture of local anesthetics (**EMLA**). To receive a prescription for EMLA, a visit to the doctor is often necessary, but if the client is well known to a physician's practice, such as the OB/GYN from regular routine visits, one can often secure a prescription by placing a call. Occasionally, doctors are willing to call prescriptions in without appointments. EMLA can be costly, but if the client has a good prescription plan, the cost can be reduced considerably. It is also worth making sure that the physician prescribes the 30-gram tube, because anything smaller lasts only a couple of treatments, depending on the area being

Novocain™
a trademark for a synthetic anesthetic drug

EMLA
a popular prescription-required topical anesthetic used by electrolysists; acronym of eutectic mixture of local anesthetics

prilocaine
a local anesthetic found in EMLA
(see preceding)

vasoconstriction
the narrowing of the blood vessels
with consequent reduction in
blood flow or increased blood
pressure

occlusive dressing
a covering that seals the area it
covers

treated. The physician can also be requested to check the refill box for up to three refills to eliminate the need for a revisit too soon, especially if the tube is misplaced. EMLA contains both lidocaine and **prilocaine** (PRY-luh-kayn) which, when combined, cause **vasoconstriction** (vay-zoh-kun-STRIK-shun) to numb the area where it is applied, making the area look blanched.

It is important to note that EMLA is a prescription. Therefore, the leaflet accompanying it should be read and the directions followed accurately. Do not spread the EMLA thickly over a large area, because it is most effective on small areas. To use EMLA, first thoroughly clean the area. The EMLA should be applied thickly so that it is opaque on the skin (approximately 4 to 6 millimeters thick). The area should be covered with a transparent plastic patch, which often comes with the cream. Some of the patches are an impractical shape and size and must be trimmed to fit well. An alternative to the patches is kitchen plastic wrap. Covering the area this way is called making an **occlusive** (oh-KLOO-suv) **dressing**. The cover prevents the cream from drying out and allows for better penetration. The EMLA must be in place for at least 45 minutes before the service. Advise the client to keep the area covered until in the treatment room, ready for the service to begin. Once uncovered, and with the manipulation of the skin, EMLA's effectiveness may only last for 30 minutes. Clients receiving a treatment of 30 minutes or longer should apply the plastic in small strips (e.g., left upper lip and right upper lip with two separate strips instead of one long one). This means that an area can be left covered and remain numb until it is time to be treated.

Nonprescription Anesthetics

Many topical anesthetics are now available without prescription. Gone are the days when clients experimented with sticky toothache and teething gels. Over-the-counter products from the local drugstore in the first-aid section usually contain 2 percent lidocaine and come in a cream, spray, or gel. The electrologist can now provide an assortment of numbing products in the form of creams, liquids, gels, and sprays and provide retail products like LMX™, formerly ELA-Max™; Topicaine™; or Laracaine™, to name a few. They usually contain 4% Lidocaine or 20% Benzocaine as the active ingredient. Do not use these products around the eyes. Liquids and sprays should not be used around the ears. It is also not recommended to use spray anesthetic on the face unless the eyes are well protected. Instead, spray cotton until it is well saturated with the numbing solution and apply it to the area. If a numbing solution enters the eyes, rinse the eyes immediately and thoroughly with plenty of cold running water for a full 2 minutes, and seek professional help. When using a numbing cream purchased from the electrologist, follow the manufacturer's directions. In general, these creams are used similarly to EMLA, except that the creams work more effectively when a small amount is massaged into the area for 30 seconds before a second, more liberal amount is applied. Most creams also benefit from the use of an occlusive dressing. When treating a large area, if the area is not pretreated with an anesthetic and requires treatment from the electrologist, the area to be treated next can be wiped with the anesthesia, allowing 2 to 3 minutes to numb the area while treating the previous area, and so on. The electrologist must follow product directions to know how quickly the numbing preparation takes to work and for how long it works to know when to apply the preparation to the next treatment area. With all these products, accurately follow manufacturers' directions for use.

Selecting the Right Modality

The choice of modality is not as important as ensuring that whatever choice is made it is carried out with skill, accuracy, and the proper training. The electrologist's goal is always to destroy the dermal papilla of as many offending hairs as possible, in the shortest time with no lasting, adverse effects to the skin. With that in mind, there is enough experience and documentation in the three modalities of electrolysis to appreciate the benefits of one modality over another, given certain variables (e.g., the type and quantity of hair to be removed).

Modality and Hair Type

Different types of hair require, or benefit from, the use of different modalities. Being educated and accomplished in the use of all three modalities affords the electrologist the choice of selecting the most effective modality for the type of hair that needs removing.

Vellus

With an extensive amount of vellus, thermolysis is the most effective modality of electrolysis. A lower-density current at a shorter duration minimizes adverse skin effects while effectively and quickly destroying the dermal papilla. However, when using thermolysis in shallow follicles like those on the upper lip, a higher intensity current and shorter duration, like the flash method, will help prevent high-frequency blowout.

Thick, Coarse Hair

Thick, coarse hair benefits more from galvanic electrolysis when there are only a few hairs, because this method is slower and the client will want all offending hairs removed in one session, if possible. The blend method would be the sensible choice if there were too many hairs to remove in one session using galvanic electrolysis exclusively. The amount of thermolysis current required to destroy the dermal papilla on strong, coarse hair could be significant enough to cause discomfort to the client and possible damage to the skin from overtreating. Coarse hair, in large quantities like that on the leg, benefits from the blend method of electrolysis.

Curly, Wavy Hair

Hair that is wavy, curly, or kinky generally has a crooked follicle. Because getting to the dermal papilla with a straight probe is not possible by sliding it down the hair follicle, the galvanic method should be the first choice if there are just a few hairs. This is because the destructive, galvanically produced chemical reaction of sodium hydroxide (lye) is able to "bleed" down to the dermal papilla to effectively damage or destroy it. The blend method is preferred if there are multiple hairs that need removing in one session, because it includes the destructive benefits of the lye "bleeding" down to the dermal papilla with the additional boost of speed from the thermolysis modality. Curly hair should have the curl trimmed off it, which will help determine the angle and direction of growth.

Distorted Follicles

Distorted hair follicles usually are formed by long-term tweezing or waxing against the hair growth and tweezing combined. Thermolysis in distorted follicles is a challenge; to succeed at it requires considerable experience and skill. It often means using that "sixth sense" that experienced electrologists develop to figure out the angle of distortion. Distorted hairs can be treated successfully with thermolysis, especially in the early anagen phase when the follicle is shallow and less distorted. The better choice for distorted hair follicles is galvanic, especially if the hairs are few and not too coarse, or the blend, if there is a significant number of coarse hairs with probable distortions for the same reasons described with curly, wavy hair. Although it is difficult to ascertain at the outset which hairs and how many are distorted, it is safe to assume that if a client has been tweezing a significant number of hairs daily or even a few times a week for a number of months or even years, most will be distorted.

Electrolysis and Skin Type

While all four skin types have a great deal in common, like the number of hair follicles (whether or not they actively produce terminal hair), thickness of epidermis and dermis, and all components found in those layers, skin types have characteristics that set them apart.

Caucasian European

Caucasian Europeans have the most varied hair group pattern, determined by heredity first, then such other influences as systemic disorders and hair-removal methods. A light-skinned, green-eyed, red-haired woman of similarly colored Irish parents, who is married to a light-skinned, fair-haired Scandinavian man can give birth to a dark-haired, dark-eyed baby, courtesy of a recessive gene from a dark-haired great-grandparent. Generally, the follicles of European Caucasians are straight unless tweezed or distorted through waxing. All modalities can be used successfully on Caucasian skin, but there are considerable variations in the degree of reaction that the skin will produce based on treatment energy and products.

Black Skin

Because the hair on people of African descent is generally very kinky, it is therefore safe to assume that the follicle will also be curved and distorted. For this reason, galvanic is the preferred modality, especially if there are only a few hairs. If there are a significant number of hairs, the sensible choice is the blend method, which has the added benefit of being faster and delivering a sufficient amount of current to destroy the dermal papilla. Black people, male and female, tend to lack a significant amount of facial hair, but when they do get some, it is more apparent because it is black, coarse, and curly. Due to the kinky nature of the hair, most methods of hair removal cause the hairs to regrow embedded, which is aggravated as the individuals develop pseudo-folliculitis barbae (see Chapter 6). It is usually most severe under the jaw and on the neck. Permanently removing these troublesome hairs will end this problem. If using the blend method on people of African descent, take care to avoid producing excessive heat. Doing so risks hyperpigmentation or keloid scarring. To help prevent ingrown hairs, the clients can use a product with salicylic acid during the treatment program. Its active ingredient helps reduce inflammation and bumps. Tend Skin™ is a well-known brand containing salicylic acid and other ingredients beneficial for preventing ingrown hairs.

Eastern Asian

The Eastern Asian include the Chinese, Japanese, and Koreans. Generally, this group of people has the least amount of facial and body hair. The most popular area for hair removal is probably the eyebrows. Electrolysis is an excellent way to gradually and permanently shape eyebrows. If the electrologist is uncomfortable establishing the shape of the eyebrow, first professionally shape the eyebrows nonpermanently either by waxing or tweezing. Electrolysis can be done as the hair starts to grow back in the optimal early anagen stage and before the new, desired shape is lost.

Middle Eastern and Asian Indian

Middle Eastern and Asian Indians, people predominately from India and Pakistan and Arab countries, tend to have the most hair on both the face and body. Because the hair follicle is usually straight, thermolysis is a fast and effective method of treating the hair permanently and therefore should be the first choice. However, to be effective, the insertion must be accurate and the hairs treated at the most effective anagen stage. The electrologist should also be careful when selecting the current intensity and duration, because overtreating the follicle could easily cause hyperpigmentation on this skin. Start with a lower intensity and a shorter duration of current until the hair releases successfully with the minimum required treatment, and carefully log the variables on clients' records for further treatments.

Moisture Gradient

The moisture gradient is the moisture content of the skin. It can vary by skin type, nationality, and age. Moisture can also be called the hydration level in the skin, that is, the amount of water in the skin's cells. The hydration level is higher deeper into the dermis and in the lower portions of the epidermis than it is up in the stratum corneum of the epidermis. It is also more prevalent in the dermis of young individuals than it is in seniors. Babies and small children shed dead skin cells rapidly, replacing them with new, plump, hydrated cells. As we age, the process of shedding skin cells and replacing them with new, healthy cells slows dramatically. We build up the less desirable dead skin cells that show visible signs of aging with fine lines and wrinkles. Skin that is dehydrated lacks moisture in the form of water. Skin that is dry lacks sebaceous activity, that is, oiliness. Even typically oily or combination skin can go through periods of dehydration. Dry skin can temporarily appear hydrated due to a hydrating moisturizer, the benefits of which are only superficial and temporary in a skin type that is genetically predisposed to dryness.

Whereas moisture reacts with and conducts current, sebum produced by the sebaceous gland acts as an insulator. Certain parts of the body naturally have higher moisture levels than others. In some areas, that moisture may be confined to the lower two-thirds of the hair follicle, like the face of a person with dry skin. In other areas like the axilla, however, the moisture may be present all the way up to the follicular opening. The hair in the axilla may be coarse, but care should be taken to avoid the heat pattern from the current from rising to the surface area of the epidermis, causing a blister. Understanding the moisture gradient of the skin and being able to analyze and recognize various skin types and their moisture levels is important, because these factors can affect the different electrolysis modalities.

The Treatment

After completing the consultation, considering all the variables, and formulating a treatment plan, the treatment session can begin. Make sure the room is ready, clean, and orderly, with all necessary supplies on hand. Sterilized items should be ready in their closed containers, and the lamp and equipment should be wiped down and turned on. Thoroughly wash the hands as described in Chapter 5, and don gloves. The client should be positioned on the table and draped. Draping is important to avoid skin-on-skin contact and thereby reduce the risk of cross-contamination. Draping protects the electrologist and the client. Draping also inspires confidence in the client that the electrologist is a professional allied-health worker. Washable goggles or damp cotton pads help when working on clients' faces to shield those clients from the glare of lamps. However, sanitize goggles between clients, and discard cotton rounds after each client. During a long, gray winter, clients may prefer the "therapy" of bright lights. Allow them that choice.

Pretreatment

The treatment area should be thoroughly cleansed to remove all traces of dirt, grime, makeup, deodorants, and so on. This can be done with a gentle, all-purpose cleanser in a light, gentle manner so as not to overstimulate the circulatory system in that area. Next, the area should be prepped with an antiseptic. **Ethyl alcohol** (ETH-ul AL-kuh-hawl) 70% is effective and not as harsh smelling as **isopropyl alcohol** (eye-soh-PROH-pul AL-kuh-hawl). While either may be effective in high bacterial areas like the groin, underarms, fingers, and toes, they may be unsuitable for the faces of some clients, because they are too drying and stimulating. Mild antiseptic lotions like witch hazel can be substituted in more sensitive areas.

After cleansing, a topical anesthetic can be applied if the client did not apply one before coming in for treatment. Anesthetics are discussed in more detail earlier in the chapter.

While the anesthetic is taking effect, wipe the needle holder with alcohol and place a clean, sterilized needle cap on it. Next, select the appropriate sterilized probe, open it in front of the client, and, using sterilized forceps, place it in the needle holder.

In the case of galvanic electrolysis and the blend technique, prepare the positive handheld electrode with the conductive gel or the moistened pad, and hand it to the client.

To collect the epilated hair, either place a cotton square in the vicinity or wrap some clear tape in reverse around the opposite wrist to the hand that slides the hair out. Discard the tape after each client.

Make all appropriate settings and proceed with the treatment.

Client and Operator Positioning

When considering client positioning consider two main factors: (1) the comfort of the client and (2) the ease of the electrologist to effectively epilate without fatigue. Factors that can affect client positioning are the sizes of the client and electrologist, the flexibility of the client, the reach of the electrologist, and the type and height of the bed/table. When the

ethyl alcohol
a colorless liquid with a fruity smell produced by fermentation; often used as a solvent; synonymous with ethanol

isopropyl alcohol
a colorless, flammable alcohol often used as a solvent

client is on the table, look for spaces along the body where the body does not contact the table. Generally speaking, those areas should be supported with anything from a towel roll or a small pillow (e.g., under the neck or lower back) to a larger bolster (e.g., under the knees). This takes the stress and pressure off certain points and provides a higher degree of client comfort. The more comfortable clients are, the more relaxed they are and the more tolerable the treatment.

When performing a treatment, electrologists usually sit on clients' right side if right handed and on the left side if left handed. The exception is when hairs grow upward (e.g., between the brows, between the breasts, and on the abdomen). In these instances electrologists have three options depending on their sizes, the heights of the tables, and maneuverability around the room. Either move the stool to the opposite side of the table or have the client lie in reverse (i.e., the head where the feet were). Standing is also an option, but it is not recommended for extended periods because it can cause fatigue and lower-back problems. It is harder to maintain the steady hand needed for accurate probing when standing.

Insertion and Treatment

The focus should always be on accuracy, rather than speed, in hair removal. Accurate probing and correct application of treatment energy make electrolysis permanent. It is not a race to remove as many hairs as possible in a session.

Do not treat hairs immediately adjacent to ones just epilated at the risk of overtreating the area and damaging the skin, particularly in sensitive areas like the upper lip or eyebrow. If working two sides of an area, use a timer to divide the session time equally and avoid running out of time before moving to the opposite area, giving an unbalanced treatment.

Start with the coarsest most obvious hairs first, progressing to the next most obvious. Avoid working in one area, which creates an obvious bald patch surrounded by more dense hair.

Gauging Follicle Depth

working point
the established treatment energy of combined current intensity and duration needed to destroy the dermal papilla

The first couple of probes should be to gauge follicle depth (Figure 13–3) and to establish an effective **working point**, which is the treatment energy required to destroy the dermal papilla, combining the current density and duration of the current. Treat one hair with minimal treatment energy going to the learned and assumed depth. Grasp the hair at the follicular opening, and slide the hair outward. If it is an intact anagen hair, hold it next to the probe tip to ascertain its length. Observing where it ends on the probe will determine the depth of the follicle. There will be some variation, but doing this to a few random hairs will approximate average depth.

Shallow insertions create a more intense heating pattern, so reduce the treatment energy if moving to shallow or early anagen hairs after treating hairs in deeper follicles. Otherwise, the skin could sustain damage at the opening to the follicle.

Working Point Establishment

Begin on an initial follicle with the lowest treatment energy recommended for the area. If the hair does not release, increase the treatment energy a second time. If the hair still does not release, try a second follicle and so on, increasing the energy until the hair releases. Do not treat the same follicle more than three times. Although it is permissible to apply the treatment energy more than once, it should be the exception, not the rule. It is far better to establish an effective working point using the minimal amount of treatment energy to effectively destroy the dermal papilla and release the hair, because doing so avoids the multiple double insertions that are both time consuming and could cause damage from overtreating follicles.

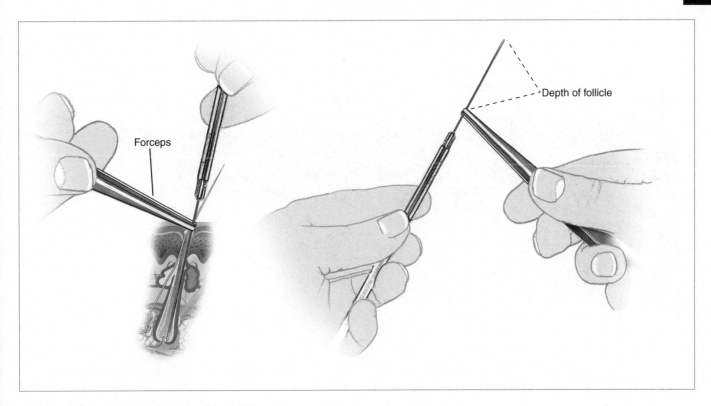

FIGURE 13–3 Gauging the depth of the follicle

Face and Body Treatment

Different parts of the face and body grow hairs in follicles of various depths and at various angles. The depths and angles mentioned in this chapter are broad guidelines that can be affected by such things as previous hair-removal methods. The measurements given should not be construed as scientifically precise but rather as empirical (Figure 13–4).

The Scalp and the Back of the Neck.   At the scalp and the back of the neck, the depth of the hair follicle in anagen stage is 3 to 5 mm; the normal angle of the follicle is 60 degrees. Place a pillow under the client's head while supine.

Occasionally, a man who is almost completely bald may ask to have the little remaining hair removed once and for all with electrolysis. The hair should be shaved or trimmed to approximately ¼ inch so that it can be grasped with the forceps after the application of current. Seat the client at the top of the table or at the side, depending on the ease of insertion. If the top, front, and sides are to be worked on, have the client lie on the back, facing upward. If the back of the scalp is to be worked on, have the client lie face down. A massage-style table is most comfortable with this position, because such a table comes equipped with a face rest. The hair is generally coarse, although there will be some finer hairs in the follicles that are weakening and dying. The needle size should be approximately the same diameter as the hair. In this area, the strength and staying power of a one-piece probe works well, because it requires a session of 30 minutes or longer to progress expeditiously.

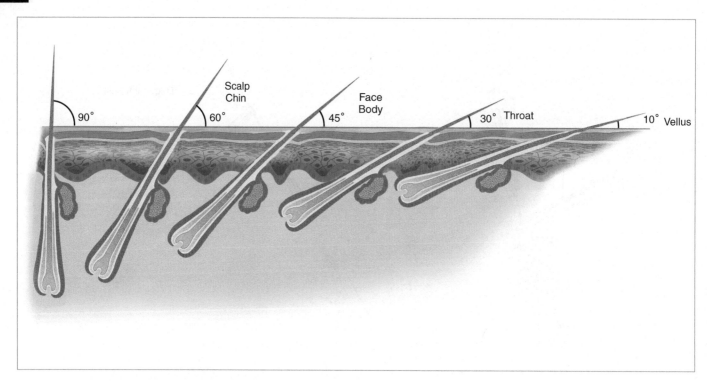

FIGURE 13—4 Angles of hair growth

The Hairline.   The hair follicle in anagen stage is 3 to 5 mm deep at the hairline; the normal angle of the follicle changes from a steeper 60-degree angle near the center of the forehead to a flatter 40-degree angle at the temple. These variations also vary with clients' individual hair-growth patterns. The hair in this area can vary from coarse, terminal hair to vellus. Often, the hair is in a widow's peak that needs softening or has a spiral growth pattern to one side. The finer the hair, the shallower the follicle in this area. Place a pillow under the client's head. Generally, it is easiest to again sit at the top of the table but to leave room to maneuver from side to side depending on the work that must be done. Sometimes, a spiral hair pattern requires greater mobility and change of position to be able to comfortably make an accurate insertion. The client's head should be adjusted from side to side as needed.

Clients who have had hair transplant treatments often require some thinning of denser, overplugged areas and more naturally defined hairlines. Careful consideration should be taken with the hairline. Consult with clients so that both clients and electrologist know exactly which hairs must go and what the desired shape should be. Clients should hold mirrors so that they can look periodically at the progress.

The Eyebrows.   The hair follicle in anagen stage is 2 to 2.5 mm in the eyebrow area. The normal angle of the follicle is 10 to 30 degrees but closer to 45 to 90 degrees in the globellar area. If the client wishes to remove more than a few hairs in the globellar area (e.g., between the brows), and you are not a trained esthetician or trained in ascertaining the best eyebrow shapes for clients, recommending that clients obtain professional eyebrow shapes they are happy with by tweezing or waxing before receiving electrolysis. Because electrolysis is permanent, there is no room for error. For a more in-depth look into eyebrow shaping, see Chapter 11.

When ready to proceed, sit at the side (to the client's right if right handed). The client should turn to face the electrologist with their head resting on a pillow. This is a good position for working under the brow line, but not for the globellar area or if this position is too uncomfortable for the client for an extended period. In that case, the other most suitable position is at the top of the treatment table. The stool should be as high as possible, and the table lowered, if possible, for the electrologist to be able to lean over comfortably. The stool should be able to roll to the right corner for the right brow, directly in the center for the globellar area, and to the left for the left brow. Due to left- or right-handedness, the electrologist will feel a need on one of the sides to move farther around the top corner of the table to achieve a correct direction of insertion. If it is difficult to reach from a sitting position, it may be easier to stand, although this can be fatiguing to do for an extended period because it is also difficult to relax the shoulder and keep a steady hand. Because of the shallow and more superficial angle of the follicle, the lowest possible current at which to destroy the dermal papilla and release the hair is recommended. The thinner skin and visible vascular network close to the follicles calls for a thinner probe and slow, careful insertions to avoid puncturing a capillary and causing a bruise. Two-piece probes work well in this area, due to their increased flexibility. Warn clients that this is an area that bruises and that if it is apparent that a capillary has been punctured, you will take all steps to minimize the bruising. To prevent a punctured capillary from developing into an unsightly bruise, as soon as it is apparent that the capillary has been "nicked," which is visible as a sudden bulge in the follicle, quickly apply firm pressure over the area. If ice is not within reach, wipe the client's forefinger with alcohol and place the finger directly on the bulge while retrieving an ice cube placed in a plastic bag. The session need not end because the client can hold ice over the bruised follicle using the hand on the side of the eyebrow (i.e., the right eyebrow with the right hand, the left eyebrow with the left hand). The ice, with pressure, should remain on the bruised follicle for 5 minutes. Gentle massage helps heal a bruise, especially in combination with **arnica** (AR-nih-kuh) **montana** oil. While the eyebrow is being iced, the opposite brow can still be worked on. To work on hairs lower in the socket, ease the skin up to the orbital bone. If a considerable amount of work is needed to reshape the brow that will not be accomplished in one session, carefully plan to divide the session time, giving equal time to both brows. The epilating should be done in the lower portions, gradually working across and upward so that at the end of the session, even though the process is not complete, the client's brows will still be even and balanced with no obvious holes or gaps. Generally, hair along the top of the brow should not be removed, because it grows downward and provides valuable density to the brow line, particularly on the outer descent. Because the brows generally become sparse with age, do not risk thinning them from the top if they grow downward and provide density to the line, and have the client regret it later. The exception is if an unusually high arch has to be softened or if the top of the arch of a brow is higher on the one brow than the other and the client is looking for a balance. Another reason one may remove hair from above is if the brow joins with the hairline and the client wants to create a distinction between the two areas. When working above the brow, it is not unusual for clients to sneeze, so place a tissue in their hands, warn them, and be ready. Due to the delicateness of the eye area, space treatments at least a week apart and allow time for the area to heal completely between treatments.

arnica montana
a plant found in Northern Europe from which oils and creams are made that are used for medicinal purposes

The Outer Ear.   In the outer ear, the hair follicle in anagen stage is 1 to 2.5 mm deep; the normal angle of the follicle varies from approximately 45 degrees on the **auricle** (AW-rih-kul) to a more severe 60 to 90 degrees on the **tragus** (TRAY-gus) (Figure 13–5). Place a pillow under the client's head, and adjust it as necessary as the client turns from one side to the other. Only the outer ear should be treated. The client should be instructed to trim those hairs with round-edged, baby scissors. Sit at the side of the treatment table with the client facing upward. Work on the closest ear, especially for work on the outer rim of the ear called the auricle or pinna. Turn the client's head to the side as necessary for work on

auricle
the part of the external ear that projects outward from the head

tragus
the pointed flap of cartilage that lies above the earlobe and partly covers the entrance to the ear passage

FIGURE 13–5
Ear hair growth directions

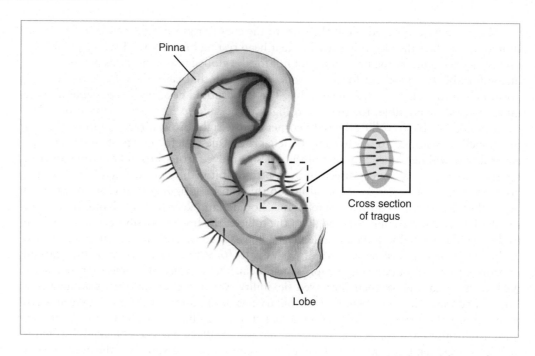

the knob or tragi, which is found on the outer rim closest to the sideburns. If reaching over to the second ear is difficult, it may be more practical to change sides. Use extreme caution when applying any pretreatment or anesthetic so that there is no risk of drips or spray entering the external **auditory meatus** (AWD-uh-tohr-ee mee-AYT-us) or ear canal. This can be extremely damaging to the ear. Do not spray the ear with anesthetic. Spray cotton and then apply to the outer rim of the ear only. Another point to consider is that the hair on the knob or tragi grows from both sides of the knob, and only one side of it should be treated in a session, allowing the area to heal before working on the opposite sides. This is because the hairs grow deep enough that the dermal papilla from hair on both sides meet in parallel. To treat from both sides risks overtreating the area.

auditory meatus
the ear canal

The Upper and Lower Lip.   The depth of the hair follicle in anagen stage is 1 to 2.5 mm deep in the upper and lower lip; the normal angle of the follicle is 10 to 30 degrees. This area often requires some anesthetic application due to its sensitivity, particularly for treatments longer than 15 minutes. A small pillow can support the client's head comfortably. Treat all areas of the upper and lower lip while seated on the same side of the treatment table. Place a cotton roll between the gum and lip to facilitate insertions. Working on the upper lip can cause the eyes to tear. This is due to the stimulation of nerve endings that in turn stimulate the tear ducts. It is not due to pain. If the area were completely numbed with Novocain™, the stimulation to the area would still produce tears. This is worth explaining to clients, because tearing can also produce feelings of sadness that are not real. After applying the treatment energy and removing the probe, use the forefinger of the hand not holding the probe to quickly tap the follicle. This helps to cut the sensation of the current and to soothe the spot. To remove the hair in a balanced fashion, make sure the time is divided equally between the two sides of the lip. Always start on the outside corner, working from the outside in and top downward. When arriving at the **divot** (DIV-ut) or bow of the lip, it is easier to make accurate insertions if the area is pinched, lifting the divot outward. The hair often grows a little more densely in this area, often in a slight horseshoe fashion. When using slanted or pointed forceps, it is important to single out and remove only the treated hair without snagging additional adjacent hairs and causing further discomfort. This is also an area that may cause clients to sneeze. Place a tissue in their hands, warn them of the potential desire to sneeze, and be on the alert. Very light hair

divot
the bow of the lip

may benefit from a follicle enhancer that is wiped over the skin and settles, causing the follicle openings to be more easily visible and allowing a faster pace of work, less searching for follicles, and less hair tugging. Follicle enhancers are available from electrolysis-supply companies. They can be removed with a gentle cleanser at the end of the treatment session. Another help with light and nonpigmented hair is to angle the lamp downward rather than directly over the area. The light then bounces off the hair, making it more apparent, rather than swallowing it up. Using purple vinyl gloves also helps lighter hair to be more visible. Because this is such a sensitive area, if extensive work of 30 minutes or more has been done, it is important to make sure the area is completely healed before the next visit, which may be approximately 1 to 2 weeks.

The Nose.   The dorsal or top of the nose has a hair-follicle depth in anagen stage of 1 mm. The angle of the follicle is 10 to 30 degrees. Place a pillow under the client's head for comfort. Hairs on the top of the nose, down toward the tip, may develop in senior years, although it is not unusual for young people to present with the problem, especially people with dark hair and olive complexions. Often, these fine hairs at a glance simply look like blackheads, but with further inspection through magnification they appear. Due to the shallow follicle, slight angle of growth, and increased sebaceous activity, this area scabs easily when treated, so the lowest possible treatment energy should be used to destroy the dermal papilla. It is also an area that is likely to draw a tear or sneeze, so give clients tissues ahead of time. Thermolysis is a fast and effective modality for these hairs, and using a low-intensity current with an insulated probe will produce good results.

Sideburns.   The hair follicle in anagen stage in the sideburns is 3 to 5 mm deep; the normal angle of the follicle varies from 10 to 45 degrees, often depending on such variables as whether the hair has been tweezed or removed against the hair growth (Figure 13–6). The hairs can be strong, coarse, terminal hairs or vellus. Often, they are a mixture. Clients may want just the terminal hairs fished out, leaving the vellus, especially if the vellus is light and is throughout the face. Place a pillow under the client's head for comfort, especially as the client turns from side to side. When clearing sideburns, it is important to establish how much hair must go. Discuss this with clients as they look in a mirror. The hair that must go can be trimmed to ¼ inch with scissors or an electric trimmer. Instruct clients that they will benefit from shaving the area 2 days before the next session to ensure

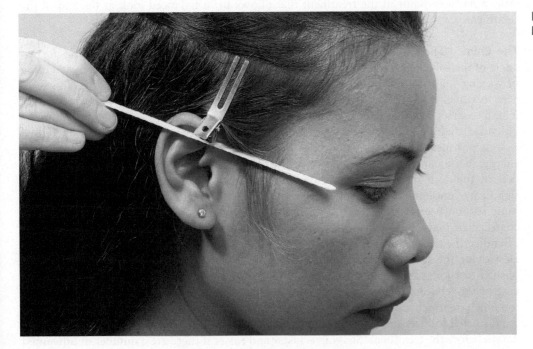

FIGURE 13–6
Markers for sideburns treatment

that only obvious anagen hairs will be treated and also to make it easier to remove the hair as it is not so long that it overlaps. Because the hair does overlap, it is difficult to work from the bottom upward, so the removal should begin at the edge away from the hairline, at the point at which the client wants the sideburn to stop, and work downward, then inward, so there is no obvious termination line. A good guideline for the start of the side-burn is an imaginary line from the tragi of the ear or the corner of the eye.

The Face.   The hair follicle in anagen stage on the face is 2 to 4 mm deep; the normal angle of the follicle is 10 to 45 degrees, again dependent on how the hair has been affected by other hair-removal procedures. A pillow should be placed under the client's head for comfort. Face hair is the hair that grows from as high as under the eye area, over the cheekbones, and down to the jawline. The hair can range from superfluous vellus with little pigment to pigmented terminal hair. As discussed before, women with Middle-Eastern backgrounds often present with superfluous facial hair. Caucasian women may develop this condition from certain medications; others may present with aggravated conditions of superfluous terminal hair caused by the continued stimulation of the vellus from other hair-removal procedures. Follicle depth should be gauged using the method described previously. Following that, the lowest possible working point of treatment energy should be ascertained, as described previously. The session should be divided into two parts using a timer to give each side equal treatment.

Begin by removing the hair that is high on the cheekbone and work from the nose side, outward and downward. Remove the most offensive hairs first, but make sure the hairs are removed in a balanced fashion. Leave no obvious bald patches that make the hair remaining appear more obvious. This is an area in which it is important to treat with accuracy rather than speed. If the insertions are inaccurate and the dermal papilla is only partially damaged or part of the hair is left in the follicle, that piece of hair and tissue debris becomes a "foreign body" in the follicle, causing a pustule to develop. Ingrown hairs may also result. With increased inflammation comes an increased chance of hyper-pigmentation.

The hair should be removed from the inner portion of the face, toward the nose, and at the highest point working downward and outward toward the ear. The hair removal should be intermittent in its spacing so that a bald spot is not created and it blends softly and gradually with the hair that still needs removing. Again, a timer can be used to deter-mine a halfway point in the treatment that allows for a balanced look at the end of the treatment.

The Chin.   The hair follicle in anagen stage on the chin is 2 to 4 mm deep; the normal angle of the follicle is 45 to 90 degrees. Angle and depth can both be affected by tweezing or waxing against growth. Place a pillow behind the client's head for comfort. This is an area in which hair growth can vary from light, nonpigmented vellus to pigmented, dark hair, to coarse, terminal hair. It is also an area in which the skin is sensitive, and on many individuals with combination skin, there is increased sebaceous activity and an increased risk of pustules. The coarser, terminal hairs require a significant amount of treatment energy, so a balance must be found to provide the maximum treatment energy possible to destroy the dermal papilla without damaging the skin. Strong, coarse hairs, requiring a significant amount of treatment energy, should not be treated too close together in the same session because so doing will cause significant tissue damage. The follicles of the coarser hair may be distorted due to tweezing. Galvanic modality would be the modality of choice if there are just a few hairs; the blend method is desirable if there are more. Destroying the sebaceous gland in the follicle is a plus in this area. This can be accom-plished by sliding the probe up and applying a second application of treatment energy to destroy the sebaceous gland. Care should be taken not to raise the probe too high or apply too much treatment energy, causing surface damage. Thermolysis can be used effectively if the distorted follicle is in an early anagen stage. Advise the client to trim or shave the hair 2 days before the treatment. Shaving is faster and easier if there are a number of unwanted hairs, but if there are only a few unwanted hairs among vellus that do not warrant removal, the area should not be shaved, because doing so could disrupt the vellus and create a problem. Instead, individually trim the few coarse hairs. Some of the hairs will have an unusually thick sheath that makes the probing difficult. They will resist sliding out of a small follicle, especially on clients with dry skin. This can be helped by using a one-piece probe that has added strength and providing the technician is confident in the depth and angle of insertion and pushes past the sheath to the dermal papilla to apply the treatment energy. Be confident in the hair extraction. There is a learned difference between the pluck of a still-intact hair and the resistance of a thicker hair sheath. If the epilation was successful, the sheath will come out intact looking like a coating of petroleum jelly around the hair. Difficult insertions under the jaw can be aided by sliding the pillow under the client's neck, tilting the head farther back and pulling the skin upward, toward the jaw bone. Pinch the skin for easier insertion, and use a curved needle holder or bend the needle at a 45-degree angle. Any or all of these techniques will help. A common problem when working on the chin is the client's desire to talk, making it a challenge to work on a "moving target." Do not be rude or ask the client to be quiet. Simply state, "While working in this area, I require the jaw to be kept as still as possible so that my treatments can go quickly and effectively." At that time, offer no comments, especially those that will cause clients to want to respond. It should be enough to occasionally say, "We're doing great, almost there!" or "Just a few more." The client should not feel the need to say, "I thought you said just a few more?" Be honest. If there are a few to a dozen hairs left, it helps psychologically to count down rather than up.

The Throat.   The hair follicle on the throat in anagen stage is 2 to 4 mm deep; the normal angle of the follicle is 10 to 60 degrees. A pillow should be placed under the client's neck for comfort, allowing the client to comfortably tilt the head back while the neck is supported. Keep the client comfortable while maintaining easy access to the follicles. Men who have been shaving regularly will have strong, deep, coarse hair that is close together. Because a significant amount of treatment energy is needed to treat these hairs, it is important not to treat adjacent hairs, because doing so will damage tissue, and there is potential for blistering and scabbing. Treating a cluster of hairs can cause a scar. The top of the throat just under the jaw is an area that can bruise easily, especially on women who are overweight and **hirsute** (hur-SOOT), perhaps due to an endocrine disorder. Even greater care should be used in treating this area on women presenting with these symptoms. A punctured capillary is visible immediately as a growing bump under the skin that looks bluish. Pressure should be applied immediately. With wiped fingers, the client can continue to apply pressure while ice is retrieved in a clean plastic bag. The area should be iced for 5 minutes to minimize the bruise. To speed the healing of the bruise, instruct the client to massage arnica montana cream or oil into the area as frequently as possible—a minimum of four times a day—until the bruise has subsided. The shaving and trimming protocol is the same as that described for the chin (see preceding).

hirsute
having a large amount of hair

The Chest.   The hair follicle in the chest in anagen stage is 2 to 4.5 mm deep; the normal angle of the follicle is 10 to 45 degrees. Place a pillow behind the client's head for comfort. This is one of those times when it is easier for the electrologist to sit on the opposite side of the normal sitting position while working on those hairs that grow upward, toward the chin, at the top of the décolleté. The hairs follow up and around the curves of the breast, gradually growing at a horizontal angle across the top of the breast and clavicle. They then change direction, generally growing downward between the breast and down to the sternum. Clients usually prefer to have the hair removed that would be most noticeable with an open-neck shirt. In later treatment, they target less-exposed areas. This is an area that benefits from shaving the area 2 days before treatment so that treatment time is spent working only on those hairs that are in the more effective anagen stage.

The Breast and Areola.   The hair follicle in anagen stage on the breast and areola is 3 to 4.5 mm deep; the normal angle of the follicle is 10 to 60 degrees. The size of the client, the size of the breasts, and the way in which the breasts fall all help determine the positioning and bolstering of the client. A petite client with small breasts may lie supine or semireclined. Clients with fuller breasts may lie supine while the technician works on the closest breast. The client can lie on their sides, bolstering their backs while the technician works on the opposite breast. Despite some controversy in the past, there is no evidence that electrolysis in any way harms the areola. The areola, however, should not be treated with anesthesia of any kind. This is an area that commonly produces two or three hairs to a follicle. Therefore, extreme care should be taken when selecting one hair in a multiple-hair follicle and when making an insertion. To treat more than one hair in a multihair follicle risks causing tissue damage and scarring the delicate area. The other hairs should be treated in later sessions. Hair growth around the areola is often irregular, and careful observation of the growth of each hair determines the direction of the insertion. This is an area in which the hair may be coarse, but the skin is delicate, which provides a challenge to the electrologist in providing a sufficient amount of treatment energy to destroy the dermal papilla while avoiding significant tissue damage. An accurate probe is crucial in keeping the treatment energy to a minimum to accomplish the task. This is an area that can produce scabbing and infection. Therefore, the client should be instructed to use meticulous care after the treatment. If scabbing or signs of possible infection should occur, the client should apply a mild first-aid healing ointment and avoid picking at scabs. Irritations can be avoided by placing a clean tissue or nursing pads in the bra after treatment and until healing is complete. This also prevents after-care lotions from getting onto the client's lingerie and clothing.

The Axilla. The hair follicle in anagen stage on the axilla is 3.5 to 4.5 mm deep; the normal angle of the follicle is 10 to 45 degrees. There is occasionally some question as to whether treating this area can cause glandular disturbances. There is no record of any problems caused in the lymph nodes when treating this area, because the treatment is confined to the dermis and the lymph nodes lie much deeper than the dermal tissue. Place a pillow behind the client's head for comfort. Place the client's arm up over the head with the hand behind the head, exposing the armpit to be treated. A pillow should be placed under the upper arm and elbow for comfort and support. Antiperspirants and deodorants should be cleaned from the axilla. Because this is a high-bacterial growth area, extra caution should be taken to be sure the area is thoroughly clean. The hair should have been previously trimmed to a ¼ inch long, eliminating any curl and making it easier to determine the direction(s) of hair growth. Again, this is an area that benefits from being shaved 2 days before the treatment to indicate which hairs are in anagen stage and are therefore most effective for removal, particularly given that, on average, only 25 percent of the hairs in this area will be anagen. In determining the pattern of hair growth, the electrologist will observe that the armpits often differ in this respect. This is an area in which hair growth is often asymmetrical. One armpit may have two directions of hair growth; the other may have three. Careful observation should determine the direction of the hair growth. Depending on the client's allotted treatment session time and the frequency of visits, the client can choose to divide the session time equally, having both armpits worked on, or choose to have one armpit worked on at a time. This comes down to personal preference, although the former is the most common. A timer should be used to determine when to move to the opposite armpit. This is an area that is more uncomfortable for most clients and benefits from being pretreated with a topical anesthetic like EMLA or LMX, formerly ELA-Max, before treatment. A one-piece probe is effective in this area, where the hairs are coarse and the skin is delicate. Insertions that are difficult due to the direction of hair growth may be accomplished more easily with a probe bent to a 45-degree angle. Hair should be removed from the outer perimeter working inward. All modalities are effective in treating this area, although if there is a significant amount of growth, as there usually is in this area, the galvanic modality will be too slow unless the multiple-needle machine is used. Because this is a high-bacterial area, the client should be advised to use no deodorants while the area is healing but to periodically throughout the day gently wipe the area with a mild, soothing antiseptic lotion like witch hazel. The client should also be advised to avoid wearing dry-cleaned clothing against the treated area until the area is healed. The residual chemicals in the clothing could create a rash.

The Arms.   The hair follicle in anagen stage in the arms is 2 to 3.5 mm deep; the normal angle of the follicle is 30 to 75 degrees. The hair on the lower arm generally lies fairly flat on the skin unless it has been waxed multiple times against its growth, in which case the angle is much steeper and the hair stands more. When working on the closest arm, the arm should be lying at the client's side, supported by a pillow. When working on the farthest arm, the client should lie on the side, facing the electrologist, with the forearm to be treated resting on a pillow. When preparing a large treatment area like this, spray it with a mild antiseptic. For cost-effectiveness and time efficiency—on average, only 20 percent of the hairs are in the effective anagen stage at any given time—this area benefits from being shaved 2 or 3 days before the treatment and only the anagen hairs treated.

The Hands and Knuckles.   The depth of hair follicle in anagen stage in the hand and knuckles is 1 to 3 mm; the normal angle of the follicle is 10 to 45 degrees on the hands and 45 to 90 degrees on the knuckles. The hands and knuckles pose a problem in that they are easily contaminated almost immediately after treatment with bacteria and require frequent hand washing. The follicles on the knuckles are steep and shallow and the hair is often coarse. This means that there is the potential for scabbing. The client should be instructed to use simple antibacterial soaps that are free of dyes and perfumes and to avoid perfumed lotions. They should also apply a first-aid ointment to the treated area periodically during the healing period.

The Abdomen.   The depth of the hair follicle in anagen stage on the abdomen is 2 to 4.5 mm; the normal angle of the follicle is 15 to 35 degrees. The client lies supine. The direction of hair growth is inward and downward to the pubic area, but it gradually changes, growing inward and upward, toward the navel. For treating the hair in the lower portion, the electrologist can remain on the usual side, but for the hair growing upward, when having difficulty with the insertion, choose to sit on the opposite side or have the client change position, placing the head where the feet were. Drapes should be placed across the top of the navel and tucked into clothing or underwear at the top of the pubic area. This area may present with fine, nonpigmented vellus and a few, unwanted, terminal hairs or darker, pigmented vellus with or without terminal hair. There may even be no vellus apparent and a significant number of terminal hairs. If it is just the terminal hairs that are going to be removed and there is no vellus, the area can be shaved 2 to 3 days before the treatment. If vellus is present but will not be treated, the terminal hairs should be trimmed individually rather than shaving the area. Again, this ensures that the anagen hairs will be easily visible for treatment.

The Genitals.   The depth of hair follicle in anagen stage on the genitals is 2 to 5 mm; the normal angle of the follicle is 20 to 60 degrees. The client can be fully or semireclined, according to preference. Some clients feel uncomfortable watching the treatment and would rather lie back, close the eyes, and relax. For those clients, a pillow should be placed under the head for comfort. Other clients may be more animated and choose to observe and chat during the treatment session. Always be professional, but particularly when treating this area. The consultation should already determine how much hair and in what areas must be removed. There should be no looks or vocalization of embarrassment, surprise, or shock. This will only cause clients to feel more embarrassed and awkward about their condition. Clients deserve the utmost professional attention. This is not a time to make tasteless jokes, even if the intent is to put the client at ease. It is not appropriate. The electrologist should provide some disposable undergarments for the client and a drape to place across the groin and upper thigh. The disposable undergarments are not only professional and sanitary, they prevent soiling or damaging undergarments with alcohol and after-care lotions and gels. If clients are to wear their own undergarments, these garments should be well-lined with a paper towel. The client should be instructed to disrobe, to put on the disposable undergarments, and to position on the table with the drape across the lap. It is unprofessional to remain in the room while clients undress. Knock on the door before reentering.

When working in this area, there is a greater-than-normal need for hygiene and sanitation. The area to be treated should be cleansed thoroughly with an antiseptic lotion. The client should have been previously instructed to trim the area 2 to 3 days before the treatment, ensuring that there are no long, dense hairs inhibiting the treatment and ensuring that the anagen hairs will be treated. Clients may also choose to preapply a topical anesthetic to the area because this is an area that benefits from a treatment time of 30 minutes or more, for swift progress. The anesthetic will minimize any discomfort that can be harder to deal with over extended periods. The drape should cover most of the area; only the area being treated should be exposed. In this area, the skin is particularly delicate and the hair coarse. This is an area in which it is important to question female clients on whether they have IUDs for contraceptive purposes, because those devices will be affected by the galvanic modality and blend technique, regardless of the hand on which the electrode is placed. The treatment energy should start low and increase gradually until a successful epilation is achieved with the minimal amount of treatment energy. The electrologist must be bold and confident in handling this area and ensure that the skin is stretched sufficiently to lift the hair and facilitate the probe. The hair should be removed from the outer perimeter inward and the top downward. If two sides are to be treated, a timer should indicate halfway through the session when it is time to switch sides. Galvanic method is too slow for the number of hairs in this area. The thermolysis modality and the blend method are better choices for their speed and effectiveness. Some of the shallow follicles that are at a flatter angle, particularly in the bikini area, are prone to scabbing. The client should be advised of the dos and don'ts of scabs to prevent long-term marks. This is an area that commonly experiences an ingrown hair problem. If this is the case, it is important to release the ingrown hairs but not remove them, instead allowing the follicle to heal and normalize around the hair. The hair prevents a scab from forming over the top that in turn may trap a new anagen hair, thereby continuing the cycle.

The Back and Shoulders.   The hair follicle in anagen stage on the back and shoulders is 2 to 4.5 mm deep; the normal angle of the follicle is 15 degrees on the sides of the back to 45 degrees on the shoulders. The client should be prone with the head resting to the side on the pillow. The client should remove the pants to avoid crumpling them during an extended service. Again, leave the room while clients undress. Clients should be given drapes to place over the buttocks and told to lie face down on the table in preparation for the treatment. Knock before reentering. If the client chooses to keep the pants on, the belt should be removed for comfort. It may be necessary to loosen the pants and to ease them downward a little to expose a starting point just below the pant line. The pants should be lined with paper towels for protection. You may need to trim the hair on the back, if it is long and curly, so that you can more easily determine the direction of hair growth. It should be trimmed to ¼ inch. It would be better to have the client trim the hair 2 to 3 days prior, so that the anagen hairs can be isolated and treated. If the client does not have a partner or roommate willing and able to do the job, it is well worth the time for them to come in 2 to 3 days before the electrolysis treatment for you to do it in preparation. The back should be wiped or sprayed with an antiseptic lotion. The hair removal should take place in a gradual, natural, blended fashion without creating obvious bald patches. This can be accomplished by starting on the outside edges, down toward the pant line and gradually working upward and inward.

The Buttocks.   The depth of hair follicle in anagen stage on the buttocks is 2.5 to 4 mm; the normal angle of the follicle is 10 to 30 degrees. The client lays prone on the table with the face to the side, resting on a pillow. The client should optimally change into a pair of disposable underpants for the same reasons mentioned in the previous section on treating genitals. The client should also be given a drape and instructed, while you wait outside, to put on the disposable undergarments, lay face down, placing the drape over the buttocks and upper thighs. Knock before reentering. If both sides of the buttocks are to be treated, a timer should be used to divide the treatment session in half. The hair grows downward, between the buttocks, and at the base of the spine and inward over the buttocks, following the curve. Due to the fleshiness of this area, special attention must be paid to stretching techniques.

The Legs.   The depth of hair follicle in anagen stage on the legs is 2.5 to 4 mm; the normal angle of the follicle varies from approximately 10 degrees on the top inner thigh to 60 degrees on the knee. Due to the shallow insertion and flat angle on the front of the shin, this is an area that can form scabs. Care should be taken not to overtreat the hairs in this area. The skin on the legs is often coarse with the scales of dead skin cells quite apparent. The knee, in particular, can be difficult to probe, so it is worth recommending to the client to do a thorough exfoliation prior to the treatment and to apply lotion so that the skin in that area is soft and supple. In the fleshier areas of the thigh, and also when treating the knees, considerably more stretching is necessary. When treating the legs and the groin, it is common for the client to produce an involuntary reaction after the current has been applied. Drawing too much attention to it only makes it harder for the client. Reassure clients that it is a common occurrence and does not bother you. A good tip is to use the fingers of the hand not holding the probe to tap the follicle immediately after the current has been applied. This helps to cut the lingering sensation of the current.

The Feet and Toes.   The depth of hair follicle in anagen stage on the feet and toes is approximately 1 to 3 mm; the normal angle of the follicle is 10 to 45 degrees. The biggest concern with treating the toes is to make sure that the client does not have circulatory problems, especially diabetes. These conditions affect the healing process, and an infection could prove to be extremely serious. Thorough cleansing and the use of antiseptics are very important in this area. The follicles on the toes are medium depth, and the angle can be steep, but this is an area that can still scab easily. After-care is very important. The treated area should be well protected from the bacteria-ridden underside of a shoe.

(Note: Directions of hair growth not illustrated here can be found in Chapter 11.)

Ingrown Hair Treatment

If hairs are of the "blackhead" type, meaning they can be easily extracted with the fingers without breaking the skin, they can be treated normally. (See Chapter 9.) If, however, the hair is embedded and visible as a thin line, it should be carefully released as close to where its normal follicular opening would be, as described in Chapter 9, and left in place and trimmed, if necessary. This gives the skin an opportunity to heal around it without forming a new scab that would block the follicular opening. That hair follicle can then be treated at the next session. Immediately treating the hair after breaking the skin causes a scab to form over the opening. If the hair removed was a telogen hair, there may well be an early anagen hair in the follicle trapped under the newly forming scab, which would also become ingrown, thereby perpetuating the problem.

Treatment End

Before completing the treatment, particularly on the face, and discarding the probe, give the client a mirror and the opportunity to check and see if the hairs that are most offensive have been removed. For clients with nonpigmented or very light hair that may be coarse, it is worth doing the "touch test" (i.e., wipe the client's finger(s) with alcohol and have the client feel for any tiny but coarse hairs that might have been missed). No one knows where those "little nuisances" hide better than the client who feels for them regularly, and nothing is more infuriating than getting in the car after a treatment and still feeling the one hair that drove you crazy and that you wanted to tweeze!

When you are satisfied that the session is complete, the probe should immediately be removed with the forceps over the sharps box or isolyser and disposed of appropriately. The needle cap and forceps should be placed in their holding containers for cleaning and sterilization. Remove the electrode from the client's hand, and prepare it for disinfecting. Return rheostat and other dials to 0. Continue with posttreatment care (see following).

Posttreatment

The most suitable after-care treatment for the client is often a question of trial and error. As with skin-care lines, and people's differing reactions to the multitude of skin-care lines, so it is with after-care products and techniques. Electrolysis-supply companies have a wide range of recommended after-care products to use on clients. Whatever one chooses, it is important to remember that the follicle itself is free of bacteria, after being treated with whatever electrolysis current. While it is important to keep the vulnerable surface area of the skin free of bacteria, the area should not be "flooded" with any liquid, particularly water, that may transport microorganisms too readily into an otherwise bacteria-free follicle. Clients who have had work done on the hairline or on the face should avoid shampooing the hair for 24 hours. They should also avoid applying hair-grooming products to the hair if the hairline has been treated and avoid getting hairspray on any treated area until the area has completely healed. Using a damp, but not saturated, washcloth or cotton with the product is key. Witch hazel lotion or gel is cooling and soothing to many people and has mild antiseptic properties. Others prefer aloe vera gel. Caladryl/Calamine lotions are effective if there are histamine-type bumps or inflammation on the skin, but they leave a chalky residue. If the area shows signs of puffiness or swelling, a few ice cubes placed in clean plastic is effective for clients to use. There are cold packs that can be prechilled and given to clients to use, but ice is more economical unless clients choose to rest in the facility with cold packs for a while. Whatever product used should be kept sterile by using a spatula if it is a jar or by pouring onto cotton if it is a liquid, without the cotton touching the lip of the bottle. If the client must return to work or has another engagement and would like the treated area camouflaged, waxing manufacturers have waxing after-care products that soothe and camouflage. Major electrolysis-probe manufacturing companies have lines of after-care products, some that are also tinted in different shades and can be applied after the treatment or purchased by the client for home use. These products are inexpensive and soothe, camouflage, and promote healing to the skin. They are preferred over makeup.

Scabbing

eschar
small, light-golden-brown crusty scab

We have learned that, in certain areas like the areola, bikini area, knuckles, toes, and a man's neck, some scabbing is normal, even inevitable. The scabbing may be a light golden color, called an **eschar** (ES-kur), and while acceptable in those areas, is unacceptable on the face. Care should be taken to avoid scabbing, and in the areas where it is expected, to keep it to a minimum. If scabbing is expected, the client should be warned of the potential and instructed in how to take care of the scabbed area, and what not to do. The scabs should be kept moist with an antibiotic first-aid cream or ointment. They should not be picked or scratched off under any circumstances. To do so could cause permanent marks like hypopigmentation (white spots). The client should also avoid exposing the scabbed areas to ultraviolet rays until it has completely healed. Even if there is only a little pinkness, the result could be hyperpigmentation (brown spots). The white and brown spots can end up being more noticeable than the hair originally, and they can be even tougher to eliminate than the hair. If the scabbing is on the face, the area should be treated with meticulous gentle care to retain the scabs until they are ready to drop off on their own accord as the skin heals underneath. Until then, continuous sunscreen of a minimum of SPF 15 or higher must be worn.

Treatment Techniques

Techniques can include various hand positioning, various insertion techniques, and different methods of application of the treatment energy. Some of the techniques, like hand position and holding the forceps, are a personal preference, while other techniques are essential to the accurate application of treatment energy to bring about the destruction of the dermal papilla. Success in the application of the treatment techniques described can be obtained by formal practical classroom training by an electrolysis educator followed by considerable practice.

One-Handed Technique

The probe is held like a writing implement, in the right hand if right handed, and in the left hand if left handed (Figure 13–7a). The forceps are also held in the same hand by the three fingers tucked underneath. When it is time to use the forceps, the probe is slipped back between the forefinger and second finger and the forceps are slipped forward in the same grip the probe was in. After the epilation, the forceps are taken back by the middle, index, and little finger with the top upward, toward the thumb, and the probe is swung back to its original position, gripped by the thumb and forefinger. With this technique, the free hand can maintain an effective stretch, along with the little finger and under edge of the dominant hand. The shorter 2¾-inch forceps fit more comfortably in the hand, with the one-handed technique.

Two-Handed Technique

The probe is held in the same manner as in the one-handed technique, but the forceps are held in the opposite hand (Figure 13–7b). There are two variables to epilating the hair using this method. The first is to epilate the hair with the hand that is holding the tweezers. This is considered faster, because there is no time wasted switching the forceps, but one may question the flexibility, steadiness, and sensitivity of using the less-dominant hand for this purpose. It may be harder to determine the resistance on the tug of a hair and whether it is truly released due to the destruction of the dermal papilla, or whether it just has a thick hair sheath. Sometimes, the more-dominant hand can make a better determination. However, with practice there is no reason that kind of sensitivity cannot be developed in the less-dominant hand.

The other two-handed method is to hold the forceps in the opposite hand to the probe but to then switch the forceps to the dominant hand for the epilation. Some electrologists consider this to be less time effective, because the forceps are still switched. Switching the forceps to the other hand also disrupts the effective stretch. However, it does ensure an accurate epilation, using the sensitivity of the dominant hand. Another consideration is the angle of the epilation. When epilating with the less-dominant hand, there is a risk of pulling the hair upward instead of outward, in the angle and direction of growth. If the dermal papilla was not destroyed, the hair may be tweezed, and in a direction that will distort the follicle. Therefore, when using the less-dominant hand to epilate, take care to ensure that the hair is epilated in the same direction and angle of the probe. This is easier to do with the one-handed method.

Stretching the Skin

The stretch of the skin, when done correctly, is vital in achieving a perfect insertion. It helps to open the follicle and lift the hair, allowing the probe to slide down the underside of the hair shaft. The stretch is always accomplished with both hands. Some fleshy areas, like the areola or a double chin, require considerably more stretching than other areas, where the skin may lay tightly over a boney protrusion, like the shinbone. The stretching will be determined by whichever hand is holding the forceps. If the probe and forceps are in the same hand, then the less-dominant hand is free to use as many fingers as necessary to accomplish the most optimal stretch. If the less-dominant hand is using the forceps to epilate, the stretching must be assumed by the little finger and the edge of the hand that follows down from it. When the less-dominant hand holding the forceps has to pass them to the probing hand, the stretch is often lost and must be reestablished. Stretching should not be heavy or forceful. It should not depress the skin, and it should not feel uncomfortable to the client. The stretch should be light and sufficient to open the follicle and lift the hair slightly for an easy and accurate insertion.

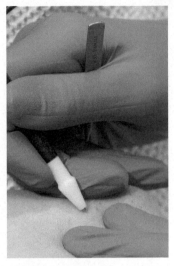

FIGURE 13–7a
Placement of forceps using one-handed technique

FIGURE 13–7b
Placement of forceps using two-handed technique

Insertion Technique

The accurate insertion of the probe into the follicle is fundamental to a safe and effective electrolysis treatment. This is especially true of the thermolysis modality. The insertion of the probe is how the treatment energy is delivered to the dermal papilla to bring about its destruction.

PEET, PERT, PEST

The PEET, PERT, and PEST techniques were developed and based on the theory that as the hair, combined with the external and internal root sheath, takes up so much of the follicle, it often impedes direct access to the dermal papilla by the probe. Through the PEET, PERT, and PEST techniques, electrologists have experienced good results in the destruction of the dermal papilla.

Preelectrolysis Epilation Technique (PEET). The hair is plucked from the untreated follicle, the needle is inserted into the empty follicle, current is applied, and the needle is removed from the follicle.

Postepilation Reentry Technique (PERT). With the PERT technique, the standard electrolysis treatment is performed first with the hair in the hair follicle, then again to the empty follicle once the hair has been epilated.

Postepilation Sustained Entry Technique (PEST). The PEST technique is accomplished using the two-handed method. The technique is to first perform the standard electrolysis treatment to the hair follicle then, while leaving the needle in place with one hand, epilate the hair with the other, repeating the current application to the empty follicle, then removing the needle. PEST is like PERT (see preceding), but by leaving the probe in the follicle, it ensures that the correct empty follicle is being retreated.

Incorrect Insertion

Incorrect insertions not only reduce the effectiveness of the current application but they can be damaging to the skin by puncturing the follicle walls or cause surface damage (Figure 13–8).

Too-Deep Insertion

Probing too deeply often draws blood, which is visible at the follicle opening. This occurs with electrologists who are not yet experienced nor adept at feeling the base of the follicle or because a probe was selected that was too long for the follicles in the area being treated. Other causes are that an accurate depth of the follicles was not ascertained at the start of the treatment (see the preceding section) or because an early anagen hair was treated because it was believed to be a full-grown anagen hair after shaving. Providing the insertion was not too deep, the dermal papilla can still be destroyed, but not without creating the unnecessary nuisance of drawing blood.

Too-Shallow Insertion

A too-shallow insertion is more of a problem with thermolysis, because it simply means that the dermal papilla will remain untreated. This is not as serious a problem with the galvanic modality or the blend technique, because the lye, if enough is produced, will bleed downward, to the dermal papilla. It will be a far more effective treatment, however, if the insertion is made to the correct depth. A shallow insertion also increases the risk of surface damage.

Insertion at an Incorrect Angle

Insertion at an incorrect angle, a common cause of drawing blood, happens when the angle of the follicle is not correctly determined. If the probe comes into direct contact with the hair shaft, it may disintegrate the hair at the point at which it comes into contact with the probe, causing the top half to break away but leaving the lower portion attached. This is again an area in which a skilled and experienced electrologist may be more adept at feel-

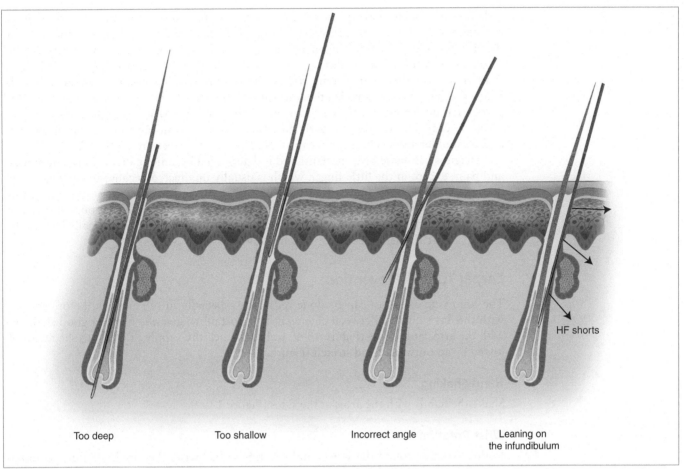

| Too deep | Too shallow | Incorrect angle | Leaning on the infundibulum |

HF shorts

FIGURE 13–8 Incorrect probe positions

ing the sides of the follicle wall, particularly with a fine, two-piece probe, but even a newly trained electrologist with a sensitive touch can make the correct determination. The angle can be affected by nearby scar tissue or a nearby mole. It can also be affected by over-stretching or stretching incorrectly.

Probe Touching the Side of the Hair Follicle

A probe touches the side of the hair follicle if the skin is not adequately stretched and the angle of insertion is incorrect so that the probe contacts the side of the follicle all the way down. This could cause tissue damage, especially with thermolysis, and the use of a noninsulated probe.

Probe Movement in the Follicle

Once the probe has slid into the follicle, take care not to move it. Focus and a steady hand are vital while applying the treatment energy to ensure there is no movement. Movement during insertion causes tissue damage. An accurate count will ensure that the probe is not being withdrawn from the follicle while the treatment energy is being applied. A description of insertion count is found in Chapter 14.

Carpal Tunnel Syndrome

Any repetitive movement with the hands over an extended period of time risks **carpal tunnel syndrome** (KAR-pul TUN-nul SIN-drom), a syndrome that can be very debilitating and that is far easier to prevent than it is to cure. Carpal tunnel syndrome affects the hands and wrists, causing considerable pain that can travel up the forearm. This pain occurs when the median nerve, which supplies sensation to the thumb and fingers (excluding the

carpal tunnel syndrome
a condition of pain and weakness of the hand caused by repetitive compression of a nerve that passes through the wrist and into the hand

little finger), fails to work properly due to pressure placed on it as it runs into the wrist through the carpal tunnel. The carpal tunnel is made of the carpal bones of the wrist on the bottom and the carpal ligament on the top. The flexor tendons also run parallel through this section. The tendons are used to flex the fingers to grasp objects. If those tendons are overworked and become fatigued and injured, they become inflamed and swell. When this happens, the swollen tendons squeeze the median nerve, causing numbness and pain. If left untreated and allowed to escalate, the condition worsens to the point at which the nerve ceases to function properly. In severe cases, the pain can travel as far up the arm as the shoulder and neck. It can incapacitate a person for weeks if not months.

Diagnosis is made by a specialist and is determined by, among other things, numbness and pain, except in the little finger, which is usually unaffected because the median nerve does not serve the little finger. Treatment usually involves wearing a wrist brace to immobilize the wrist so that it can heal and using anti-inflammatory medications followed by physical therapy. In extreme cases, treatment may be a surgical procedure called the Endoscopic Carpal Tunnel Release, for which recovery is 4 to 6 weeks.

Carpal Tunnel Prevention

The following exercises can be done regularly, especially in the morning before starting with the day's clients. Between clients, it is important to give the hands a good shakeout with the arms at the side (Figure 13–9) to bring a healthy supply of blood to the area, followed by an outward hand stretch (Figure 13–14).

Hand Shaking

Shake the hands with the arms at the sides (Figure 13–9).

Wrist Rotation

In this exercise, rotate the wrists multiple times clockwise, then multiple times counterclockwise (Figure 13–10).

Invisible Piano

To do the invisible-piano exercise, imagine playing the piano by tapping on the lap or treatment table (Figure 13–11).

Finger Pulses

Place the hands in a prayer position with the shoulders and arms relaxed and match finger to finger (Figure 13–12). In turn, apply pressure and resistance from matching finger to finger.

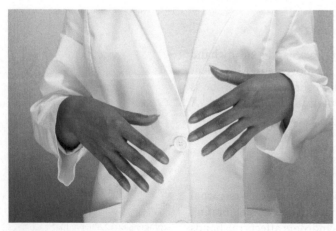

FIGURE 13–9
Shaking hands increases blood flow

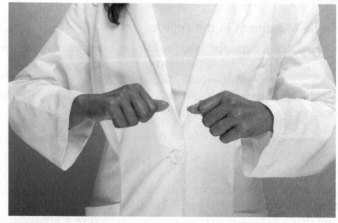

FIGURE 13–10
Wrist rotations strengthen and improve flexibility

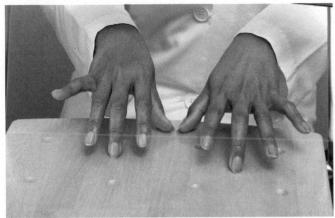

FIGURE 13–11
"Invisible piano" – tap fingers on lap or flat surface

FIGURE 13–12
Finger pulses increase flexibility and strength

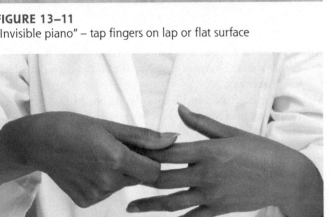

FIGURE 13–13 Massage each finger individually

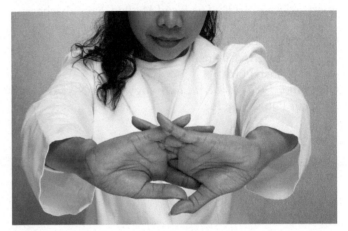

FIGURE 13–14 Outward hand stretch

Finger Massages

Massage each finger individually, starting at the base and working toward the tip (Figure 13–13). Pay special attention to the knuckles.

Hand Stretches

Clasp the hands together, interlocking the fingers, then, turning the hands so that the knuckles are opposite the chest (Figure 13–14), push downward and outward, stretching the palms and fingers outward.

Conclusion

The effectiveness of electrolysis as a safe and permanent method of hair removal depends on its correct application, and on candidates who qualify for the service without contra-indications. Knowledge of the different modalities and the pros and cons of each modality allows the electrologist to make judicious choices of which modality to use for a safe, effective, and comfortable treatment. A thorough and effective consultation will help determine the most appro-priate course of action. Ending the treatment with good after-care and providing home-care instructions will ensure that the client will have a minimal negative reaction and fast healing. All in all, an effective treatment that causes the minimum adverse reaction and promotes fast healing ensures a happy and satisfied client who will continue to return until the unwanted hair is permanently removed.

Discussion and Review Questions

1. List three pros of electrolysis.
2. List three cons of electrolysis.
3. List five contraindications of electrolysis.
4. What are four things clients can do ahead of time to have more comfortable and more effective electrolysis treatments?
5. What are three things clients should avoid immediately after receiving electrolysis treatments?

6. What are two main ingredients in a topical anesthetic?
7. What is an important concern when treating the tragi?
8. Discuss how to gauge the depth of a hair follicle.
9. What is PEET?
10. What is carpal tunnel syndrome?

Additional Readings

Bono, Michael. 1994. *The Blend Method.* Santa Barbara, CA: Tortoise Press.

Gallant, Ann. *Principles and Techniques for the Electrologist.* Cheltenham, U.K.: Stanley Thornes (Publishers) Ltd.

Glor, Fino. 1987. *Modern Electrology.* Great Neck, N.Y.: Hair Publishing, Inc.

Hinkle, Arthur Ralph, and Lind, Richard W. 1968. *Electrolysis, Thermolysis, and the Blend.* Los Angeles, CA: Arroway.

Meharg, G. E., R.N., and Richards, R. N., M.D. 1997. *Cosmetic and Medical Electrolysis and Temporary Hair Removal,* 2e., Toronto, Ont: Medric Ltd.

CHAPTER 14

Thermolysis

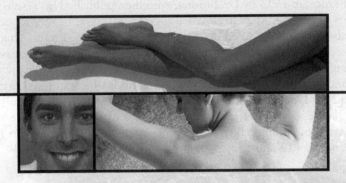

Chapter Outline

Learning Objectives ■ Key Terms ■ Introduction ■ Types of Thermolysis Machines
How Thermolysis Works ■ Thermolysis Treatment ■ Thermolysis Techniques
Conclusion ■ Discussion and Review Questions ■ Additional Readings

Learning Objectives

By the end of this chapter, you should be able to:

1. Differentiate between manual and computerized thermolysis machines.
2. Know the basic thermolysis techniques.
3. List the pros and cons of thermolysis.
4. List the indications and contraindications of thermolysis.
5. Know how to apply thermolysis to various parts of the body.

Key Terms

current density
electrocoagulation
megahertz

pulsing
working point

Introduction

The first treatments of thermolysis as a method of hair removal were performed in Paris, France, in 1923 by Dr. Bordier, who then published his results in 1932. Thermolysis takes its name from the Greek word *thermo*, meaning heat, and *ysis*, meaning to dissolve. It is also commonly called diathermy, a more outdated term; "high frequency," for the AC it uses; and "shortwave," again for the high-frequency shortwaves that produce heat-inducing action via a needle to destroy the dermal papilla. The facts that it is fast and effective and relatively (compared to other methods of electrolysis) easy to learn make it a popular method, and it is still the most common method of electrolysis around the world. This chapter covers the rudimentary aspects of thermolysis that are unique to this modality. Areas of commonality to the other modalities of permanent hair removal are covered in Chapters 12 and 13.

Types of Thermolysis Machines

Thermolysis epilators can be classified three ways:

1. manual
2. semi-manual
3. computerized.

They can range from units that are very basic but reliable and do an adequate job of destroying the dermal papilla with diathermy to very sophisticated pieces of equipment that have all kinds of "bells and whistles" and require substantial training by the distributor. Once mastered, however, this equipment provides an excellent service for the client through programmed records of clients' treatments. Whatever the choice of equipment, the operator must completely understand the equipment, how it works, and all the variables that belong to it so that the client may have a safe and effective hair-removal treatment.

Manual Thermolysis Machines

With the manual thermolysis machine, the intensity of the current is selected using a rheostat and controlled by the operator, as is the duration of the current, which is controlled by the foot pedal (or, in some countries like the United Kingdom, a button on the probe). The current intensity may be displayed in a sequence of numbers ranging from 0 to 10 or in increments of 10 ranging from 0 to 100. To accurately interpret the numbering on the dials, the operator should always refer to the unit's operating manual.

Semi-manual Thermolysis Machines

Semi-manual thermolysis machines were developed later, as concerns arose about the duration of the current. The lengthy and often clumsy use of the footswitch or inaccurate counting with the hand-operated button resulted in the overtreatment of the hair follicle and damage to the skin. To prevent the extended application of current, a dial with an automatic timer was added, allowing the operator to preselect the duration of the current once the footswitch is tapped. The intensity control (rheostat control) is still set on a dial by the operator.

Computerized Thermolysis Machines

Computerized, or automatic, thermolysis machines can be programmed for galvanic, thermolysis, the blend, and pulsing and flash techniques. They can also be programmed to apply the appropriate amount of current for hair type. Some have additional features, such as a hair-count feature and a feature that allows adjustments of the flow of current down the needle in the middle of an insertion. Some computerized epilators are also programmed to work in "auto mode," without the use of the footswitch. Another useful feature of the computerized machines is their ability to hold in memory clients' files, which enable the operator to continue an effective treatment at the "flick of a switch." A growing number of electrologists claim that their clients talk of feeling less discomfort with the programmed treatments and achieve better results. Less discomfort could be due in part to the super-flash feature, which is a sequential feature designed with the first "flash" destabilizing and "distracting" the nerve endings that transmit pain, so that when the next actual treatment flash is emitted, it is not felt as strongly.

How Thermolysis Works

Unlike the galvanic method, which requires a conductor to complete the circuit, high-frequency sound waves can travel through air, so the only conductor that is needed is the probe that is placed in the hair follicle. The waves oscillate at a rapid, alternating speed of 30 **megahertz** (MEG-uh-hurtz), or 30,000,000 times each second. The terms megahertz (Mhz) and megacycle are used interchangeably.

megahertz
1 million hertz (cycles per second)

The high-frequency current, when passed down the probe, which is the conductor, alternates between a flow of positive electrons and negative electrons (Figure 14–1). When the probe is placed in the hair follicle, it creates a magnetic field, exciting the atoms in the tissue. The atoms contain both positive and negative protons, and it is those protons that

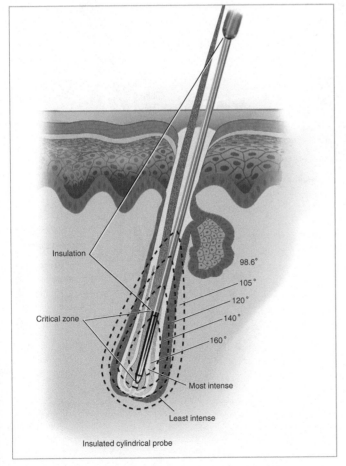

FIGURE 14–1
High-frequency heating pattern with an insulated probe

Insulation

98.6°
105°
120°
140°
160°

Critical zone

Most intense

Least intense

Insulated cylindrical probe

are attracted and repelled, alternating in a push-and-pull action as the positive and negative electrons alternate on the probe. It is a case of opposites attracting and likes repelling.

This excitement or agitation of the atoms in the tissue generates heat, in an action similar to the way that microwaves heat substances. The heat that is generated coagulates the tissue, and hopefully the dermal papilla, if the probe is correctly inserted into the hair follicle. The normal body temperature is on average 98.6°F/38°C; any temperature above 110°F/44°C irreversibly damages cells. At temperatures above 212°F/100°C (the boiling point of water), desiccation, the drying of tissue, occurs. Anything above 240°F/116°C can result in severe burning and scarring. With the action of thermolysis, the heat causes the cells to coagulate and become dysfunctional. This is known as **electrocoagulation** (uh-LEK-troh-koh-ag-yu-LAY-shun).

Variables Affecting High Frequency Waves in the Follicle

The current density, intensity, and duration, along with the type of probe, depth of insertion, and moisture gradient are all variables that affect high frequency waves in the follicle and determine the effectiveness of the treatment.

Current Density

Current density is the number of electrons flowing out of a conductor. In thermolysis the conductor is the probe. Once the current density is established by the diameter of the probe, the current density stays the same and does not change, but the tissue in the follicle will get hotter the longer the current is applied (Figure 14–2).

electrocoagulation
the process by which heat causes cells to coagulate and become dysfunctional

current density
the amount of current (electrons) flowing from a conductor (the electrolysis probe)

FIGURE 14–2
High-frequency intensity and duration in follicle

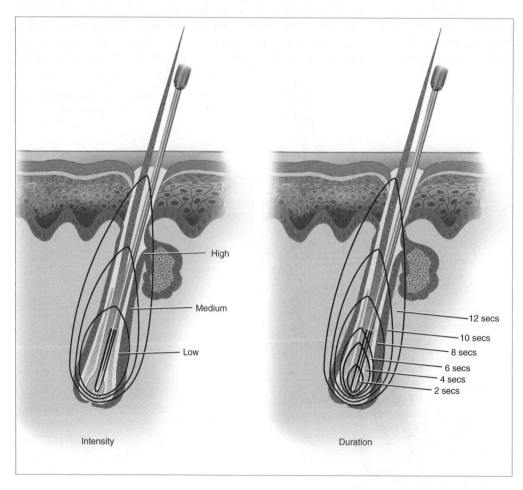

High

Medium

Low

12 secs

10 secs

8 secs

6 secs

4 secs

2 secs

Intensity

Duration

Current Intensity

It is measured in radio frequency watts and amperes. One ampere flowing with the pressure of one volt produces one watt of power. Because of the tiniest electrical charges used in thermolysis, we measure the current in milliamperes which are 1/1000 of an ampere. For thermolysis, the range of intensity is controlled by a rheostat: The higher it is turned, the more heat it generates in the hair follicle. It is measured in milliamperes. For thermolysis, the range of intensity setting is from 40 to 99 percent.

Current Duration

The longer current is applied, the more heat that escalates in the follicle. The thermolysis dial indicates the time for the pulse of current, which for thermolysis ranges from 0.05 to 0.15 second.

Insertion Depth

The depth of insertion of the probe in the hair follicle (Figure 14–3) significantly affects the skin's tissue. The deeper the insertion, the less heat that is produced at the probe tip. This is because the high-frequency current is dispersed over a greater area of tissue with less concentration and therefore less heat. With a shallow insertion, the high-frequency causes a more concentrated application of heat in the upper portion of the hair follicle. This can cause considerable damage to the skin. If a shallow insertion in indicated, then the treatment energy must be reduced, either by reducing the current density or the current duration. With thermolysis, the most important factor in probe insertion is that it is correct and that the tip is at the dermal papilla when the current is applied.

Deep anagen hairs that are coarse benefit more from a treatment of lower-current intensity and a longer current duration. Care must be taken when moving to a shallow hair to shorten the duration to avoid overtreating the follicle and blanching the skin.

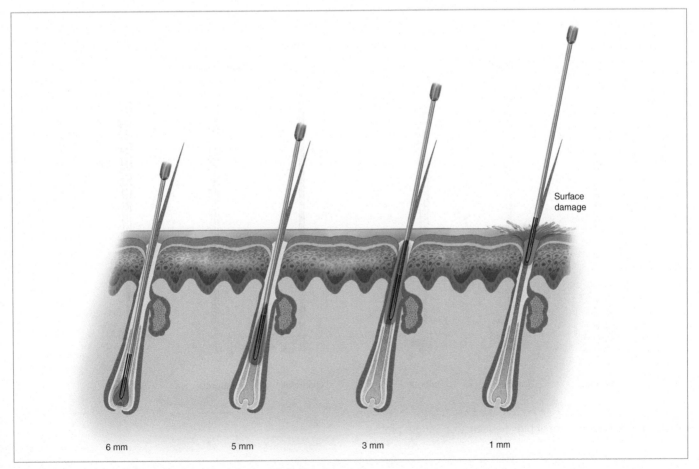

Surface damage

6 mm   5 mm   3 mm   1 mm

FIGURE 14–3 Effect of high frequency on deep and shallow insertions

Moisture Gradient

The moisture gradient is discussed in more depth in Chapter 13. Extra care should be taken when working on very moist skin, in areas where the follicles are shallow, or with early anagen hairs to avoid having the treatment energy unnecessarily high. The heat may rise to the surface and cause blistering. This could happen if the treatment energy is not adjusted when moving from deeper insertions to shallower ones.

The Probe

The probe is the conductor of high-frequency, so the type, size, and shape of the probe can have a tremendous effect on the tissue of the hair follicle when the high-frequency current is applied. As discussed in Chapter 13, the shape of the probe and its tip has a significant effect on the distribution of the heat pattern when using high frequency.

Insulated Probes

Insulated probes are most effective when using thermolysis modality, because they produce the current and therefore the heat at the base of the follicle, where it is most desired to destroy the dermal papilla. It is important to note, though, that the heat is three to four times greater at the tip of an insulated probe than at a noninsulated probe (Figure 14–4), because it is more dense with a smaller surface area for the electrons to pass in to the follicle. Therefore, adjustments should be made to the epilator to reduce the treatment energy when using insulated probes to avoid high-frequency blowout.

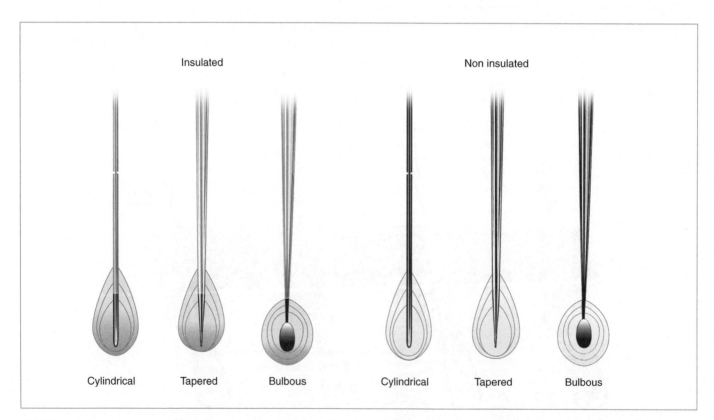

FIGURE 14–4 Heat pattern of high frequency on various probes

Tapered, One-Piece Probes. Tapered, one-piece probes should be the first choice when using thermolysis, because they produce the best point effect, which helps to prevent damage at the surface due to overtreating and therefore work well in areas of high moisture, like the upper lip. Because they are considered sturdier than two-piece probes, one-piece probes are also an excellent choice for areas in which the hair is coarse and dense and for sessions lasting longer than 30 minutes.

Cylindrical, Two-Piece Probes. Cylindrical, two-piece probes are an excellent second choice for thermolysis, especially if insulated. For many, they are the first choice, especially if electrologists rely on the sixth sense of touch to guide them down the follicle with the more delicate probe.

Noninsulated Probes

Noninsulated probes have no insulating coating along the blade and are therefore able to emit electrons the entire length of the probe instead of just the tip. The shape of the tip, however, can still alter the heating pattern so understanding the heating patterns caused by noninsulated probes help in the selection of the appropriate probes.

Tapered Probes. Noninsulated tapered probes are not as preferred as insulated tapered probes, because the heating pattern can still rise higher in the follicle, but it is still a good choice when a sturdier probe is called for, for longer session times.

Cylindrical Probes. Noninsulated, cylindrical probes are not preferred over insulated ones, but when used with the correct treatment energy, they should not be problematic either. The reasons are the same as those for insulated cylindrical probes (see preceding).

Bulbous Probes. The shaped tip of the noninsulated bulbous probe is no better or worse than the standard cylindrical or straight probe with regard to the point effect or heating pattern. However, the bulbous tip may make insertions more difficult, particularly where the follicular opening is very small. Some electrologists feel that the bulbous tip generates too much heat at the dermal papilla and therefore less treatment energy should be used.

PROS & CONS

Pros of Thermolysis

- Thermolysis is the most straightforward method of electrolysis to learn.
- Thermolysis is fast and can treat a number of hairs. A skilled electrologist can treat a new hair every few seconds.
- Fine vellus can be treated with thermolysis with very little regrowth.
- There is no risk of "tattooing," a complication with galvanic electrolysis.

Cons of Thermolysis

- Thermolysis is not as effective on coarse hair, because the required amount of heat, sufficient to destroy the dermal papilla, could cause a negative reaction in the skin. A lower current means that there will be some regrowth, which can be eliminated on a lower current with a subsequent visit.
- Thermolysis is not as effective on distorted follicles, but multiple treatments to a once-distorted follicle do eventually straighten it, making thermolysis still possible for permanent removal.
- The thermolysis equipment does not provide for the opportunity to deliver an after-care treatment of cataphoresis to soothe the skin.

INDICATIONS & CONTRAINDICATIONS

Indications of Thermolysis

- Superfluous vellus
- Fine terminal hair
- Hairs with shallow to medium follicles

Contraindications of Thermolysis

Follow the contraindications listed in-depth in Chapter 13.

It is difficult to treat distorted hair follicles caused by excessive tweezing with thermolysis.

Curly, kinky hair, like those associated with people of African descent, are difficult to treat effectively with thermolysis due to the curvature of the follicles.

The general rule of thumb in selecting the best diameter is to match the probe thickness to the thickness of the hairs being epilated, bearing in mind that, with thermolysis, given all the same additional variables of current intensity and timing, the finer the probe, the hotter it is. This is because the high-frequency current has a smaller area with which to disburse its current. An analogy would be forcing the water through a small stream attachment on a hose nozzle, causing it to fire out with more force, as opposed to adjusting the nozzle to a larger hole, through which it comes out more sluggishly. The thicker probe can be likened to the larger hole in the hose attachment, a larger area equaling less density.

Thermolysis Treatment

Thermolysis is the easiest of the three electrolysis modalities to learn, but it is also the most difficult to master. Once the theory and techniques have been learned, it takes considerable practice to continually make the accurate insertions necessary for permanent hair removal.

Treatment Preparation

Have an easy-to-follow system of preparation, incorporating hygiene, appropriate client preparation, and the following guidelines. A good system will allow for a smooth start to the electrolysis service in a timely manner and free from error.

- Some manual thermolysis machines are designed to also perform galvanic electrolysis, so before using them in thermolysis mode, check that the positive (handheld) attachment is removed.
- Untangle and unimpede all remaining cords to prevent disruption of the current flow or a shorting, particularly in the case of the needle holder.
- Turn on the equipment. (Some older manual machines take a couple of minutes to warm up and so should be turned on a few minutes ahead of time.)
- Select thermolysis mode, if it is the preestablished method.
- Test the equipment to ensure that the current is flowing by initially observing the light indicator. If there is any question, use the lightbulb tester.
- Position the client comfortably on the treatment bed and drape appropriately.
- Wash hands in front of the client according to the manner described in Chapter 5.
- Don gloves.
- Pretreat the client's skin.
- Analyze the client's skin and hair under magnification.
- Select the desired probe, and remove the presterilized forceps and needle cap from their covered containers.
- Using the forceps, insert the needle into the probe.
- Select current density and flow time on the dials following manufacturer's guidelines (intensity × duration = treatment energy).
- Begin epilation with the insertion.

Epilation

As the effectiveness of thermolysis is dependent on an accurate insertion and correct application of the treatment energy, an effective working point should first be established. Using the following guidelines will establish an effective working point for the epilation process to begin.

- Slide the probe down the selected hair follicle.
- Depress the footswitch to allow the current to flow. A small light on the control face usually indicates the flow of current. With semi-manual and computerized machines, the current shuts off after the preselected amount of current has been applied. With manual machines, the operator must focus and count the footswitch depression, corresponding to the desired amount of current flow.
- After applying the current, lift the foot off the footswitch and slide the probe out of the follicle. Using the forceps, gently slide out the epilated hair. If the dermal papilla has been destroyed, the hair removal should meet with no resistance. If it does meet with resistance, make adjustments in one of the three following areas:
  1. probe accuracy
  2. current intensity
  3. duration of the current application

  A higher current may be required, but it should not exceed the manufacturer's recommendations for that area.
- The current density and duration of current flow combine to form the treatment energy and the working point.
- After the working point has been established, make a new insertion and apply a new application of current.
- After the hair has been removed without resistance, signifying that the dermal papilla has been destroyed, move to another hair follicle, completing the treatment. Make adjustments to the current intensity and duration as the individual hairs dictate.

Insertion Count for Manual Thermolysis

Particularly for manual machines, the four-count method is standard when learning the thermolysis application of current. It consists of steadily counting "one-two–three-four." The total four-count should last between 1.75 and 2.0 seconds.

1. On the "one" count, insert the probe into the hair follicle.
2. On the "two" count, apply the current by depressing the footswitch or button on the probe.
3. On the "three" count, lift the foot off the footswitch or lift the finger off the button, stopping the current.
4. On the "four" count, remove the probe from the hair follicle.

This count method is a good habit to get into initially, because it helps prevent the electrologist from sliding the probe up and down the hair follicle while the current is flowing, causing possible skin damage.

Note: It is important to ensure that the foot is off the footswitch and that there is no risk of the current being applied while the needle is sliding in or out of the follicle, because doing so could cause damage, particularly to the epidermis, leaving undesirable marks on the skin.

Treatment End

After the treatment is completed, turn back the dials to 0 and turn off the machine. Immediately remove the needle using the forceps and place it in the sharps container. Apply after-care to the client.

Thermolysis Techniques

There are various techniques of current application used with thermolysis to destroy the dermal papilla in a manner that is comfortable for the client. These techniques are described, along with some of the adverse reactions that can happen with the incorrect application of treatment energy to the follicle.

Working Point

working point
the treatment energy required to successfully epilate hair; determined both by current intensity and duration of current flow

pulsing
the process by which a current is applied to the same follicle in two or more intervals, instead of in a continuous burst

The **working point** is the point at which the lowest current intensity and shortest current application length have been established to destroy the dermal papilla with minimal discomfort to the client and a minimal negative reaction to the skin. The lower the intensity, the longer the required current application, and vice versa. High intensity with a short burst of current, called the "flash technique," is addressed in the following.

The working point is arrived at by first applying the lowest intensity recommended for the area with a shorter burst of current, then grasping the hair with the forceps to see if the hair slides up without resistance. If not, make adjustments, increasing either or both the current intensity and length of the current application to the same follicle. This can be done up to three times in the same follicle to establish the working point at which the hair releases with one application of current. To do this more than three times risks overtreating the follicle and causing damage. A new follicle should be tried if three attempts are unsuccessful at releasing the hair.

Required Timing

The timing of the current application can be as varied as one quick high intensity burst lasting only a fraction of a second, multiple bursts at a medium intensity, or a longer, lower intensity burst that lasts 2 seconds. Timing techniques are determined according to the hair type, the area to be treated, and the clients' tolerance and comfort level.

Pulsing

In **pulsing**, current is applied to the same follicle in two or more intervals, instead of in a continuous burst. This is often done in areas that feel more sensitive to the client (e.g., the upper lip). Pulsing is achieved by tapping the footswitch, or it can be programmed into the equipment. Pulsing can be applied in multiple ways that can deliver the same amount of current (Figure 14–5). There is an advantage to pulsing if an effective amount of heat is produced in the follicle, sufficient to destroy the dermal papilla, however if the spacing

FIGURE 14–5
Pulsing of current applications

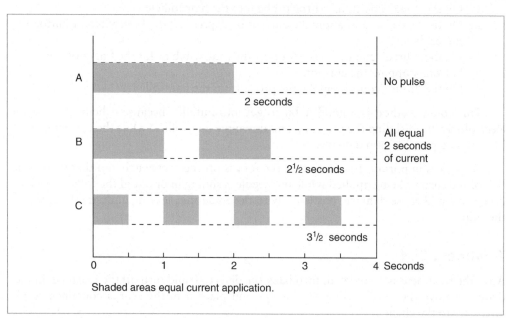

Shaded areas equal current application.

between the bursts of current is too long the temperature in the follicle may drop resulting in insufficient heat to destroy the dermal papilla.

Flashing

The flash technique should only be used on fine, straight hairs. It is effective most on fine, straight hairs with medium to shallow follicles. The premise of this method is to use a higher-density current for a shorter time, usually 0.20 to 0.50 of a second, although manufacturer's guidelines for individual machines should be observed. The heating pattern is intense but narrow in the field of destruction, destroying the dermal papilla without damaging the skin or causing high-frequency blowout. The more shallow the follicle, the lower the dial should be. The current can be applied in a few bursts. Check between bursts to see if the hair has been released and the dermal papilla destroyed. The benefit of the flash technique is that clients often have higher tolerances for shorter, higher intensities, the premise being that it happens faster than the nerve endings register the discomfort. However, too high an intensity can excessively damage the skin.

Thermolysis Overtreatment

The overtreatment of a follicle can be apparent by observing surface tissue damage, a crackling sound as the current is applied, or debris stuck to the probe. Recognizing the signs of overtreatment will help the electrologist to know when to reduce the treatment energy.

High-Frequency Blowout

"High-frequency blowout" (Figure 14–6), a term described by Dr. James E. Schuster, occurs if the treatment energy is too extreme. It results from either too high an intensity of current or too long an application of current at the tip of the probe. The fluid in the soft tissue may "boil," producing steam in the follicle. Because steam is a poor conductor, the

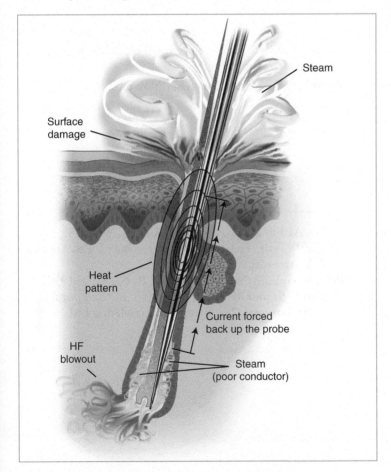

FIGURE 14–6
High-frequency blowout

Steam

Surface damage

Heat pattern

Current forced back up the probe

HF blowout

Steam (poor conductor)

current is forced to rise back up the probe, to the surface, causing undesirable effects on the skin's surface. As the current rises up the probe, soft tissue debris adheres to the probe. When this happens, a crackling can be heard. High-frequency blowout can be avoided by reducing the treatment energy.

Crackling

Crackling happens when the probe is too hot and steam has been produced in the follicle. Reduce the time and/or current intensity.

Probe Debris

If there is debris on the probe after one application of current to the hair follicle, the probe is too hot and the time and/or current intensity should be reduced.

 ## Conclusion

For clients with dense, unwanted hair growing in straight follicles, electrolysis offers a fast and effective method of permanent removal. This modality of electrolysis is the easiest to learn but the hardest to master. It takes considerable practice and evaluation before it should be applied on clients. Practice the insertions on the arms and legs of friends or fellow students until the insertions are accomplished with ease and accuracy. When the teacher is confident that the students' insertions are accurate, the current can be turned on and hairs on the limbs treated. The hairs should slide out with the hair bulb intact and with minimal reaction to the epidermal tissue, indicating a safe and effective treatment. Treatments in this area should be mastered before moving to other parts of the body. The face should not be treated until an electrolysis educator has determined the safety and accuracy of the insertions and treatments. When thermolysis is mastered, it can be a very satisfying and worthwhile treatment.

 ## Discussion and Review Questions

1. What are the main differences between manual and computerized electrolysis machines?
2. What kind of sound waves does thermolysis produce?
3. What is electrocoagulation?
4. What is the first choice of tip shape for the thermolysis modality?
5. Thermolysis is *not* the preferred modality of choice on which type of hair?
6. What causes high-frequency blowout?

 ## Additional Readings

Bono, Michael. 1994. *The Blend Method.* Santa Barbara, CA: Tortoise Press.

Gallant, Ann. *Principles and Techniques for the Electrologist.* Cheltenham, U.K.: Stanley Thornes (Publishers) Ltd.

Glor, Fino. 1987. *Modern Electrology.* Great Neck, N.Y.: Hair Publishing, Inc.

Hinkle, Arthur Ralph, and Lind, Richard W. 1968. *Electrolysis, Thermolysis, and the Blend.* Los Angeles, CA: Arroway.

Meharg, G. E., R.N., and Richards, R. N., M.D. 1997. *Cosmetic and Medical Electrolysis and Temporary Hair Removal,* 2e., Toronto, Ont: Medric Ltd.

CHAPTER 15

Galvanic Electrolysis

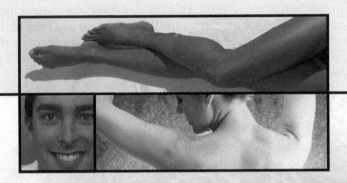

Chapter Outline

Learning Objectives ■ Key Terms ■ Introduction ■ How Galvanic Electrolysis Works
Variables Affecting Galvanic Electrolysis in the Hair Follicle ■ Conclusion
Discussion and Review Questions ■ Additional Readings

Learning Objectives

By the end of this chapter, you should be able to:

1. Understand how the galvanic modality works.
2. List the pros and cons of galvanic modality.
3. List the dos and don'ts of galvanic modality.
4. Know how to perform a galvanic treatment.
5. Know how to perform a cataphoresis treatment.

Key Terms

galvanism
hydrochloric acid

lye
lye gradient

shocking
tattooing

Introduction

galvanism
the application of DC, forming a chemical reaction

Galvanic electrolysis is *true* electrolysis. Although electrolysis has become the general term for permanent hair removal, including thermolysis and the blend, **galvanism** (GAL-vuh-niz-um) is true electrolysis. This chapter covers the various aspects of the galvanic modality of electrolysis, how it is applied, and the pros and cons of this method over others. The end of the chapter has a section on cataphoresis, an effective after-care treatment using the galvanic equipment. The indications and contraindications of galvanic electrolysis are discussed in Chapter 13.

How Galvanic Electrolysis Works

Galvanic electrolysis—sometimes referred to as "true electrolysis"—is the original modality used for permanent hair removal. Galvanic does not work with the speed of thermolysis, but what it lacks in speed can be made up with accuracy as the chemical reaction caused by the galvanic current is able to "bleed" down distorted follicles to destroy the dermal papilla. The accuracy of insertion is not as crucial for galvanic as it is with thermolysis, making it a good modality to learn with.

- Galvanic current is DC, that is, current that moves continuously in one direction (Figure 15–1).
- DC in a saline (salt-water) solution causes the separation and rearrangement of the chemical components, that is, water (H_2O) and sodium chloride (NaCL) into new substances, the main substances being sodium hydroxide, also called lye (NaOH), and hydrogen gas. This process, called electrolysis, occurs in similar fashion on the soft tissue in the hair follicle.
- The galvanic machine is plugged in and turned on, which is shown by the indicator light. The power source used to be a battery, but now electrolysis devices use AC with rectifiers built in to produce the DC needed for electrolysis.
- The rheostat is set to control the intensity of the current flow.

FIGURE 15–1
Diagram of the galvanic machine

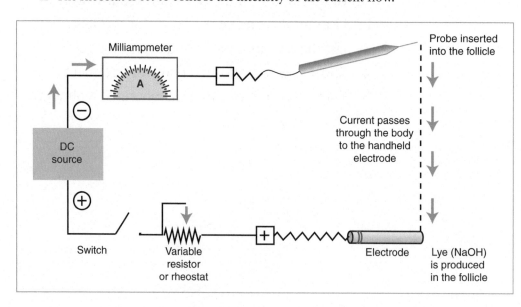

FIGURE 15–2
Galvanic electrolysis treatment

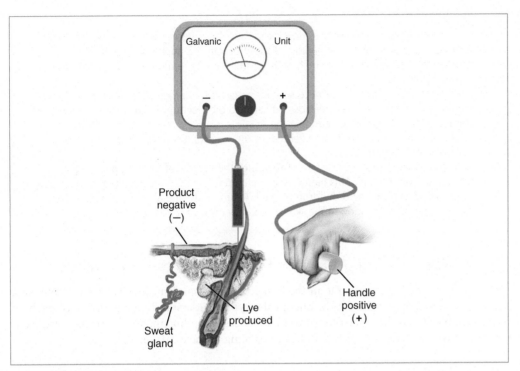

- The milliampere meter gauge measures the flow of galvanic current.
- The positive applicator chord is attached to the positive jack, and the moistened electrode is attached to the client or given to the client to hold.
- The needle holder is attached to one end of the negative cord, the other end of the cord is attached to the negative jack on the unit.
- The footswitch is attached to its jack, usually found at the back of the unit.
- The probe is placed in the client's hair follicle.
- The footswitch is depressed, releasing a flow of DC that runs from the negative pole (i.e., the needle) via the shortest route through the client's body to the positive pole (i.e., the electrode attached to or held by the client) (Figure 15–2).
- The chemical action of the current in the moist tissue of the body occurs at the tip of the probe inserted into the follicle, producing lye.
- The electricity returns to the positive terminal of the DC source.

PROS & CONS

Pros of Galvanic Electrolysis

- Galvanic electrolysis offers the highest success rate in lack of regrowth.
- An accurate insertion is less important with galvanic electrolysis than it is for thermolysis, because the caustic **lye** (LYE) that is produced "bleeds" down to the dermal papilla, causing its damage or destruction. As a result, galvanic electrolysis is a good choice of modality for the newly trained, less experienced electrologist.
- Distorted and wavy hair follicles can be successfully treated, because although the probe may not bend and go all the way down to the dermal papilla, the lye will continue to bleed down to the base and effect the necessary change.
- The lye produced in the hair follicles continues destroying the hair follicle even after the treatment session is over.

Cons of Galvanic Electrolysis

- Galvanic electrolysis is the slowest method of permanent hair removal. The chemical action needed to produce sufficient lye to destroy the dermal papilla can take a number of minutes on each hair.

continues

lye
a strong solution of sodium hydroxide or potassium hydroxide in water

- The extended application of the current can cause an irritating sensation for the client. A client with a high-strung or nervous disposition may be unable to tolerate the slowness or discomfort. It may be harder for the client to remain still throughout the current application.
- The client's full cooperation is necessary for successful treatment. This includes remaining still for extended periods and keeping the electrolysis circuit flowing by continuously holding the electrode.
- While lye can continue to treat follicles after the session, it can continue to be a source of discomfort and irritation.
- An incorrect cord setup can result in **tattooing**, the process of forming permanent black marks on the skin. This happens when the positive pole is connected to the probe, causing **hydrochloric acid** (hy-droh-KLOR-ik AS-ud) in the metal of the probe, which creates a permanent tattoo in the skin that is very difficult to remove.

tattooing
a mark on the skin caused when the positive pole is connected to the probe, creating hydrochloric acid in the metal of the probe

hydrochloric acid
a strong, colorless acid formed when hydrogen chloride gas dissociates in water

Variables Affecting Galvanic Electrolysis in the Hair Follicle

The variables that affect galvanic in the hair follicle are current density, current intensity, current duration, insertion depth, and probe type. Understanding the effect of each of these variables helps the electrologist to make necessary adjustments to produce sufficient lye to destroy the dermal papilla without producing tissue damage.

Lye Gradient

lye gradient
the concentration of lye produced in the hair follicle

The **lye gradient** (Figure 15–3) is the concentration of lye produced in the follicle. It can be affected by the treatment energy (i.e., the current duration and current density), and its

FIGURE 15–3
Lye gradient

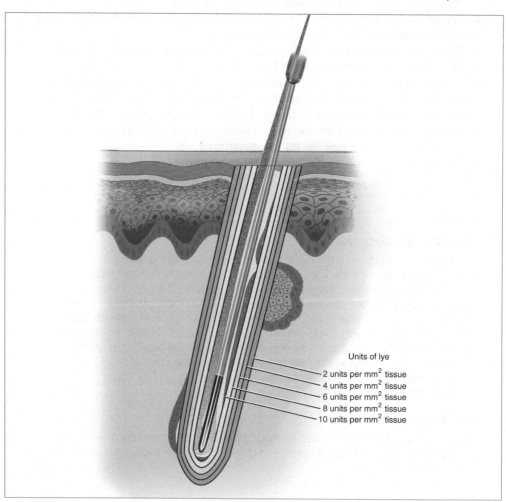

Units of lye

- 2 units per mm^2 tissue
- 4 units per mm^2 tissue
- 6 units per mm^2 tissue
- 8 units per mm^2 tissue
- 10 units per mm^2 tissue

pattern can be affected by the tip of the probe. The concentration of lye is stronger close to the probe, weaker farther away. The critical zone is the area of the most concentration of lye, where tissue damage is most affected. If part of the dermal papilla lies outside that critical zone, the lye will not destroy it and regrowth will occur.

Current Density

Current density is the amount of electrons that flow into the surrounding tissue from a given surface area, in this case, the probe. Current density can be affected by the size of the probe, the depth of the insertion of the probe (the density is greater, for instance, on a thinner probe than it is on a thicker one, when using thermolysis), the time the current flows, and the strength or intensity of the current. The greater the density, the more lye that is produced. A shallow insertion creates greater density.

Current Intensity

Current intensity is the strength of the current flowing from the probe to the surrounding tissue, is measured in milliamperes (ma). It is applied in a range of approximately 0.1 to 1.0 ma, the most comfortable levels being between 0.3 and 0.7 ma. For multiple-needle galvanic, the range would be lower—0.01 to 1.0 ma—with the most comfortable setting being around 0.08 to 0.12 ma.

Current Duration

Current duration is the length of time the current flows from the probe into the surrounding tissue. The duration of the current can be preset, but it is applied by the footswitch. In older, manual models, the current flows as long as the footswitch (or, in some countries, the button on the probe) is depressed. With galvanic electrolysis, the current must flow, on average, for approximately 30 seconds to produce sufficient lye to destroy the follicle. Although the average duration is 30 seconds to 1 minute, the range can go from 30 seconds to 3 minutes. With the multiple-needle galvanic, the duration can be considerably longer, up to 5 minutes. This is in sharp contrast to the blend method, in which the galvanic current is combined with thermolysis and need only flow for a quarter of that time.

Faraday's Law/Treatment Energy

$$\text{intensity} \times \text{time} = \text{lye produced}$$
$$\text{(in ma)} \quad \text{(in seconds)}$$

In application, 1 ma applied for 5 seconds produces the same amount of lye as 0.1 ma for 50 seconds or 5 ma for 1 second.

The treatment energy required for treating different hairs varies considerably, from 8 units of treatment energy for vellus up to 80 units for coarse hair.

Insertion Depth

Insertion depth does not affect the density of current when using the galvanic modality, but it should be considered when using the galvanic modality with the blend technique, because it is affected by the use of thermolysis.

Pulsing or Tapping

Pulsing is unnecessary and should not be used when using the galvanic modality alone. However, it does have a use with thermolysis and the blend technique, as addressed in their respective chapters.

Shocking

shocking
discomfort the client experiences
due to the careless application of
the electrical current; often in the
form of a sudden jolt or burning

Shocking consists of the various types of discomfort a client experiences due to the careless application of the galvanic current. It can be experienced in the form of a sudden jolt or a tingling or burning sensation.

There are three main types of shocking:

1. General shocking, which is experienced when too much current is applied to the hair follicle.
2. Mass effect shocking, which occurs in multiple-needle electrolysis, also occurs when too much current is felt. However, with multiple-needle electrolysis, there may be a lower level used in each follicle than that causing the degree of discomfort in general shocking. The collective sensation of multiple needles at lower current levels, however, can still cause discomfort.
3. Make-break shocking is usually experienced in the form of a sudden jolt when the galvanic current is turned on and off suddenly or abruptly. To minimize this, epilators today are designed with a "ramping" feature that enables the application of the galvanic current to gradually build when turned on and to gradually decrease when turned off.

Probes

Both insulated and noninsulated probes can be used with galvanic, although they produce different lye patterns in the follicle. Some are preferred over others, and care should be taken to make adjustments in the application of treatment energy with some shaped probes. Knowing the variables will help in the selection of the most suitable probe.

Insulated Probes

Insulated probes are covered two-thirds of the way down with insulated, plastic coating. Because the electrons must flow through the tip only, there is a greater point effect at the tip. Therefore, lye is produced only at the tip of the probe, and, while they can effectively destroy the dermal papilla, sebaceous glands may remain unaffected. One school of thought holds that for effective and permanent hair removal, the sebaceous gland should also be destroyed. According to James E. Schuster, MD, the intensity of heat is three to four times greater at the tip of an insulated probe than on a noninsulated and that therefore adjustments should be made to the epilator to reduce the treatment energy when using insulated probes.

When using an insulated probe of the same diameter as a noninsulated probe and applying the same milliampere, there will be equal strength but greater density of electrons at the tip of the insulated probe; they will be distributed over the length of the noninsulated probe. There may also be some question as to the durability of the insulation on the probe and whether the lye produced by the galvanic current would break it down. Consult with the probe manufacturer to determine if the insulation on the probe could withstand the effects of lye.

Tapered Probes.   With galvanic, insulated, tapered probes react like cylindrical probes; the greatest point effect is at the tip. Therefore, they are not the first choice for the galvanic modality if one feels the sebaceous gland must also be destroyed.

Bulbous Probes.   Insulated or not, bulbous probes are effective with the galvanic current. They create the greatest amount of lye at the tip. For those who believe that permanent destruction of the hair follicle must include sebaceous gland destruction, these would not be the probes of choice. For those who feel that only dermal papilla destruction is necessary, these are good choices.

Cylindrical Probes.   The effects caused by insulated cylindrical probes are similar to those of insulated and tapered probes described above.

Noninsulated Probes

The pattern of lye production differs with each of the three types of noninsulated probes.

Tapered Probes.   Noninsulated tapered probes are not suited to galvanic current because they are wider at the top and therefore generate a stronger lye gradient closer to the surface of the skin at the opening of the hair follicle, where it is least desirable and least effective.

Bulbous Probes.   The bulbous-shaped tip of this noninsulated probe is suitable for the galvanic modality, particularly if you are not of the school of thought that believes that the destruction of the sebaceous gland is essential to permanent hair removal, because most of the lye would be concentrated at the tip of the probe.

Cylindrical Probes.   The noninsulated cylindrical probe is preferred for the galvanic modality because of the even concentration of lye along the probe, permeating into the surrounding tissue the length of the follicle destroying the sebaceous gland and the dermal papilla.

Probe Diameter

With galvanic electrolysis, the rule of thumb is to choose a probe of the approximate diameter of the hair. More on probe diameters is found in Chapter 12.

Positioning of Handheld Electrode for Shortest Circuit

Current always searches for the shortest, most direct route between positive and negative poles. This is true in the human body. Therefore, place electrodes to bypass any metal objects (Figure 15–4) and to direct the current along the most comfortable route.

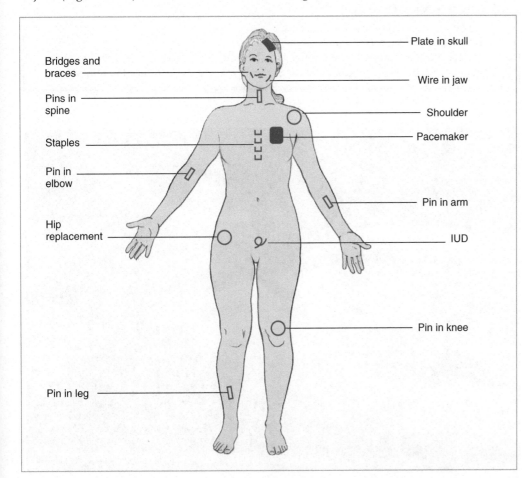

FIGURE 15–4
Location of metal in the body

Upper Lip. When working on the upper lip, place the indifferent electrode in the client's hand on the same side as the side of the upper lip being worked on (e.g., in the right hand for the right side of the mouth, in the left hand for the left side of the mouth). This prevents the current from passing all the way around the mouth and creating a metallic taste.

Pregnancy or IUD. Arrange electrodes so that the current does not pass through the pelvic region. Avoid the galvanic modality when working on the abdomen and bikini area of women with an IUD and use thermolysis instead. Avoid working on the breasts or abdomen during the third trimester, and reread the section on pregnancy contraindications in Chapter 13.

Cataphoresis

Cataphoresis (Figure 15–5) is also known as positive surface galvanism. A carbon roller with a positive (anode +) pole is used to distribute galvanic current to the surface of the skin, enabling a more effective penetration of a substance, whether it is a medication or simply a soothing agent. Cataphoresis can be very beneficial after galvanic electrolysis to

---

DO'S & DON'TS

Do's of Galvanic Electrolysis

- Follow all guidelines of the machine's manual.
- Use the shortest current route to minimize discomfort.
- Make sure the negative cord with the probe is attached to the negative jack to avoid tattooing the client.

Don'ts of Galvanic Electrolysis

- Do not use tapered or insulated needles.
- Do not pulse with galvanic current.
- Do not attach the probe to the positive jack, because doing so creates hydrochloric acid at the tip of the probe, which marks the skin with a tattoo that is difficult to remove.

FIGURE 15–5
Cataphoresis

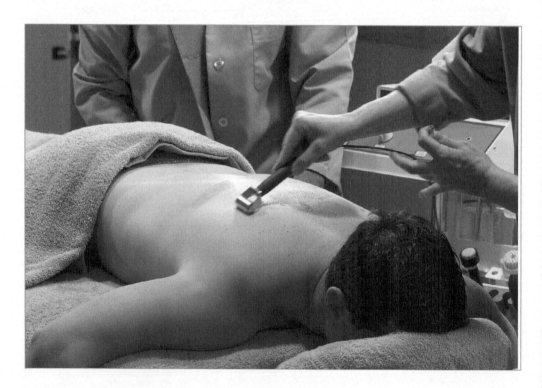

reduce redness and provide more effective antibacterial protection. It should not be applied after thermolysis or the blend, but it can be applied after galvanic electrolysis.

Make sure that the roller is stainless steel and not the now-defunct carbon. Apply 2.0 ma. Warn the client that if a metallic taste is experienced in the mouth, it is not metal but a reaction on the taste buds.

There are two ways of applying the gauze, which can be premoistened with witch hazel. Either wrap it around the roller or apply directly to the skin. Move the roller across the gauze, or apply the moistened gauze directly on the skin being treated.

Iontophoresis in galvanic electrolysis is achieved using two rollers. One roller is attached to the negative (cathode –) pole, the other to the positive (anode +) pole. The client need not hold an electrode. Lotions or a gauze soaked in a solution are applied to the skin, and the rollers are passed over the gauze, causing ionization.

More on cataphoresis is found in Chapter 12.

Conclusion

The galvanic method of electrolysis is preferred for occasional distorted follicles and on light-density hair with curved follicles. It lacks the speed of thermolysis, and with less accuracy than thermolysis can significantly and permanently damage the dermal papilla and, with the correct choice of probe, the sebaceous gland also. For dense amounts of hair with curved or distorted follicles, the blend method, explained in Chapter 16, is preferred.

Discussion and Review Questions

1. What is lye?
2. Why are noninsulated probes the probes of choice with the galvanic modality?
3. Which probe tip should be used?
4. What is another name for cataphoresis?
5. What are the three main types of shocking?
6. What causes tattooing in galvanic electrolysis?

Additional Readings

Bono, Michael. 1994. *The Blend Method*. Santa Barbara, CA: Tortoise Press.

Gallant, Ann. *Principles and Techniques for the Electrologist*. Cheltenham, U.K.: Stanley Thornes (Publishers) Ltd.

Glor, Fino. 1987. *Modern Electrology*. Great Neck, N.Y.: Hair Publishing, Inc.

Hinkle, Arthur Ralph, and Lind, Richard W. 1968. *Electrolysis, Thermolysis, and the Blend*. Los Angeles, CA: Arroway.

Meharg, G. E., R.N., and Richards, R. N., M.D. 1997. *Cosmetic and Medical Electrolysis and Temporary Hair Removal*, 2e., Toronto, ONT: Medric Ltd.

CHAPTER 16

The Blend Method

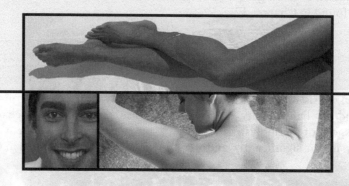

Chapter Outline

Learning Objectives ■ Key Terms ■ Introduction ■ What Is the Blend?
Types of Blend Epilators ■ Indications and Contraindications ■ Pros & Cons
Variables of the Blend Technique ■ Conclusion
Discussion and Review Questions ■ Additional Readings

Learning Objectives

By the end of this chapter, you should be able to:

1. Describe the blend technique.
2. List basic differences between the manual, semiautomatic, and automatic blend-epilator machines
3. Compare sequential and simultaneous current application.
4. Calculate a basic formula for using the blend.

Key Terms

causticity   porosity
neuronial blockade   turbulence

Introduction

The blend technique is just that: a technique or method applying DC (galvanic) and AC (high frequency) through one probe or filament that is inserted in the hair follicle. The blend method was developed by Arthur Hinkle and Henri Saint-Pierre in California in 1938. Hinkle patented the technique in 1948. Since then, others have developed the technique, adding research, testing, and experience to come up with their own formulas for effective blend-method hair removal. The blend method has now become the most popular and frequently used method in the United States. This chapter covers basic formulas, kinds of blend-method epilators, and advantages and disadvantages of the blend, overviewing the blend technique, and how it might be used. This chapter is not designed to be the sole reference for this very complicated technique, rather a brief introduction and guideline that should be used in conjunction with formal, hands-on classroom training under the supervision of a skilled electrolysis educator.

What Is "The Blend"?

Is the "blend" a method or a machine? Michael Bono used an analogy that likens the blend to cooking: One must have the recipe and the skills and, like one can do of a good meal, ask, "Did the stove make the meal, or did the chef?"

The blend method is the application and use of the two different types of current applied simultaneously or sequentially (Figure 16–1). Those currents are galvanic (DC),

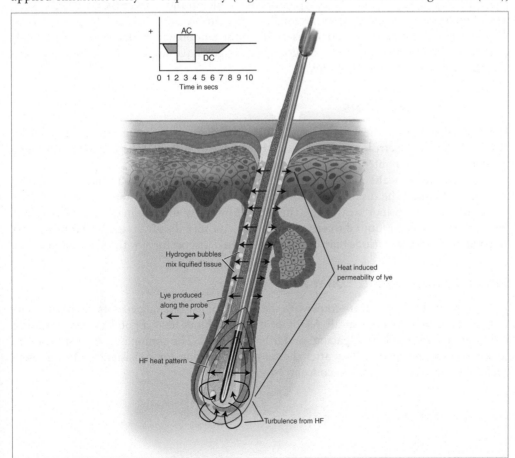

FIGURE 16–1
Effect of the blend on a hair follicle

FIGURE 16–2
Combined AC/DC

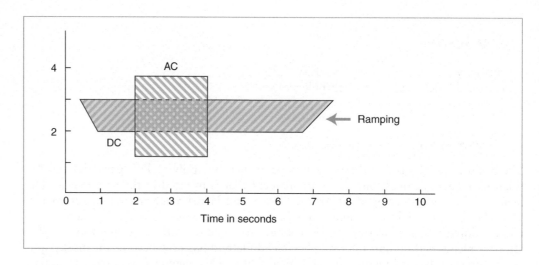

which is slow yet the most effective in hair-follicle destruction, combined with thermolysis (AC), which brings speed to the method (Figure 16–2).

The galvanic current or DC produces a chemical reaction that breaks down the water and salts in live tissue, creating sodium hydroxide (lye). When heat is introduced by the AC of thermolysis, the chemical reaction is accelerated, producing significantly more lye, three to four times more, in a shorter period, and better permeability to the surrounding tissue. Hinkle teaches that heated lye is six times more caustic than lye at normal body temperature and with each 10°C increase in temperature, the speed of the chemical reaction doubles.

Types of Blend Epilators

There are a wide selection of blend epilators available on the market today, to suit every type of budget and business, from the smaller home business to the large, busy electrolysis clinic where more than one electrologist will use the equipment. Epilators can be manual, semiautomatic or automatic. Their ergonomic designs have improved considerably over the years and are more user friendly.

Manual Blend Epilators

The manual mode is when the timing and stop and start of the current application is controlled by the electrologist. In the case of the blend method, the galvanic and high-frequency current is controlled with one or two foot pedals.

The advantage of the manual method is its versatility, being able to individualize the treatment of hairs. The disadvantage of this method is that inconsistencies are inevitable in the timing of each hair treatment. Timing and intensity may be inaccurate. Continual concentration is also required to ensure accuracy. Another disadvantage is that using two footswitches for long periods may cause work-related discomfort for the electrologist.

Semiautomatic Blend Epilators

Semiautomatic blend epilators come with the option of using a single-footswitch, two separate footswitches, or none at all. Many of these machines have a good variety of timing and intensity, with pulsing, spacing, and a hair counter. The timing and intensity can be preset to cease the current flow after the set time, allowing for consistency. Once presettings have been established, less concentration is required.

Automatic Blend Epilators

With the automatic blend epilator, timing is controlled entirely by the machine. It calculates and consistently applies the appropriate timing and intensity of both blend currents once it has been programmed with the hair type. Features include a galvanic after-count and a hair counter. This means there is a lot less brainwork for the technician to do. These machines also come with one- or no-footswitches.

The disadvantage is that there are fewer options to make adjustments for individual hairs. Many electrologists may at one time have felt intimidated by the computerization of these machines, but as computer technology becomes more prevalent, intimidation becomes less of a concern.

INDICATIONS & CONTRAINDICATIONS

Indications of the Blend Method

■ Works for a significant number of hairs
■ Works for curly and kinky hairs that have curved follicles
■ Preferred for anagen to high telogen hairs

Contraindications of the Blend Method

■ Consider the contraindications of the galvanic electrolysis and thermolysis modalities when evaluating a client's suitability for the treatment (see Chapter 13)

PROS & CONS

Pros of the Blend Method

■ The blend modality is an effective and versatile method of treating a wide range of hairs on all parts of the body.
■ Using high frequency for a longer time on a lower-intensity setting and following it with the galvanic is effective for treating hairs from their early anagen stage right up to their high telogen stage.
■ Blend allows for effectiveness of galvanic electrolysis but the benefit of a speedier treatment with the application of thermolysis.

Cons of the Blend Method

■ The blend modality is the most difficult to learn and master. Its planning and calculating of accurate effective treatments is complex, and while those tasks might be made easier by an automatic machine, the complexities of computerization may remain a challenge.
■ Damage from high-frequency blowout.
■ "Gas blowout."

Variables of the Blend Technique

Recommended parameters for face and body techniques should be observed, as should the client's comfort level. Continued dialogue with the client will ensure the treatment is minimally painful. Clients are usually vocal about their comfort levels.

Face Technique

The techniques used on the face are designed to ensure an effective treatment with minimum adverse reaction to the skin on the face. Adverse reactions could be eschars, blanching, pitting, and dimpling of the skin due to the overtreatment of an area or excessive application of treatment energy. To avoid these adverse reactions, follow the guidelines recommended by the manufacturer of the blend-method epilator, as well as guidelines covered in formal classroom training. With face technique, it is important to note that the high frequency is considered the "master current." As the high frequency is applied, creating heat in the follicle, the goal should be to cease the high-frequency current before the heating pattern rises to the surface, damaging the skin and allowing the heated lye to continue destroying the dermal papilla and surrounding follicular tissue. The rule of thumb is to apply a moderate level of high frequency for long enough to epilate the hair, between 6 to 20 seconds. Do not epilate the hair with a high-frequency current less than 6 seconds, because this indicates that the high frequency is too high and the result could be damage and scarring of the face. Slower, shorter treatments, over longer periods reduce the risk of permanent damage and the chance of overtreating a delicate area.

Body Technique

When working on the body, where there is often more hair that requires removal, the goal is to provide a faster, safe, and effective treatment with minimum regrowth. There is not the same concern of posttreatment irritation on the body that there is for the face. Areas like the bikini line or along the shinbone on the front of the leg are more prone to eschars, which rarely leave permanent markings. The client is often more interested in the fact that the treatment permanently eliminated hairs and prevented regrowth and the need for repeat visits over an extended period. The longer the session, the harder it is for clients to tolerate higher levels of discomfort. They may cross certain thresholds causing them to want to cut short their treatments.

Use a higher-intensity high frequency for 1 to 2 seconds with the simultaneous application of DC in two bursts, gradually increasing the bursts to provide a more effective treatment. When treating the large areas of the body, have the client shave 2 days before the treatment so that the technician's time will be spent only treating observable anagen hairs.

Calculating Formulas

There are differing schools of thought when it comes to calculating the formula for a blend treatment. One popular blend formula, the earliest, was established by Arthur Hinkle and Henri St. Pierre, who found that by using the minimal intensity high frequency required for the hair type, and referring to Hinkle's Units of Lye Chart, for the units of lye required to destroy the hair with galvanic electrolysis, that only one-quarter of those units of lye were needed when heated by high frequency speeding up the treatment.

A single unit of lye is the amount of lye produced when one-tenth of one miliampere of current flows for one second.

1/10 of 1 ma for 1 second = 1 unit of lye
5/10 of 1 ma for 1 second = 5 unit of lye

Hinkle's Units of Lye Chart	
Hair Type	**Lye Quantity (in Units)**
Shallow vellus (found on cheek and lip)	15
Medium deep terminal (sides of face, chin, and arms)	45
Deep terminal (women, chin and legs; men, back and shoulders)	60
Very deep terminal (men's beards)	80

Hinkle found that when high frequency was added, only one-quarter of the lye units (UL) were needed for the galvanic treatment of the same size hair.

Establishing the Working Point for the Blend

1. Turn on the machine and allow it to warm.
2. Ensure the client has good contact with the positive electrode.
3. Use the two-handed method described in Chapter 13.

4. Establish the working point (intensity and time) for thermolysis that is needed to epilate the hair on a low intensity and up to, but no longer than, 10 seconds. Increase the intensity if necessary, but without going over the 10-second duration.
5. Type the hair in units of lye measurement.
6. Establish the galvanic working point (intensity and time) needed to remove the same hair.
7. Divide UL/HF seconds = galvanic setting in 10/ma.

Example – Coarse chin hair found on a woman

HF seconds = 10 seconds

UL value = 60 units

60/10 = 0.6 ma (if this is a tolerable level for the client)

Average Blend Settings				
Hair Type	H.F. Time (seconds)	H.F. Intensity (percent)	Galvanic Time (seconds)	Galvanic Intensity (ma)
Vellus/fine	0.2 to 0.3	5 to 10	8	0.25
Fine/medium	0.2 to 0.4	5 to 10	10	0.35
Medium/coarse	0.2 to 0.4	5 to 15	12	0.45
Very coarse	0.2 to 0.5	5 to 15	15	0.55

Settings are to be adjusted with these settings, allowing for the release of the hair on the lowest setting and accommodating the client's tolerance.

Simultaneous Application

Both high-frequency and galvanic currents are applied at the same time, resulting in great speed of treatment, but some feel this method produces a higher degree of discomfort for the client.

Sequential Application

High-frequency and galvanic currents are applied in a sequence of pulses. There is a theory known as **neuronial blockade** that suggests that nerve endings are either damaged or fatigued by high frequency or galvanism, whichever current is applied first, decreasing the level of discomfort experienced from the application of the following current.

Hinkle prefers to lead with high frequency to reduce the discomfort of galvanism, whereas Shuster has found that the theory is inconsistent and that there is little difference in pain sensation relative to the lead current.

Leading with galvanic is helpful if there is blockage in the follicle, because it clears it and allows the probe to more readily slide down to the dermal papilla. It does not need the kind of force that could cause the probe to "overshoot" and rupture below the dermal papilla.

neuronial blockade
the theory that nerve endings are damaged by thermolysis or galvanism, whichever current is applied first, decreasing the level of discomfort experienced from the application of the following current

Action of the Blend Method in the Follicle

When high frequency and DC are applied together to the hair follicle, either simultaneously or sequentially, reactions result that are unique to the combined application of those currents as opposed to the reactions of either used alone.

Causticity

When sodium hydroxide is heated, it proves to have considerably more **causticity** than when unheated, 2 to 16 times more caustic according to Hinkle. In tests on organic tissue, the reaction rate of sodium hydroxide doubled with temperatures above 115°F/44°C, for every 22.4°F/12°C increase in temperature. When significantly produced heat is applied to

causticity
the state of being burned by chemical action

the galvanically produced sodium hydroxide, the simmering action agitates the sodium hydroxide, thereby intensifying its chemical action on the follicular tissue.

Porosity

porosity
the extent to which something is porous

Providing that the application of high frequency is not too high, and not generating too much heat that would dry out the follicular tissue, the high-frequency current will coagulate the tissue, changing it into a more spongy, cellular substance. **Porosity** is the degree to which this occurs. Following with the application of the DC, the sodium hydroxide that forms around the probe will be more readily absorbed into the coagulated tissue, as opposed to the cellular tissue that has either not been affected by the high frequency or completely dried out by too intense an application of high frequency.

Turbulence

turbulence
a departure from a smooth flowing to an irregular motion

The agitation caused by the high-frequency current heating the sodium hydroxide is called **turbulence**. This is a similar action observed with a casserole simmering in an oven dish. The soupy bubbles create a stirring action, working their way into the "nooks and crannies" of the surrounding follicular tissue and the bends of curved or distorted follicles. With the increased advantages of causticity and porosity, this advantage also ensures the complete destruction of the dermal papilla and the follicular tissue surrounding the hair.

Adverse Reactions

Adverse reactions for the blend method can be caused by miscalculating the treatment energies for either thermolysis or galvanic, and not making the necessary allowances and adjustments when the treatments are used in conjunction with each other. Adverse reactions can also be caused by not selecting the appropriate probe for the treatment. Some of the adverse reactions are described following.

High-Frequency Blowout. "High-frequency blowout," a term described by Dr. James E. Schuster, occurs if the treatment energy is too extreme, caused by too high an intensity of current or too long a duration in the application of current at the tip of the probe. The fluid in the soft tissue may "boil," producing steam in the follicle. Because steam is a poor conductor, the current is forced to rise back up the probe to the surface, causing undesirable effects on the skin's surface. As the current rises up the probe, soft tissue debris adheres to

---

DO'S & DON'TS

Do's of the Blend Method

- Follow all the guidelines of the machine, as laid out in its manual.
- Use the shortest current route to minimize discomfort when applying DC.
- Make sure the negative probe is attached to the negative jack to avoid tattooing the client.
- Always consider high frequency the dominant method and use it at a moderate level.
- A fast, high-intensity blend technique should be used for parts of the body that do not scar easily and that are not sensitive to pain.
- A noninsulated, cylindrical probe is the most effective to use with the blend.

Don'ts of the Blend Method

- Do not rush the blend—observe the 6-second rule, never working faster than 6 seconds with this method, except on vellus.
- Do not use noninsulated tapered needles.
- Do not pulse with galvanic current.
- Do not use flash mode with high frequency.
- Do not attach the probe to the positive jack, because doing so will create hydrochloric acid at the tip of the probe, which will mark the skin with a tattoo that is difficult to remove.

the probe. When this happens, a crackling can be heard. High-frequency blowout can be avoided by reducing the treatment energy.

Incorrect Probe and Use.   Insulated and noninsulated probes can be used with the blend. The recommendations for the particular modalities should be followed. For example, while noninsulated tapered probes are not good to use with galvanic electrolysis, they can be used with the blend. With insulated probes, check with the manufacturer that the insulation will withstand the galvanic current. Thinner-diameter probes generate more heat with thermolysis, so the high frequency should be reduced or a thicker-diameter probe is preferable for the blend. The probe tip should be accurately placed at the dermal papilla for the blend. If it is too shallow and there is no reduction in the high frequency application, high-frequency blowout could result. If a tapered probe is used with excessive galvanic applied first, the result could be a silent blowout in the bulb area at the base of the follicle.

Gas Blowout.   When galvanic is applied, and followed by high frequency, the hydrogen gas and water vapor rise to the follicle opening, and if the probe has too large a diameter and blocks the pathway, or the follicle opening is small, the gas cannot escape. A gas bubble may be seen at the surface. If too much gas forms, the base of the follicle ruptures and the gas bubbles leak through the bulb area into the surrounding tissue. It can be helped by using a finer nontapered probe, which allows the gas bubbles to travel freely to the surface and also reduces the galvanic current.

 ## Conclusion

The blend method is the fastest growing method of electrolysis in the United States for good reason, because it combines the speed of thermolysis with the effect of lye production in the follicle to destroy the follicle and dermal papilla. The accuracy of the probe, while still important, is not as essential as it is for straight thermolysis. While the blend is the hardest method to learn and master, it has become more popular due to better-designed, more user-friendly equipment, and improved training. This method is preferred, especially in areas of densely growing hair with curved or distorted follicles, like those on clients who have tweezed significant numbers of hairs over a long period of time, and those of African heritage with kinky hair.

 ## Discussion and Review Questions

1. What is turbulence?
2. How can gas blowout be avoided?
3. What is the difference between simultaneous application and sequential application?
4. What is the 6-second rule?

 ## Additional Readings

Bono, Michael. 1994. *The Blend Method*. Santa Barbara, CA: Tortoise Press.

Gallant, Ann. *Principles and Techniques for the Electrologist*. Cheltenham, U.K.: Stanley Thornes (Publishers) Ltd.

Glor, Fino. 1987. *Modern Electrology*. Great Neck, N.Y.: Hair Publishing, Inc.

Hinkle, Arthur Ralph, and Lind, Richard W. 1968. *Electrolysis, Thermolysis, and the Blend*. Los Angeles, CA: Arroway.

Meharg, G. E., R.N., and Richards, R. N., M.D. 1997. *Cosmetic and Medical Electrolysis and Temporary Hair Removal*, 2e., Toronto, Ont: Medric Ltd.

SECTION V

Laser and Light-Based Epilators

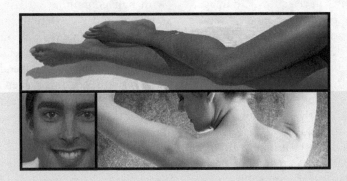

There continues to be considerable controversy surrounding laser hair removal and its effects, specifically whether those effects are permanent or long lasting. The FDA's Medical Device Division has now given permission for advertising some of these devices as effective in the permanent reduction of unwanted hair, though not for the permanent removal. FDA clearance for permission to market a device does not permit the manufacturer to advertise that device for permanent hair removal. Hair-removal specialists should be aware of this and inform clients who are looking for laser hair-removal treatments. Only devices that manufacturers have demonstrated, with sufficient data, to back up the claims of permanent reduction (not removal) are permitted to advertise as such._

Controversy also exists over the long-term effects that laser and intense light exposure might have on the body. It was not too long ago, in the 1920s, that men and women sought X-ray as a method of hair removal. It became apparent that the safer, weaker X-rays only temporarily removed hair. As stronger X-rays were applied, in the hope of permanent results, patients experienced serious injuries, including bone loss, skin-tissue scarring, dis-figurement, vascular lesions, hyperpigmentation, and hypopigmentation. X-ray as a form of hair removal was eventually banned in the 1940s. However, it was not until many months to years later that X-ray–related cancer reared its ugly head, resulting in a number of deaths. The Institut National de la Recherché Scientifique at the University of Quebec reports that collagen fibers in the skin are damaged by 40 j/cm (40 joules per cubic centimeters,

continued

continued

squared). Because it takes intensities of more than 40 j/cm to effectively remove terminal hair, there is the possibility of collagen damage, which in turn causes visible signs of premature aging to the skin.

While a degree of destruction does take place at the dermal papilla, it is not always a complete, irreversible destruction. Histological examinations, performed after laser treatment, have shown damaged follicles dispersed among intact follicles randomly, questioning the exact mechanisms of hair destruction by laser. However, with billions of dollars invested in the laser industry for hair removal, and the positive results being documented from clinical studies, clearly laser hair removal is going to be around for a long time to come. Just as Edison took many attempts (more than 10,000) to create and perfect the lightbulb, laser hair removal is moving toward the kind of permanency electrolysis now enjoys.

Laser hair removal's growing popularity may concern some electrologists, because they may feel that their profession may be in jeopardy. The opposite may in fact be true. As the laser industry grows, and equipment manufacturers and people offering the service continue to advertise and to promote the benefits of hair reduction, there will be a greater need for electrologists to "finish the job" by permanently removing the remaining hair, as well as the nonpigmented hairs that were not suitable for laser hair removal. This may be the time for certified electrologists to align with offices that practice laser hair removal by earning the trust and confidence of those offices who may refer the clients who are not good laser candidates or to remove the few remaining hairs after completing a series of laser treatments. Perhaps electrologists and laser offices can work out cross-referral agreements. As research and development continues, there may well be a time when the FDA permits the advertising of laser for "permanent" hair removal, at least on certain types of hair. Laser hair removal may eliminate hair faster on some large body areas, but there will always be a need for electrologists to finish the work permanently.

Laser equipment is extremely costly to purchase or lease, making the treatment cost high. The cost of treatment may be justified when permanency results, but the unscrupulous promise permanent results with hair containing little or no pigment, knowing full well that the results will be poor. Such people do this out of desperation of meeting their high leasing payments (see the case history at the end of this chapter). Perhaps, and this is even more serious, those people were not paying attention during training to the physics governing laser hair removal.

It is important for any hair-removal specialist to keep informed of the technologies affecting the hair-removal industry. Regardless of whether specialists choose to enter laser or intense-light hair removal, hair-removal specialists should have a basic knowledge and understanding of *all* methods of hair removal, including laser and photoepilation, so that they can answer clients' questions in a honest, balanced, and informed way. This section, which informs the hair-removal specialist of the basic aspects of laser and IPL epilation, should not be considered the sole material for learning this method of hair removal. There are schools around the country that educate and train individuals in photoepilation and that offer more extensive manuals and training materials. The manufacturers and distributors of laser and IPL equipment also offer training and further information. This section, however, should arm interested readers with enough information to further investigate this method of hair removal and give those readers enough background information to understand the manufacturers' sales representatives, know which questions to ask, and be able to make comparisons when shopping for photoepilation units.

Note: To learn which manufacturers have been cleared by the FDA to advertise permanent hair reduction, check the FDA's Web site at *www.fda.gov/cdrh/databases.html* or call the FDA's Center for Devices and Radiological Health, Consumer Staff, at 1-888-INFO-FDA or 1-301-827-3990.

CHAPTER 17

Laser Physics, Equipment, and Safety

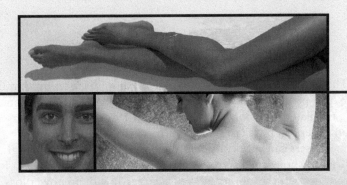

Chapter Outline

Learning Objectives ■ Key Terms ■ Introduction ■ Laser Removal ■ Photoepilation
Laser Devices ■ Laser Physics ■ Treatment Parameters ■ Safety Issues ■ Case History
Conclusion ■ Discussion and Review Questions

Learning Objectives

By the end of this chapter, you should be able to:

1. Explain how laser and ILP hair removal work.
2. List the different types of lasers.
3. Understand the basics of laser physics.
4. Describe the effects of laser light on human tissue.
5. Understand what is meant by the Fitzpatrick Skin Phototype and the Lancer Ethnicity Scale.
6. List the treatment parameters of laser hair removal.
7. List all the important safety issues.

Key Terms

active medium	energy source	optical cavity	resonator
amplification	excited states	oxyhemoglobin	selective photothermolysis
argon	Grothus Draper Law	Photodynamic therapy	singlet state
chromophore	ground state	photon cascade	spontaneous emission
coherent light	in phase	photons	spot size
collimated	joules	polychromatic	stimulated emission
cryogen	metastable	pulse duration	thermal relaxation time
dermal scattering	monochromatic	pulse width	thermal storage coefficient
energy fluence	nanometers	pumping	wavelength

Introduction

The term *laser* is an acronym for light amplification by stimulated emission of radiation. Nobel-prize-winning physicists Albert Einstein and Max Planck first defined the theory of "stimulated emission" in the 1920s. In 1960, the first true laser was built and patented by an American physicist named Gordon Gould.

Lasers can vary considerably in size, from as small as a grain of salt with the ability to drill 200 holes on a spot the size of a pin head to as long as a football field with the ability to reflect off the moon and return to earth with no power loss. Lasers have the strength to pierce nature's hardest substance, the diamond, to perform orthodontic procedures on the gums, or to conduct ophthalmic procedures on corneas. Although in the 1960s Dr. Leon Goldman began testing the effect of lasers on the hair follicle using a ruby laser, it was not until the 1980s that the laser was first introduced as a method of hair removal. This happened quite by chance when it was noted that, when birthmarks were treated with certain types of lasers, the hair that was present had ceased to regrow. In 1996, the first laser devices to be used for hair removal were cleared by the FDA.

Whereas electrolysis works on a hair-by-hair basis, laser uses a wide beam that can treat multiple hairs at once.

Sidebar definitions

selective photothermolysis
the selective targeting of an area using a specific wavelength to absorb light into that target area sufficient to damage the tissue of the target while allowing the surrounding area to remain relatively untouched

wavelength
the distance between two consecutive peaks or troughs in a wave

monochromatic
light of one wavelength, which therefore appears as one color

Laser Removal

Laser hair removal is based on the principle of **selective photothermolysis** (foh-toh-ther-MAH-luh-sus), which is the selective targeting of an area using a specific **wavelength** to absorb light into that target area sufficient to damage the target tissue while allowing the surrounding area to remain relatively untouched.

Lasers are intense beams of **monochromatic** (mahn-uh-kroh-MAT-ik), coherent light that are produced from laser devices containing gases, or minerals (Figure 17–1). There are four main kinds of lasers:

1. solid-state
2. semiconductor
3. gas
4. dye

When those gas and mineral properties are stimulated by an electric current, they excite atoms that in turn emit cohesive, narrow, parallel beams of light of one wavelength. When this light focuses for a fraction of a second on hair with dark pigment (natural melanin), and in particular the dark pigment of the matrix close to the dermal papilla, and is absorbed by the pigment, it heats the pigment and vaporizes the dermal papilla. The more intense the light, the hotter it gets. The result is hopefully a severely damaged if not destroyed dermal papilla. Laser is ineffective on hair that has little or no pigment, such as blond or gray hair or vellus. Laser is most effective on dark hair surrounded by light skin.

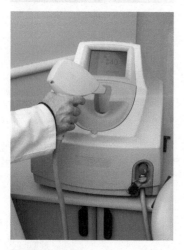

FIGURE 17–1
A laser machine

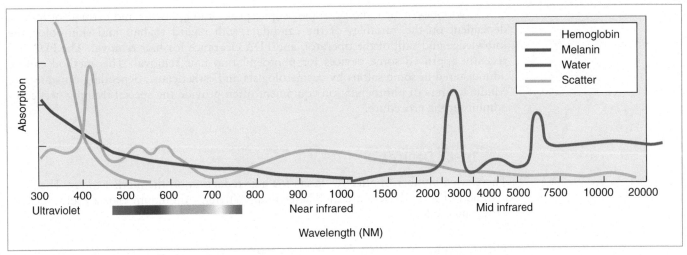

FIGURE 17–2 Electromagnetic absorption

Early devices used an **argon** (AR-gon) laser, but because results were poor, such devices were abandoned in favor of the ruby rod and Nd:Yag, both of which target melanin without affecting the red blood corpuscles in the surrounding tissue. Two lasers not suitable for hair removal are the argon laser, which emits a green light that targets red blood corpuscles, and carbon dioxide (CO_2), which is used in skin resurfacing by ablating the entire epidermal area that is exposed to it.

Laser is most effective on hair in its anagen phase, when there is an actively growing hair attached to the dermal papilla. The theory is that if there is pigment in the hair shaft going all the way down to the dermal papilla, then when the coherent light is focused, it will follow all the way down and, in turn, vaporize the dermal papilla. The question is whether there is, on average, enough melanin down at the dermal papilla to effect the dermal papilla's destruction.

The wavelength of visible light ranges from 390 to 770 nm (Figure 17–2). Lasers for hair removal operate in this range effectively without damaging dermal tissue. **Oxyhemoglobin** (ahk-sih-HEE-muh-gloh-bin) and water are competing chromophores, absorbing much less energy at those wavelengths. Any light source that operates between 700 and 1000 nm effectively targets melanin in the hair shaft.

argon
a chemical element in the form of an inert gas used in the creation of early lasers

oxyhemoglobin
the bright-red form of hemoglobin; a protein in red blood cells

---

Wavelengths of Lasing Mediums (nm)
- Argon: 488 or 514.5
- Ruby: 694
- Alexandrite: 755
- Diode: 810
- Nd:YAG: 1064

Photoepilation

Photoepilation is also called intense pulse light (IPL), intense light source, or flash lamp hair removal. The pros and cons, indications and contraindications, protocol, and safety concerns of photoepilation are all very similar to those of the more well-known lasers, but IPL is generally considered safer. The basic concept of IPL hair removal is similar to that of laser. The main difference is the emission of one wavelength of laser versus the full spectrum of noncoherent light in the visible spectrum, including blue, yellow, red, and infrared appearing as white light with low-range, infrared-radiation spectrum of approximately 400 to 1200 nm. The operator eliminates and filters out the lower wavelengths to allow a specified range of wavelengths to be used, those that will be most effective. IPL is delivered in one to four pulses of 1 to 1200 milliseconds duration, the average being approximately 35 milliseconds and using an **energy fluence** range of 2 to 7.5 joules/cm². The light is reflected, refracted, scattered, resisted, and absorbed.

energy fluence
the energy level of a laser; measured in joules (see following)

As with laser hair removal, some people speak of long-lasting and permanent results, dependent on the variables of the candidate with regard to hair and skin color, the knowledge and skill of the operator, and FDA clearance for hair removal. The FDA has recently approved some devices for photoepilation hair removal. This method can be administered in some salons by cosmetologists and estheticians, depending on state law. Manufacturers of photoepilation equipment often provide the special training needed to administer the procedure.

Laser Devices

There are a number of effective lasers for hair reduction on the market today. The most common of these devices are the NeoDymium Yttrium Aluminum Garnet, ruby, alexandrite, and diode.

NeoDymium Yttrium Aluminum Garnets

NeoDymium Yttrium Aluminum Garnets (Nd:/YAGs) have a longer pulse, making them more effective for longer term and even permanent hair removal. The Nd:/YAGs use a carbon-based lotion for greater effectiveness, and while they once professed permanent hair removal, published clinical data dispute that claim. Subsequent data collected by operators using this laser with the carbon lotion reported a 27 to 66 percent reduction at 3 months after one treatment. This device, now cleared by the FDA to advertise its ability to produce long-term or permanent reduction, is considered by some to be less painful when compared to the alexandrite laser treatment, particularly those devices with cooling ability, and with fewer side effects than ruby or alexandrite on more pigmented skin.

Ruby Lasers

Ruby lasers, cleared by the FDA for hair removal in 1997, use shorter wavelength systems. However, clinical research showed that the laser damage did not seem to extend far enough down the hair shafts to result in permanent hair destruction at the dermal papilla. In addition, when used on individuals with dark skin or tans, these lasers caused hyperpigmentation.

Alexandrite Lasers

Alexandrite lasers were cleared by the FDA for hair removal in 1997. While this is currently a very popular device for laser hair removal, there is still insufficient data to clear it as a permanent method, and there are also issues regarding the negative effects of this type of laser on skin with substantial pigment.

Diode Lasers

Diode lasers were cleared by the FDA in 1997. This type of laser has proven to be successful in the treatment of ingrown eyelashes. No data has yet been published proving its effectiveness. This type of laser at this time seems to produce reactions on the skin's surface resembling hives, but has still proven effective in hair reduction.

Laser Physics

A typical laser has three main parts (Figure 17–3):

1. **energy source**
2. **active medium**
3. **optical cavity**, also called a **resonator**

To understand how laser light is produced, consider a laser hair-removal device using a ruby rod for the active medium, making it a ruby laser (Figure 17–4).

energy source
the device in a laser that supplies energy to the active medium

active medium
the part of a laser that absorbs and stores energy

optical cavity
the part of the laser that contains the active medium

resonator
another term for "optical cavity" (see preceding)

FIGURE 17–3
Generation of laser light

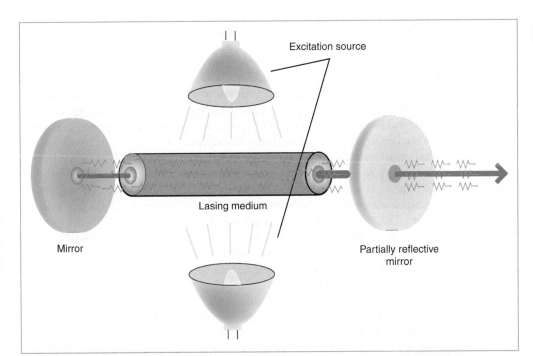

FIGURE 17–4
The ruby laser: synthetic ruby
crystal (top); flashlamp with
housing (bottom)

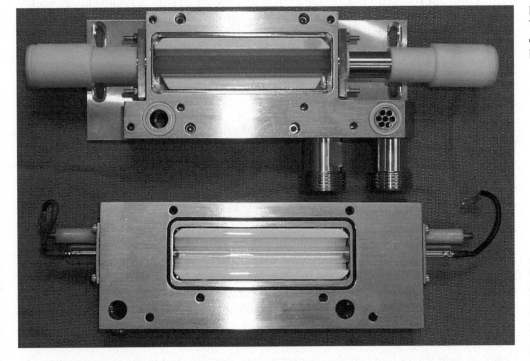

pumping
the process whereby the energy
source supplies energy to the active
medium

ground state
the condition of a physical system
in which the energy is at its lowest
possible level

excited states
the conditions of a physical system
in which the energy level is higher
than the lowest possible level

singlet state
a state of higher energy of atoms
arrived at upon excitation

metastable
in an apparent state of equilibrium,
but likely to change to a more truly
stable state if conditions change

The energy source is a device that supplies energy to the active medium in a process called **pumping**. Lasers, particularly for hair removal, use electricity as the energy source.

The substance or element of the active medium contains atoms that can absorb and store energy. Lasers are distinguished by the elements they use. Some elements used in hair-removal or dermatology laser devices are alexandrite, carbon dioxide, Nd:YAG, and ruby.

Electricity, as the energy source, pumps and excites the atoms of a substance that normally exist in a state of lowest energy, called **ground state** (atoms can also exist in higher-energy states called **excited states**). Atoms in ground state considerably outnumber those in excited states. When atoms in ground state are "excited," they arrive at a higher-energy state, called a **singlet state**.

After the singlet state has been reached, some of the atoms immediately begin to drop back to an intermediate level, called the **metastable** state. Some, not all, of the atoms arrive at the metastable state. The atoms that can sustain the metastable state are capable of lasing.

As the atoms in the metastable state return to their ground state, they emit energy in the form of **photons** of light, which are minute units of electromagnetic radiation. The photons of light are reflected, absorbed, transmitted, and scattered. Excited atoms can hold extra energy for only a fraction of a second before releasing their energy as other photons and falling back to ground state. This process is called **spontaneous emission**. Some atoms store energy for relatively long times in excited states, up to 2 seconds, which is much longer than most excited states, which are 1/1,000 of a second.

As long as the energy source is applied, a continuous chain reaction occurs. The photons of light strike other atoms in the metastable state. This collision causes the atoms to return to the ground state and, in so doing, creates another photon of light in a process called **amplification**. This second photon has an equal amount of energy and moves in the same direction as the original photon. This process is called **stimulated emission**.

All the activity produces photons of light colliding with each other that are of the same energy levels, parallel, of the same wavelength in the visible color spectrum, and **in phase**. The result is a **photon cascade**.

The optical cavity contains the active medium, in this case the ruby rod. At either end of the ruby rod are mirrors: one that is fully reflective on one side and another two-way, partially reflective on the other (like the one-way mirrors used in police interview rooms) that reflects the light back into the active medium. The photon cascade crashes back and forth in the ruby rod, reflecting off the mirrors and becoming stronger until enough energy is produced to cause the photon cascade to blast through the two-way mirror in the form of a narrow beam of laser light.

In this case of laser hair removal using the ruby laser, the beam of light is introduced and applied to the body's tissue, in particular the pigment of hair for absorption.

Light in Its Different Forms

To understand laser light we should first understand the different types of light in their different forms. These types of light are traditional, coherent, monochromatic, and collimated.

Traditional Light

Traditional light is **polychromatic** (pahl-ee-kroh-MAT-ik), that is, it contains all colors and wavelengths of the visible light spectrum, including ultraviolet and infrared. Traditional light waves go in all directions, lighting the surrounding area according to strength. Light from most sources diverges rapidly. The farther traditional light moves away, the dimmer it gets; the closer it gets, the brighter it gets. Light from a flashlight, for example, fans out quickly and fades after a short distance. Examples of traditional light are the sun (our strongest traditional light source), a lightbulb, and a candle.

Coherent Light

Coherent light waves that travel in perfect unison, parallel, and in the same direction are called "in phase." They are like people marching together in line and in the same direction, as opposed to crowds bustling randomly on a busy street. Because coherent light travels in straight lines, it does not appear to dim as it moves away. Laser light is coherent light that is amplified by a laser device, but laser light travels in a very narrow beam, even over long distances. A laser beam's coherence allows it to travel long distances without losing intensity. For example, a typical laser beam expands to a diameter of only 1 meter after traveling 1,000 meters, or only 64 inches per mile.

Monochromatic Light

Each type of laser light has its own color determined by its single wavelength. In hair removal, that color determines how the laser will react with the pigment in the hair

---

photons
miniscule units of electromagnetic radiation or light

spontaneous emission
the process whereby an excited atom, after holding extra energy for a fraction of a second, releases its energy as another photon, then falls back to its grounded state

amplification
the creation of a new photon of light, resulting from a chain reaction involving the collision of other photons

stimulated emission
the process whereby a newly created photon of light (generated through amplification) acquires energy equal to the photons that created it and travels in the same direction

in phase
a property of light characterized by waves traveling in parallel and in the same direction

photon cascade
excited, parallel photons of light of the same energy, wavelength, and in phase

polychromatic
consisting of light of multiple wavelengths, appearing as different colors

coherent light
light waves that travel in parallel and in the same direction

and skin. The pigment it is attracted to and reacts with is called a **chromophore** (KROH-muh-fore). All lasers react to different chromophores, which is why they are so versatile in the medical world, as well as in the worlds of cosmetic dermatology and esthetics and dentistry.

chromophore
a group of atoms in a molecule that produces color through selective light absorption

Collimated or Intense Light

Collimated (KAHL-uh-may-ted) light refers to a very thin beam of laser light, in which all rays run parallel.

Laser light differs from ordinary light in two major ways: (1) it has low divergence (spreading), and (2) it is monochromatic (single colored). Light with these two characteristics is known as coherent light. For a device to "lase," it must produce light waves that are monochromatic, intense, and coherent.

collimated
an intense, very thin beam of laser light in which all rays run parallel

Effects of Laser-Light Absorption

Certain principles affect laser light absorption. These principles include the chromophore, which absorbs the laser light using the Grothus Draper Law to generate heat in the target chromophore.

Chromophore

Atoms and molecules of various substances selectively absorb photons of light from specific laser devices. That substance is a chromophore. Because different lasers operate at different wavelengths, the substances (e.g., hair or skin) will be chromophores to one wavelength but not to another. Chromophores allow for selective targeting. For example, the ruby laser targets the melanin in hair (the chromophore), which absorbs the photons of light, converting them to thermal energy or heat that destroys the hair. The red blood cells of the hemoglobin, and therefore the surrounding tissue (providing there is little melanin in the skin), remain relatively unaffected. This is because the red of the blood does not absorb the photons of light because it is not a chromophore to the ruby laser. Therefore, the laser will target the pigment in the hair but leave the surrounding dermal tissue, which contains blood, unaffected. Laser devices used to treat vascular conditions target the hemoglobin, which in that case is the chromophore.

Grothus Draper Law

Grothus Draper (GROH-thus DRAY-pur) **Law** states that light absorption must take place for an effect to take place in biological tissue and that, without absorption, no effect or damage is observed. A certain wavelength of light may be absorbed by one type of tissue but be scattered or transmitted by another.

Grothus Draper Law
the physical law that states light absorption must occur for an effect to occur in biological tissue and that, without absorption, no effect or damage is observed

Heat

The absorption of laser light in pigment generates thermal energy or heat, which is the effect desired for hair removal.

When laser light chemically alters molecules, the chromophores of certain substances in a photochemical reaction, the process is called **Photodynamic therapy** (PDT). For the purposes of laser hair removal, however, this is still more of a theory, and is still in the early stages of research as an application for use in hair removal.

Photodynamic therapy
the process whereby the chromophores (see preceding) of certain substances are altered by laser light

Treatment Parameters

Treatment parameters vary from one piece of equipment to another, so manufacturers' guidelines should be followed in their entireties.

Wavelength

nanometers
each one billionth of a meter

joules
units of energy or work

Registered in **nanometers** (nm), wavelength determines the chromophore. The wavelength of a ruby laser is 694.3 nm, which is red in the visible range of the electromagnetic spectrum, making its target melanin. The greater the wavelength, the deeper it will penetrate the target chromophore selectively absorbing the wavelength.

Energy Fluence

Used in pulsed lasers, energy fluence is measured in **joules** (j) per square centimeter, (j/cm²). The larger the laser beam's spot size, the more fluence that is necessary to produce the same effect. Lower fluences have been observed to cause higher rates of double hairs in regrowth. Cooling the skin allows for a higher and more effective fluence. Fair skin types I to III can take a fluence level of 25 to 40 j/cm².

Thermal Storage Coefficient

thermal storage coefficient
the measure of heat stored in a chromophore (see preceding)

The **thermal storage coefficient** (Tr_2) is the storage of heat in a chromophore. When a chromophore is heated beyond its Tr_2, the heat spills over and is diffused into the surrounding tissue. Hair has a higher Tr_2 than the epidermis. Coarse hair has a higher Tr2 than finer hair. To minimize damage to surrounding tissue by not exceeding the Tr2 of the chromophore, the laser operator should understand this principle and follow the recommended guidelines of pulse duration and energy fluence.

Pulse Duration

pulse duration
the duration of an individual pulse of laser light; usually measured in milliseconds; also see "pulse width" (following)

pulse width
see "pulse duration" (see preceding)

thermal relaxation time
the amount of time it takes a substance (e.g., dermal tissue), after heating, to return to its normal temperature

Pulse duration (or **pulse width**), which is measured in milliseconds (ms), is the timing of light energy. Most laser hair-removal devices have a maximum pulse duration in the 20 to 40 ms range. The pulse duration should match the fluence needed to damage the target hair follicle. A longer pulse duration is generally required for melanin in the hair than for fragile capillaries in the epidermis. The coarser the hair, the longer the required pulse duration generally. Longer pulse widths are considered more effective with fewer side effects, because they allow for more skin types to tolerate higher fluences. This should be particularly true of dark skin, although to date no significant scientific studies have proven this theory. The pulse should also be longer than the **thermal relaxation time** of the epidermal tissue but shorter than the thermal relaxation time of the hair follicle, keeping the heat in the hair follicle. This is aided by the use of cooling agents or mechanisms applied to the epidermal tissue. New studies suggest that individuals presenting with tans can still be treated with a pulse width starting at 100 ms and achieve effective treatments. When treating areas with dense hair, use caution when using a longer pulse width. Thermal conduction can occur between the closely adjacent hair follicles.

Spot Size

spot size
the width of a laser beam

dermal scattering
the change that occurs between the laser's spot size at the surface of the skin and the spot size deeper in the tissue

Spot size, measured in millimeters, is the size or width of the beam effecting treatment. The larger the laser beam's spot size, the more fluence that is necessary to produce the same effect. A spot size of 7 to 10 mm is considered acceptable for laser hair removal. The spot size can be affected by **dermal scattering**, which affects the relationship of the spot size deeper in the tissue due to its size on the skin's surface (i.e., the spot size is smaller deeper in the tissue and gradually becomes larger on the surface). The spot size also affects penetration depth. A general rule of thumb is that the spot size should be about four times as wide as the target is deep.

Thermal Relaxation Time

Thermal relaxation time (TRT) is the time it takes for 50 percent of heat energy to be conducted away from the target tissue. It can be registered in ms. For skin it is between 600 and 800 microseconds. Because the TRT of the hair follicle depends on the follicle's diameter, the laser source must have a range of pulse widths capable of damaging different size follicles. Knowing the TRT and making the necessary adjustments in the treatment of different size follicles in different areas minimizes collateral thermal damage to the dermal tissue.

Epidermal Cooling

By cooling the epidermis, it is possible to use a higher fluence and provide a more effective treatment. The cooling not only helps prevent epidermal tissue damage, it reduces the discomfort of the treatment. A new theory of using a cooling treatment continuously before, during, and after the laser application means that dark skin can be treated. Means of cooling the skin during treatment are:

- *cryogen spray*—used before and after each laser pulse
- *gel*—a chilled, clear gel applied to the skin
- *contact cooling*—cold water circulates through a window on the laser head, cooling the skin on contact
- *chilled tip*—some devices, like the diode laser, use a cold sapphire window on the handpiece to cool the epidermis before, during, and after each laser pulse

cryogen
a substance used to produce extremely low temperature

Handpiece Shape

The shape of the handpiece has a considerable effect on the treatment, because it affects the overlapping from section to section, thereby affecting treatment time. A circular beam requires a certain amount of overlapping to cover the treatment area. This in turn creates a percentage of wasted time and overtreatment. On the other hand, beams that are square, rectangular, or hexagonal (Figure 17–5) can be more easily aligned without overlapping, thereby reducing overtreatment and offering faster treatment.

The laser treatment process (Figure 17–6) allows for the selective absorption of light energy by the melanin in the hair shaft and dermal papilla with adequate energy fluence per unit area combined with pulse durations that are equal to or less than the thermal relaxation time of the targeted follicles in human skin, between 10 to 100 ms.

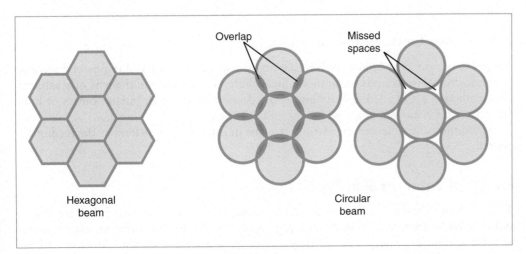

FIGURE 17–5
Hexagonal beam versus circular beam

Treatment Parameters of Laser Hair-Removal Devices*

Device	Wavelength (nm)	Trade Name	Pulse Duration (msec)	Spot Size (mm)	Features
Long-pulse ruby laser	694	Epilaser (Palomar)	3	10	Cooling handpiece
		Epitouch (ESC/Sharplan)	1.2	6	Dual mode, gel cooling
		RubyStar (Aesculap)	2	up to 12	Dual mode, cooling system optional
Long-pulse alexandrite laser	755	Gentlelase Plus (Candela)	3	8–18	Cooling handpiece
		Apogee, PhotoGenica LPIR (Cynosure)	5–20	12.5	Cooling handpiece, scanner available
		Epitouch Plus ALEX (ESC/Sharplan)	2–40	5, 7, 10	50 mm scanner optional
Diode laser	800	LightSheer (Coherent)	5–100	9	Cooling handpiece
		Apex 800 (Iriderm)	5–40	7, 9, 11	9 mm cold tip
		LaserLite (Diomed)	50–250	2–4/scanner	24×20 mm scanner
		MeDioStar (Aesculap)	N/A	12	Contact cooling
Q-switched Nd:YAG laser	1064	Softlight (Thermolase)	5–10	7	Pretreatment with carbon suspension
		Medlite IV (ConBio)		4	
Long-pulse Nd:YAG laser	1064	Lyra (LaserScope)	10–50 adjustable	3–5/scanner	SmartScan Plus 20 mm scanner/cooling device
		CoolGlide (Altus)	10–100	9	Integral chiller
		Athos (Quantel)	3–5	2, 4, 5	Scanner available, multipurpose mode
		Depilase (Depilase NA)	5–100	2–6	40 mm scanner available
Intense pulsed light	590–1200	EpiLight (ESC/Sharplan)	2–7	10×45	Cooling device

*This is just a sampling of laser/IPL hair-removal devices, not all on the market to date.

Pulse versus Continuous-Wave Lasers

Pulsed lasers emit laser light in pulses that are measured from quadrillionths of a second, or nanoseconds, to seconds using mechanical shutters like those on the lens of a camera. This method is also called Q-Switching. Pulsed lasers emit rapid, intense bursts of light that effectively remove pigmented lesions and tattoos.

Continuous wave lasers emit strong streams of intense light as long as the medium is excited.

Effects of Laser on Skin Type

While all four skin types—(1) Caucasian European, (2) African descent, (3) Eastern Asian, and (4) Middle Eastern and Mediterranean—have a great deal in common, like the number of hair follicles (whether or not they actively produce terminal hair), thickness of the epidermis and dermis, and components found in layers, they have other characteristics that set them apart.

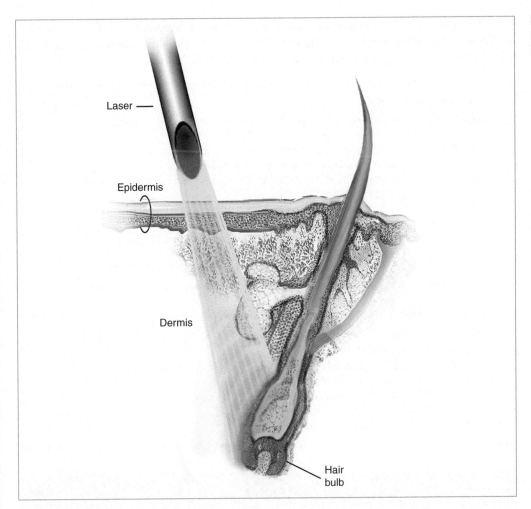

FIGURE 17–6
Laser penetration and hair-bulb destruction

Caucasian European

Caucasian Europeans have the most varied skin type and hair and eye color variations, as determined by heredity. The effectiveness of laser hair removal on these individuals depends on hair and skin color and can be ascertained using the Fitzpatrick Prototype and Lancer Ethnicity Scale (see accompanying boxes).

African Descent

With dark brown skin, Africans, African Americans, African Europeans, and African Caribbeans are poor candidates for laser hair removal, because the laser light absorbs into the skin pigment, possibly causing burns and scars, including keloids. In addition, the intense laser beam draws away from its target area (i.e., the dermal papilla). Nevertheless, studies and research of new variances with laser devices and cooling agents are being done to see if safe and effective treatments can be offered.

Eastern Asian

Eastern Asians include the Chinese, Japanese, and Koreans. This group of people generally has the least amount of facial and body hair. In terms of laser hair removal, they are good candidates due to their dark hair and minimal skin pigmentation.

Middle Eastern and Mediterranean

Middle Eastern and Mediterranean people tend to have the most hair on face and body. Skin color varies from dark white to medium brown. Individuals with lighter skin may be candidates for laser hair removal. Some candidates choose to use skin-bleaching agents like 4% hydroquinone to lighten the skin as much as possible, making the laser treatment as effective as possible while reducing the risk of burning the skin. There is an increased risk of causing hyperpigmentation on the skin of this ethnic group.

Fitzpatrick Skin Phototype

- Skin Type I— Very fair skin accompanied by blonde or light-red hair and blue or green eyes. Never tans, always burns.
- Skin Type II— Fair skin accompanied by light-brown or red hair and green or brown eyes. Occasionally tans, always burns.
- Skin Type III— Medium skin accompanied by brown hair and brown eyes. Often tans, sometimes burns.
- Skin Type IV— Olive skin accompanied by brown or black hair and dark-brown or black eyes. Always tans, never burns.
- Skin Type V— Dark-brown skin accompanied by black hair and black eyes. Never burns.
- Skin Type VI— Black skin accompanied by black hair and black eyes. Never burns.

Lancer Ethnicity Scale

- Skin Type I—Light white plus ethnic origin
- Skin Type II—Medium white plus ethnic origin
- Skin Type III—Dark white plus ethnic origin
- Skin Type IV—Light brown plus ethnic origin
- Skin Type V—Medium brown plus ethnic origin
- Skin Type VI—Dark brown plus ethnic origin

Lancer Ethnicity Scale	Fitzpatrick Skin Type
I	I
II	II
III	III
IV	Could be IV, V, VI
V	Could be IV, V, VI
VI	Could be IV, V, VI

Safety Issues

The safety issues for the client and technician differ from those for other methods of epilation but are nonetheless extremely important. While there is no concern of drawing blood and contaminating probes and other critical items, or the risk of infection unless the skin is burned, there is concern for eye safety. For this reason, certain guidelines have been laid out by various organizations. Complying with these guidelines ensures the safety of the technician and a safe and effective treatment for the client. These organizations are:

- *Occupational Safety and Health Administration (OSHA)*—A branch of the Department of Labor, OSHA's major concern is worker safety. Because laser is a treatment that is still relatively new outside a medical facility, OSHA has not yet published its own set of safety guidelines, instead recommending the laser-safety standards specified by the American National Standards Institute (ANSI) (see following).

- *American National Standards Institute (ANSI)*—ANSI is not a government agency but a nonprofit organization that coordinates and administers the U.S. voluntary standardization and conformity assessment system. The organization is made of voluntary representatives from companies, professional and trade associations, and consumer-protection organizations. Collectively, these representatives set standards that are adopted by government agencies.
- *Food and Drug Administration (FDA)*—The FDA, a governmental agency, first legitimizes a device by ensuring that it safely and effectively does what it purports and advertises. Second, it conducts more in-depth regulation through its branch called the Center for Devices and Radiological Health (CDRH) (see following).
- *Center for Devices and Radiological Health (CDRH)*—The CDRH, a specialized branch of the FDA, provides professional expertise and technical assistance on the development, safety and effectiveness, and regulation of medical devices and electronic products that produce radiation.
- *The Society for Clinical and Medical Hair Removal, Inc. (SCMHR)*—The SCMHR strives to investigate all the merits of new technology for hair removal on behalf of professional electrologists, who currently make up the greatest percentage of membership in the organization. SCMHR's goal is to take the lead in bringing educational and business opportunities and support to its membership with regard to laser and light-based hair removal, as well as other methods of hair removal, believing that, as a profession, hair-removal specialists should ultimately be defined by the service itself rather than the equipment used to perform that service.

In the United States, laser devices are all subject to stringent Mandatory Performance Standards and must meet the federal laser product performance standard, including specifying safety features for the benefit of the patient and operator.

Operating Safety

The room used for laser or IPL, even though it may be used for other treatments, such as electrolysis, should be set up following the strictest guidelines associated with laser equipment. The equipment distributor or manufacturer will usually set up the equipment. It is a poor idea to buy used laser equipment, unless it comes from a distributor, has been checked and serviced thoroughly, and comes with a guarantee.

The room should have:

- a door that can be locked during the treatment and/or a warning light outside that indicates treatment is under way to prevent or warn individuals from entering
- protective eyewear outside the door of the room for individuals who may enter during a treatment
- no windows, or windows blacked out with protective coverings
- an electrical outlet that is grounded and includes proper amperage, voltage, and its own circuit breaker
- no mirrors or other reflective surfaces (e.g., steel containers or trash cans)

The equipment should:

- rest on a flat surface
- have plenty of ventilation around it
- be grounded and have its own circuit breaker
- be serviced and calibrated according to manufacturer's guidelines
- have the key removed from the laser equipment when it is not in use
- be regularly cleaned of carbon buildup

The operator:

- should be well trained and qualified in the use of laser hair removal and all its aspects, including histology and client care, and have insurance coverage for accident and malpractice claims
- should remove all reflective clothing and jewelry and be dressed sensibly and professionally with a lab coat and comfortable shoes
- must, along with any other individual in the room, wear ANSI-approved protective eyewear to avoid laser blindness

The client should:

- have received a detailed and thorough consultation and patch test, before the treatment, along with pre- and postcare instructions
- receive all pertinent information to be able to make an informed choice regarding laser hair removal, understanding benefits and risks
- remove all reflective clothing and jewelry
- be given ANSI-approved protective eyewear and be instructed to keep the eyewear on throughout the treatment
- receive a treatment in line with manufacturer's guidelines for the skin, hair, and area of the face or body, including the appropriate settings for laser fluence, spot size, and pulse width, to prevent over- (and under-) treating and risking skin damage
- receive appropriate after-care instructions that include what to do and what not to do

Case History

Jean, a 55-year-old, postmenopausal woman who was a light-redhead (almost strawberry blonde) before graying, came to the office discouraged and bothered by the coarse hairs on her chin and under her jaw. The visible hairs numbered around 60 that day. Jean told me that she had been receiving laser treatments by a dermatologist and had received three treatments to date, at a total cost of $1,500. She was frustrated that she had seen very little difference posttreatment, because she was told in her consultation that the target areas would probably require only three treatments. When Jean returned to the dermatologist 6 weeks after her third treatment, the doctor told her that it would probably take an additional three treatments, because her hair was light. Jean was told that she should shave daily to encourage the hairs to grow in darker. On examining Jean's hair, I observed that many among the vellus were in fact gray and without pigment. The remaining hairs were a light, translucent ginger.

I asked Jean if she had ever seen gray beard stubble on a man who shaves daily, to which she replied, "Yes, my husband." I told her that once a hair has gone gray and no longer produces pigment, it never will, and no amount of shaving will change that. Laser will never effectively permanently remove those hairs. We proceeded to eliminate Jean's hairs with electrolysis. She will carry the "sting" of the $1,500 cost of laser treatments with her for a long time.

Conclusion

Whether one chooses to offer laser hair removal as a service, or even recommend the service to clients, it is important to understand how it works and to understand the physics of laser hair removal so that the service can be clearly and accurately relayed to curious clients. It is also important to understand the physics of laser hair removal to appreciate the developments in this method as they occur. The decision of whether or not to recommend or provide this service should be done after studying the method and after thoughtful and careful consideration. Experiencing laser hair-removal treatments may also factor in the decision to offer or recommend the service.

Discussion and Review Questions

1. For what does the acronym LASER stand?
2. What are the four main types of laser?
3. What are the three main components of a laser?
4. What is the scientific term for the substance that acts as a target to the laser light absorbing it?
5. List five treatment parameters of laser hair removal.
6. List three important safety considerations for the treatment room.
7. List three important safety considerations for the laser equipment.
8. List three important safety considerations for the operator.
9. List three important safety considerations for the client.

CHAPTER 18

Laser Hair-Removal Treatment

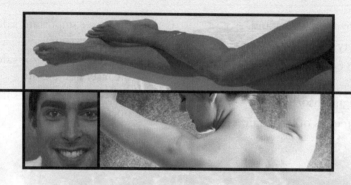

Chapter Outline

Learning Objectives ■ Key Terms ■ Introduction

The Consultation ■ Indications and Contraindications ■ Pretreatment

Pros and Cons ■ Treatment ■ Posttreatment ■ Home Care

Conclusion ■ Discussion and Review Questions

Learning Objectives

By the end of this chapter, you should be able to:

1. List the pros and cons of laser hair removal.
2. Identify the indications and contraindications of laser hair removal.
3. Understand photosensitivity and phototoxicity.
4. Conduct a client consultation.
5. Know the rudiments of treatment application, including pre- and posttreatment, and home care.

Key Terms

albinism

hydroquinone

Nikolski sign

photosensitizing

splattering

Introduction

This chapter informs and educates the hair-removal specialist as to what to expect when removing hair with a laser. It is not designed to be the only educational tool for this method of hair removal, rather an introductory overview to be built on with formal, detailed, and intensive training through a specialized educational program specializing in laser hair removal. This chapter explains how the procedure works, compares it to other methods in this book, identifies its pros and cons and indications and contraindications, and outlines its general treatment protocol.

The Consultation

Clients are willing to pay more for laser hair removal than for any other hair-removal method. With this willingness to pay more comes an expectation of more effective results. Clients may have questions regarding the treatment, and they may have researched it on the World Wide Web or read about it in magazines. It is the role of the hair-removal specialist to ensure that clients are informed as to whether they are good candidates for laser hair removal and to ensure that those clients understand what the service entails to be effective. Make no promises of complete and permanent hair removal.

PROS & CONS

Pros of Laser Hair Removal*

- offers a fast, long-lasting hair removal
- may produce some permanent results
- can treat large body areas with greater speed by treating multiple hairs at once, unlike the hair-by-hair method of electrolysis
- no risk of disease transmission via blood
- not considered as uncomfortable as electrolysis, though subjective
- regrowth is often finer and lighter

*Depends on the laser hair-removal device being cleared by the FDA for "permanent hair reduction."

Cons of Laser Hair Removal

- costly, requiring an average of three to six or more treatments
- safety and effectiveness issues over the long term
- ineffective on light and nonpigmented hair, like blonde, red, or gray/white
- depending on the laser, generally ineffective on dark or tanned skin
- safety concerns for the eyes and need for protective eyewear
- some discomfort
- no guarantee of satisfaction
- inadequate and inconsistent state regulatory controls and guidelines

---

While it is currently accepted that laser is ineffective on blonde, light red, gray, or white hair, research and testing is currently being done on the application of a melanin-containing solution to nonpigmented hair twice a day for a period before the treatment. The hair absorbs the pigment. The hope is that the now-darkened hair will respond by becoming a target for the laser. The lotion requires no FDA approval, because it is a cosmetic product, not a drug. The main question is whether sufficient pigment absorbs into the hair down at the dermal papilla, where it is needed to attract and absorb laser light to effect destruction. This research, in its early stages, has to date yielded insufficient data to determine its effectiveness in removing naturally nonpigmented hair.

INDICATIONS & CONTRAINDICATIONS

Indications of Laser Hair Removal

- all parts of the body, except the area under the eyebrow and the ear
- most effective on light skin and dark hair

Contraindications of Laser Hair Removal

- pregnancy
- epilepsy
- diabetes
- herpes simplex (cold sores or fever blisters)
- **albinism** (AL-bi-niz-em) (absence of pigment in hair and skin)
- gray hair
- nervous disorders
- sunburn
- open wounds
- birthmarks, moles, or beauty spots on the area to be treated, unless treatment is approved by a physician
- history of keloid scarring
- hirsutism, until the cause has been diagnosed and treated
- certain oral and topical medications (see accompanying box) known to cause photosensitivity or photoallergic reactions
- **photosensitizing** (pho-toh-SEN-sih-ty-zing) medications like Accutane, tetracycline, or Retin-A

Medications That Cause Photosensitivity or Photoallergic Reactions

- *Accutane*—Discontinue the medication 3 months before a laser hair-removal treatment
- *Tetracycline*—Discontinue 6 weeks before a laser hair-removal treatment.
- *Retin-A*—Discontinue 6 weeks before a laser hair-removal treatment

---

albinism
the congenital lack of normal pigmentation in the skin and hair

photosensitizing
producing an increase in sensitivity of an organism to electromagnetic radiation

Before treatment, the client should have filled out the client consultation form (Figures 18–1 and 18–2 on page 256). Review it to see if the client has any contraindications (listed in the accompanying box), and to see, based on hair and skin color, if the client is a viable candidate for one successful treatment or series of successful treatments. (See the Fitzpatrick Skin Phototype and the Lancer Ethnicity Scale in Chapter 17.) Next, examine the area to be treated to see if there are any visible signs of contraindications.

After it is determined that the client is a good candidate for laser hair removal, give the client a brief and basic overview of laser hair removal, including the variables affecting treatment, the most important of which are the three stages of hair growth that occur at different times and in different follicles in the same area. Because a percentage of hairs are not going to be at the optimal stage (growing stage), more than one session or treatment is prescribed. Generally, three to six treatments are needed for optimal, long-lasting reduction.

To reduce the number of required treatments, cease all methods of hair removal other than shaving or depilatory creams at least 10 weeks before treatment. Removing the hair from the follicle by tweezing, waxing, or electrolysis throws the hair follicle into a resting stage, delaying the effectiveness of the laser hair removal. The target hair must be in the follicle to absorb the laser energy at the time of treatment for the laser to damage or destroy the follicle. Shaving or clipping may be done up to 2 days before treatment. By shaving 2 days before the treatment, the technician can ascertain the percentage of growing hairs and will then shave the area before the treatment.

Acknowledge cost versus effectiveness. If the client only has a few hairs, or if the client is at the point after a number of laser treatments where there is a considerable reduction in hairs, it would be more economical for the client to finish the removal process with electrolysis. Subsequent light or fine hairs that do not respond to laser may also be permanently removed with electrolysis.

Subsequent hair growth in the treated area is the result of newly active follicles, follicles that were empty and in a resting stage, and missed hairs. The number of needed treatments depends on the pattern of hair growth, hormonal influences, and plucking or waxing done before the laser treatment. If hormonal imbalances or medications are influencing hair growth, maintenance will be necessary to treat new hairs as they appear. Laser can only remove hair that is present, not hair that will develop.

A few clients have little or no success with laser treatments. These clients are called nonresponders, and there is no way to predict which patients will be nonresponders. Even with all optimal conditions, such as hair in the anagen phase and melanin in the hair shaft, laser is still unpredictable.

After laser hair removal, there may be swelling, crusting, temporary redness, or skin discoloration (hypo- or hyperpigmentation). Hyperpigmentation may be treated with 4% **hydroquinone** (hy-droh-kwin-OHN), which is skin bleaching cream, but hypopigmentation cannot be reversed. Clients must strictly adhere to follow-up instructions for their comfort and protection. Clients should expect to see tiny black spots in the follicles over a few days. These "singed" hairs, called **splattering**, will gradually and naturally expel from the skin and can be wiped away.

Take photos of the area to be treated. These photos are visual evidence of treatment progress. Clients may sign forms allowing the photos to be used anonymously for educational and promotional purposes.

Insurance and Cost

Laser hair removal, because it is considered cosmetic, is not covered by insurance. Each laser treatment is separate and usually incurs a separate charge unless a specific treatment package is arranged. Treatment costs are related to the expense of purchasing and operating laser equipment. Therefore, tell clients that charges are subject to change without notice.

hydroquinone
a white, crystalline compound used in skin bleaching

splattering
the appearance of tiny black spots, which are singed hairs, in hair follicles; caused by laser treatments

Laser Hair-Removal Consultation/Record Form

Name _____ Date ___/___/___

Address _____

Telephone Home (___)_____ Work (___)_____ DOB ___/___/___

Attending physician _____

Medical History: Allergies _____ Keloid scars _____
Infectious diseases _____ Cancer/melanoma _____
H/L blood pressure _____ Heart disease/pacemaker _____
Hormone therapy _____ Thyroid condition _____
Herpes _____ Nervous disorders _____
Epilepsy _____ Laser resurfacing _____
Diabetes _____ Pregnant _____
Lupus _____ Vitiligo _____
Scleroderma _____ Other _____

OB/GYN History _____

Medications and herbal supplements currently and recently taken _____

_____

Area(s) to be treated _____

Natural color of hair: ☐ brown ☐ blonde ☐ red ☐ gray/white   Hair pelosity: ☐ coarse ☐ medium ☐ fine

Skin tone

☐ Very fair: Always burn, never tan, blue eyes   ☐ Fair: Mainly burn, sometimes tan
☐ Medium/olive: Mainly tan, rarely burn   ☐ Dark: Never burn, dark hair, dark eyes

☐ Tattoos or permanent makeup   ☐ Gold and salt injections

Previous Hair Removal

Temporary means of hair removal _____ Frequency _____
Permanent means of hair removal _____

Date began _____ Last treatment _____ Approximate number of treatments _____

I, the undersigned, do hereby certify that the answers to the above questions are correct to the best of my knowledge.

Signature _____ **Date** _____

Signature of parent/guardian if under 18 years of age _____

FIGURE 18–1 Client Consultation and Record Form (front)

Anesthesia

The client should be able to purchase an effective topical anesthetic cream from the laser treatment clinic to apply before the treatment, or, if the treatment is done in a doctor's office, the client should be given a prescription for an effective anesthetic. Detailed information on anesthetics and their use can be found in Chapter 13.

Date	Laser Device	Area(s) Treated	Fluence	Pulse Width	Spot Size	Additional Comments

FIGURE 18–2 Client Consultation and Record Form (back)

Complications and Side Effects

- shorter-wavelength lasers using high fluences produce erythema and edema, most of which subsides within 20 minutes to a few hours
- longer wavelengths produce tiny bumps resembling "goose bumps" and additional edema, which should also subside within a matter of hours
- significant pigmentation in the skin, or errant hairs that were not trimmed adequately can experience some superficial blistering
- in cases of extreme erythema, there may be some skin discoloration in the form of hyperpigmentation and hypopigmentation

The Patch Test

A patch test is important for two reasons. First, it gives the technician an opportunity to gauge clients' tolerances to the treatment and to select the appropriate fluence levels. Second, it gives clients an opportunity to experience the laser and to perhaps relieve some of the anxiety that might be associated with the treatment.

An initial, single pulse should be performed at a test site near the treatment area and observed for damage to the epidermis in the form of blistering or an epidermal separation caused by lateral pressure on the skin, called the **Nikolski** (nih-KAHL-skee) **sign**. If such a reaction occurs, lower the fluence by 5 to 10 j/cm^2. Record the test results on the record form.

Nikolski sign
a condition on the skin characterized by blistering or epidermal separation, caused by lateral pressure on the skin

Pretreatment

Appropriate pretreatment steps prepare the client for a safe, effective, and comfortable treatment. Client preparation also reflects professionalism. All steps should be followed in their entirety.

1. Instruct the client to remove all necessary clothing, and provide a gown and drapes. Leave the room, and knock before reentering.
2. Take photos, if none were taken during the consultation.
3. Cleanse and free the area of lotions, deodorants, perfumes, and cosmetics.
4. Shave the target area.
5. Cool the skin before treatment to help reduce side effects.
6. Give the client the safety goggles to wear.

Treatment

Follow all treatment steps in their entirety for a safe, effective, and comfortable treatment. Communicate with the client throughout the treatment to monitor their level of comfort.

1. Unlock the laser device.
2. Don safety goggles.
3. Set the treatment parameters according to manufacturer's guidelines for the area, hair, and skin and according to the response at the test site.
4. Perform the treatment at the highest fluence the skin can tolerate for the most effective hair reduction. The time needed to cover the area depends on the spot size of the beam and the scanning pattern of the handpiece.
5. Compress the skin firmly with the handpiece to disperse the oxyhemoglobin (a chromophore that competes with melanin) away from the treatment area. Doing so, which allows for greater absorption of the laser light (Figure 18–3a), reduces the risk of epidermal damage as well as maneuvers the dermal papilla closer to the surface, which makes for a more effective treatment.
6. During the treatment, between some of the pulses, clean the handpiece with alcohol to free it of the carbonized hair that collects on the window. The buildup makes the window feel hot and impedes the flow of the laser beam.
7. Client comfort level is affected by the treatment fluence and treatment time. Adjust either according to the client's tolerance if other attempts, like topical anesthesia and cooling remedies, have not reduced the discomfort (Figure 18–3b).
8. At the end of the treatment, turn off the laser device and remove the key.
9. Because the handpiece contacts the skin, wipe it clean with a disinfectant between treatments.

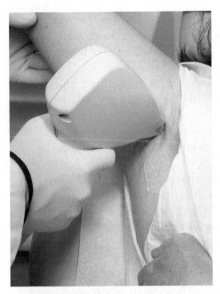

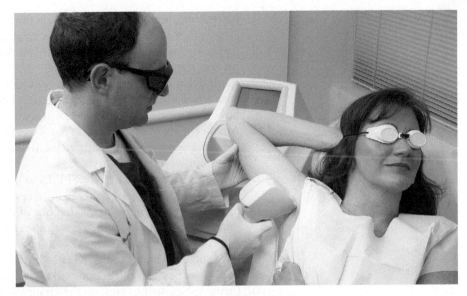

FIGURE 18–3a Treatment closeup   **FIGURE 18–3b** Client positioning for laser treatment

Approximate Treatment Times

Facial areas—10–15 minutes
Underarm and bikini—30 minutes
Back—30 minutes to 1 hour, depending on the extensiveness of the area
Chest—30–45 minutes
Full leg—45 minutes to 1 hour
Half leg—30 minutes
Half arm—30 minutes

Posttreatment

Posttreatment procedures will help minimize client discomfort and prevent negative post-treatment reactions. A client should never leave the facility without appropriate after-care.

1. Use ice in a vinyl surgical glove for after-care. Uce cold packs, aloe vera, or any other cooling preparation to ease temporary, mild burning.
2. Apply a total sunblock, if the area will be exposed to ultraviolet light.
3. Apply makeup as long as the skin is not broken. Makeup also serves as additional sunblock. Use new, uncontaminated makeup product, and apply it with a clean sponge.
4. Advise the client to return within 6 to 8 weeks. Ensure that any hair follicles that were in the resting stage during the initial treatment are in a growing stage at the time of follow-up.

Home Care

Encouraging the client to follow the recommended home-care guidelines will promote faster healing and prevent adverse reactions like hyperpigmentation and hypopigmentation. Make sure that the client fully understands their responsibility in following the guidelines.

1. Recommend quick, warm showers. If areas other than the facial area are treated, advise no hot baths for 24 hours.

2. Place additional clean, cold packs on the treatment area. Bags of frozen peas, as long as they are clean, or protective, clean cloths under the bag, work well.

3. Apply a soothing, healing ointment like Aquaphor™. Keep the area lubricated to prevent tissue crusting or scabbing.

4. In the event of blistering, apply a topical antibiotic cream or ointment and cover with a nonadhering dressing. Have the client notify the technician and/or physician overseeing the laser treatment.

5. Advise clients to avoid the sun for 3 weeks following treatment to avoid hyperpigmentation. Also advise them to avoid tanning if they are planning to have follow-up treatments.

6. Apply a sunscreen of at least SPF 15 to any area that could be exposed to ultraviolet light as long as there is an erythema. If further treatment is needed, have the client commit to staying out of the sun. Sun exposure creates certain minor complications, which should be discussed fully with the client.

7. Apply makeup and lotions the next day or when signs of irritation or erythema have subsided and if the skin is not broken. Use uncontaminated makeup, and apply it with clean fingers or a new, clean sponge.

8. Instruct the client to contact the facility and the technician or physician if there are any concerns or questions.

Conclusion

This chapter should not be considered the only theoretical tool in providing laser hair-removal treatment. It, with manufacturer's guidelines, is meant to inform and educate on what is involved in a typical hair-removal treatment and to complement the hands-on formal training delivered at a licensed laser hair-removal school.

Discussion and Review Questions

1. List three pros of laser hair removal.
2. List three cons of laser hair removal.
3. What are eight contraindications of laser hair removal?
4. What are the three steps of pretreatment?

5. What are the three components of treatment?
6. What are the four steps of postcare?
7. List three points of advice to give a client for posttreatment.

SECTION VI

Business Practices

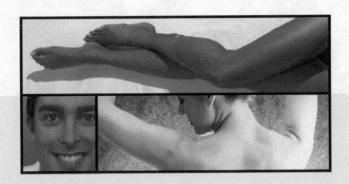

It may well be that, after receiving certification for any or all aspects of hair removal described in this book, the technicians choose to work in existing spas, salons, clinics, or doctors' offices, or they may choose to open a new business, or purchase an existing facility. This section covers the many variables to be considered when starting a hair-removal business from scratch or purchasing an existing one. In addition, this last section of the book addresses the importance of certification and licensure, professional-association membership, continuing education, and professional ethics.

CHAPTER 19

Licensure and Starting a Practice

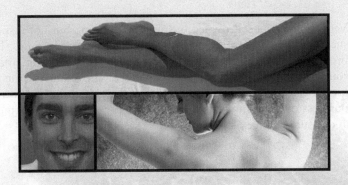

Chapter Outline

Learning Objectives ▪ Key Terms ▪ Introduction ▪ The Business Plan
Location and Facility ▪ Home Businesses ▪ Insurance and Litigation ▪ Service Charges
Employee Relations ▪ Accounting and Finances ▪ Advertising and Marketing
Conclusion ▪ Discussion and Review Questions

Learning Objectives

By the end of this chapter, you should be able to:

1. Form a detailed business plan.
2. Differentiate between types of business ownership.
3. Have the theoretical tools necessary for selecting a
   business location and facility.
4. Use the theoretical tools necessary to set up a business.
5. Conduct an employee interview.
6. Choose the most suitable forms of advertising based
   on a budget.

Key Terms

Better Business Bureau
bookkeeper
business plan
capital
certificate of occupancy

certified public accountant
(CPA)
corporation
doing business as (DBA)
entrepreneur

federal tax ID number
lease
liability
loan request
malpractice

partnership
sales tax ID number
shares
stock
zoning permit

Introduction

Venturing into a self-owned business is daunting but not insurmountable. Businesses can succeed, they just take careful and thoughtful planning. This chapter describes and broadly outlines all the considerations of buying, owning, and running a business. Other sources of information should supplement this material; this section should not replace lawyers, CPAs, or other business professionals, people who not only advise and protect business owners' interests but clarify many aspects of starting a new business or buying and assuming an existing one.

The Business Plan

A business begins with knowledge, experience, and capital. Capture ideas and a vision for the business on paper as a proposal, then "sell" the idea to those whose help and expertise are needed to open and run the business (e.g., private investors, bankers, lawyers, realtors, leasing agents). A **business plan** is like a blueprint for a project. It is an organized paper filled with facts and details about the envisioned business venture. The business plan starts with brainstorming, listing and compiling every piece of information that crosses the mind; it is a primary list.

business plan
a document detailing all aspects of the business as it is at present and as it is envisioned

The Primary List

Following are some of the items on the primary list to consider:

- hair-removal services to offer (e.g., waxing, sugaring, threading, electrolysis, laser, or a combination of the aforementioned)
- demand in the area for those services
- main client base
- desired client base
- business location
- type of facility
- name of the business
- style and image of the business
- mode of raising funds to start the business
- structure of the business (e.g., sole owner or multiple owners, sole employee or multiple employees)
- bookkeeping format; handling of business/bookkeeping aspects, possibly by a **bookkeeper**
- expansion plans
- business license
- **zoning** permit
- insurance
- advertising

bookkeeper
individual who records the accounts or transactions of a business

zoning permit
permit issued by town hall in the town of the proposed business indicating approval for the business in a particular neighborhood

The Secondary List

Once the initial primary list has been made, form a secondary list by giving one page to each item on the primary list. The secondary list should be a brainstorming list of the thoughts and ideas related to each of the primary-list items.

An example of the secondary list is:

Type of facility
>Home
>Doctor's office
>Strip mall

Insurance
>To cover **malpractice** for multiple services
>Fire/water/property damage
>Personal disability
>Payroll/workers' compensation disability

malpractice
the dereliction of professional duty or failure to exercise an accepted degree of professional skill

Business-in-a-Binder

Once the initial lists have been made and it is easier to see which information must be obtained through research, it is helpful to organize the areas into a "Business-in-a-Binder," which is a three-ringed binder with dividers and pockets that both helps organize information and holds the documentation and certificates needed when meeting with various people. Depending on its level of importance and the amount of information that could be compiled, each item on the list should have its own page or section in the binder. Once the binder is organized, begin gathering detailed information on the items.

When contacting government offices and business for information, not only note their information, log the name, job title, and phone number of the contact person, as well as the date and time of the call.

Types of Ownership

A business can be a sole venture or with one or multiple partners and investors. The types of ownership are:

1. sole proprietorship
2. partnership
3. corporation

Sole Proprietor

In a sole proprietorship, there is one self-employed owner and manager of the business. The success of the business is the sole responsibility of the owner.

There is no need for a **doing business as (DBA)**, unless the name of the business is going to differ from that of the owner.

doing business as (DBA)
permit required if a business is going to be conducted under a name other than the business owner's own name

Partnership

A partner gives the opportunity of shared ideas, shared responsibility, and shared **liability**. A business partner is often an opportunity to generate additional investment capital.

When two or more people own a business, the business is called a **partnership**. The partner may be a husband and wife sharing equal ownership, but ownership need not be equally shared. If the partner is not a family member, it is important to know the partner extremely well, and to ascertain the depth of that person's involvement in the business. Will the person be involved at every level, in all decision making, or will the person be a silent partner, providing additional capital and receiving a share of the profits but with no involvement in the development or running of the business?

liability
obligation incurred due to position or situation

partnership
a legal, contractual relationship between two or more people in business

Corporation

corporation
a business that is shared by one or more individuals who are identified in the corporation by a state-mandated charter and that is subject to mandated regulations and taxation

A **corporation** can be a business that is shared by three or more individuals who are identified in the corporation by a state-mandated charter. However a sole owner may form a corporation and may hold all the titles and incorporate the business. State governments subject corporations to mandated regulations and taxation. Decisions and policies are generally made by a board of directors, then voted into corporate policy by shareholders. An executive officer, however, may hold all the business's stock and capital.

Becoming incorporated is important, whether there are one or more employees, because incorporation offers protection from liability. In the event that a client sues for malpractice or a client or an employee sustains an injury on the premises and decides to sue, a claim cannot be made against a business owner's personal assets.

stock
the value of a company; can be registered and listed on the stock exchange for the purpose of selling shares to the general public to generate revenue for company expansion

shares
the unit value of company stock which the public can purchase and become stockholders

When a business has grown to the degree that, with the right influx of cash, it can expand nationally or internationally, it can be registered and listed on the stock exchange. This is called "going public." The value of a company is called its **stock**. Stock is listed as **shares**, which have a unit value. The public can purchase multiple shares in a company and become stockholders. The bulk of the money made from selling the stock is used to take a business to a greater level in the hope of generating greater profit. The profit is shared among the shareholders, who, in the event of a downturn, cannot lose more than their original share investment.

Financing and Budget

capital
the amount of cash available and the amount of money that must be raised to see the venture to fruition

A very important part of the business plan is the gathering and listing of all the finances relating to the proposed business, everything expected to pay for leasing, utilities, equipment, insurance fees, and so on; monies that have been saved, along with personal assets; and the amount of money needed to make the business happen. **Capital** refers to the amount of available cash and the amount of money that must be raised to see the venture through to fruition. If extra capital is not going to be raised through private individual investors, a bank loan will be necessary. When considering the sum of the loan request, consider requesting more than the amount on paper so as to have a reserve pool available in the event of some unforeseen problem. There should also be sufficient capital to support the business for at least a year until it becomes well established and profit making.

loan request
solicitation of funds for a temporary period

Before taking a business plan to the bank for a **loan request**, call or visit the bank and ascertain what information and documentation the bank requires for a loan application. Having all the necessary and required information up front not only expedites the loan process, it instills confidence in the bank's loan officer that the owner is organized, professional, and a good risk.

Business Laws and Regulations

Before deciding to open a business, learn the business laws and regulations that will affect the business. Doing this may help the business owner determine whether to start a business, or continue as someone else's employee. Laws and regulations can come from multiple sources, from a local level to a federal level, and include not only general laws governing businesses, but regulations covering the personal services of hair removal.

Local Regulations

Local governments may have guidelines for parking, building codes, and so on.

State Laws and Regulations

On the state level, there are stipulate and regulate sales taxes, licensing and worker's compensation, payroll taxes, and reporting and industry census reports.

Federal Laws and Regulations

The federal government regulates payroll taxes and reporting plus Social Security, unemployment compensation or insurance, and, through OSHA, such guidelines as the MSDS discussed in Chapter 5.

Not knowing or understanding laws is no excuse for violating those laws. The business owner and hair-removal specialist are responsible for finding out all the relevant laws, regulations, and guidelines and abiding by them.

Location and Facility

After considering the finances and form the business should take (e.g., sole proprietor or corporation), choosing the location and type of facility are probably the next most important decisions. There are a number of questions to be asked, the answers of which will invariably affect the business's type and location:

- Does the area have a large enough population to sustain a business?
- Do you plan to be the sole operator, or do you plan to bring other hair-removal technicians into the business?
- Do you plan to lease a business that gives you room for growth or to lease something smaller and, down the road, vacate and move to a larger facility?

The answers to these questions may depend on the capital available and the amount of funds that can be raised or the kind of loan secured. Most banks will want to see in a business plan the business's kind of facility, location, square footage, and leasing cost before committing to a loan.

Initial information on the kinds of available commercial properties can be obtained from the business and real-estate sections of the newspaper. Such information is also available online by visiting the Web sites of major realty companies. If online services are not available, trips to local realty offices will give a clear idea of what is available and for what leasing cost.

Some of the variables that are important to consider when selecting a facility are the:

1. location
2. floor plan
3. lease

Location

There are many advantages to being located along a thoroughfare: The business is easily accessible, easy to find with simple directions, and clearly visible (e.g., at an intersection visible from multiple sides or in a strip mall where pedestrians and slow-driving cars will notice the business). Is the business on the route of public transportation? It may be an office in an executive park, which would provide a good, immediate client base, provided a large percentage of the offices are leased, not vacant. Does the facility have good frontage appeal and a place for an eye-catching sign? A good window for drawing clients in for services or products? Does it have adequate parking? Will the parking area be safe and well lit if the business is to remain open after normal business hours? Who would be responsible for clearing away snow? Is the area zoned for such a business? Are there other desirable businesses in the vicinity that will help attract a clientele?

The Floor Plan

The right floor plan is key. When looking at a facility, it is important to have in mind and on paper an idea of what would be minimally acceptable and what would be ideal, given

the financial situation. The facility should have adequate square footage with handi-capped accessibility, and, if it is on a second floor or higher, an elevator. The facility should open into an immediate reception area (Figure 19–1), have one or more treatment rooms large enough to hold all necessary equipment, an office, a dispensary, storage space for supplies, possibly laundry facilities, and restrooms that are clean and attractive. Finally, it should have good lighting and good ventilation.

The Lease

lease
contract that conveys real estate,
equipment, or facilities for a
specified term and a specified rent

Comparing locations is essential when looking for a business location. Consider different options with regard to the location, things like square footage, local regulations, and history of small businesses in the area (do businesses seem to "turnover" regularly?), and compare them to the cost of the **lease**. After selecting a few possible locations, list the pros and cons of all the facilities, then prioritize them. Consider advantages and disadvantages with the particulars of the different leases. It is not enough to simply ascertain the cost of the lease. Study other variables of the leasing agreement, including who foots the bill for major and minor changes to the premises, electrical installation, and plumbing changes. Is the lease long term or short term? If the lease seems like a great deal for the first year, allowing for buildup of the business, look into by how much it can increase in the second year. This is often the downfall of so many new businesses. A new **entrepreneur** is attracted to a low introductory leasing cost, which helps when getting started, but, after 6 months or a year, or when the contract expires, leasing costs can soar. The property owner hopes that, because the tenants are committed to the business, they will pay the additional cost, but for many it means looking for new locations or simply going out of business. Before signing any lease, have a lawyer look it over for hidden pitfalls. Leases are negotiable. It is worth the effort of reaching mutually agreeable leasing terms based on strong negotiation.

entrepreneur
individual who organizes,
manages, and assumes the risks of
a business or an enterprise

certificate of occupancy
required permit that indicates,
after inspection, that the building
is safe for the purpose of the
described business

If any new construction is to be done before leasing the facility, it will have to be inspected by a town's building inspector. If the facility passes the inspection, a **certificate of occupancy** will be provided, which must be displayed.

Home Businesses

The benefits of a home business are the lack of high overhead, tax-deductible features, and no commute. The downsides are that the job is ever present and strangers invade a private domain. Because of the "hidden" nature of the business, it is predominantly a referral business. Keeping that part of the house clients will see presentable can be tricky, especially if there are young children and pets in the house. Children (and pets) must be taught to recognize when clients are "in house" and to not interrupt so that the clients feel they are getting a professional service with the operator's undivided attention. Some clients enjoy the personalized touch of a home business, feeling like they have landed on the "best-kept secret in town."

Home businesses have regulations to follow that include registering a business name (DBA), if the name is going to differ from the owner's name, and getting a special residential zoning permit. Zoning permits are usually obtained from town halls. They can be straightforward to obtain in some areas, difficult in others. It may be easier if it is apparent that there are other small neighborhood businesses in the area. After completing and filing the form to request special zoning, the town sends a letter describing the business's intent to people in the neighborhood, inviting those people to a town meeting at which the business owner will describe, present, and defend the request for a home business. If friendly with many of the people in the neighborhood, it may be worth drafting a petition and going door to door, discussing the venture and answering any concerns neighbors may have. Assure them that their concerns are noted and instill trust that the business will be conducted in a manner that will not erode the integrity of the neighborhood. Doing this ahead of time takes away the surprise of a note from the town board and gets the word out to potential clients who may love the convenience of the local business.

At one of the town meetings the business owner will be invited to present the proposal for a home business and to address any questions or concerns. The main points of concern are if there will be more than one person working in the home, meaning multiple clients and multiple parked cars. Generally, towns look more favorably on singly-operated businesses. The "town" also prefers "off-street" parking for clients, a restriction of clients in one day, and enough of a break between clients so that those clients are not continually lining up and down the street. The "town" also usually frowns upon any sign, particularly on the front lawn. Having a clear presentation, including a petition; photos of the outside of the property showing adequate parking; and house and lot plans all help to produce a favorable vote. At the end of the meeting, providing all issues are covered and all concerns are addressed that evening, there will be a vote by the "town" and an immediate result as to whether the business is approved. The bottom line is that the town board is well aware that many people have home income not registered or approved of, and they generally appreciate those who wish to conduct business legitimately and to pay taxes on their income.

Existing Businesses

When considering buying a business, it is important to solicit the advice and guidance of a lawyer and/or an accountant with expertise in this area. For a fee, such professionals will serve to look out for the buyer's interest and ensure that the business is worthwhile. An accountant can thoroughly go over a business's finances from the previous few years and ascertain its value, as well as look for any default of payments or existing debts and ascertain if the current owner is responsible for those debts or if the buyer should assume responsibility. A lawyer can also thoroughly go through important documents, like the written purchase-and-sale agreement and the lease agreement and transference of an outstanding bank note or mortgage.

Some questions to ask are:

- Why is the business for sale?
- Can the name of the business be continued for a certain time?
- Will employees stay on under new ownership?

■ Will the cost of leasing the premises go up? If so, how much?
■ What equipment and fixtures will remain with the business and be negotiated into the sale?

Legalities and Licensure

The next step with any business, including a home business, is to obtain the necessary business certificates to comply with local, state, and federal laws and regulations (Figure 19–2). The business certificate can be obtained from the county clerk's office. If the business is going to be registered under a business name other than the owner's legal name a DBA or a "conduct of business under assumed name" certificate is necessary. The latter is also available for a few dollars from the county clerk's office. The clerk will then provide the information needed to obtain a federal or sales tax ID number. Once all the certificates and licenses are in hand, steps can be made to set up the business.

Office Setup

The first order of business after the lease is signed, is to ensure that all utilities (e.g., electricity, phones, gas, and heat) are turned on.

The next section discusses the setup of a hair-removal business from the outside in, remembering that there is never a second chance to make a first impression.

Business Facade

An appealing frontage or facade will make the business more desirable to enter. If the property was leased at a low rate because it was in disrepair, take steps to make it clean and attractive. Paint is cheap, and peeling windows will not attract clients like a crisp, clean facility. Flowers and landscaping in the front of a business, even a home business, are often tax deductible, so it is worth checking with a CPA to see how much is worth investing in the front of the building. The business name and its sign should be easy to read, spell, and pronounce. With the high cost of advertising, good, strong name recognition offers a lot of advertising power for minimal cost. There are regulations for types of signs. Town permits are usually required for them. The permit can be obtained from the town hall.

Windows

Windows (Figure 19–3) can either cause people to walk by without noticing the business or draw people in, if only out of curiosity, to pick up a price list or brochure. Windows are

FIGURE 19–2
All appropriate licenses and certificates must be in hand to set up the business

FIGURE 19–3
An attractive window beckons customers inside to inquire about services

also an opportunity to display the stickers that acknowledge membership in nationally recognized associations.

Reception Area

When entering the facility, clients and potential clients should be greeted by an attractive reception area. After the first impression from the facade of the business, the reception area is the area that sets the tone of the business. An individual's initial impressions as to whether to return for treatments often form in the reception area. If the reception area doubles as a waiting area, it should contain comfortable seats; attractive artwork; lamps for a warm, soft effect; and plants. If possible, there should also be some seats in a less obvious part of the facility for clients with topical anesthesia and occlusive dressings on their faces who may be embarrassed at being in full view. The reception area should also contain a closet for coats and an umbrella stand near the entrance. A wall in the reception area is a good location to display professional licenses, certificates, and diplomas in attractive frames. They instill immediate confidence in clients.

Wall, Floor, and Window Coverings

Walls, floors, and window coverings should all be in soothing, restful colors and easy to clean and disinfect. In treatment rooms, the walls, floors, and other surfaces should be able to withstand the solvents used for removing depilatory wax spills.

Office and Office Supplies

Organization is the key to an efficient office and an efficient business. The office will probably serve as double duty for accounting and bookkeeping tasks, and for interviewing staff, prospective employees, and representatives from other businesses. The office, at a minimum, should have a desk with the usual array of office supplies (e.g., pens, pencils, tape, stapler), two chairs, a phone and a fax, a file cabinet, and a notice board and bookshelves for supply catalogs. Other useful items in today's business are a personal computer with online access and a safe for spare cash.

The Restroom

The restroom should be handicapped accessible and clean. It should contain liquid soap in a pump, toilet tissue and paper towels, and a trash can with a lid. Other items that make the restroom attractive are a vanity mirror, an air-freshener spray or bowl of potpourri, and a box of tissues. Public bathrooms are notorious for running into plumbing problems, often due to a patron putting too much toilet tissue into the toilet bowl. It is acceptable to put a sign in the bathroom that states:

> Please refrain from placing paper towels and feminine products in the toilet bowl. Use the receptacle provided. Your cooperation is appreciated. Thank you.

The Laundry/Utility Room

When starting out, a business may lack a facility that supports a laundry area. While helpful, it is not essential and just means that used linens must be bused home to launder. If there is an opportunity to install a washer and dryer along with a utility sink, it is worthwhile. A utility room with a utility sink is necessary for general cleaning supplies, the vacuum and broom, the mop and bucket, with a "Caution: Wet Floor" sign, and bathroom-cleaning supplies.

The Dispensary

The dispensary contains all the supplies for the services, as well as the ultrasonic cleansers and disinfectant solutions, which should be stored carefully on secure and stable shelves. The dispensary can also house the sterilization unit.

The Break Room

The break room is optional unless there are employees who work 5 hours at a stretch. Such a room should contain a sink, a trash can, a table and chairs, a fridge, a microwave, an employee notice board, and a clock.

Treatment Rooms

Treatment rooms especially should have walls, floors, and surfaces that are easy to clean and disinfect. They should be uncluttered with as much product as possible hidden until needed to make cleaning and disinfecting between clients possible. If possible, the laser device should be in a suitable room by itself, one used solely for that purpose following the guidelines in Chapter 17. Waxing and electrolysis services can be carried out in the same room. The guidelines for those rooms appear in Chapters 11 and 13. In addition, any background music should be low enough as not to interfere with the normal tones of conversation. The music should be soothing and relaxing and, if possible, instrumental to avoid lyrics that may cause embarrassment.

Phone Techniques

Phone manners are essential to any business providing sales and services to the public. It is often the client's first contact with the business. The first impression is a lasting one and may determine if the potential customer chooses to receive services there. Staff answering the phone should always provide their names; doing so makes them accountable. Each call should be conducted in a friendly and courteous manner from beginning to end. The phone operator should remain in control of the call, promptly eliciting the pertinent information; offering clear, brief answers to questions; and generally avoiding lengthy calls and tying up the phone lines. If clients want to discuss services in depth, they should be politely invited in for consultations that are required for certain services anyway. At that time, all the questions could be answered in more depth. Experience has shown that the more booking choices a client is given, the more difficult those clients are to book. Ask clients if they would like weekday or weekend, day or evening appointments, then offer two choices (e.g., "we have an opening on Wednesday at 6 pm or Thursday at 7:15 pm. Which would you prefer?").

Callers should never be put on immediate hold without a greeting or ascertaining the purpose of the call. Doing so is rude and may cause clients to not call back or to call the next number in the phone book. Callers may have emergencies, and it is irresponsible to assume a call is not important enough to be allowed a few seconds.

If a client calls to complain about a service and very little can be done without observation, invite the client to come in as soon as possible so that the matter can be addressed. If, however, a situation would benefit from a technician recommending an immediate and appropriate home-care remedy, verify the client's name and number, when receiving the treatment, what the treatment was, and who provided the service. Then reassure the client that a call is forthcoming as soon as the technician is finished with the current client. The phone operator should maintain self-control, be courteous and reassuring, and let the client know that the concerns have been heard and noted and will be passed promptly to the appropriate person.

Booking Techniques

An appointment book on the reception desk as opposed to a computerized system is initially an inexpensive way to schedule appointments and can reduce the cost of opening a business. Appointments scheduled manually in an appointment book should always be made in pencil so that they can be easily erased in the event of a cancellation or rescheduling. A daytime phone number should always be placed next to the client's name to confirm the appointment.

The advantage of a computerized booking system is that it can conveniently store other pertinent information belonging to the client as well as booking history and a record of items purchased. The computerized system can help with stock and inventory control. Booking systems often allow technicians to print their daily schedules. Reports can be easily stored and retrieved, as can information on technicians' services and sales. Information in the computer saves space and is easier to retrieve. The computerized booking system is also linked to the cash drawer and credit-card scanner and speeds the cashing-out process, leaving less room for human error.

Services should be confirmed by contacting the client 1 to 3 days before the service. Appointments can be guaranteed with credit-card numbers, particularly if the clients have failed to show for appointments before. If there is a policy of charging the client for appointments not cancelled within a 24-hour period, post it clearly for clients to see, and mention the policy at the time of booking and confirmation

Equipment Purchase and Lease

Leasing equipment, especially expensive equipment like laser equipment, allows businesses to get the latest equipment without penalty or buy-back cost. Equipment should only be leased or bought from well-established companies that preferably have a number of years in the allied-health, beauty, or medical industry. The equipment should come with an appropriate guarantee and offer service and support and a toll-free customer-service hotline. It is also helpful if the company can provide loaner equipment while the leased piece is being serviced or repaired. Information for the purchase or lease of credit-card machines and services can be obtained from local banks or from any major credit-card company. Major conferences and conventions are excellent opportunities to shop for equipment, talk to salespeople, observe demonstrations, test equipment, and have questions answered. Manufacturers may offer "show prices" with significant discounts if equipment is purchased or leased during the show.

Insurance and Litigation

There are many types of insurance to learn about, regardless of the size of the business. There are a variety of reasons that a business or technician can be sued. To ignore the importance of being covered by insurance is reckless and could seriously jeopardize the business.

Malpractice Insurance

Different services may have to be covered under different insurance companies, although it is more cost-effective to shop for one company that covers all services under one umbrella. The insurance company will want verification that those providing services are well trained and certified.

When insuring equipment, especially costly equipment like laser devices, it should be clear as to whether the coverage is valid for use by operators other than physicians or whether they just need names and documentation verifying sufficient equipment training.

As mentioned earlier, corporations provide better financial protection in the event of a lawsuit.

Business Owner's Liability Insurance

Business owner's liability insurance covers many important areas, including clients or employees being injured on the premises. It offers similar protection to that of home-owner's insurance.

Fire and water insurance can be purchased, as can protection for any natural disasters that may occur in the area of the business (e.g., hurricane insurance along coastlines, tornado coverage in tornado-prone states, earthquake coverage for businesses on earthquake fault lines and in high-risk earthquake areas). Also seek coverage for theft. Before covering the business in these categories, representatives may visit to examine the business and ensure that appropriate steps are taken to prevent or reduce major damage (e.g., the installation of a fire sprinkler system, effective door locks, and a security system).

Personal Disability Insurance

Personal disability insurance is very important in the hair-removal industry. People who suffer major accidents that prevent them from continuing to work will benefit from the financial protection this coverage offers.

When working with insurance companies and policies, it is important that there is no lapse in the payments that will cause the policy to lapse. Having payments made by automatic withdrawal will help prevent that, but it is important to check monthly statements to ensure payments are being made.

 ## Service Charges

A CPA can help identify the service charges that will generate a healthy, acceptable profit margin. Service charges should be calculated by considering such variables as overhead, technicians' salaries, and acceptable fee in the service area.

Cost of Services

Service prices should be calculated according to overhead, materials, and labor costs, whether salary or commission. Timing for each service should be ascertained and documented. State whether the services are labor intensive (e.g., a full leg and bikini wax) or technically advanced (e.g., electrolysis).

Overhead

Overhead includes things like rent/lease and the costs of equipment leasing, products, supplies, advertising, cleaning and laundry, utilities, and employee salaries. An accountant can help calculate and determine the fees, which should be comparable to those of businesses in the area.

 ## Employee Relations

Being competent in the hiring, training, and managing of employees contributes greatly to the success of the business and the creation of a professional and harmonious atmosphere.

Hiring

Prospective employees should complete applications. Once reviewed, bring in suitable candidates for personal interviews. The interview should include:

- review of the application and verification and documentation of eligibility to work legally
- viewing of certification and licensure
- review of the job description and responsibilities
- discussion of candidates' training and experience
- tour of the facility
- identification of all duties and tasks required in the position
- review of the employee manual (e.g., dress code)
- salary and pay schedule
- benefits, if offered
- work schedule, days and hours

At the end of the interview, allow the candidate to ask any questions, and answer those questions. Thank the candidates and state a date by which a decision is expected.

If the applicants are undesirable, tell them as soon as possible so they can continue job searching. If the interview is favorable, take a day or two to verify references and previous employment. Inform the candidate within a week of the interview.

As soon as an offer is made, ask the new employee to come in to receive the employee handbook and to fill out the required employee-processing information, including federal and state tax withholding forms (W-4 form) and the federal employment verification forms (I-9). Employees must provide appropriate documentation to verify their eligibility to work legally in the United States.

Employee Manual

An employee manual that details personnel and policy issues is a good idea. It can list everything from dress code to areas of unacceptable behavior and vacation time. Ask new hires to read the handbook, then sign a form stating that they have read and understood it.

Employee Evaluations

Hold employee evaluations at least once a year to assess employees' performance and growth. Privately address concerns and problems, encourage and recognize strong work, and review items in personnel folders. Also, ensure that all licenses are up to date and that continuing-education hours are being completed, if they are required. Ideally, hold evaluations close to anniversaries of hiring dates.

Termination of Employment

Terminating employment is probably the most difficult task for a business owner who hired an individual in good faith and wanted that person to succeed in the business. Review infractions and disciplinary write-ups before terminating employment. Termination should be done in private. State why it is necessary. Ready the paperwork ahead of time. Then, escort the employee immediately from the premises in a comfortable and non-threatening manner.

Accounting and Finances

The success of a service industry business not only relies on providing a quality service, it relies on observing sound principles of money management and knowing the laws and regulations regarding taxes and payroll. Using a CPA or bookkeeper can be profitable and prevent negative repercussions from an audit.

Federal Tax ID Number

A **federal tax ID number** is only necessary to have with employees.

federal tax ID number
registered tax identification number needed only with employees

State Sales Tax ID Number

A state **sales tax ID number** is only necessary if when planning to sell products or when offering taxable services. For instance, in New York State, hair-removal services, but not products, are nontaxable. To learn a state's regulations, contact that state's Department of Tax and Finance.

sales tax ID number
a registered tax identification number needed only when selling products or taxable services

Bank Account

As soon as the business plan is to be implemented, open a business bank account with funds. Ensure checks for payments and withdrawals include tabs for documentation.

"Cashing Out"

Unless a sole proprietor, and if more than one person uses the cash register, two employees share in the task of cashing out and ensuring the day's proceeds match the charges for the services and products. Cash out after all entrances are locked, for safety and security reasons.

Deposits

Cash is insured, but a person's safety must be protected. Going to a bank deposit box in the darkness of night is not a good idea if the banking can be done in the morning. Place revenues in a safe in the office overnight, along with a cash reserve.

Monthly Statements

View and analyze monthly statements every month to avoid any escalating problems.

Drafts and Notes

Drafts and notes happen when there are insufficient funds to cover a check. They should be avoided. Pay bills promptly to maintain good credit.

Payroll

A professional payroll company, an accountant, or computer software package are cost-effective, time-efficient ways of handling payroll if it is not within the owner's expertise.

Taxes

certified public accountant (CPA)
individual who has met the requirements of a state law and has been granted a certificate in accounting

Using a **certified public accountant (CPA)** or bookkeeper to track business-related taxes is recommended. These professionals make it their duty to learn and understand state and federal laws and often pay for their professional services with the money they save businesses with their expertise.

A bookkeeper or a good bookkeeping system ensures that income and expenses can be tracked, keeping businesses informed and current with regard to profitability, which in business is the bottom line. Neglecting bookkeeping will prove costly, because doing so prevents profitable business decisions. For example, changing expenditures and service prices based on inaccurate records skews results.

Advertising and Marketing

Advertising is crucial in a new business. With leases and initial high loans, a stream of clients as soon as the business is open is essential for success. Generating an initial client base with immediate advertising will begin the snowball effect of repeat business and word-of-mouth referrals. The form of advertising should be well thought out and planned to get the maximum possible exposure for the money. When negotiating the business loan, factor in adequate advertising funds.

Also desirable is frontage with a sign and a name that is easy to read, spell, and pronounce.

Referrals

A client-referral incentive is a good way to help a new business grow. A client can receive a discount on service after referring other clients who receive a service.

Business Cards and Brochures

An attractive brochure and menu of services, with the business's philosophy, is an effective way to advertise. Pass out business cards at opportune moments when it can be done personally.

Recommendation of Additional Services

Gently invite regular clients to try other services, if those clients show interest. For example, if a client regularly receives an eyebrow wax, the operator may observe that the client's facial hair could benefit from electrolysis. A client may, in passing, discuss an upcoming cruise vacation, so suggest a bikini or leg wax. There is no substitute for "the power of suggestion" when increasing clients services. Do not underestimate clients who come in for quick lip waxes. Sell further services.

Chamber of Commerce

The local chamber of commerce can give invaluable help and advice in business promotion.

The Better Business Bureau

One cannot simply become a member of the **Better Business Bureau,** but after 5 years of providing quality services, without major complaints, the invitation may be offered to become a member for a fee. If invited, consider membership. This organization indicates that a business is recognized for its reputation and service.

Better Business Bureau
organization whose membership indicates that the business is recognized for its reputation and servic

Television/Radio/Newspaper

Depending on the extensiveness of the ad, TV is the costliest form of advertising. Radio offers a better deal and is especially effective if the area is high traffic/high commute and the ad is played during the busiest commuting times.

Having the trust of a handful of doctors is an excellent way to build a business. A visit to doctors' offices with brochures and credentials is a must. Dermatologists, especially, would be happy to cross-refer; so would endocrinologists.

Placing ads in art programs shows support for the community. People attending these functions like to reward businesses who support such events. The advertisements are also tax deductible.

Mass Mailings

Placing an advertisement, with or without coupons, in vendor mass mailing circulars can reach a number of local households and potential clients.

World Wide Web

The World Wide Web (WWW) is an economic and effective way to be identified in an area. A Web site means that people using Internet searches can find and contact businesses easily.

The Yellow Pages

The yellow pages are the most common form of advertising. New clients generally refer to the yellow pages for conveniently located businesses offering desired services.

Goodwill

Advertisements in programs for cultural or sporting events are a cost-effective way to advertise, and they instill a feeling of goodwill in the area. Also, donations in the form of gift certificates for charitable organizations are effective and demonstrate civic responsibility. People feel good about patronizing businesses that support community programs. In addition, the cost of the advertisement or value of the gift certificate are tax deductible.

Controllable variables
- poor leasing negotiations
- poor location
- too high overhead with too little initial capital or continued revenue to outstanding bills
- neglected bookkeeping

> **Uncontrollable variables**
>
> ■ Poor economy—people will always want their hair removed, whatever the state of the economy.
> ■ National or natural disaster—A regional disaster can be devastating and may mean the closure of a business. After September 11, 2001, many businesses not only experienced collateral damage, causing them to close temporarily, many could not reopen because they depended on the patronage of the many who worked in the World Trade Center. This kind of disaster is completely out of the business owner's control. Hurricanes, tornadoes, earthquakes, floods, and forest fires are the kinds of disasters that, although also outside the business owner's control, can be insured against.

Conclusion

There is nothing more exciting and daunting than considering owning a business and becoming the boss! For many, a business is a life-long aspiration; for others, it is a dream. With the aspirations and dreams come the need for the right tools, guidelines, information, and funding so that, from the earliest planning stages, responsible choices can be made to make that dream a reality.

Discussion and Review Questions

1. How many types of ownership are there?
2. Name two state-regulated items.
3. Name two federally regulated items.
4. What are four points to consider when choosing a business location?
5. What are the three types of insurance that are important to have as a business owner?

CHAPTER 20

Professional Ethics, Professional Organizations, and Continuing Education

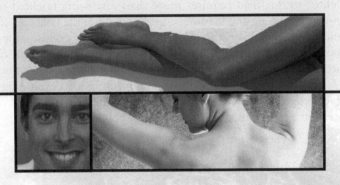

Chapter Outline

Learning Objectives ■ Key Terms ■ Introduction ■ Professionalism ■ Ethics
Keeping Abreast of the Latest Technologies ■ Professional Organizations
Continuing-Education Classes and Credits ■ Conclusion ■ Discussion and Review Questions

Learning Objectives

By the end of this chapter, you should be able to:

1. Understand the importance of being professional.
2. Define ethics.
3. Appreciate the importance of keeping up on the latest technologies in the field.
4. Explain the importance of joining professional organizations.
5. Understand the importance of earning continuing-education credits.

Key Terms

continuing-education
credits

ethics
professionalism

Introduction

Many individuals are drawn into the hair-removal industry because they enjoy working with their hands and feel a sense of satisfaction from the services they provide. To be "elite" in this field requires more than just being talented with one's hands. It requires in-depth training and learning everything about the field and seeking and applying methods and techniques from the masters in the field to continue developing those skills. It also means developing the people skills needed for dealing with clients who have hair-growth problems and the emotional distress those problems can cause.

This chapter deals with the importance of developing professionally in terms of knowledge and practical skills, as well as the importance of conducting oneself appropriately, in a professional manner, in all aspects of work.

Professionalism

professionalism
skill, competence, and character expected of a member of a trained profession

Conduct in work on a daily basis, with clients, employers, and colleagues, reflects our attitude toward **professionalism** (Figure 20–1). This is demonstrated by punctuality, dress code, and the kind of language used when talking to people in the workplace or when dealing with people outside the workplace. One never knows when a person will become a client. A young hairstylist had a traffic altercation in which inappropriate words were exchanged. To the stylist's horror and dismay, the individual showed up in her chair later that afternoon, having booked an appointment as a first-time client a week before. It was, needless to say, embarrassing for both parties and could have been avoided if professional conduct had carried over into private life.

FIGURE 20–1
Professional conduct is important to the salon's overall success

Professionalism means punctuality: arriving at work with enough time to complete all necessary tasks before greeting the first client.

Professionalism means dressing appropriately: not exposing cleavage or offensive tattoos. It means being clean and well groomed with the hair neatly off the face so that it does not get in the way of the work that must be done. It means wearing a clean lab coat. A lab coat that shows dirt around the sleeve cuffs or pockets is unacceptable and reflects poorly. Professionalism also means being meticulous in personal hygiene, paying careful attention to body odor and breath, freshening between clients or popping a breath mint, and being judicious in the use of perfumes and colognes.

Professionalism means politeness: a cheerful greeting using the client's name and avoiding expletives, religious words that might offend, and crude and vulgar language. It means keeping the conversation appropriate and avoiding subjects that may offend (e.g., religion, politics, and weight). Inappropriate topics include gossip about other clients and staff and personal problems. Appropriate conversations are client progress and reassurance. If a client is receiving a waxing service before a special occasion like a wedding or vacation, talk about the occasion. Listen to the client, and remember details from the conversation to refer to in subsequent visits. This reinforces to the client that the technician listened and was interested.

Professionalism means appropriate conduct. In intimate or delicate circumstances, be even more mindful of professional conduct. This means providing a drape for a client, leaving the room while the client undresses, and knocking before reentering. It means avoiding crude and tasteless jokes. It means not commenting with tasteless humor to the client about excessive hair growth in the bikini area. It means not talking loudly in the reception area about the service, or a client's health issue. Anyone who has had to have a thorough examination from a physician should be able to appreciate the importance of professional conduct and look to that as an example.

Professionalism means striving for high standards in the workplace, not just individual high standards, but wanting to be part of a team that promotes high standards of work and high standards in the business as a whole. Offer help, support, and encouragement to colleagues and generate a positive work environment.

Ethics

Ethics is defined by the *Merriam-Webster Dictionary* as (1) the discipline dealing with what is good and bad and with moral duty and obligation, (2a) a set of moral principles or values, (2b) a theory or system of moral values, (2c) the principles of conduct governing an individual or a group, (2d) a guiding philosophy.

ethics
moral standards and principles governing appropriate conduct for an individual or group

Professional ethics is deeper than just what is right or wrong regarding our professional conduct with clients, colleagues, and employers. It is what is right and wrong morally in conduct in the work environment. We know it is wrong to take someone else's tools and equipment. That is black and white to most of us. However, there will be occasions when we have to make ethical choices, and who we are in terms of our professional character is determined by our choices. An example is the individual who works part time in a salon or clinic but has the means to provide similar services in the home. What happens when an individual sees an advertisement, comes into the salon or clinic because of it and becomes a regular and enjoyable client of yours, and then in passing finds out that you offer the service at home for a slightly reduced rate and asks to come to your home instead? What do you do? The ethical thing to do is to say, "Thank you for your confidence in me. I do enjoy having you as a client here. As you walked through these doors here first, I am unable to have you come to my house as a client. I enjoy my work here and the professional relationship I have with my employer because I have these ethical boundaries. My employer trusts that I will not take clients in my house that were solicited to this business first." You will be respected by the clients and your employer for your stance, and you will have increased self-respect that will spill over into an enjoyable work experience.

Professional ethics also means not making unsubstantiated or unproven claims or promises with regard to a particular service. It means being honest and realistic in discussing the results. Making unrealistic claims is shortsighted. The client will figure out in time. This will reflect poorly on you, the technician, on the salon or clinic, and on the industry. When proper ethical conduct is not upheld, you are considered in violation of the rules of ethical conduct.

Keeping Abreast of the Latest Technologies

The hair-removal industry is an expanding and changing industry. New methods are being researched, tested, and introduced. It is important to keep abreast of any new technology, even if not embracing it. The information superhighway has never been as vast. Where clients once received information by browsing through magazines, they now have a multitude of television channels with infomercials and magazine news shows continually informing viewers. The Internet also affords clients the opportunity to research almost every subject imaginable and into as much depth as they choose. Our clients are becoming more informed, more selective, and more discriminating as they investigate and educate themselves on services available. Technicians, too, must in turn stay abreast of the latest technologies so that, when asked about a method or procedure, they can respond in an educated and informed manner. This can be done through reading books on the subjects, researching the subject online, and attending conferences, conventions, seminars, and trade shows.

Professional Organizations

Memberships in professional organizations offer numerous benefits, including:

- abiding by the high standards and codes of ethics that they set, which inspire us to continue to raise our level and standard of service.
- avenues to improve techniques and continue education at conferences with the association of others in the industry where ideas are exchanged.
- association newsletters and other literature, which inform and educate, as well as brochures and pamphlets, to distribute to clients.
- a standard level of acceptance for membership, which means achieving a level of education and training that is acceptable. This is very important, particularly in states with no licensing in the profession. As of 2003, electrolysis is still unlicensed in the state of New York, for example. In a state where anyone can purchase equipment and, without formal training, go into business, a certificate from a nationally recognized organization helps instill trust and confidence in the new client.
- online directories, which can steer new clients in your direction, and press packets to help you promote your business.
- legal counsel and discounted insurance rates.
- advanced credentialing, which recognizes the commitment to continued learning, advancement, and mastery of our chosen field.

The American Electrology Association

American Electrology Association
106 Oak Ridge Road
Trumbull, Connecticut 06611
U.S.A.
Tel.: (203) 372–7119
Fax: (203) 372–7134
Web site address:
www.electrology.com

The American Electrology Association (AEA) is one of the most respected electrology associations in the world. Since it was incorporated in 1958, the AEA has taken an active role in stressing the need for legislation and licensure in every state, promoting the need for improved education and higher standards of infection control and other safety issues. It continues to promote public awareness on the benefits of electrolysis and acts as a liaison between its members and the public. It has also taken a platform of raising public awareness to the negative use of laser devices in hair removal, and, in particular, the concern with the use of laser devices by nonmedical people. Association members are encouraged to seek further education and advancement in the field by taking the CPE certification exam and becoming certified professional electrologists. Doing so allows them to use the designated letters CPE after their names.

The International Guild of Professional Electrologists, Inc.

The International Guild of Professional Electrologists, Inc.
803 N. Main Street, Suite A
High Point, North Carolina 27262
U.S.A.
Tel.: (800) 830–3247
Web site address:
www.igpe.org

Established and incorporated in 1979, the International Guild of Professional Electrologists, Inc. (IPGE), has members in all 50 states, as well as 11 foreign countries. They offer similar benefits to those of the AEA (see preceding), promoting the probe method of electrolysis as the only permanent method of hair removal. However, the guild also supports electrologists' right to expand their scope of practice to include laser hair-removal devices and their use of new technologies as approved by the FDA.

The Society for Clinical and Medical Hair Removal, Inc.

The Society for Clinical and Medical Hair Removal, Inc.
7600 Terrace Avenue, Suite 203
Middleton, Wisconsin 53562
U.S.A.
Tel.: (608) 831-8009
Fax: (608) 831-5485
Web site address:
www.scmhr.org

Established and incorporated in 1985, member affiliation in the Society for Clinical and Medical Hair Removal, Inc. (SCMHR), offers similar benefits as the other associations, but this association has an aggressive platform of also promoting the benefits of laser hair removal as a method of permanent hair reduction. They support efforts to monitor and encourage legislation that allows electrologists to offer laser hair removal as a service. Another purpose is to educate the public on the benefits of electrolysis and the laser and IPL methods of treating unwanted hair. They also offer two levels of certification through their independent affiliate, the Professional Examination Services of New York City. Candidates who are successful on the first level exam may use the designation letters for Certified Clinical Electrologist (CCE) after their names. They can then take the second, advanced-level exam. If successful, they can earn the designation Clinical Medical Electrologist (CME).

 ## Continuing-Education Classes and Credits

continuing-education credits
nationally recognized further education units that can be earned relating to a specific profession

Attending classes offered at conventions is an excellent way to continue improving skills and gaining knowledge and tips in the trade. Many classes are offered by various manufacturers who focus on their products. These classes are often complimentary and are covered by the cost of general admission. Other classes are offered in the form of symposia attached to conventions. They are given by leaders and experts in the industry. They often cost an additional fee and offer **continuing-education credits** (CEUs) for attending the class or seminar. Attending association conferences also provides a venue for continued education. Associations like the American Electrology Association and the Society for Clinical and Medical Hair Removal require specified continuing-education credits for continued active membership. These are obtained by attending the conferences, and, for those who cannot attend, by taking small, single courses online or by mail. By doing this, these associations ensure that their members are not just members in name only but are continuing to gain knowledge and expertise in their profession. In an ever-changing field, learning never stops, and we must stay informed and strive to gain more in-depth knowledge in all aspects of our profession.

 ## Conclusion

It is not enough to just learn the basics in the hair-removal industry. We must strive to gain knowledge and improve our skills to be ahead of the competition. Do not fear competition. One thing that makes America great is an abundance of choice. Choosing to acknowledge this principle can hold us all to a higher standard in our services.

We should strive to conduct ourselves in a professional, ethical manner at all times, and thereby earn the respect of our clients, colleagues, and peers in the industry. To stand still in a profession that is moving forward is tantamount to going backward.

Discussion and Review Questions

1. What is meant by the term "professional ethics"?
2. Give an example of unethical behavior.
3. Name four unprofessional actions.
4. List four benefits of membership in a professional association.

Glossary/Index

Note: Numbers in bold denote page on which terms are defined.